the SPORTSCASTER'S DOZEN

Off the Air with Southeastern Legends

Matt Fulks

MASTERS PRESS

NTC/*Contemporary Publishing Group*

Library of Congress Cataloging-in-Publication Data

Fulks, Matt.
    The sportscaster's dozen : off the air with southeastern legends / Matt Fulks.
        p.   cm.
    ISBN 1-57028-203-X (trade)
    1. Sportscasters—Southern States—Interviews.   2. Radio broadcasters—Southern States—Interviews.   I. Title.
GV742.4.F85   1998
070.4'49796'0975—dc21   98-11321
                                                                 CIP

Cover photographs courtesy of Otis Boggs, Bob Fulton, and Woody Durham

Cover design by Nick Panos
Interior design by Heather Lowhorn

Published by Masters Press
A division of NTC/Contemporary Publishing Group, Inc.
4255 West Touhy Avenue, Lincolnwood (Chicago), Illinois 60646-1975 U.S.A.
Copyright © 1998 by Matt Fulks
All rights reserved. No part of this book may be reproduced, stored in a retrieval system, or transmitted in any form or by any means, electronic, mechanical, photocopying, recording, or otherwise, without the prior permission of NTC/Contemporary Publishing Group, Inc.
Printed in the United States of America
International Standard Book Number: 1-57028-203-X
98   99   00   01   02   03   VL   6   5   4   3   2   1

To one of my radio mentors, Tom Lawrence. Thank you for your guidance, encouragement, and, most important, your friendship.

Contents

Foreword
VII

Acknowledgments
XI

Introduction
XIII

Otis Boggs
1

Al Ciraldo
37

Jack Cristil
65

Woody Durham
91

Paul Eells
127

John Ferguson
153

John Forney
173

Bob Fulton
195

Bob Harris
231

Cawood Ledford
271

Larry Munson
301

Jim Phillips
331

Foreword

"**B**orn to be a play-by-play man!" I truly believe there's a fraternity of sportscasters that really believe in that statement. ¶ Some of us are extroverted type-A's who are simply extensions of ourselves when we're on the air. Some of us are utilizing our alter egos, expressing a side of our personality that few ever witness when we are without a microphone, transmitter, and most importantly, an audience.

Some of us view ourselves as electronic journalists of sports, never losing our objectivity, reporting only what we see and never choosing sides.

Some of us get caught up in the idea that we are the so-called "mouthpiece of the fan," understanding that our audience is fanatical and lives vicariously through the success and failure of their teams.

The only thing we all have in common is a bond of passion that brought us to the business and a never-ending desire to nail our next broadcast.

I was born in 1956, the classic baby boomer who never knew what life without sports on television was like. I'm the son of a radio and television pioneer of sorts in my hometown of Shreveport, Louisiana. Like a lot of second-generation broadcasters, I was introduced to, and enjoyed, radio as much as television.

In fact, all the great sports commentators from the World War II generation that I was watching on television in the 1960s *and* 1970s had vast radio experience. Those were the ones that charted the course with unwritten rules for sports play-by-play, and broadcasting in general, that we still live by today.

Legendary names like Curt Gowdy, Ray Scott, Jim McKay, Jack Buck, Chris Schenkel, Jim Simpson, Lindsey Nelson, and, yes, even

The Sportscaster's Dozen

Keith Jackson were all influenced by, or perhaps worked alongside, the men who blazed radio's play-by-play trail; men like Bill Stern, Mel Allen, Marty Glickman, and Red Barber.

Gowdy influenced me the most. He did it all: football, basketball, baseball, the Olympics, and on Sunday afternoons (who will forget?) "The American Sportsman." As a young sportscaster in New Orleans I had Curt on my own sports talk radio show. He was candid and enlightening in previewing the upcoming Final Four, but it was our conversation the next morning that I will never forget.

At the tender age of 25, my only play-by-play experience had been on radio, while I desperately wanted to break into television. Gowdy told me never to apologize for the privilege of doing radio play-by-play.

Curt had already reached the twilight of his television career, and he was in the Crescent City to work alongside the legendary voice of the Kentucky Wildcats, Cawood Ledford, for CBS Radio's coverage of the Final Four. It was here that he pointed out to me that Ledford and others like him who had chosen to stay near their homes had made very wise career choices.

Curt said these guys had just as much talent and perhaps more well-rounded lives than some of the "network types" that I had looked up to for so long. Now, don't get me wrong, it's not as if I didn't always respect the voices of the 'Dogs, 'Cats, Tigers, etc., but Curt simply reminded me that these announcers would have long broadcasting lives. In many instances, their tenures would be longer than some of the head coaches and athletics directors at many of the various institutions.

The truth is that while I will forever be a fan of Gowdy and others like him, fans of college football and basketball in the southeast will have long since forgotten network announcers as they continue telling stories of Jim Phillips at Clemson, tales of Otis Boggs at Florida, Al Ciraldo at Georgia Tech, Bob Fulton at South Carolina, Bob Harris at Duke, and John Forney at Alabama.

Television is a medium best suited for dialogue between the play-by-play man and analyst. By contrast, radio is more narrative. The dramatic voice inflection of a good radio announcer gives the listener a theatrical description of what they canSt see but would love to visualize. It is that aspect that sets radio and it's play-by-play commentator apart.

It has been my good fortune through the years to get to know most of the men that you will be reading about. I must admit each of them brings his own unique quality to the airwaves, whether it's Larry Munson's insecurity over his outweighed 'Dogs that always have to "hunker down"; or Woody Durham's passion for Carolina blue; or the smooth staccato styles of Paul Eells, John Ferguson, and Jack Cristil.

What follows is their view of how they were able to become the legendary voices of the Southeast.

Tim Brando
CBS Sports

Acknowledgments

It would be impossible to thank everyone who helped with this book, but if I didn't, this would be a blank page. (And I apologize in advance if I forget to name you.) With that in mind, I would like to personally thank the following, who provided unending support and encouragement, and who helped turn this idea into our book: Malcolm (Brad) Bratcher, Randy Carney, Ken Dugan, Kurt Dugan, Scott Grissom, Crystal Henderson, Mike Mansfield, Mike Milam, Chuck Morris, Todd Reel, and Pam Snowden.

To the Sports Information Directors, and their staffs, for providing media guides, ideas, and various stories for the book. Some of those who helped include: Brian Binette, Tim Bourret, Rick Brewer, Norm Carlson, Mike Cragg, Claude Felton, Mike Finn, John Humenik, Tony Neely, Mike Nemeth, Rick Schaeffer, Herb Vincent, Larry White, and Rod Williamson.

Thank you to the sportscasters' wives and families, some of whom I've gotten to know: Helen Boggs, Ruth Ciraldo, Jean Durham, Marjorie Forney, Phyllis Harris, and Frances Ledford. Thank you for all that you ladies did, whether it was offering a cup of coffee, editing your husband's chapter, showing us hospitality at a university luncheon, sending us a Cat's Meow (that wooden block), or taking my wife shopping at the mall.

To Wes Durham, one of Woody's sons and a future legendary sportscaster, thank you for your advice, support, and friendship. Thank you to the "young" legendary voice of the Alabama Crimson Tide, Eli Gold, for your comments on John Forney as well as your thoughts for the Introduction ... Bama fans are lucky to have you. Special thanks to the voice of the Tennessee Volunteers, John Ward, for helping formulate the list of legends and for encouragement

The Sportscaster's Dozen

throughout the project. Even though you're not in this book, you're still included in this list of "legends."

Thank you to Tim Brando, another future legendary sportscaster, for your willingness to write a great foreword. Keep hitting that little white ball straight.

A special thank you to the sportscasters for opening up your memories to someone you didn't know from a hole in the wall. Without you guys, this would still be a blank page. Thank you for your willingness to be included in the book and the generosity extended to me over the past two years. It has been an honor and a pleasure working on this book and getting to know each of you; I'm a better person for knowing you. You guys can turn anyone into a fan of the schools you represent.

Thank you to Ken Samelson and Holly Kondras at Masters Press for believing in this project.

To the group of friends and family who serve as my core support, guidance, and constant encouragement, I owe a mountain of gratitude: my media mentors, Rudy Kalis, Tom Lawrence, and Jonathan Seamon ... you three were the backbone to this project; Logan "Gig" Fulks, my legal support and "big bro"; John, Alicia, and Addi Wood; Morey "MoJo" Joseph; Ronnie, Sharon, and Colton Carnahan; Barry Landes, who sat through those Sundays at East Village Grille pulling for the Chiefs and the Giants; Kevin, Sarah "Yasmine," and Ashlyn Oats; Kevin, my marathon training partner and Arturo counterpart, had to hear stories about the book on our long Saturday runs because he couldn't get away; the best young agent in the business, Sabrina Cashwell, and her husband, Chris, both of whom provided endless support and advice; my in-laws, Todd and Pat Burwell, who also transcribed a couple interviews; Jesus Christ, through whom all things are possible; my family, Pop, Mom, and Joshua, for your love and for making me what I am; and above all, my wife, Libby, who not only loses her sanity to help me keep mine, but also makes sure I meet my deadlines. Thank you.

Introduction

Well, good evening everybody, and welcome to tonight's game. ¶ Ahh, music to any sports fan's ear, whether those words are coming out of a car radio on a brisk, fall night; a clock/radio on an office desk during an afternoon March Madness game; or from a transistor radio with an earplug that a boy has smuggled into class in April to catch opening day of the baseball season.

It's a special feeling when your favorite team is on the radio, because it usually means your favorite sportscaster is on the air, painting a brilliant word picture which is so vivid, you feel like you're at the game. It's that familiar voice (or voices) to let you know that everything is going to be OK.

For more than 50 years, colleges and universities in the southeast have been known for their athletic teams' accomplishments and the unique players they have developed. These teams have produced exciting and unforgettable Atlantic Coast and Southeastern Conference games in basketball, football, and baseball. More often than not, the radio broadcaster is the link between the fan and these teams.

Through that link the broadcaster and fan develop a bond, whereas the sportscaster naturally becomes known as the voice of the state; in many cases, they are the fabric of that state and institution. Often, all that a fan knows about a particular school is by what the athletic teams do, and therefore by what the radio announcer says about those teams.

There have been 12 such men, who week in and week out have served as the voice of college athletics in the southeast. This book is their story, in their words, as they tell about their experiences covering some of the top athletic programs in the country.

The Sportscaster's Dozen

Why has the southeast developed some of the most outstanding sportscasters not only at the local level, but nationally, as well? Does it have to do with the socioeconomic status of the area when many of these broadcasters were growing up? Is it the dialect? Are Southerners bred as better storytellers? It's not known for sure why the southeast has had an uncanny ability to produce top talent, and it probably never will be known; but the fact remains that several of the best radio sportscasters in the history of the business have called the southeast home. Sportscasters who have painted word pictures so vivid that the listener can see the action ... from his radio.

The voices of major league baseball broadcasting icons such as Red Barber, Mel Allen, Lindsey Nelson, and Ernie Harwell have come from such southeastern cities as Sanford, Florida; Bessemer, Alabama; Knoxville, Tennessee; and Atlanta, Georgia. Current voice of the Alabama Crimson Tide, Eli Gold, grew up in Brooklyn, New York, listening to Barber and Allen call the Yankee games.

"Growing up, I was a big New York Yankee fan, and fans were spellbound by these southern announcers. Keep in mind this is in a city who's fans can be pretty rough sometimes," he says. "In New York city, we used to listen to these southern guys make the games sound so romantic. They could paint incredible word pictures in a soothing way.

"For a kid out of Brooklyn to hear this southern-tinged voice that actually talked to you and not at you was something special. You never forget those memories of your youth. I will never forget these guys."

It's ironic, maybe somewhat funny, that Gold, who is also one of the main announcers for NASCAR, gained most of his radio play-by-play values from southern sportscasters.

As Gold describes, "During the last few years of Mel Allen's life, we would laugh about how he went from Alabama to New York to call games for a team that is so traditional with the North that it has the nickname of 'Yankees,' while I came from New York to the South to do University of Alabama sports and one of the most storied southern football programs, as well as NASCAR, a sport with its roots deep in the south."

One southern sportscaster who deserves to be in this book is John Ward from the University of Tennessee, who has spent over 30 years as the voice of the Volunteers. Ward has a distinguished style, somewhat deliberate, that sends chills up the spine of any UT fan each fall when he bellows out, "It's football time in Tennessee!" True to form, Ward's touchdown call has a deliberate uniqueness with his patented,"He's at the five ... four ... three ... two ... one ... give ... him ... six!"

Ward takes a businesslike approach to broadcasting that possibly goes back to the law degree he holds from UT. In fact, in one letter he wrote to me during this project, he said of game day preparation, "Never break the routine; don't do anything to alter focus on the most important thing ... the game broadcast. Focus on the game broadcast."

John Ward is focused. He prepares for each broadcast very meticulously, which shows on the air through in his calm demeanor. He prepares as hard today as he did as a young broadcaster in the late 1960s. Even though he brings an excitement each time he is on the air, Ward gives the listener the feeling that everything is under control.

In a business which seems to breed egos the size of Tennessee's Neyland Stadium, Ward is extremely humble. He has always declined offers from other authors and publishers wanting to write his biography. Originally he had wanted to be a part of this project, but shortly before completion he had to retract his acceptance due to a possible personal conflict of interest with the University of Tennessee.

Even though, selfishly, I had planned on including the voice of the Volunteers in this book and was disappointed when he changed his mind, I have nothing but the utmost respect for John Ward. He has been instrumental throughout this entire project, including the suggestion of several of the legends and offering various pieces of advice in regards to the book and to broadcasting.

John Ward is a legendary sportscaster.

But what makes a sportscaster legendary? There are really no true qualifications to be considered a "Legendary Sportscaster." There is no secret formula. A sportscaster does not necessarily have to be a 20-time Sportscaster of the Year award winner in their state or belong to a particular Hall of Fame. Generally over the course of time, the great sportscasters receive the accolades they deserve. The great ones are mainly concerned with putting a quality broadcast on the air that tells the story of the game, regardless of which team is playing well and which one is playing poorly.

If for no other reason, the men in this book qualify as legendary through two distinct qualities they each possess; they have been in

The Sportscaster's Dozen

the business for at least 25 years, and they are highly respected in their profession. Each of the 12 have a phenomenal photographic memory, often remembering players and details which time has forgotten.

It takes a unique person to be a good play-by-play announcer, let alone a legendary one, especially in today's technologically-driven society. Today, the idea of radio as a main medium is a slipping thought, while three-network television is long gone. Many of today's up-and-coming sports announcers choose television over radio. Some, like Joe Buck and Thom Brennaman, have been able to successfully juggle both. Others, like Tim Brando, earned a break in television and ran with it. As Brando says, he now has an opportunity to reside in the city where he grew up and spend quality time with his family.

The general consensus, however, is that the money in play-by-play is mainly found in television. That may be justified, but from what I've seen and heard, the radio announcer develops a closer relationship with his listeners ... a bond forged by representing one school with its own fans.

Radio is a wonderful medium and a wonderful art. Frank Lloyd Wright once said that, "Television is chewing gum for the eyes." If that is true, then radio must be chewing gum for the mind ... for the imagination, with a good announcer providing the flavor.

This is a project I started because of my special interest in sportscasting, as a former play-by-play broadcaster for WAKM radio in Franklin, Tennessee and with Lipscomb University in Nashville. I also have a nostalgic love of the business. Doing radio play-by-play is how I first met my wife (she was a basketball player) and it was eventually the avenue by which I asked her to marry me, during a coach's show.

The idea for *The Sportscaster's Dozen* first came to me while working at WAKM on Saturday mornings, and I would hear University of Tennessee fans express their love for John Ward during the 'Kick-Off Call-In Show.' Traveling to other states in the Southeast, I heard other fans react similarly to their particular broadcaster.

For me, growing up in the Kansas City area during the 1970s and 1980s, the perceptions of "my" teams were provided by radio greats such as Max Falkenstien from the University of Kansas; Fred White and Denny Matthews with the Royals; plus Bill Grigsby and Kevin Harlan with the Chiefs. (In fact, two of my life's biggest thrills have been getting to know Fred White over the last few years, as well as receiving a letter of encouragement from Max Falkenstien during the writing of this book.)

Any time any of these sportscasters were on the air, I tried to be close to a radio. It was not uncommon during the Big 8 Conference basketball tournament or major league baseball postseason for me to be in class with Grandma's transistor radio hidden in my coat with a simple ear plug to see how the Jayhawks or Royals were doing. (It's OK to 'fess up to that now, isn't it?) Even though I was in school, I was on top of the world!

Georgia Tech broadcaster Wes Durham, a super broadcaster in his own right, said he used to do the same thing growing up in North Carolina listening to the ACC tournament. Part of his dreams were realized when he went from Vanderbilt to Georgia Tech and was able to broadcast ACC tournament games.

I have truly been blessed, because I have been able to gain first-hand experience in radio, television, and newspaper. Now, I wouldn't trade my experiences thus far as an author for anything in the world, but there's nothing like getting behind the microphone to represent an institution and a team ... take a listen ...

M.W.F.
12/31/97

*There's heroes and there's legends.
Heroes get remembered,
but legends never die.*

> *The Sandlot*
> David Mickey Evans and Robert Gunter

OTIS BOGGS
UNIVERSITY OF FLORIDA

Growing up I loved sports; I particularly loved baseball and football. I spent some of my formidable years on the campus of Clemson University. I loved their sports, so I used to sell peanuts and soda pop at baseball and football games. ¶ Through that association at Clemson, I got to know a famous Indian named Joe Guyon. That name may not ring a bell to most people, but he played football under coach John Heisman at Georgia Tech. Joe Guyon had played as a blocking back for Jim Thorpe at Haskell College in Lawrence, Kansas, and then he transferred down to Tech before the 1917 season. Eligibility was not something that was followed too closely in those days. He was full-blooded Chippewa. One day I went into his office and I looked at this picture of a guy in a turtleneck sweater, and I said, "Coach, who is that man?"

He said, "Son, that's the greatest coach who ever came down the pike. That's John Heisman."

(It was Heisman who coached the Tech team that beat poor little Cumberland, 222-0.)

I got to know the Chippewas pretty well. Mr. and Mrs. Guyon used to come to our school to lecture and bring Indian art craft. So I learned a lot about Indians from Joe Guyon and his wife.

My father was a railroad man and worked for the Southern Railroad, which obviously runs through most of the South. During the Depression he moved over to the Seaboard Airline, the main artery of which ran down through the state of Florida. (That's why I have Florida connections although I was born in Clemson, South Carolina.)

> We make a living by what we get, but we make a life by what we give.
> ~ Sir Winston Churchill

The first game I ever saw was Clemson against Davidson, a small school in Charlotte, North Carolina. I was eight years old. Clemson won it 6-0. There was no "fun-n-gun" there like Florida has today—you got one touchdown and that was it. I had a natural love of sports.

Somewhere along the line, though, I decided I wanted to go into chemistry. My basketball coach in high school in Auburndale, Florida taught me chemistry and told me he thought I should go into that field because I was a natural at it. So before I got out of high school, I took college chemistry for two semesters at Clemson where I stayed with my aunt.

I probably would have gone to Clemson for college and lived with my aunt and uncle, but they moved the summer after my senior year in high school. So my dad suggested I go to the University of Florida where I would be closer to home. So I did. I was very lucky I made that move because they didn't have any type of radio school at Clemson, while Florida had WRUF, which is a campus-owned station that turned out Red Barber and a flock of other great radio people. That's how I kind of fell into the radio deal; I would not have had that same radio opportunity at Clemson.

Growing up I used to listen to Red Barber do baseball and I always thought that would be something interesting to do. A buddy of mine in college found out they were having auditions at WRUF, which was primarily operated by students. We went down to the station (this was the middle of my sophomore year). I passed the audition, and a gentleman by the name of Dan Riss was in charge of the new announcers and had a training school for us. He said for the people interested in sports to meet him at the field the next day (the Gators were having spring practice in March).

Each guy got to do a little mock play-by-play at that practice. Two days later Dan told me he wanted me to help out with color for a basketball game during the state high school tournament they were having in the last week of March. I jumped at the chance, little knowing what I was letting myself in for.

I got over there and the first game got off at 8 o'clock, and the guy who was to do the play-by-play couldn't make it for some reason. Jimmy Walton said, "Otis, you're going to have to do the play-by-play."

I had never done play-by-play. So in 1939 I jumped in there and did my first basketball game. It was between Green Cove Springs and Mulberry. For the poor people who listened to that ballgame, I hate to think of the pure torture they must have been subjected to listening to me do my first basketball game. I did so poorly, at least in my own mind, that I thought that was the end of my radio career.

About three or four days later a good friend of mine, Dave Russell, who was on the boxing team said, "Otis, they've been waiting on you to get down to the radio station so you can start your shift." I asked him if he was kidding me.

"No," he said, "You better go down there this afternoon!"

That's how I got started. At WRUF you got to do a little bit of everything. In fact a lot of people look at me when I can speak of classical music and opera and wonder how a sportscaster ever got to learn all of that. Well, I had to write a one-hour show every day called "The Hour of the Masters." And believe me, when you do that you become familiar with it, and you either learn to love classical music or you go crazy.

Later on when I worked out at WFAA in Dallas, I had a chance to do a couple of shows with Antol Dorati, the famous Hungarian who conducted the Dallas Symphony. My background put me in good stead; I wasn't completely lost doing the shows. Dorati asked me, "How did a country boy like you ever learn anything about Beethoven and Strauss?"

In the old days of radio you had to learn a little about everything, and you tried to fall into that niche that fit you best. From my lucky standpoint, sports happened to be that niche, I guess.

Dan Riss, who had been the sports man at WRUF moved to Texas and Dave Russell, who had been an understudy of his, became the football play-by-play man for the Gators for the 1939 season. Of the three people who auditioned for sports on that March day, I was the lucky one (I guess I stuffed the ballot box enough) to be the color man that season.

When Dave Russell moved to Texas in 1940, I became the play-by-play man for the Gators. With the exception of the three years away for Uncle Sam during World War II and one year in Dallas, I held the position of play-by-play man until 1981. All in all I was the voice of the Gators in baseball, basketball, and football for 37 years.

Radio's Pioneers

Back when I was a kid, the first announcer I heard do football was Graham McNamee. He was one of the pioneer broadcasters. Later on CBS had an announcer named Ted Husing. I liked Husing

The Sportscaster's Dozen

Otis Boggs (center, with microphone) broadcasting the European Basketball Championships in Munich, Germany, in 1946. Second from left is former University of Alabama All-American center Joe Domnanovich. Third from left is former Green Bay Packer Cecil Miller.

although I found out later that technically he didn't know a lot about football. But he had the most marvelous vocabulary. To hear a man express his thoughts the way Husing could was just beautiful. He did the big games up East and he did the Orange Bowl.

Husing's use of the English vocabulary was unbelievable and he had a beautiful voice to go along with it.

I also used to like to listen to Bill Stern because he was the dramatic type. He had a great sense of drama. I used to like to listen to Stern and a show in which he would tell a story. He did that in the most dramatic fashion. I looked up to all of those people because they were several plateaus ahead of me. I also learned a little from each of them.

Vocabulary and expression, I think, are things that have helped make Pat Summerall an outstanding sportscaster. Some sportscasters are not too glib with the King's English, but Pat had taught English literature, and when you listen to him you realize his grammar is spectacular. He won't burn your ears up, I'll tell you that.

When I was a little kid, my dad was working at a teeny stop up the road from Gainesville called Highland. In those days they didn't have double tracks. They had single tracks and you had to have operators around there to give orders for the fast trains to go through, or the slow trains to get off on a siding. It required a lot more personnel in running a railroad because they didn't have all the electrical equipment that they do today.

We knew a gentleman named Mr. Wimberly who was also an agent in that town. My dad worked the midnight to dawn shift. Mr. Wimberly had one of the first radios around there. This was in 1925. I was five years old.

Mr. Wimberly invited us over one night to hear his radio. It was one of those radios that you needed to used earphones because it didn't have a speaker. The only station they could pick up during the daytime was out of Jacksonville, WJAX, and it was a city station. They had a young family who put on a country music family show. That family's name was Canova, which included Judy, Annie, and Zeke. (Judy later went on to be a famous comedian in Hollywood.) Hearing them was my first introduction to radio.

Our family didn't own a radio until 1931 when I was 11 years old. I found out that the neighbors listened to football on Saturdays, so that's where I would hang out. I would worm my way into wherever they were listening to a football game. I never missed one.

As a kid growing up, in my mind there were only two teams: Clemson (because I grew up there on the campus) and Alabama (because they represented the South, and went out and beat everyone in the Rose Bowl. Later on I obviously had to root against the Tide).

I think you form these allegiances as a youngster, but they can change quickly depending on which side your bread is buttered. For example, I had a cousin who grew up in Atlanta and went to Tech High and thought that was just the greatest thing in the world. All of a sudden he went to school at the University of Georgia and learned to hate Georgia Tech.

I think now of all the baseball announcers, Red Barber, who was a dear friend of mine, was far and away the best. Before I really got to know Red, I asked Burt Shotton, who managed the Dodgers during the Jackie Robinson days, "What kind of a guy is Red Barber?"

Shotton said, "Otis, if I had to turn my ballclub over to one person outside of baseball, without hesitation I would turn it over to Red.

He knows the ballclub inside and out, top to bottom. He knows the pitching rotation. He knows the league. He knows the players, and he's a great humanitarian. He'd make one helluva manager."

To me that's one of the greatest compliments I've ever heard a baseball man pay to a broadcaster. I've never forgotten that.

Red Barber

Red Barber was very intense. He grew up in Florida. His dad was a railroad engineer for the Atlantic Coast Line, while my father was a ticket agent for the Seaboard Airline Railroad. That's where the similarity ends, because Red was more famous and made a lot more money than I'll ever make.

He was very engaged in humanitarian projects. He was one of the leading blood donors during World War II. He worked for the Red Cross and many similar organizations.

I learned the real technique of knowing the game inside and out from Barber. He taught me about knowing the rules and knowing the players. Something he never did, and I think a lot of our modern-day sportscasters feel they need to do it, is serve as the manager, the umpires, and the personnel director. Red told me one time about how [former baseball commissioner] Judge Kennesaw Mountain Landis once called all the World Series announcers together and told them how the most important thing was not to umpire the ball, not to editorialize on why the manager made this change or that change, because they were getting paid to do their jobs and you were getting paid to broadcast the ballgame.

Red asked him, "Do you mean to just tell it like it is?"

To which the judge replied, "Here's what I mean ... if in the heat of the battle, some player gets mad at the umpire, gets mad at me, and gets mad at baseball in general, and gets a dip of water with tobacco in his mouth, comes over to my box and he spits the whole shooting match right in my face ... you tell whether I took it standing up or sitting down, and which way the wind was blowing. Give it the whole pitch, just don't editorialize on why he did it."

Red told me he never forgot that.

He helped start a lot of people in radio. One of his best known "gifts" to radio was a young fellow named Vince Scully who had never done any broadcasting. Vince came over to Red's office one day, and Red was impressed with Vince's knowledge of the game, his voice, and the way he expressed himself. So Red helped turn

Scully into one of the nation's best baseball announcers. For about 40 years, Vince has been with the Dodgers organization. I know Red was always proud of what Vince had done in broadcasting.

I used to listen to Red do baseball. He also used to sing with a hillbilly band at WRUF named the Orange Grove String Band. As a young boy he had wanted to be a minstrel, but then he got into sports and forgot all about being a minstrel. We had a show with the Orange Grove String Band that Red used to emcee. My dad used to listen to it. That's how I got introduced to Red Barber.

We had a week at the University of Florida where we invited top sportscasters to come down and deliver a lecture series on what they did. We had about 10 or 12 outstanding sportscasters, including guys like Al Helfer who used to do the "Game of the Day" for Mutual. That's when I first actually met Red. He lectured about broadcasting and how he got started. From that day on he became a fast friend.

When Red moved back to Florida, my wife and I would go up to Tallahassee see him and his wife, Lilah. (It was kind of interesting that my wife had gone to church in Key Biscayne and Red had been a lay reader in the Episcopal Church, and she had met him there and loved his reading of the Word.) It was a good friendship.

We lost a great broadcaster when he passed away.

Homecoming With the Guy on the Lights ...
What a First Year!

As I mentioned I started out doing color for the Florida Gators in 1939, and during that first year we had a unique situation. During our next to the last game of the year, we played Georgia Tech. Tech had a great team that year led by quarterback Johnny Bosch, and they had already received a bid to the Orange Bowl for postseason play. The Yellow Jackets came down to Gainesville to play us for our homecoming.

In those days our broadcasts were handled by the NW Ayer Agency for the Atlantic Refining Company. They also sponsored the Georgia Tech games. We had young Dave Russell doing play-by-play on our games, and Tech had a veteran by the name of Marcus Bartlett. (Marcus later became the general manager of WSB radio in Atlanta. In fact, Marcus is the one who hired Detroit Tiger Hall of Fame broadcaster, Ernie Harwell.)

Since both of our broadcasts were handled by the same ad agency, they decided to let Marcus do the play-by-play, and I would do the color. (That way they had a Tech guy doing the game and a Florida guy doing the color.)

At that time, Florida Field only seated 22,000 people. [In 1997 capacity was 85,000.] The light towers were up at the top of the rim of the stadium. There were three light towers on either side. And over on the student side (the east side), there was a platform up by the lights which had a ladder leading up to it so they could change the lights.

> *Otis was a good broadcaster. Even though we really didn't know each other, I know the people in Florida loved him.*
>   ~ Bob Fulton, University of South Carolina

On the field Julius Battista of Florida blocked a punt, scooped it up and ran it in for a touchdown. The Gators and the Jackets were tied 7-7 at halftime. Off the field, however, right before halftime, there was a student who had been smoking reefer (we called it "reefer" then, it's "pot" now) and was high. Evidently his girlfriend had just dumped him. He was beside himself because of that. He smoked a couple strings of marijuana, and he climbed the northeast light tower on the student side only being spotted by a few people.

He got up to that platform where they changed the lights, and he was doing hand stands and skin the cats on the railing. Hell, people forgot all about the football game! (Women were literally fainting in the stands.)

The police sent two plain clothes officers from their SWAT team (there weren't actual SWAT teams back then, but they had comparable groups) up to the top of the tower. The band came on the field to do their halftime show. I was going to be doing the halftime show and color, but I didn't get to do it because all of the attention was on the center ring over on the northeast light tower.

The first of the two officers to get up there almost got kicked off when the kid tried to kick him in the face. The police had to do a combined attack. In the meantime the band's playing, but nobody's listening to them although nobody was leaving the stadium. (Back in those days the *Atlanta Journal-Constitution* didn't have color pictures, but they had a wonderful pictorial section. The day after this game they had a few pictures of the band and the game, but most of them were of this kid on the tower.)

The two police finally got a hold of him, knocked him out, handcuffed him and tied him down. They didn't lower the kid down until after the game was over.

It got some bad publicity for the University of Florida because here's one of their students about to commit suicide on the light

Boggs receives an achievement award from Batman and Wonder Woman at Sea World in 1976.

tower during the homecoming football game! (Tech won the game, by the way, 21-7.) That was the most unusual thing that has ever happened to me in broadcasting. For sheer diversion you can't beat that.

My introduction to color was surely horrendous; the band show went down the drain. I thought, man, this could be more exciting than play-by-play! I'll never forget that.

Then 1941: World War II

I got a good break a few years later at the start of World War II. Tom Leib was coaching the Gators, and we had a pretty good team for Florida standards at that time. We had scheduled UCLA. (The two schools had played a series before I got to school.) This particular year, 1941, we were scheduled to play the game in Jacksonville. Since we weren't playing on the West Coast, the game was not canceled. We played it around December 14.

UCLA had a great team that year. Florida gave the Bruins a good game, but UCLA won it 30-27.

That happened to be my second year of doing play-by-play. The Mutual Network got the rights to the game coast to coast, and they invited me to do the play-by-play while a California guy did the color. So not only was that my second year of doing games, but that was my first time of doing a game for a coast to coast audience like MBS; I'll never forget that experience, either.

Deep in the Heart of Texas

After spending the 1946 season at the University of Florida, I moved to station WFAA in Dallas in 1947. During the time I was there, Rip Engle brought Penn State in to play Southern Methodist University in the Cotton Bowl. SMU featured the outstanding halfback Doak Walker who won the Heisman Trophy in 1948.

Rice University has a great tradition in that it's a leading academic school. Years ago, if your grades were such that you were in the upper 4 percent of high school graduates in the state of Texas, they would let you in to Rice for free. (At one time the Rice institution owned part of Yankees Stadium in New York.)

I used to like to go down to Rice because the coach there was Jess Neely. When I was a little boy growing up at Clemson, he had coached at Clemson and hunted on my grandfather's farm. I got to know Coach Neely later when he was at Vanderbilt, but he was quite a guy and a good coach.

Neely was coaching at Rice when an Alabama player came off the bench to tackle one of his players about to score a touchdown. I guess the guy just couldn't stand it when he saw Rice was going to score so he came off the bench and made a super tackle!

I guess after seeing that I figured I had seen it all and headed back to Gainesville for the 1948 Gator season.

Bob Woodruff and Ray Graves

Bob Woodruff is a dear friend of mine. When he came to Florida as the football coach, if the Gators won two games in a season back then, friend, it was cause for a celebration. It was also thought that as a coach you could never build a winner at Florida just by recruiting in Florida alone. So many of the coaches before Bob went out of the state to recruit. For instance, a lot of our linemen in the 1930s had come from Pennsylvania because the coaches felt the only way to get good, big linemen was to go out of the state.

(Of course all of that has changed now. There is a wealth of instate talent today. In fact, if you could recruit all the good players from the state of Florida, you could probably suit up four or five teams. We've got three pretty good ones down here from year to year with Florida State, Miami, and Florida. Not in that order necessarily, but the whole scheme has changed.)

Woodruff came to Florida when things were kind of lean. He gave the school a new identity. Number one he was a builder. Bob loved football, don't misunderstand me, but when he came to Florida he started building other programs. He increased the size of the stadium, he got the tennis program up, and he got the baseball program up. To this day I've never forgotten him, and Florida fans will never forget him. We still had a number of years to go before we got the first Southeastern Conference football title, but Bob was the first one to move us in that direction.

Then along came Coach [Ray] Graves who had played at Tennessee, just like Bob Woodruff had. Coach Graves had coached with Bobby Dodd at Georgia Tech. He had a sense of putting a good recruiting program in and of playing wide open football.

I think the most exciting game that I ever saw was Coach Graves' first year here (1960) when he went up against his old tennis partner and fishing buddy, Bobby Dodd. That Florida-Georgia Tech game was one of the most exciting ones ever for Gator fans. Tech was favored to win. Coach Dodd's wife is sitting over in the stands. Her son, Bobby Dodd, Jr., is playing for Florida, her husband is coaching Georgia Tech, and one of her favorite players at Tech, Pepper Rogers is the offensive coordinator at Florida. There was more emotion and sheer drama in that ballgame than any you'll ever see.

I can recall to this day Billy Williamson, who was an athlete out of Miami, running for a touchdown to give Tech a 17-10 lead late in the fourth quarter. It looked like the Florida dream was not going to come true. But the Gators got a hold of the ball. The younger Bobby Dodd completes a throwback pass to one of the wideouts who fumbled but then recovered on about the 3-yard line.

On the next play, Lindy Infante took a pitchout and ran it in just inside the flag in the north end zone for the touchdown. That made the game 17-16 with under a minute to play in the fourth quarter. Coach Graves went for a two-point conversion (which had just been put into place the year before), and we converted on a pass play to the fullback to win, 18-17. Florida proved that season they could win some big games. After that game things improved for the better as the team went on to the Gator Bowl and beat Baylor to end the season.

That Tech game was in 1960. After that game we went down to Miami and played Rice. There was a feeling that we needed to recruit in the Miami area so we gave up a home game to the Orange Bowl in Miami and played there. Rice shut us out 10-0, but the Gators went on to have a very good year, losing only one conference game (to Auburn). They wound up playing Baylor in the Gator Bowl and won it 13-12.

It was a good year ... Pepper Rodgers and Ray Graves had lots of fun.

I was close to Coach Graves and Coach Woodruff. In fact Coach Woodruff used to call me in to his office, because he knew I got excited when the opponents completed at least 15 passes against our secondary. He told me one time before a Rice game how they had a pretty good short yardage passer, but he couldn't hurt us deep, so we were going to let him have a few short ones. Coach told me not to get too excited if they completed 10, 11, or 12 passes that day. I appreciated that because it kept me from hitting the panic button. Coach Woodruff was that kind of a guy; just a very straightforward person.

Each coach, not just Bob Woodruff and Ray Graves, has contributed something to this Florida program. Doug Dickey, for instance, had some tough years here, but he was the first coach to take a Florida team over to Jordan-Hare Stadium in Auburn, Alabama, to beat the Tigers. The Gators dominated the Auburn Tigers and won 12-8 (the game wasn't as close as the score indicated).

Charley Pell gave a new sense of pride and went orange. (On a side note, we had a situation when he took a Gator team up to Atlanta to play Georgia Tech. Florida was beating the Yellow Jackets pretty good, and a tremendous rain and thunderstorm came out. The game was held up for 20 minutes because of the lightning, so we had to fill up that air time. When something like that happens, you are reaching for everything; you talk about tradition helping out ... that's when you reach for tradition!) Pell also did some great recruiting while he was here.

"The" Comeback ...
Not Our Comeback but the One That Sticks Out

The biggest comeback I remember was not a Florida comeback, but rather a Duke comeback. We went over to Jacksonville in 1962 to play the Blue Devils, and it was the first time Florida had played Duke. Coach Graves was the Gator coach at that time.

Florida jumped out to a commanding lead early and was leading at halftime, 21-0.

(There was a period in football when there was an offensive player they called the "lonesome end." It was a player who wouldn't even come in and join the huddle, but he was used as a flanker. There was this formation where the end was a pass receiver.) Duke used the "lonesome end" and scored 28 points in the second half to beat the Gators, 28-21.

Ray Graves was pretty upset. Obviously when you blow a 21-point lead, that's pretty bad. To me that's one of the most amazing comebacks because Florida could have and should have beaten Duke that day but didn't. Coach Graves later told me that was one of the few times he had actually cried over a football game.

We don't play Duke much anymore.

The Bear and Bobby

There are two opposing SEC coaches that come to mind immediately and who I would say were the best we faced ... Paul "Bear" Bryant at Alabama and Bobby Dodd from Georgia Tech (when they were in the SEC).

In the 1950s Coach Dodd and his teams pretty much dominated the SEC. And I think seeing us beat Bear Bryant and Alabama in Tuscaloosa was one of my biggest broadcasting thrills. We beat them 10-6 in 1963.

Those are the two opposing coaches that stick out; that's not to put the other coaches down by any means.

General Bob Neyland, for instance, in the early days set the scene at Tennessee. I remember going up to Knoxville and watching his teams play (and he loved the single-wing offense).

The Sportscaster's Dozen

Otis broadcasting a 1954 spring football game at the University of Florida. Note the electronic spotting board.

That's one of the interesting things about Steve Spurrier coming to Florida as a player. He grew up in Johnson City, Tennessee, and Ray Graves' brother was postmaster in Knoxville (which is close to Johnson City). Ray's brother called Coach Graves and told him there was a great high school quarterback in Johnson City. Steve liked to throw the ball, which you do some in the single-wing but it's more of a grinding offense. Ray told him it would be an open throwing-type offense with the Gators, which appealed to Steve, so he came to Florida instead of becoming a Volunteer at Tennessee.

Steve Spurrier

I think the real epitome of Florida football is what has happened with Steve Spurrier. He has rewritten the offensive books as a player and now as a coach. Some people don't agree with some of the things he does, but I tell them this is the most exciting brand of Florida football I've seen since I started broadcasting in 1939. I enjoy every minute of it.

Some people cry about him running up the score, but I can remember the day Georgia beat us 75-0 ... Coach Spurrier isn't even close to running up the score yet. That's all in jest because I have some friends and relatives who went to Georgia, but I guess what goes around comes around.

For the fans who follow the Gators under Coach Spurrier, they'd probably buy 50,000 tickets on road games, if they could get them; that's how popular it is.

Away from the field Steve is a very likable person. When I retired from play-by-play in 1981, he was an assistant at Duke University, and he wrote me one of the nicest letters I received. In fact I still have that letter in one of my scrapbooks.

Steve Spurrier is very competitive whether he's coaching football or playing golf; he's just a natural born competitor. He likes to win, and not to brook with mediocrity too much. The defense, for instance, had never come up to his expectations, so he brought in Bob Stoops as a defensive coordinator and the 1996 defense helped give the offense the ball as much as any defense could. (Steve likes for the offense to have the ball. I don't blame him ... that's his game.)

I broadcasted every game that Steve Spurrier played in college and had the pleasure of doing the games the year he won the Heisman Trophy in 1966. I remember the game when he kicked the winning field goal against Auburn at Florida Field. He normally didn't kick field goals, but he had a strong leg. In that particular game, our main field goal kicker wasn't in good shape, so since it was late in the game and we were tied 27-27, he figured we needed three points. He went to Coach Graves and told Coach that he wanted to kick the field goal. So Coach let him go for it.

To this day I can still see that field goal. Most field goal kickers when they kick, get a tremendous altitude. Spurrier's was a line drive. It traveled about 40 yards and looked like it was on a clothesline, as it barely got over the crossbar. I remember wondering if it was going to go just above or just below the crossbar. Hitting that field goal and thus winning that game may have helped give Steve the Heisman. (Of course he had a lot of help from people we had in our battle plan like Norm Carlson who was the sports information director and a very fine man. A player doesn't make the Heisman on his own, he has to have some publicity and hype from other people. Norm Carlson came through.) Steve certainly deserved the Heisman.

Steve was the first quarterback to come to Florida who could run the two-minute offense. The Gators were never out of a ballgame with Steve in there. Generally speaking he didn't lose too many.

The Sportscaster's Dozen

He could run the two-minute offense and utilize the clock, which I think is still apparent today with the way the teams Steve coaches can work the clock at the end of a game. They do things today on the spur of the moment; they'll call an audible with five seconds to go sometimes. Every once in awhile you get socked with a 5-yard penalty for delay of game, but that's just part of it I guess.

The Gators

There have been so many great football and basketball players here. John Reaves was an exciting football player. John played here with the "Fabulous Sophomore" group that Coach Graves and his staff recruited and gave way when Coach Doug Dickey came down here from the University of Tennessee. Reaves and [Carlos] Alvarez were sophomores together in 1969. I'll never forget the way Reaves and Alvarez worked together as a great passing combination.

> Otis is one of the great people in the world. He used to always have a gallon of fresh-squeezed orange juice for us when we went to Florida. He did a heck of a job for the Gators.
>   ~ Cawood Ledford, University of Kentucky

We were playing a Houston team that had been picked to win the national championship, and in that particular ballgame at Florida Field, the Gators came out on the first play from scrimmage—Reaves hit Alvarez on a 70-yard touchdown play. From then on the fun had just begun because the Gators wound up and scored 39 points in the first half.

People listening in to their radios (we didn't have a great deal of TV coverage back then) in places like Ocala and Daytona Beach couldn't believe it; they thought I was making it all up. People couldn't believe the Gators scored that many points on Houston!

They had the greatest ticket sales at halftime that they had ever had at a Florida game. The ticket people figured we had about 5,000 people come in from other parts of the state within driving distance just from listening to the first half. Houston had a fun-n-gun offense of their very own and they scored quite a few points that day. It was a fun game! The Gators won that opening day game in 1969, 59-34.

But the combination of John Reaves to Carlos Alvarez was outstanding. Carlos is now a prominent attorney here in the state of Florida and has done very well in the legal profession.

Later, Florida fans found that if anybody knew the game of football it was Cris Collinsworth. He knew the game from two angles;

originally he was recruited as a quarterback (and he still holds the Gator record for longest touchdown play when he threw to Derrick Gaffney for a 99-yard touchdown at Rice in 1977), but then they found out he had such good hands and could catch it and that he was much more valuable as a receiver. Cris later gained his fame as a receiver with the Cincinnati Bengals in the National Football League. He was a very articulate person which has helped him land jobs in radio and television.

Wes Chandler was one of the early great receivers we had at Florida. We have four or five receivers of that caliber now, but Chandler was the guy that if you got him the ball, he could probably score a touchdown. He had great moves with good speed, and he later had a fabulous career with the San Diego Chargers as a receiver.

Rick Caseras was a tremendous football player back in the day when it was 5 yards and a cloud of dust. (He lettered from 1951-1953.) He played fullback and did the quick-kick. You don't see the quick-kick much anymore. I guess there's no place for the quick-kick in the fun-n-gun. In the old days of football if a team was deep in its own territory, a coach might send out that good kicker of his on second or third down and have him drop back two steps and bang it away. Caseras could punt from deep punt formation, but his forte was kicking the quick-kick. It was like it had been shot out of a cannon when he hit it. He kicked some 70 yards on the roll ... it was just amazing.

Caseras was just a great athlete. He also played basketball. I'll never forget John Mauer, who was our basketball coach in the 1950s, used to say, "When you get in a scramble under the basket with Rick, don't hang on too long because he'll stuff you right through the hoop." And John was right, because Rick was one tough dude.

On the basketball side, the University of Florida has never really had that many great players. In fact the basketball Gators did not capture their first SEC title until the 1988-1989 season which was the last season for Coach Norm Sloan. (That's when Dwayne Schintzius was the big player underneath.)

Neal Walk was a really fine big man who played here in the late 1960s. There have been some other fine players, but Neal is the one that comes to mind as being a very good big man for the Gators.

Basketball, I think now, with the better recruiting in the 1990s, will be bigger at Florida. I think the fans will start getting into it more. Basketball for some reason has only had two high water points;

the year Norm won the SEC and in 1992 when Coach Lon Kruger took the team to the NCAA Final Four. Basketball was the stepchild of Florida for a long, long time.

For years and years in the Southeastern Conference, Kentucky was the king of the hill with Adolph Rupp as their head coach. I think Coach Rupp beat teams so badly that school officials realized they better get a basketball program going, instead of having their football coach do both (which some of the schools did).

But I think basketball at the University of Florida will improve.

I don't think the caliber and number of outstanding college basketball players rival the caliber and standard of outstanding football players that we have in the state of Florida. There are some great basketball players in the state of Florida, but I think there have been and continue to be more outstanding football players here.

"Fergie" Ferguson

I think another great athlete (and this one goes way back) was Forest "Fergie" Ferguson from 1939-1941. He was on some of the Florida teams that just won three or four games, but he was tremendous athlete from the state of Florida. He was a boxer, a baseball player, and a great javelin and shot put man. He played all of his life in Florida but never got too much recognition. He got third team All-America honorable mention after his senior year as an end.

I recall the first coach I ever really became acquainted with was Tom Leib. Tom had been a great player at Notre Dame and played tackle for Knute Rockne, but he always wanted to play fullback. Quite frequently, after he started coaching at Florida in 1940, he would demonstrate how to run plays. At the time Florida was putting in a draw play, similar to the one where the quarterback takes the ball and after holding it for a moment he gives it to the fullback who waits for a couple seconds then breaks through.

Leib wanted to demonstrate this draw play. Fergie was always pulling pranks on Coach Leib, and the day the draw play was going to be demonstrated was no exception. Coach Leib, with his baseball hat and baseball pants on, came running up the middle as the fullback on this draw play. All of a sudden to cut off the hole Leib was going to run through comes Fergie. Ferguson was about 6 foot 3 and 210 pounds which was all bone and muscle. Fergie hit Tom Leib at about the midsection (Tom weighed about 230 pounds), lifted him straight in the air and dropped him flat on his back!

When Leib hit the ground it knocked all of the wind out of him. He started shouting, "Fergie, why did you do that?"

"Well, Coach," Fergie replied, "If you had broken that tackle, you would've been a blue-chip All-American." Leib was too weak and hurt to strike out at Ferguson; he just wanted to know why.

The coach at Boston College from 1939-1940, who was later to become almost as big of a legend at Notre Dame as Knute Rockne, was Frank Leahy. He actually had 107 wins in his career compared to 105 wins for Rockne. Leahy did not lose a regular season game at Boston College except for the one he played against Florida.

The Eagles lost to the Florida Gators, 7-0 in 1939, primarily because of a great defensive effort by Fergie Ferguson. He had a ton of tackles and big defensive plays; it was truly one of the best defensive performances in Florida Gator history.

When World War II broke out, they formed two service teams. Fergie played on a team coached by Wallace Wade and the other team was coached by General Neyland from Tennessee. These two service teams met out on the West Coast, and played in the Rose Bowl. Fergie had never played in a big game on the West Coast, so he dashed out on to the field at the Rose Bowl, got down on his knees, kissed the ground and said, "Thank God I finally made it!" Fergie was so good that he started at end and Holt Rast, who was a two-time All-American from Alabama, sat on the bench.

Fergie later died of wounds he received in World War II. Today there is the Fergie Ferguson Award. He was a fantastic player.

Nobody today running around Florida Field remembers Fergie Ferguson, but they still give an award in his name and it's very deserving because he was outstanding.

The Cigar Bowl

Back in the early days the networks had the bowl games locked up, so it was more difficult for us radio broadcasters to do the games. During my career, however, I did three bowl games. I did the first Cigar Bowl game ever played, which was between Rollins College of Winter Park, Florida, and the University of Delaware. Bill Murray, who would later become an outstanding coach at Duke, was coaching Delaware at the time. That game was fed to people in Florida and Delaware.

The second bowl game I did was between Florida and Miami of Ohio in the 1973 Tangerine Bowl. That was the first of four straight

The Sportscaster's Dozen

Otis Boggs (left) receives the Distinguished Alumnus Award from then-interim University of Florida President Robert Bryan in 1989.

bowl games for the Gators under Doug Dickey. The game was played at Florida Field in Gainesville because they were rebuilding the Tangerine Bowl stadium in Orlando. The Gators lost that one 16-7.

The final bowl game I did was the Tangerine Bowl (or Citrus Bowl) between Florida and Maryland in 1980. Florida won that game 35-20. That was Charley Pell's second year as head coach.

Nowadays the play-by-play man for the school gets a pretty big break radio-wise because they're allowed to broadcast the bowl games. I think it's a good break for the voice of the team to be able to do a game like that.

The First Gator Bowl

The very first season we went to a bowl game (1952) sticks out in my mind even though I didn't get to broadcast the postseason game. Coach Woodruff had taken over the program from Raymond Wolf in 1950, and took the Gators to the Gator Bowl against Tulsa two years later. Florida had never even seen a bowl game up to that point, much less played in one!

In the game leading up to the Gator Bowl, Florida closed out the regular season with a win over Kentucky, 27-0. That was the first of only two times in Florida's history that we beat a Bear Bryant-coached team. Under Ray Graves in 1963, the Gators took a team over to Tuscaloosa and beat Alabama, 10-6. That's the only game the Bear lost in Tuscaloosa until the final year of his career when Southern Miss beat them over there.

The Florida teams in those first few years under Woodruff boasted of such top players as Rick Casares and an outstanding quarterback by the name of Haywood Sullivan. Haywood decided to play pro baseball instead of football. We've had a lot of great quarterbacks at Florida, but I'll never forget Haywood because he had such tremendous hands (he was a catcher in baseball). It didn't matter if it rained or not, because Haywood's hands were so big that he could easily hold on to that football; he could throw in the rain all day long.

Doug Dickey was Sullivan's understudy, and even though he didn't have the same physical characteristics as Haywood, he had a very good mind for the game. Dickey was the quarterback for the Gators when they beat Tulsa 14-13 in the 1952 Gator Bowl.

With that Gator Bowl win, Florida football had made a big step in the right direction.

"THE SWAMP"

The noise level in the Swamp, where the football Gators play their home games, is really deafening. To give you an idea of how loud it can be, the university made a special deal for Red Barber and his wife a year before he died. Since he had left Florida, the new group of people over there had heard about him, but they had never worked with him. So they decided they wanted to do something for Red and have him come down to one of the games.

So in about 1991, someone from the athletic department called him and told him they wanted him and his wife to be the guest of the university at the Florida-Tennessee game. The sports information director at the time, Norm Carlson (he's now an assistant athletics director), asked me if I would fly with him up to Tallahassee to pick up Red since they had never met.

We flew up early on a Saturday morning (the game was scheduled for that night) to get Red and his wife. When we got back to Gainesville, there was a nice, big limousine to meet us at the airport. There was a luncheon for the Barbers, and then I taped a TV interview with Red.

Red and Lilah were seated in the President's box which is right under the press box. The noise in the Swamp was so tremendous that Red and his wife had to leave and go back to their hotel at halftime.

It's true that a quarterback coming in and trying to get a snap count off and call an audible can find it almost impossible because of the noise. The Florida football stadium is a very unique place.

The Florida fans help make it such a unique place. There are some Gator fans out there, and some of them get obnoxious every once in a while. I guess, probably, the Gator fans had experienced losing for so long, then all of a sudden they're treated to the caviar of the sports world as winners; for some people it's difficult to get used to that.

Florida fans are so avid they would travel to about anywhere to see a Gator football game. I sometimes wonder how they keep their jobs. Look at the Florida memorabilia out there; it's incredible. I am absolutely a Gator fan.

GATOR RIVALS: THE "OTHER" FLORIDA SCHOOLS

Florida State is a bigger rival to the Gators than the University of Miami, simply because Florida and Florida State play on a regular basis whereas the Gators and the Hurricanes don't.

> *Otis is a longtime professional; an accurate, complete radio broadcaster. Florida was fortunate to have him all those years. He had old-time, solid broadcasting skills*
>
> *& John Ferguson, Louisiana State University*

I did the first game between Florida and Florida State in 1958 when the Gators won in Gainesville, 21-7. Then we turned around and beat Miami 12-9 before losing to Ole Miss in the Gator Bowl.

The 1966 game (Spurrier's senior year) sticks out in my mind. The Gators won that one 22-19. That was just an outstanding game in Tallahassee.

Florida State came to Gainesville in 1971 undefeated at 5-0 while the Gators were still looking for the first win of the season, sitting at 0-5. (To start off the season, Florida had lost to Duke, Mississippi State, Alabama, Tennessee, and LSU.) The Gators scored off the opening kick off. Florida also picked off several passes that day and completely dominated the game. The Gators never trailed and won the game 17-15.

Florida won three of its last five games, defeating Maryland, Kentucky and Miami. Even though the Gators finished the season 4-7, I feel the FSU game was the turnaround of the season.

The last football game I ever did was the 1981 Florida-Florida State game at Florida Field, and the Gators won it 35-3. That was a big margin of victory for Florida at that time. In fact, during Charley Pell's first season as head coach in 1979, the Gators had a record of 0-10-1. The closest that team came to a win was a 7-7 tie with Georgia Tech.

Getting back to the Hurricanes, I think Coach Steve Spurrier would like to play Miami, but I don't really think the scheduling in the Southeastern Conference now would allow for it. In the SEC you must play eight conference games, plus a possible title game if you're good enough. That leaves you with three outside foes. Florida plays FSU so now there are only two games left. Florida has traditionally played a team for homecoming that, relatively speaking, is a soft touch.

Miami and Florida could be a great series and a great rivalry. I think it would be a great money game for the schools.

Florida Pride and Tradition

It's good to broadcast for a school with a tradition like Florida because it gives you an opportunity to call a lot of great games.

Gene Ellenson at one time was the head of the Gator Boosters down here. Gene was a very good football man; he had played for Wally Butts at the University of Georgia and he was very knowledgeable. I used to tell him we needed to get more tradition. He kept saying how the Gators are working on it and how we would have our tradition one day.

Gene played in 1942 on the Georgia team that came down to the Gator Bowl and beat the Gators 75-0! I always tell people not to get too hooked on scores and start comparing scores between three teams, because you can get fooled by comparative scores. We had played Auburn University here at Florida Field and beat them 6-0. Then we went over to Jacksonville and played Georgia in that 75-0 loss. (Georgia scored 27 points in the first quarter of that game. They hadn't even broken a sweat before scoring 27 points. You talk about a long afternoon ... try sitting in a blow out like that while trying to keep some semblance of interest for your audience.)

The week after Georgia trampled the Gators, they played Auburn in Columbus, Georgia, and lost 27-13. At that time, that was a major upset in the Southeastern Conference. So we beat Auburn 6-0, lost to Georgia 75-0, then Auburn beat Georgia 27-13. That's why I advise not to compare scores between three teams.

I can also well remember the first time I ever saw Florida win from Georgia. It happened my freshman year before I even thought about getting into radio. In those days, the freshman had to wear a ratcap (a beanie), and you had to write on there "Rat" and your last name ... so I was Rat-Boggs. (There were some interesting combinations, like Rat-Coffee or Rat-Love.)

They had a tradition going that IF you beat Georgia in Jacksonville, then you didn't have to wear your ratcap to classes and around campus and those sorts of places. That year (1937) the Gators blocked a kick and beat the Bulldogs, 6-0. That was the first time Florida had beaten Georgia since 1929.

But overall, a program's tradition gives you something to peg information on. It gives you recall of things that have happened. Florida now has a wonderful tradition.

The best thing that happened for the Gator program was the fact that there are such great athletic programs in Florida's high schools. Back in the 1930s and early 1940s, we just didn't have the talent in the state.

For a long time, we were the doormat of the SEC. That's the reason when people complain about Steve Spurrier and the present-day Gators running up the score, I don't really care ... let him run up the score.

Oops ... two Sidekicks in a Bad Press Box

We used to have a lot of fun traveling on road trips.

One time Fred Abbott, who was an outstanding linebacker for Florida in the early 1970s, was talked into doing some color commentary. We were playing Miami, and with about 3 minutes remaining in the game and Florida leading, Fred got mixed up and said to the other color announcer (Bob Leach), "Bob, if we watch our time here we'll get the two-minute warning and we'll be able to get an extra timeout in."

Leach said, "Where are you? This is a college game, this isn't the NFL!"

Sometimes I think having two color commentators may have added a little confusion to the broadcast. That was started when they decided they wanted a former athlete as a color man. Leach had been a longtime anchor on the networks, and he had a great voice, so he kept doing it.

There were good features and bad features about it. One of the bad features when you had three guys in there you didn't know who's going to talk when. But overall it didn't work out too badly.

The bad part came in a couple stadiums where we worked. Tulane

Otis (left) with cousin, and baseball great, Wade Boggs.

University in New Orleans used to play their games in what was the actual Sugar Bowl. They had the most unbelievably small place to work from; you could barely fit one person in your space, let alone two or three. If you were sardines in oil, you might be able to fit all four of your people in there. I never really cared to work out of there. Now they have the Super Dome, and the facilities in there are great. I've done a couple games in there and it's very nice.

I never did like working from the Orange Bowl in Miami. In their facility you were restricted in what you could do. They tried to build it up as something great, but it wasn't.

A couple of the nicer places I've done games from include the Rose Bowl and the Coliseum in California. Northwestern and LSU were also two good facilities from which to work. Georgia Tech also always gave us a good booth. I always liked Alabama games in Tuscaloosa as well as Auburn games.

For the Love of Football

I had played baseball and basketball in high school, but despite some of our broadcast positions, I loved doing football play-by-play the most. There is so much strategy involved; it's like legalized warfare. I grew up watching football when the players went both ways. A guy would be in there on offense and as soon as his team lost the ball, he would go on defense.

Then the game became specialized in the late 1940s or early 1950s and a guy would only play offense or defense, but he was excellent at what he did. I think that really improved the game for the fans.

The game has reached a real high point offensively today here at Florida with what Steve Spurrier has done with his "fun-n-gun." He has loaded his lineup with great receivers, a good passer, and good runners. Whenever you see a Spurrier team play, he may lose, but he is going to put some points on the board. I think the fans really enjoy that.

Learning what the fan needs to hear was most difficult for me in those first few years. For the radio fan, you need to paint a picture of a thousand words. For instance, he's got to know where the ball is and where the down is. I think the person who comes up doing the radio broadcasts really learns the game inside out, or you leave sportscasting and go back to driving a truck or pumping gas. I'm glad I came up in that period, I must say that, because I think it was very valuable.

One of the ways I tried to paint that picture was through one of the main phrases I used. People always used to accuse me of saying someone kicked a "high, end over end spiral." When you think about it, that can't happen.

I was describing one day the trajectory when you kick a high spiral, and the minute it hits the ground it becomes end over end. That end over end got me in trouble. (Besides when you think about it, an end over end kick isn't true ... when you kick a ball going clockwise, it's end under end and not end over end.)

I think one of the tough things for me, and I'm sure for other announcers, was learning more players when football became specialized. It went from knowing 11 players for each team to knowing 22 for each team. The play-by-play man needs to be able to identify—with the help of a spotter—who makes the tackle, who makes the block and so on. That put tremendous strain on the play-by-play man at that time. However, the guys doing the play-by-play broadcasts today do a marvelous job.

When the game became specialized, I developed an electronic spotting board where I had it so rigged up that you could throw one switch and 22 lights would change on both sides of the board. For example if Florida lost the ball, I would throw the switch, and the offense would go dim and the defense would light up. Same way for the opposing team. I had it four-men deep. It operated on 120 AC.

That really helped out until one day at the Sugar Bowl in New Orleans, my spotter plugged it in to a 220, and it burned out every bulb on the board. That was a day for sure.

The simple way is the best way today but that electronic board was a lot of fun. It helped me out a lot.

Living with a Sportscaster

I don't think being married to a broadcaster is like being married to a doctor where you could lose your husband at any time of the night to an emergency. There are tough times, however, when you aren't at home with your family, but you want to be there with them. And there are other times you would like to take your wife to a ballgame but you can't do that. If my wife Helen wanted to go to a game she would either have to go alone or take a friend with her. Things work out, but you're never at a sporting event with your wife because you're always working.

On the other hand, this business has some advantages because you get invited to places you normally wouldn't be invited to like parties and various functions.

In 1989 I was given the Distinguished Alumnus Award from the University of Florida. I was told beforehand by one of the deans that they were going to give me the award at graduation on a Saturday morning. There were about five of us who got that award. (On the Friday evening prior to the presentation, they had a special dinner at the house of the university president. They really rolled out the red carpet for this dinner.)

But at the graduation the next morning, the five of us were sitting up front while the graduates were being introduced. One of the graduates was Mary Wayte who worked with me at WRUF. (She was also an Olympic gold medalist swimmer in 1984.) When she came up to get her diploma she stopped and laid a huge kiss on me!

One of Mary's friends whom I had met at the station called me up and jokingly told me I almost got into trouble with Mary landing that kiss on me.

She said, "Did you know Mary's boyfriend was in the audience today and saw every bit of that kiss and was very upset?"

"Aw c'mon," I replied, "Doesn't he know I'm an old man?"

"That doesn't matter to him; and he could bring some serious pressure to bear on you."

I didn't know if he was a policeman or what. Come to find out Mary's boyfriend was Prince Albert of Monaco! Their relationship lasted about a year, but he was at the graduation and saw that kiss.

When the award presentation was made and my name was announced, the entire group from the school of communications stood up and started cheering. That was really something special.

If I had any regrets, however, I wish I could have been around to do a football season when Florida won the SEC title. Outside of that I don't have any regrets. It's like verses from the Bible that Red wrote on a note to me about there being a time for everything. When you think it over, there is a time, and I've come to realize that.

I am very thankful I had a chance to do play-by-play for Florida. Certainly their fans are the greatest; they really love their football team. Through play-by-play I didn't get rich, but I was able to make some great friendships. It also helped me meet my second wife, Helen, who's turned my life into something really nice. (My first wife and Helen's husband had both died. She and I knew each other for 16 years and were married in 1981.)

THE BOGGS FAMILY TREE

Baseball player Wade Boggs and I didn't really know that we were kin. He bought a fish camp for his dad about 12 miles outside of Gainesville. After he did that and his name got out, I called his dad, Winfield, and told him I had been wanting to talk to him because there was a chance we were related.

As we started talking, I found out that Winfield was born in South Carolina and had grown up in Marietta, Georgia. I asked him what part of South Carolina.

"A town you've probably never heard of," he replied. "It's a little place called Townville which has about 400 people and is close to a town called Seneca."

I was born about six miles from Townville on the edge of the Clemson campus.

He said, "My goodness, we're related. Why don't you come over and have supper with me tonight."

Winfield was in the Marines and fought in the Battle of Guadalcanal in World War II. When the Korean War came along, he was a civilian but still eligible for the Marines, and they wanted him to come back. He decided when the Korean War broke out, though, that he wanted to do something different, so he signed up with the Air Force.

During his time in the service, Winfield was a great fast-pitch softball pitcher. He was good enough to make several military all-star teams. General Curtis LeMay liked athletics so he and Winfield hit it off just like that.

After Winfield and I reunited, we started to compare family notes. For instance we found out that our great-great-grandfather, Henry Thomas Boggs, lied about his age to get into the War of 1812 (he was a bugler) but eventually saw combat action. After the war he came back to a town called Liberty, South Carolina, and bought a mountain. If you ever saw "The Waltons" television show they had Walton Mountain; in Liberty, South Carolina, there is a Boggs Mountain. Our great-grandfathers grew up on that mountain.

John "Red" Cochran's dad was a fine athlete at Clemson University. After the elder Cochran graduated he moved to Birmingham and played baseball during the summer months for the Birmingham Barons of the Southern Association. Red Cochran and his two brothers, Bob and Ralph, all played college football; Red played at Wake Forest while his brothers played at Alabama.

Then there's Wade Boggs, who has played baseball for the Boston Red Sox and the New York Yankees. I have trouble making it to baseball games, but on March 19, 1996, the Yankees changed their spring training home from Fort Lauderdale to Tampa.

The old Al Lopez Stadium was torn down, and they built what is now called Legends Field in Tampa. In the old stadium, the field and the parking lot were located on the south side of the street. With the new stadium it's on the north side and the public parking is now on the south side of the street (the stadium is too big to have both on the north side), while the parking for the players is next to the stadium.

To make a long story short, Winfield told Wade he was bringing me to a game and they arranged for us to park in the player's lot.

I really enjoyed seeing the ballgame and watching Wade play. After the game we went to Wade's new home. (He had just built a house in a very nice residential community in the Tampa area.) The house was incredible! One room was nothing but trophies; his five batting title bats were in there with two Gold Glove Awards and then six or seven trophies for being named the pro athlete of Tampa, plus various other awards and memorabilia.

The Sportscaster's Dozen

Legendary broadcasters (from left to right) Red Barber, Otis Boggs, and Pat Summerall.

He's also an avid fisherman and hunter, so in another room he had personal gaming trophies of things he had caught or shot. It was just a fabulous home.

There was another huge Italian villa next door and I asked Wade who his neighbor was. He told me it was Pete Sampras. So Wade and Pete are good friends and neighbors. He told me a funny story about how anytime he does something well (like winning a batting title), Pete would send him a bottle of champagne. Wade did the same thing when Pete won a big tennis title. But he figured he was losing money in that deal because Pete has more chances to win titles in a year than Wade does.

That was really a great time!

My No-hit Dream

Even though I was able to do some wonderful games and call some great Florida moments, emotionally speaking, if I could pick out one event to do, it would be a no-hitter in the seventh and deciding game of the World Series. Why do I say that?

Johnny Vander Meer was invited to come up to a broadcasting conference we had in the journalism building at UF. Johnny had been at Cincinnati and pitched back-to-back no-hitters. Red Barber used to tell the story about seeing Johnny's second no-hitter, which was at Ebbets Field.

People used to tell Red how much they enjoyed his broadcast of that game, but he said they didn't announce that game. At any rate he put together a tape to play after Johnny spoke to this broadcast group. Vander Meer was sitting at a table with my wife Helen and I. When he heard that tape, Johnny Vander Meer was frozen and emotionally shook; it was one of the most emotional things I've ever seen.

To me, to do a no-hitter in a World Series would be phenomenal because the pressure on each and every pitch, and each and every play is so great. That's what I would have loved to have done.

Red did Don Larson's perfect World Series game in 1956. In fact, Red and Mel Allen were in the booth together, and Mel just about had a heart attack because you generally didn't mention a no-hitter after the first couple innings, but Red said he realized there were people out there listening who didn't know Larson was pitching a no-hitter. He told Mel he was going to broadcast it, and he did. Red later told me that Allen about passed out in the booth when it was mentioned on the air. I think Red was prouder of doing that game than any other thing he did in his baseball broadcasting career.

Red also used to tell me about Jackie Robinson and what a great person he was. After Jackie finished his career, he went up to Red and thanked him for all the broadcasts he had done. Even though Red felt Jackie did a lot for him, he was still honored and thrilled that Jackie said that to him.

Know and Respect the Players

There are so many areas in radio in which a person could work. The first piece of advice I would give a person going into broadcasting is to respect the people you work with. When dealing with players you have to be very careful sometimes with what you say to them.

Red was telling me one time about broadcasting an important baseball game and a pitcher may have a bad inning. The tendency is to jump on that player and say how he doesn't have it today. But you don't know if that player had been up all night with a sick child at home, or something like that; you really have to respect that situation. I think the same is true with any sport you deal with, and not just baseball. The same rule also applies to the officials and umpires. I knew Butch Lambert very well, and he was a very good official. (His son is now officiating.) He was an old Mississippi guy.

I was never one to say on the air that an official missed a call. It's like Red Barber's story about former baseball commissioner Judge Kennesaw Mountain Landis telling Red that it wasn't his job to critique umpires; his job was to broadcast the game.

That's not to say that sportscasters follow that rule, though; they sometimes have a slip of the tongue and criticize players and officials. It's also not to say that sportscasters don't have a different slip of the tongue and say embarrassing things.

Oh sure, that happens. It's almost impossible to sit there and talk for two and a half hours each week, without slipping somewhere. I hear guys do it today when they make a misidentification of a player or something like that. If you can get into that rhythm, you don't slip very much.

Luckily there aren't any for me personally that stick out in my mind. I've been very fortunate. I was never a great person for profanity, anyhow, which is a big help if you're messing around with a microphone. If you use profanity regularly and you use it behind the mike, you could lose your job; there goes the old family estate right down the drain.

One thing I would encourage broadcasters to do (and I think this would've been good advice for myself) is to not be a homer any more than you have to; give the other team credit. If you give the other team credit and show them as being a good team, then it makes your own team look better and well coached. I tend to agree that the job of the broadcaster is to broadcast the game and not try to be the coach or umpire ... just the broadcaster.

Personally, I was a homer to this point ... I don't think anyone ever doubted that I was a Florida Gator broadcaster, but I always tried to build up the other teams and the things they did well. I was never guilty of saying "our Gators" or "we," but I think with the enthusiasm I showed on the Florida side, people knew who I was for. (After all, we were broadcasting on a regional network.

I never believed in tearing another team down or talking about how lousy they were; that was not in my style of play at all.

Speaking of the other team, today I would also tell a young broadcaster to prepare. I didn't have much choice but to learn how to

After receiving the Outstanding Sportscaster Award for the state of Florida in 1961, Otis (left) is congratulated by North Carolina Governor Terry Sanford and Miss North Carolina.

prepare. Since the Florida football Gators were in a constant state of flux early on, the first thing I would do at the start of the season is learn our team. Over the years we maybe put a little more emphasis on the players on the line, so I studied them more. Don't miss a good play by someone.

I would also work all the practice sessions and the scrimmages before the season started. Then I would talk to the coaches; if the coaches trust you, then they will give you all sorts of useful information that will help the broadcast.

For the opposing team, the sports information director was a key source. They could always provide me with statistics and background information on their players or coaches.

To me the preparation and meeting the people were a couple of the more fascinating things about broadcasting. I always enjoyed meeting people outside of the SEC.

Turning off the Mike

I think my wife, Helen, would tell you that the first six months or so after I retired from play-by-play were tough. I was pretty shaken up because I had lived Florida athletics for so long.

Red Barber, who was a very religious person, was one of the people who wrote me a letter. In that letter he quoted a section out of the Bible from Ecclesiastes (3:1-8) that talks about how there is a time for everything. That part of the Bible really helped put things in perspective and simplified things for me.

It's difficult to do something for so long and turn it over because you can come to a point when you miss it. But don't get me wrong, I listened to the games that first year away, and I still do. Actually, I continued in broadcasting (although not play-by-play) doing a morning show here in Gainesville. That caught on pretty quickly, and I've enjoyed doing that. There are still times, though, on Saturdays when I wish I could be out doing the games. (Although, physically I know I could not do that now because of the type of schedule you can have and because you need good vision.)

When I got out it was a situation where I was 61 years old. The athletic association wanted an in-house man (I did not work for the athletic association; I worked for WRUF radio) who could do a number of things like play-by-play on radio, the TV shows, plus travel with the alumni association around the state and make various speeches. I'm not sure I would've wanted to do just sports.

Mick Hubert is doing the games now, and I think he does a very good job and has been well received by the alumni groups. People still come up to me and recognize me as the voice of the Gators, which is nice to be remembered like that; it's a nice compliment. For a big Hollywood star it's an everyday occurrence, I'm sure, to be recognized, but when a small regional guy like me is recognized, it's special.

In the fall of 1996, my wife and I were in a little town outside of Gainesville and were pulling up a driveway to a grocery store. I was driving in the parking lot with a row of cars on both sides of us, and all of a sudden there was a big pickup truck backing up and there was no way I could avoid him. Even if I sped up he was going to get me. Sure enough he nailed my rear quarter-panel.

When he got out of his truck I noticed that he was a younger fellow, about 35 years old, and the first thing I asked him was if he had insurance. He told me not to worry, that he was the insurance man. Come to find out as he was giving me his insurance information he worked for an insurance agency out of Tampa and was also an adjuster for an insurance company. What are your chances of getting hit by an insurance adjuster?

As he was getting my information he asked my name, and I told him. He said, "Otis Boggs? I grew up in Tampa listening to you. I've always wanted to meet you!"

I told him it was good to meet him although I wish it had been under different circumstances. He was very nice about everything.

King Solomon and Stormin' Norman

Our particular situation at WRUF was that we had students coming through and working, unlike most commercial stations. Because of that I had a chance to work with a lot of them.

Thinking about some of the students I've worked with, I had one former spotter who became a general in the Marines. I had another student who got injured playing football (his wife worked at the radio station as a traffic operator), he was another spotter for me and later became a famous judge in Jacksonville.

Then I had another young man from Jacksonville who was a spotter, and just a perfect picture of health. After he graduated he in-

> *I go back with Otis as long as I do with anybody, because he was in the SEC when I got here. He did a splendid job for the University of Florida and was a very knowledgeable broadcaster. He was also a great social guy; he was very full of life and always seemed to have a great time wherever he went; he was extremely jovial. We really got to know one another early in our careers and socialized quite a bit together.*
>
>   Jack Cristil,
> Mississippi State University

herited one of the largest Ford dealerships in Jacksonville. Sadly, he called me about 15 years ago to tell me he had Lou Gehrig's Disease. He said, "Otis, one of the most treasured moments I have to remember is when we worked together in the broadcast booth and the trips we made." That really hit me deep down.

On a lighter side, we had another young man by the name of Solomon (we called him "King") who worked with the basketball team. One night during the 1962-1963 season we had a game in Charleston against West Virginia back in the days when they had a tough full-court pressure defense. (This was the first game of a three-game trip as we played West Virginia, Kentucky, and Tennessee.) With West Virginia's tough defense, I don't think we got the ball across midcourt more than four times in the first half. The Gators ended up getting beat 114-67.

Norm Sloan, who had a fiery temper, was the coach of that team, and he always came to the booth after the game to do an interview. On this particular night Solomon comes to the door, and I asked him what he was doing there. He replied, "Well, the King is going to have to be with you tonight because Stormin' Norman ain't going to be here." Solomon later went on to become the top sports editor for the *Washington Post*.

The associations I've had in this business have been wonderful. I often tell people that I never made a lot of money in the business, but I made a lot of friends, which I think is very important in this lifetime.

AL CIRALDO
GEORGIA TECH

I grew up in Akron, Ohio, and can remember when our family got our first radio in about 1930, when I was 9 years old. All I would try to do was pick up ballgames. There weren't a lot of radios around then. Back then we would listen to baseball games and then to football and basketball. Basketball was young then; we didn't have pro basketball, but we had the semi-pros. We would listen all the time, and people would gather around radios then, much like people do with televisions today.

> *I will study and I will prepare; and perhaps someday my chance will come.*
> ~ Abraham Lincoln

In our house, the radio was always on. Again, there weren't a lot of radios around then; there was one in probably every two homes. Then it got to be big, and car radios started coming into play which got to be a big audience.

In baseball it was the Cleveland Indians; since they are so close to Akron, I would listen to all their games. When I broke in as the number two man doing the Akron Yankees, I became more involved and at night would tune in the clear stations like KMOX in St. Louis.

There was a man by the name of Ted Husing who did football for CBS. I did the soap box derby for several years in Akron, and Husing came in there for CBS. We developed an acquaintance and talked quite a bit.

He had more influence on me than anyone else. The main reason is because when he was at Columbia he was a quarterback on the football team and so when broadcasting, he would paint a picture where he got you involved in the ballgame. He would get the point across with a lot of empathy, then you as a listener would be going through the motions like you were that quarterback. He really had a style.

Growing Up on the Radio

I was 15 years old and in my hometown of Akron, when one of the radio stations had a contest looking for the number two man to do minor league baseball. On a dare I went in there and won the contest, to make a long story short. Before that time, I had never been in a radio station in my life. The town we lived in was about 300,000 people, and when you have an announcer who is 15 years old, it's a big deal. They made a big deal about it.

I played a lot of sports growing up and was very fortunate to have a photographic mind. I could read about Babe Ruth or someone like that in the sports page, see the statistics, and that was all it took for me to remember. Early in high school I played baseball, basketball, and football, but then said forget that; and I concentrated on radio. From that point on, I read any type of sports pages I could get my hands on.

My first partner, Bill Griffiths, had an advertising agency. He steered me right when he said, "Look Al, forget about this damn announcing, the money is in the advertising and the sales." He let me work in his advertising agency, plus I did the minor league baseball games for the Akron Yankees. That was in 1938.

I did three innings of the Yankee games, and Griffiths did the rest. After that I branched out into football, basketball, and everything else around.

We didn't travel with the team, so if, for instance, Akron was at Erie, Pennsylvania, we recreated the game from the studios using the Western Union guy at the ballpark. A lot of announcers felt that was tough, but I didn't think it was because you knew everything that was going to happen there, and you could add your own style. I think it worked out well.

The United States was deep into World War II when I graduated from high school, so before college, it was off to basic training in Mississippi. After basic training, I went to the Pacific where I was at [General] MacArthur's headquarters. From Australia I went to New Guinea, then Manila. We were preparing for the invasion of Japan, and I was working out of San Francisco. As soon as the War ended, I got the hell out of there as fast as I could.

Originally I was going to go to school at Notre Dame (my dad wanted me to go into law), but when I got into radio, it was tough to get it out of my system. All of a sudden, the idea of studying law at Notre Dame wasn't as exciting. My dad was upset when I decided to concentrate on radio; he just didn't understand when the radio bug hit me. Regardless, though, Dad wanted all three of his boys to be college graduates.

I had checked about two or three schools that were good in radio, and for awhile I thought that I'd maybe go to Ohio State, but then I picked out Florida. So instead of going to Notre Dame to become a lawyer, I was going to be a Gator and be a broadcaster. Florida has a great broadcasting school at the university, with a 5,000-watt radio station, WRUF.

Red Barber is the one who got me to go there. Back then Wheaties cereal sponsored all of minor league baseball, and Red was in Cincinnati, Ohio, and was in charge of all the Wheaties' announcers in the Midwest. I was talking to him when I was about 16 years old, and he said, "What you want to do if you decide to stay in radio, is go down to the University of Florida." I took his advice and was in Gainesville from 1946 to 1948, when I graduated early.

Red was a great guy; they don't come any better. You meet some great ones in sports announcing, but then you meet the other type, too. Red Barber was a good one.

Otis Boggs was in school the same time I was there. He worked for WRUF, and I free-lanced to supplement my income so I could take as many hours as possible to graduate as soon as I could. Otis was there for years as a broadcaster for the university.

Personally, I got some breaks along the line, which I think you need to have. The best break I had was getting with Georgia Tech. It was a break because they owned the radio station, and when I first broke in with them, no one was doing Tech basketball. It was just a matter of going in there year, after year, after year.

The Industrial League

My first experience broadcasting basketball was in Akron. That's going back to the days when there were industrial leagues; there weren't pros. Goodyear and Firestone, for example, which were in Akron, Ohio, would go out and hire the All-American basketball players to work for the company for big money. That was the best in basketball in those days.

Indianapolis had a team in there. Chicago was in there. Akron was in there with two franchises. Oshkosh, Wisconsin, was in there. New York had a franchise. Big factories would back these teams, and they'd draw between 7,000 to 8,000 fans.

As soon as a youngster was ready to finish college, and he was a senior star basketball player, a company would sign him up. The kid would work with the company, and eventually they all became presidents of corporations. But that was called the Industrial League.

Starting out in Ohio, I did a lot of those Industrial League games as well as high school games.

I always found basketball was easy. All you need is a good vantage point to do the games; and with five players, what the heck? In those days, with a photographic memory, I could just read something or see the players in the dressing room and could remember. I would always go by the numbers as a safety valve, but that was it.

I always enjoyed broadcasting football and basketball the most. I loved baseball, but it was just too slow. Remember, this is before television, and in those days, you got a chance to do things in basketball and football. You could do things in baseball at that time, but not as much.

You would get on there and paint the pictures. Since there was no TV, you could probably do a better job in football and basketball with all the excitement.

Preparation

In the beginning of my broadcasting career, I used to really prepare ... I mean every day I would do something. Let's go back about 10 years or so with Georgia Tech.

There really wasn't anything that was difficult for me in preparing because I enjoyed doing it. It could be tedious because there was something to do every day of the week. By doing all of that, you can do a better job.

A lot of the announcers today will have someone else do the spotting boards, then they'll just come in on Friday or Saturday and think they're ready. Well, they aren't very acquainted with the teams that way. I'll say, though, that radio announcers still prepare a lot more than TV announcers.

I was always in good with Coach [Bobby] Dodd, which helped. I could go into his office, and we'd look at films of the games, and he'd give me the scouting report and the game plan. Because of the preparation we did together, I could actually do the games without spotters (even though I always used them just to be sure). Of course, as I got older and older, I used spotters more and more. It was something to actually prepare with Coach. Then I'd go to the game and

Al Ciraldo publicity photo from Georgia Tech, 1996.

knew everything as far as Georgia Tech's plays as well as what the other team was going to do.

I prepared every day. I did my own boards in football, and I would read up on everything. I would also go to the sports information directors for the opposing schools and get all the information I could from them. When Saturday afternoon came, heck, I was ready.

Broadcasters don't do that today; very few of them prepare. In those days you had a lot of substitutions, whereas today you generally know who's going in. Georgia Tech, for instance, is two deep and you know that. Today the plays are about the same. Bobby Dodd used to have a lot of trick plays (we called them gadget plays). But he would always tell me when they were going to use something like that.

I always prepared a lot because I started out young and thought I had to. The announcer I worked with, Bill Griffiths, didn't prepare at all. As a result, when I did a game with him, I had a heck of a background on everything that he didn't have. I could never figure out why he didn't work at it. As I got older, even though I always prepared, I realized why he maybe didn't prepare.

When Georgia Tech was in the Southeastern Conference, back in the late 1950s, I figured out that a lot of the announcers then didn't prepare because they would get Tech's starting lineup from me then start asking a lot of questions. You could just tell they hadn't prepared properly.

There are a lot of announcers today, especially in television, who just show up. Keep in mind that they always have a monitor in front of them.

As time went by, I began to rely more and more on spotters. I would always put together the information for the spotters and make it easy for them. In fact, my son still spots for Georgia Tech. He and the other Tech spotter, Tommy Barber, have both been there for 20-something years. They're Tech graduates, and they love to work the games. You could do a game with them because they just don't miss anything.

Wes [Durham], the current Tech announcer, is a guy who really prepares, which is part of the reason he'll be a success. He prepares a lot more than any of the announcers I've been around. Although he depends on spotters, he could do a lot without them.

Bobby Dodd Way

Bobby Dodd was great, in my estimation, as a football coach; I've seen him do it all. I was very close to him, where he would let me know what was going on with the plays and the quick-kicks, things like that. Today with a lot of broadcasters, coaches won't let them come in and see all of this stuff. They let some of them look at film, but that's usually the extent of it. Coach Dodd would tell me everything.

I would say that if a fella is going to be successful broadcasting college athletics, it is important to have that closeness with the coach. That way, you're likely to be included in recruiting and game strategies and that sort of thing.

In my case, for instance, if we were playing in Birmingham at the University of Alabama, we'd cut the "Bobby Dodd Show" that Saturday morning about 10 o'clock, right before we took off for the stadium. He would tell me at that time pretty much everything they were going to do, even though he wasn't always right.

We played Alabama at Bobby Dodd Stadium one year, and he told me, "We haven't got a chance." That was when Bear Bryant was at Alabama, and they were undefeated and No. 1 in the nation two straight years. We beat Alabama 7-6. That was their first loss. It was just a big bombshell, but Coach Dodd didn't think we'd win. He was a realist and would tell me exactly how he thought about games, just like that one.

I knew Alabama coach Bear Bryant very well because of Coach Dodd. Bear used to call Coach Dodd almost every day and they would just talk football. It's hard to get to know the opposing coaches because you don't see them so much; you see them once a year when you play them, but Coach Bryant is one I knew.

Bear knew Coach Dodd had the secret to winning, so every time we played Alabama he would come in early, and we would sit and talk awhile. When Tech played basketball at Alabama, I would see Bear in one of the hotels, and we would chat there.

Even away from the field Coach Dodd was great; the public liked him, but he was very reserved. You might think he was an egotist or something, but he wasn't that way; he didn't like crowds. On the road we would always be next door to each other in the hotels, and he'd ask me to go down and get him a paper because he didn't want to see all the people around in the lobby.

But in his day, he was the No. 1 football coach; everybody loved him. He didn't go to meetings, like the different Southeastern Conference meetings. Instead, he would send the assistant athletics director, again because he didn't like crowds.

We used to do all kinds of shows together, and during one I said, "Coach, I want you to do a show where you'll answer questions. We'll filter the questions of people who call in, and I'll have a list of the questions. That way you can answer the ones you want to."

"Nope, I don't want that," he replied.

He had been an All-American at the University of Tennessee. He was a natural athlete; he played football, basketball, baseball as a youngster in high school and then in college, plus he could shoot pool. I think that's why he was a great recruiter, not only because he won a lot of games. (But in order to win a lot of games you have to have great recruits.) Georgia Tech is a high academic institution. So he would go into a home to recruit, and the father would be there wanting his boy to have a good college education. I used to call Coach "old syrup mouth" because he was so good with the right answers. The fathers and mothers loved him and would send their sons to Georgia Tech. As a result, we had the best kids in Mississippi. We had the best kids in Alabama ... we had the best in the whole South. Even parents in places like Cleveland, Ohio, would send some kids down to Atlanta.

He got a player by the name of Billy Lothridge out of Gainesville, Georgia. He was ready to go to the University of Georgia, and our assistant coach came back and said to Coach Dodd, "Billy Lothridge is going to Georgia, so I need your help." Coach went to Billy's house and noticed they had a pool table there, so he went in and shot pool. Before you know it, Billy Lothridge is going to Georgia Tech. Bobby Dodd was just a great recruiter.

Under Coach Dodd we consistently went to the Sugar Bowl, Orange Bowl or the Cotton Bowl; it seemed like we went to a bowl game every year. We went through a stretch from 1950 to 1953 where we won 26 straight games. (The team was undefeated in the 1951 and 1952 seasons.) We had powerhouses; nobody even came close to us.

I went with him on recruiting trips quite a bit. Our radio station at Georgia Tech then, WGST, was located adjacent to the Coliseum on the Tech campus. So a lot of the coaches, when they went out to recruit, would bring the kids by the radio station, and I would sit down and talk to them. Since I was in sales, the coaches felt I could sell the kids on Tech. In those days I could do those things, but now I can't go out and recruit or do anything like that. The rules are rough now.

There was a kid named Charlie Dudish who was probably the best high school player in America. Everybody wanted him. There was all kinds of illegal recruiting going on with him. Finally I sold him on Georgia Tech, and he came here.

(It was things like that I was able to do. I did a lot more in basketball because the basketball office was right below our radio station on the campus. Coach [Whack] Hyder would bring every recruit upstairs he ever brought in to the campus. As a result I got to know all these kids when they were in high school.)

Coach Dodd was also a great motivator; kids would listen to him. There was a kid one time out of Alabama that Dodd wanted. The player came to a game with his daddy and afterwards said, "Coach, I'm coming."

His dad said, "Wait a minute, now. What are you going to do for me, Coach Dodd? You told the boy he was going to get a good education and laundry money. What are you going to do for me?" (At that time, athletes got $15 laundry money.)

> When I first came down here I found out Al was from Akron, Ohio. He was a throwback to the old broadcaster. Al was a tremendous guy.
> ~ Jim Phillips, Clemson University

Coach Dodd said, "I'm not going to do anything for you. We give each boy tickets to the game, so I guess he can give you a ticket."

"My boy's not coming to Georgia Tech," the father replied. "I've had other, better offers."

The player's daddy had owned a small grocery store in Alabama. The athlete went to another school. His daddy ended up with a supermarket.

Coach Dodd would always caution our alumni, and everybody in the program, on illegal recruiting. That's part of the reason why if Tech was going to do anything illegally, our grads were scared to do it. Coach would call all the alums in and say, "Look, this is all you can do, and that's it. This is what you can do for the kid and you can take the father out to eat."

Again, that's just the way Coach Dodd was. We had some great athletes come through here. In those days it was a little broader. Now the NCAA rules are rough. Back then you could take the daddy to a lunch, or something like that.

Coach Dodd's Vision: Athletes in Broadcasting

I think it's good to have former athletes as color commentators; most of the announcers don't like it, though. Most announcers who don't like the idea of former athletes getting into broadcasting figure the athlete didn't go to the school of hard-knocks. But I think it's great.

The Sportscaster's Dozen

Ciraldo (left) speaking with Georgia native, and former president, Jimmy Carter in November 1977, while Tech was in the area for a football game with Navy.

Kim King was picked as my color man. Coach Dodd even liked the idea of having a former Tech player doing the color. Kim was chosen because of his knowledge of the game.

There are a lot of announcers who don't like a color man with them at all during a broadcast. I think it makes a great broadcast having a former jock in the booth. Having Kim in the booth is almost like a having a coach in there. I think most of the jocks nowadays do a great job; they give you insight that you normally don't get.

The play-by-play guy does a good job at describing a play, but he doesn't know why it happened. He doesn't know why a quarterback did this or that, or why the team did this. The listener now is educated to where he wants somebody to tell him why the team made that play. If you have an expert in there like a former jock, he's usually right about 99 percent of the time.

Bobby and George

Bobby Ross was successful because he felt even though it was Georgia Tech, he would check up and make sure the kids were going to class. A coach shouldn't have to do it, but he felt like he had to.

Bobby is a workaholic. He's in his office at 5:00 in the morning and leaves at midnight. He told me one time, though, that he had to do that to make up for Georgia Tech's situation. He said that coaches at other schools didn't necessarily have to worry as much about player's grades as he did.

He is very intense. He's a helluva coach—one of the best—and he's proving that in the pros. He's been very successful at that level, but he's another person who is very reserved. I'm not sure how much our alumni liked him because he wouldn't go speak to them all the time because he was working. He figured if you're doing all of that, then you're not working. I talk to him maybe three or four times a month, and he's working just as hard in the pros and finding that the pros are a lot different to coach.

In football the 1990 national championship was the only one we have had here at Tech, and Coach Ross guided us to that one. (Back in the early 1950s when the team went undefeated, there wasn't a national championship like there is today. In 1952 we went 12-0 and shared the national championship with Michigan State.) It was a very big deal when we won it in 1990 ... that was a lot of fun.

George O'Leary was an assistant under Bobby Ross when we won the national championship. O'Leary's first year as a head coach was 1995, and he went 6-5. And his teams will get better over the next few years. He's a disciplinarian; the kids respect him, and they love him. He's the same way in recruiting in that he does a heck of a job getting the players.

He also has a great staff. They're with the kids as much as he is. If you want to be successful as a coach, you better have yourself a staff. I don't know of anybody who has been successful without a great staff. And that great staff will leave one by one, and you've got to replace them.

Coach O'Leary will be a great one.

Whack Hyder: From Minor League Baseball Player to Tech Basketball Coach

Basketball coach Whack Hyder was at Tech for 22 years. A funny story about him was when he was a minor league baseball player with the Akron Yankees. When I was a kid broadcasting, he was in Akron and we got acquainted.

Back in those days when a player hit a home run, the-breakfast-of-champions Wheaties would bring him a carton of 24 boxes of Wheaties. The players were just young kids in the minor leagues then, and they were all living in a small hotel or a small apartment somewhere, and didn't have a lot of use for the Wheaties. Well, Whack was the oldest one of the bunch, and every time he hit a home run he gave me all his Wheaties. I don't know how many cartons of Wheaties I used to have. I lived on Fifth Avenue in Akron. When he gave them to me, I would always give some to all my buddies on the street. So every time Whack hit a home run I would say, "There goes one for the folks on Fifth Avenue."

Then when I came down to Georgia Tech, Hyder was an assistant basketball coach and assistant baseball coach. That's actually how I started doing Tech basketball, because no one was doing the games. (They had a little gym at the time and didn't really encourage it. They had television coverage about once a month.) In 1953 Whack suggested to me to do the games, so we got everything worked out and that started my 43 years doing Tech basketball and football.

I probably got as close to Whack Hyder as I did to any coach. On Tech road trips I always roomed near him, so I got all the information I needed or wanted. He's still living (he was born in 1912), and we have him on at halftime every once in awhile. He was a fine person that everybody loved.

He never used profanity. We were playing Virginia one time at their old gym, and all of a sudden the officials called a technical foul on the Tech coach. Doing the games there in Virginia, I was near the Tech bench and could hear everything Whack said. When the official called the technical he said to Whack, "You're using profanity, and I'm not going to take it."

Well, Whack never used profanity, he would just say "cheese and crackers" when something would go wrong. The officials called another technical on Whack and threw him out of the game. The official again said he was using profanity. Come to find out what had happened, the head of the officials of the SEC was at the game, and this game official wanted to show how he could control the game. That was the only time Whack ever got thrown out of a game, or even had a technical called on him.

He was a battler. He beat Adolph Rupp and Kentucky twice in one year. Adolph at one time had a streak of 126 straight wins at the Coliseum there in Lexington, Kentucky, and Whack upset them. They came down here to play us, and Adolph was thinking that losing to Tech the first time was a fluke. They came in here and Tech beat them again. We just had a mediocre team, but any time Whack went up against Kentucky, he got fired up.

"Toe Meets Leather" with Jacket Nicknames and Butterflies

I brought a lot of jargon in when I was doing the games at Tech. A lot of it came from the fact that I played a lot of ball. Growing up, when we would play basketball in the streets, or wherever, kids were in a habit of broadcasting while they were playing. We all did that, which helped me develop the jargon that I later used. For example in Akron, Ohio, there was a kid when he kicked off I would say, "Toe meets leather."

When I came to Georgia Tech, I used a lot of the same sayings like that and people liked it. During basketball I would say quickly but simply, "Good!" Again I would say that to be different. Even when I pass people on the streets today a lot of them will say, "There's toe meets leather."

I used "we've got a thriller brewing here" and "brother and sister" quite a bit; I brought those with me down from Ohio. I've heard other people use those, and if they're copying me, that's fine. I also tell youngsters to get their own style and not copy what someone else does. I got a lot from Ted Husing, but I never got a chance to listen to him; I just used his advice.

You should not only come up with your own style, but also sayings and nicknames for the players. I think you ought to do that because that's what people love. Fans can associate the player and that nickname.

> Al was a legend at Georgia Tech. Anybody who did what he did, as long as he did it, and as well as he did it, would certainly classify as a legend. Personally, when my son, Wes, went to Georgia Tech to do the games, Al took Wes under his wing to help make the transition a smooth one. Al not only did a terrific job as a sportscaster, but also as a person.
> ~ Woody Durham, University of North Carolina

I also tried to come up with different nicknames to use every year for the players, but I didn't really change my jargon. I would ask the players if they had a nickname. If they didn't, then I figured I had to come up with one for them. I asked Dennis Scott if he had one, and he said no, so I started using "The Great Scott." That one stuck with him even to the pros.

For the most part I didn't get a lot of butterflies before a broadcast. When I was starting out at 15, I got butterflies because it was something new.

At the same time, I would advise anyone getting into this business that some of those butterflies are good for you when you're broadcasting. I think you're better off going into a broadcasting job with some of those butterflies, but not too many.

As you do something over 40 years, you don't really get them as much. In those early days there was no television so you had to paint the picture. If you have an exciting game, you can really do something with it, just like a painter; create the excitement. What I do is get that excitement in me to get it out to the audience.

We used to have so many barn-burners over at the Coliseum, I would say, "Brother and sister, we have a thriller brewing here." I started using the word "brewing" early on in Akron, Ohio. When I was at the station there, they wanted me to do a commercial for Duquesne Pilsner Beer, but my dad said, "You're not going to do anything like that."

So about the only thing I could do was say something like, "We've got a thriller brewing here for Duquesne Pilsner," when we were doing the game. Dad didn't want me telling other kids through the commercials about beer. With TV now, it's different. Even if they have the TV on with the sound down, listening to you, they can create their own excitement now.

The Tech Athletes

In basketball there are two great players who stick out right off the top of my head: Roger Kaiser and Mark Price.

When Whack recruited Roger Kaiser in the late 1950s, we only had about five basketball scholarships. When Roger got here in 1959, he really had this town going crazy over Tech basketball. The Coliseum was 7,000 capacity, and he jammed it with people. He was the greatest shooter from the outside, plus he was a great free throw shooter; he hit about 87 percent every year he was at Georgia Tech.

When Kaiser was playing here, Tech basketball was big. Roger was an All-American for two years, and they held clinics with him every year. There would be about 7,000 kids show up for these things.

Tech had played at Furman one year on a Saturday. Georgia and South Carolina had gotten a lot of snow that weekend, and we were driving back to Atlanta on Sunday. Roger was in the car with me. He told me to stop when we got to a certain church there in north Georgia. He hadn't missed Sunday school in something like 12 or 13 straight years, and he wanted to go. The other players with us in the car all waited with me while Roger went to Sunday school. That's the type of kid Roger was.

He's coaching now at Life College and has won some championships. In fact his team won the 1996-1997 NAIA national championship.

> *Al Ciraldo loved what he did, loved the Yellow Jackets. And he was the type of guy that you like to be friends with.*
>
> — *Bob Harris, Duke University*

Mark Price is that same way. I sat down with Mark Price back in the 1980s and talked to him about Georgia Tech. He was also a fine youngster. When we sat down to lunch Mark said, "I heard Coach (Bobby) Cremins uses a lot of profanity."

"No, I've sat in on practices with the team and haven't heard him."

After Mark was here about two years he asked me, "I thought you said Coach doesn't use profanity?"

I said, "I didn't go to every practice session, so I didn't hear it all."

But anyway, Bobby would say, "Mark, I'm mad right now, so close your ears because here I go."

Roger Kaiser and Mark Price are the two basketball players who come to my mind immediately as two of the best from Georgia Tech. Both were great free throw shooters. If you're not a great free-throw shooter, then you're not a great shooter because if you can shoot from the outside, you ought to be able to go up to the line and shoot 85 or 86 percent. Dennis Scott was a great shooter; he could really bomb away from 35 feet.

But there have been so many great players over the years. We went through a stretch in the early- to mid-1990s where we had more players in the NBA at one time than any other school. About 15 players at one time were in the pros from Georgia Tech.

In football there were guys like Eddie Lee Ivory, who was out of Thompson, Georgia. He gained a ton of yards while he was a running back here. As a matter of fact, the one football game that sticks out in my mind was when we played the Air Force Academy back in the 1970s. Ivory had an incredible game. He ran one touchdown for over 70 yards and another touchdown for over 80 yards ... and the field was icy. It was so cold that day that my color man, Kim King (who is still the color guy for Tech), had to keep getting up and wiping the glass in front of us because it kept icing and freezing over.

We've just had so many great athletes here at Georgia Tech, it's hard to remember all of them. In basketball I could name one after another. In basketball you get a lot closer to them than you do in football because you have five starters and only about 10 players on the whole squad. With football you have between 65 and 70 players, and so you just get acquainted with the so-called stars.

Bobby Cremins: The Jacket from New York

Bobby Cremins really had to do a lot of talking to get the Georgia Tech basketball job because first the school wanted a coach from Pennsylvania. At the time Bobby was at Appalachian State and wanted to come down here to interview for the job. He was persistent until he talked his way into an interview. He'd call up Homer Rice, the Tech athletics director, and tell Homer that he wanted the job. From there it became a process of elimination.

To make things look good, Homer Rice acted like Bobby was his first choice and that he told Cremins while he was still a player at South Carolina that he wanted him as a coach one day. But really, Cremins just badly wanted the job and he got lucky. That was more than 17 years ago.

You're in stitches around Coach Cremins. He's the type of person that what you see is what you get; he's as honest as he can be. There were times (and I used to give him a hard time about this) when a reporter would ask him a question and Coach would talk about growing up on the playgrounds in New York and about how he was going to jail and how they would steal stuff. I told him he shouldn't say things like that, but that's just the way he is. He doesn't hide a thing, and he shouldn't.

When Bobby came here, our basketball got more publicity than our football. That may have been because we had so many players in the NBA at one time, or maybe the publicity helped us get so many players in the pros at one time.

Coach Cremins is one of the top sports personalities in Atlanta. He makes a lot of speeches and does a lot for different charities without looking for any type of fee or anything like that.

Despite the basketball program getting more publicity than football when Coach Cremins came here, it certainly didn't lose any ground when the football team was co-national champion with Colorado in 1990. That was the year the basketball team reached the NCAA Final Four.

That was a thrilling ballclub. We were in the regionals where we beat Louisiana State, Michigan State and Minnesota. Those were some thrilling games that we were able to pull out with last second shots from guys like Dennis Scott and Kenny Anderson.

When we got to the Final Four we played this great team, University of Nevada-Las Vegas. That is the year UNLV won it. We were leading UNLV by about 10 points in the second half, and Anderson picked up his fourth personal foul. When Coach Cremins took him out, we had a lead that disappeared in a hurry. UNLV won the game 90-81. The Jackets finished the 1989-90 season with a record of 28-7.

CREMINS TO SOUTH CAROLINA?

As close as I get to these coaches, a lot of times I hear things early. That was the case when Coach Cremins was headed to the University of South Carolina. I heard about it during the season. His former roommate from South Carolina was always coming in to Georgia Tech from Columbia to watch Coach's games. And this roommate always had another guy with him from South Carolina.

I asked them, "What brings you two fellas around here?"

They told me they were just coming around to work out and shoot, that type of thing. I didn't think anything of it until I saw them come back about two weeks later. I asked them again what they were doing, and they told me the same thing.

Finally, I went to Bobby Cremins and I said, "Coach, what the hell is going on? Are you thinking about going to South Carolina?"

He said, "Well, I'm not thinking about going there, but they're making me offers and that sort of thing. I told them I wasn't going to do anything until the season was over."

Bobby's the type of guy that can't say no to anyone, especially his friends. I started to see this South Carolina deal coming more and more. I finally decided in my mind that he was going to go there, so I went to talk to his wife about it.

She said, "Al, I don't know what he's going to do, but I know that he's gotta make up his mind when the season's over, and he's either going to South Carolina or he's going to stay at Georgia Tech."

As time passed I kept asking Coach about it and tried to show him the bad points of leaving and going to South Carolina. By that time he was talking more and more about going there.

Later that season we were in the ACC tournament in North Carolina, and we won it. I went down to the locker room after the game and I said, "Coach, you're going to stay here now, aren't you?"

Very sincerely he said, "I haven't made up my mind yet."

So I went to two of the players (Coach would do anything for his players), and I told them about the possibility of Bobby leaving and that they may have been the only two people who could talk him into staying. These two guys talked to Coach about it and basically told him that they came to Georgia Tech because of him, not because of Georgia Tech.

With that we turned the table around, and he was going to stay. In fact, South Carolina officials called Coach Cremins on a Tuesday night to make sure he was going. He told them that he had changed his mind and decided to stay at Georgia Tech.

The South Carolina people stayed persistent until Coach finally decided to take them up on an offer to fly to Columbia and look around. It was during this trip that he decided to take the job.

Everything was announced and he took the head coaching job at South Carolina. After about two days there, though, he decided he wanted out. He called his wife and told her to go pick him up in Columbia and bring him back to Atlanta. Even though everything had been announced, the job at Tech was still open and the officials welcomed him back.

It was just a matter of Coach being so good-natured that he couldn't turn down South Carolina. I think I've figured out the deal with the two guys that kept coming around. They stayed persistent and he started to think how he enjoyed himself while he was a player in college for four years and as an assistant coach there, and he felt that he owed the school something.

He's sure glad he came back ... and so are we.

In the Crow's Nest

Duke University for basketball is an awful place to broadcast from because they put you up in the rafters with television. You have to climb a long way up there, then when you get there, it's hotter than hell. When you invite a guest up there at halftime, it's tough, because usually they don't want to come up there either.

In football there aren't as many bad places, but I can remember doing a game at Duke (this is way back) and they were working on the press box. Since they were under construction, they put us in an auxiliary press box in the end zone. You don't ever want to do a game from the end zone; it was tough.

Conditions were a lot worse in the old days.

We were doing a Georgia-Georgia Tech game in Athens back

around 1950. At that time, they put you up in the bleachers of Woodruff Hall in with the crowd. Georgia had a lot of fans that would sit there and razz us, but we had to keep our cool. This one guy started making it tough. He started cheering things in the background that could be heard over the air. Again, it's a lot better now, but back then you really had to go into places like Athens in good graces or people would yell a lot of profanity into that microphone.

Back in the 1950s places like Mississippi and Mississippi State didn't have good basketball facilities because they didn't have anyone interested in doing their games.

Creating Excitement When Tech Wins 220-0:
The Blowouts and Comebacks

I could have called Tech's 220-0 win over Cumberland in 1916, but in a game like that you're not going to create that thrill. Every time the Jackets came down the field they would score a touchdown. (They led 126-0 at the half.) If you can get a thriller, you can do a job. If you get a game that's 45-0, how the hell are you going to make that thrilling?

Announcers today, though, are all shouters. I used to shout, but you have to be sure to bring it up at the right time. Today, announcers shout about exciting plays, they shout for their team, and they shout at the officiating.

I would insinuate something about the officials during a game, but not to the extent where I would say that a specific ref blew a call. The public would know by listening to me that the call was blown. If there was a bad call I would say something about the coach getting mad about it on the bench.

Even though a lot of announcers do it, I don't believe in actually saying on the air that someone blew a call because I'm human and I'd try to visualize myself if I was officiating. The crowd's going to have an effect on you, and you're going to blow some ... what the hell? Announcers blow it sometimes too.

I was a homer, but I would always give credit to the other team. If you were playing for Notre Dame and you ran 70 yards for a touchdown, I'd give you credit for what a great play it was. More and more today, announcers are just rooting for their team; they are cheerleaders. If the other team scores, you can tell in their voice; they are very monotone. If it's their team, boy, you can't even hear their voice because the crowd is roaring and the announcer is screaming. I think that's what the public wants, and as a result, the announcers give them what they want.

We've had some comeback games that have been exciting, and it's not difficult to keep up that excitement level. There have been so many comebacks in basketball. Dennis Scott won several games for us on last second shots from 35-40 feet out; I couldn't even tell you how many of those there were.

I remember one game where Roger Kaiser hit a shot from the corner with 5 seconds to go to beat Kentucky. Roger also led his team to the NCAA tournament (there were only eight teams in the tournament instead of 64 like today). That was the year, 1960, Ohio State won it with Jerry Lucas and that group.

Going back to 1990 in football, since that's fresh in my mind, we were playing football at Virginia. Both teams were undefeated. Tech ended up winning the game, 41-35. But it was just a helluva game. We were down pretty big in the game but were able to come back, win, and stay No. 1 in one poll and No. 2 in the other poll.

The most exciting football game for me, though, was in 1962 when we played Alabama at Bobby Dodd Stadium. It was a game where Alabama came in here undefeated. We beat them 7-6 and stopped their winning streak. It wasn't only a thriller because it was a close game, but it was a chance to snap their streak; you could feel the tension. Anytime 'Bama came in here, Coach Bryant would come out early and walk around the field with his players behind him, just like an army. We were supposed to lose that game by 21 points, so naturally with a game like that you can put a lot into it, which I did.

Humor on and off the Field

One time one of our scorekeepers spilled a Coke all over Kim King. Kim just blew a fuse. I tried to get him to calm down, because it was just an accident. That scorekeeper was scared of Kim from that moment on. That was pretty funny.

There used to be an announcer doing Georgia games by the name of Ed Stalinius. A lot of times they would be in the booth next to us when we played Georgia. He would have a meeting with all of the people involved in the broadcast that would last about two hours before the game. He used to think I was crazy for not having meetings. Hell, our guys had been doing it for so long, they would just show up right before the broadcast.

Ciraldo (right) interviews Georgia Tech basketball coach Bobby Cremins at the Omni after a game in the early 1990s.

There have been some humorous things happen on the field. There was a basketball game here several years ago when one of the player's shorts came down. The crowd went wild. You see things like that happen every so often.

In the booth during the old days, I used to be a one-man gang; I did play-by-play, color, stats, and engineer. We were up in St. Louis one year, which is a union town. The union there always had a "standbys" to make sure the union was being taken care of. This particular year when we were there, there was this guy who kept staring at me. He finally came up to me before the game, introduced himself to me, and said, "I represent the union as a standby, and you guys are going to pay me. We'll send a bill to your station." I just ignored him. He asked me another question, and I just kept ignoring him. He kept hanging around throughout the game.

When the game was over, he said, "I want my money."

I said, "I'm not giving you any money. You listen here." Then I got pretty rough with him, got his name, and told him I was going to turn him into the union in Georgia.

When Whack Hyder came after the game to do the coach's show, this guy was still around. When I told Whack about what happened, he told me to watch out or I was going to find myself in the river. Whack was really worried about it. I wasn't too worried about it.

Georgia Tech-Georgia

In football Georgia Tech's biggest rivalry is definitely with Georgia; although in basketball it may now be with North Carolina.

There aren't as many big rivalries today in sports like we had in the old days. When the rivalry with Georgia was big, during the game you could feel the fans outside yelling; electricity was in the air. You still get some of that today, but it's just not as common.

The Georgia Tech Fan

Georgia Tech fans are not as fanatical as other fans because the student is different there. He goes to Tech to just get an education, and the competition in the classroom is big. As a result athletics are not an outlet like they are at other schools. Georgia fans, for instance, used to be fanatical; they would even skip class to go to games. Tech fans are not that way, although they're starting to get like that.

The Varsity Drive-In restaurant is an institution here. Fans go over to the Varsity before and after Tech football games. (It's right next to the Tech campus.) My wife and I got married in 1950, and after our kids were born we'd take them there. I got acquainted with Frank Gordie, who was the founder of it, and he was a great man. One of the waiters there, Flossie, used to sing out, "What'll Ya Have?"

When I take visitors in there, they are just amazed at what is going on. It's not quite as big now as it was 20 years ago, but it's still an Atlanta institution. I can remember when they had hot dogs for a nickel and two hamburgers for 15 cents. That place used to be packed with Georgia Tech students. I don't see a lot of them over there anymore; I don't think they appreciate it as much today. Now there are two McDonald's on campus which I think affects the Varsity a little bit as far as the students are concerned.

But going back to the fans, there was one time a few years back when I knew the fans were not only pulling for the team but also for the announcer. Georgia Tech let another station bid for the rights to the games. That station, WCNN, wanted to bring its own man in to do the games. At first they wanted me to work for them, but I told them no because I had been at WGST for years and didn't want to leave them. (But those were the days when you were loyal.)

The town was going nuts; it was in the papers all the time that WCNN wanted to bring in another announcer. I've never had so much publicity; there were headlines on the front page. The president of Georgia Tech at the time called me and told me that I would be in there doing the games. (This was about six months before all of this started.) He told me to just keep it quiet. When everything came out in the papers, the fans were in an uprising. I literally got about a thousand letters telling me to stay at Tech.

Georgia Tech has a big "T" on top of the president's office. (It's probably about four or five feet tall.) One morning, while all of this was going on, I came out of my house and there was this damn "T" on my front porch! There was a note with it that basically said, "They're either going to let you do the games, or they're not getting the 'T' back." It was like some type of ransom. I called the school's security, and they came to pick it up.

The school ended up hiring me to do the games, and I still worked at WGST on their sales. WCNN went in to the athletics director, Homer Rice, and told him they wanted me to sell for them. After that meeting Homer told me he would appreciate it if I would go with WCNN, so I did. It was tough for me because I had been at WGST for over 20 years and that loyalty was there. That whole episode made me feel great.

Through episodes like that and spending so long at a place, I'm a fan of Georgia Tech. I went to the University of Florida — and don't get me wrong — I like to see them win, but I'm a Tech fan. Way, way back when Tech would lose, I would have a hell of a week; it would just eat the inside of me. It doesn't affect me as much now because I've learned to win, and I've learned to lose. But winning is so great. Watching your team win does something to you inside.

After 40-plus years, you can't help but be a fan of a team, especially with what the school has done for me; they made me an institution.

Life After Al

I'll tell you something weird ... I had my heart attack and never had any type of pain having it. I went down to the end of our driveway to get the newspaper one day and started wheezing and couldn't figure out why. I called my doctor, and he said it sounds like it could be my heart, so I went to the hospital and let them do the EKG. According to the tests everything was ticking all right, but eventually they found two blocked arteries (and they had to take a picture of it before they could figure that out). In 1989 I had bypass surgery.

Then I continued doing the pregame shows, the postgame shows, the coaches shows, and all the halftime. I got away from preparing to do the play-by-play, which took a big load off my mind.

Bob McCann, who was the number two man when I was doing the games, started doing the play-by-play at that point and I did the halftime shows, the coaches shows, etc. Bob did the games for two or three years. We have a unique situation here at Georgia Tech that a lot of schools probably don't have; Kim King and I stay in the booth right after the game is over while one of our assistants takes a microphone to the dressing room, and we can do the locker room show from the press box.

Then we have the coach's show, which lasts about an hour, and it includes the coach and the scouting report. We also do that from the press box to the locker room.

Before we did it that way, I used to run like heck to get down to the locker room after a game. I wised up one day about 10 or 15 years ago and realized we could do it with microphones in the two locations.

Wes Durham — who was doing Vanderbilt University games at the time — heard that the job was open, and he went after it. He has turned out to be a great one. I'd say, unless he wants to stay here in Atlanta, he's got a great chance to move up the ladder and maybe go national.

Turning Over the Reins

Turning over the mike to Wes is no problem; he's so knowledgeable and so professional. It would be rough to turn it over to someone else. I don't mind it now. Wes is so exciting. My doctor told me he wanted me to keep doing the things I was doing, but he wanted me to get an office at the house and turn over some of the play-by-play duties to someone else.

Since I still sold advertising for Georgia Tech broadcasts after I stopped doing play-by-play, it kept me going. In fact, one thing has led to another, but every job I've ever had has included sales and sports announcing. It's a great combination, but it's tough. If you're in sales, you've gotta hustle.

There have been some years I have sold around $1.9 million in advertising. But that's my job and that's where I make the majority of

Al Ciraldo in a 1950s publicity photo for WGST radio in Atlanta.

my income. I've been selling Georgia Tech for over 40 years. During that time, I got to know the top people for these companies that I sell.

For instance, I know the chairman of the board for Delta Airlines. He was going to school at Tech when I was broadcasting, and he told me he would always take care of Tech. Same thing with the people at State Farm Insurance; I've known them for years and years. For the Tech clients, it's really just a matter of renewing their contracts each year.

It can become rough with some of the smaller companies when they just buy a coach's show. People a lot of times ask me what my secret is to successfully selling this advertising. There's no secret to success in the fact that it's a lot of hard work, and it's getting in there and knowing everybody.

It's the same way with Anheuser-Bush. I knew the number two man in there, and he would just tell their people, "Whatever Al wants, just buy it." It's easier than when I was out there pounding the pavement.

With the selling, even though I could have gone on to bigger jobs, I was making too much money to leave. When the Hawks came to town as the NBA team, they wanted me to do their games. They offered me $25,000. I said no because I was selling. It's like a coach who gets $200,000 for a Nike endorsement and $110,000 from the school he's coaching.

This Is a Fun Business

I have no regrets about getting into this business ... I think it's fun. I even think the selling part of it is fun. Everything I've ever done in this business has been fun. At the advertising agency in Akron, I was in there with the broadcasting—I call it singing and selling—and it was fun. Heck, I was a kid making great money and having a great time.

Even though there have been offers to go other places, I thank myself for staying at Tech. If I would have left, I would have had to give the selling game up. And I didn't want to do that, so I turned the offers down. Other offers may have also taken me away from my family more. In some ways it was tough on my family life. Since I started so young, it helped me see what type of time and travel it took to do baseball and helped me realize I couldn't do that and be around my family. When a young broadcaster asks me for advice, I tell them if they are single, then OK; but if they're married, then they really need to think about it. You also have to get some breaks along the line.

I have one son and three daughters. My son, Al Jr. still spots for Wes Durham on the Tech football broadcasts. My son knows more about Georgia Tech than I'll ever know.

Competition is so tough today that you have to have breaks along the line. A key is to know somebody. Then once you get in there, you do a good broadcast when you get the listener involved with the play ... when they feel like they are the quarterback, and in their minds they are going through the motions of that player. I got in the business at the right place at the right time and tried to make the listener feel like they were in the game, but, again, I was lucky. And I think for the most part I was able to give the fans a good account of the game.

In the minds of fans, I have been considered a legend and a celebrity. I don't feel that way; I was doing a job that I loved. I just got the breaks. The biggest break I got was staying at Georgia Tech and Georgia Tech owning the radio station there. The big break, also, was that I was selling.

Now I wouldn't mind people thinking of Al Ciraldo when they think of Georgia Tech. If you want to be a legend, just stay at the same place for 20 or 25 years.

It's great to be associated with a school that has as much tradition as Georgia Tech. In 1986 the school had a day for me. The team played North Carolina State that day. I'm an honorary graduate of Georgia Tech. I've been the Marshall for the Georgia Tech homecoming parade two times. I'm one of the family here, and that's great. There's the Al Ciraldo Award which is a big trophy, presented to the outstanding newspaper, radio, or television man in Atlanta.

As a longtime broadcaster you also feel good when someone comes up to you and introduces you to their son and says how they grew up listening to you.

I have people come up to me now and say, "I used to listen to you as a kid when I was five years old. I grew up with you." Everyone pretty much knows why I got out of it, and so a lot of people will come up to me now and ask me how I'm feeling. The Georgia Tech fans are very special people.

When I was doing a game here in 1986, it was "Al Ciraldo Day." This was a big deal all over the town; they had buttons made up for it, and it was a full crowd. The buttons that were made up had "Hello Al" on them.

That day was very special. The Governor was there, plus Bobby Dodd made a presentation. Then they took my wife and I for a ride around the field in that Rambling Wreck car. That was all in the halftime ceremony. It's a big thrill because it happened that way; it was something special.

I think the biggest compliment, where my ego would be tested, is when I would go to the games and have a cheering section near the band, and they would yell, "Hello, Al!"

It felt good to hear that each time.

Editor's Note: On November 7, 1997, Al Ciraldo died of complications resulting from congestive heart failure. He was 76.

JACK CRISTIL
MISSISSIPPI STATE UNIVERSITY

One of the greatest plays I remember calling would have been in 1955 when Mississippi State was playing Kentucky at Stoll Field in Lexington. It was my first trip to the University of Kentucky. The Bulldogs led the game 13-7, until late in the game when Kentucky put together a scoring drive, converted, and led 14-13 with 1:17 left in the game. Kentucky kicked off to Mississippi State, and we brought the ball out to about the 17-yard line. Bill Stanton threw a pass to William Earl Morgan, who caught it behind the Kentucky defender and ran for an 83-yard touchdown catch and run. I remember saying when William Earl caught it that the Kentucky defender was chasing him but wouldn't catch him, even if he was on Citation. State won the game.

> *The quality of life is determined by its activities.*
> ~ Aristotle

There have been game-winning shots in basketball and that type of thing, but that one football play sticks out more than anything else.

THE MINOR LEAGUES

I started my broadcasting career in minor league baseball. After World War II and up until about 1952, minor league baseball was a very live entertainment feature for people. In fact, there were about 52 different minor leagues operating until about 1952. At that point the room air conditioner came into being, and in the metro markets television was beginning to make an impact. Between the two of them, the people who had those so-called television sets and watched that snow on television gathered the neighborhood around for their entertainment. Those who were fortunate enough to buy room air conditioners, particularly in the South, installed one of those and quit going to ballparks. So minor league baseball became almost nonexistent. In fact, in 1953, only eight leagues were operating.

I had wanted to get into broadcasting sports and got started with Clarksdale of the old Cotton States League, which was a Class C league—Class D being the lowest. I worked the Cotton States League; Anniston, Alabama, in the Southeastern League; Jackson, Tennessee, in the Kitty League; and Memphis in the Southern Association. I did that for a five-year stretch, and in 1952 it became evident that the leagues were collapsing, and I had to go to work for a living.

I went back to Clarksdale where I had a very dear friend who was the assistant manager at the radio station. In the spring of 1953 he gave me a job on staff, plus I did a little sales work on the side. The Mississippi State football play-by-play job became available in the fall of 1953, and I secured that job and have been there ever since.

Baseball was my first adventure into broadcasting. I really haven't done baseball since the mid-1970s, when the Mississippi State team went from a 25-game schedule to a 50- or 60-game schedule. I made my living in radio sales, so I just couldn't take three or four days off each week to do baseball.

I guess in the early part of my career, I would have liked to have broadcast major league baseball full time. I was a single man in those days, so the travel was no problem even though it wasn't as convenient as it is now. It didn't take much money to live in those days as a single man, and I had no responsibilities to anyone other than myself. I enjoyed good health. It was all good. I was enjoying what I was doing at the time and making a living at it; that's hard to beat.

> *Jack is a friend who I've known for a long, long time. Tupelo, Mississippi has two claims for fame ... Elvis Presley and Jack Cristil. He's a very good broadcaster and a guy I've traded a lot of stories with.*
>
> & *Otis Boggs, University of Florida*

Later I turned down an opportunity to do major league baseball for personal and family reasons. By that time, we had two small daughters and were living in Tupelo, Mississippi, and my late wife and I thought that was a great place to rear children. We had a chance to move to St. Louis and work with the Cardinal organization, but we had been married about 12 or 15 years then, had two small children, and liked what we were doing with Mississippi State football and basketball.

If I had to pick the sport I enjoy the most now, it would be basketball. I love the game of basketball; it's a fantastic game. It's probably more of a true team game, if there is such a thing, in relationship to others. Obviously, you see a lot of great individual performances,

Off the Air with Southeastern Legends

Jack Cristil (center) tees it up with Mississippi State University coach Rocky Felker (right) and MSU athletics director Larry Templeton in 1989.

but it's team-oriented in its concept. Regardless of the score in a basketball game, you always see great plays being made and great athletes making these plays.

In baseball many times late in the game, the teams go through the motions. Obviously in football they do. But in basketball you're still going to see great individual plays. It's played in a relatively confined area so you see it all, and weather conditions usually don't play a factor except for maybe travel ... so to me it's ideal. I just love basketball.

Growing Up with the Pioneers

I was a sweet, lovable child; the apple of my mother's and father's eye, I'm sure. I was one of six children, three boys and three girls in the family. I was born and reared in Memphis. My father died when I was about 12 years of age, so my mother reared the kids.

Basically, I guess growing up under those circumstances, the one thing you learned was to make your own decisions—to think through a given situation and make your decision because your brothers and sisters weren't going to make it for you, and you had no parents to make it for you.

The most important decision I ever made was at the outbreak of World War II. I knew I wasn't going in the Navy or Marines, so I volunteered for the Army and got into the Air Corps. I came home, told Mama what I had done, she signed the papers and away I went.

I had an excellent childhood; it was just marvelous. We never had any problems. We never had any money, but we didn't need any. I played ball all the time in the neighborhood and had a great area in which to grow up. We had a number of ethnics—there would be a little Greek descent, and Italian descent, and Russian descent, and Irish descent, and German descent, and we were all in the same neighborhood and spoke two or three languages colloquially.

There was Mrs. Cappodolis, for example, had three sons who were Greek, and she spoke no English, except "Charlie." That was the name of her youngest son. His Greek name was Custer, and his English name was Charlie. We all called him Custer, but she called him Charlie. I knew "how do you do" and "I'm doing fine" in Greek. We learned how to cuss in Italian, and so forth and so on. It was just a superb neighborhood. And the guys and the girls that came out of that neighborhood obviously did well for themselves. It was all up from there.

I wish I could paint this picture for you of my earliest radio memory—we lived in a neighborhood in which the municipal waterworks was located. There was always a game going on at the waterworks. In football season it was football, or in baseball season it was baseball, or ran track; we did everything over there.

I was at the waterworks one day and was a kid probably six, seven, or eight years old then. My sister Zelda, who's a year and a half older than I, came running over and said, "Come home, we've got something you have to see." Mama had bought a radio. They plugged it in the wall socket, and "One Man's Family" came on.

Late at night, or at least it seemed late at night to me as a child, I could dial through that thing and find a baseball game. I used to get KDKA in Pittsburgh or WLW in Cincinnati, and you could hear a

Bill Stern or a Ted Husing or Graham McNamee. I would find a ballgame somewhere. That's when I first started listening to radio and first knew that's what I was going to do; I was going to broadcast games on radio.

My oldest brother Harold, who's now deceased, used to raise all manner of hell because he never particularly cared for ball, and he sure didn't want it on the radio. We used to have a running fight all the time, and he generally won. But that was my first exposure to radio.

The Lewis and Clarks of Sportscasting

Early on, I listened to Ted Husing, Bill Stern, and Jack Brickhouse, people like that; these were the pioneers of the business. Nobody had done it before them, so they had to develop this thing called radio broadcasting. How they did it, I don't know, but those of us who came along a few years later at least had some teachers who pioneered this and had done some of the right things and some of the wrong things. You just tried to discern what was proper and what was improper. I don't know that I necessarily patterned myself after any one particular individual, but I have great admiration for them all.

They were the Lewis and Clarks of the radio business. It was out there once the radio was invented, and they had to make the determination as to how this thing was going to be presented and how it was going to be accepted. They created the vocabulary for it, and the whole shooting match. They had tremendous usage of the English language. Obviously, they had great imaginations, and they had the ability to communicate one-on-one, which is the beauty part about it. They didn't talk to millions, they talked to one person. They did it absolutely superbly. It was unbelievable how these people could deliver a sporting event ... you could picture it by looking at the radio (which is what we did in those days). You could look at that box and see the game. Red Barber was the same type of guy.

You have to have tremendous admiration for these people, because no one had ever gone down this road before. Not only did they go down that road, but they did it very, very successfully. They paved the way for everybody else and made it so easy for the rest of us. If you're going to paint, paint like Van Gogh. If you're going to be a broadcaster, be a Bill Stern, or a Ted Husing, or a Red Barber, or a Jack Brickhouse, or whomever.

The Sportscaster's Dozen

Play It Again

Gordon McLendon was the greatest of all in recreating baseball games, absolutely fantastic. He was out of Dallas and began to recreate major league baseball, and when the Mutual Network had the "Game of the Day," he did a "Game of the Day" for the Liberty Network. Gordon sat in Dallas, with a man relaying information from Ebbets Field, or wherever, and recreated major league baseball.

We would turn on two radios, one with Mutual's game with them sitting in the ballpark, and McLendon doing the exact same game from Dallas for Liberty. He would wear the Mutual guys out. He was a phenomenon.

Gordon called himself "The Old Scotsman." He was a young guy, but would tell people on the air that he was 80-something years old. He worked with Wes Wise, who later went to the West Coast. They even had sound effects on these recreations where you could even hear a public address system. Remember, this was in the late 1940s and early 1950s.

A lot of the recreation depended upon your operator. When I first started doing it, you had a Western Union operator sitting there on a tick-tick-tick machine to the operator, for instance, in New Orleans. I would be sitting in Memphis, and the team would be playing in New Orleans. The operator could tell me if we were going to have a good broadcast depending on who was working on the other end.

They weren't allowed to use a lot of color words, but some could use some phraseology with that click-click-click machine. With some of them you would just get the straight stuff like ball one, strike one, ball two, strike two, and so on. Later they had a machine called a teleprinter instead of an operator taking it. It was a great invention, but I didn't like it because I preferred the live operator.

I didn't find recreating games difficult even though you would obviously rather be at the ballpark. You got the basic information you needed. The only time you really ran into a problem was during rain delays, and you didn't really know what to make up because you didn't know what the situation was at the stadium.

Preparation: The "Typical" Week

There is no such thing as a "typical" week when it comes to my football preparation. Now, keep in mind that obviously the longer you do a given job, it's easier to prepare. For me, the longer I've been

Cristil (right) with Jim Ashmore, all-district basketball All-American in 1957.

in the Southeastern Conference, the less time it takes for preparation because I've met so many people in the league: coaches, administrators, and officials, and these people don't turn over every year.

The same thing with players. If you're going to play the Georgias and the Auburns and the Alabamas, there are some players on those teams who played last year or the year before that you're familiar with and have some knowledge of. So you're just learning those people who are relatively new. I think for a guy who walks into the league for his first year, it would be extremely new and could be extremely difficult and take a great deal of preparation. The longer you stay with the same basic group of opponents, then the knowledge you've gained over the years is there for you and consequently the preparation time is less.

In football probably four or five numbers is all you really need to know, which includes the running backs, the wideouts, the kick return guys, the punter, and maybe a linebacker if he's a great one. But with all due respect, you don't learn the numbers of interior linemen.

The way the conference is set up now with Eastern and Western divisions—we're in the West, so we play everybody in the West, and I keep up with everybody in the West. If we're going to play, for example in football, Tennessee, Georgia, and Florida out of the East, then I'll keep up with Tennessee, Georgia, and Florida. I don't necessarily worry about the other teams in the East because we won't play them. You build on that, and it's generally not too difficult.

I start getting some information together during our Sunday morning television show that we do during the football season. Obviously, we're going to play somebody the next Saturday, so you have to make some remarks about them on the show. We do a radio show on Thursday. Usually by Wednesday I've got facts and figures and almost complete stats put together and written down before the call-in show. I write it down for me and the coach, since he doesn't have time to mess with that type of thing.

This way the phone caller may ask the coach how many receptions a receiver for the other team has. The coach can look on my board and say, "Well, he's caught 19 up through last Saturday's game and five were touchdowns, so we'll really need to guard him." Usually by Thursday, I'm in good shape, which gives me Friday to refine what I need to do.

Basketball Preparation

Basketball is very, very similar because you see teams and individuals play, and they don't change a lot. Take, or example, Vanderbilt and Frank Seckar, who we saw as a freshman. By the time you see him his senior season, you know things he can do, you know he wears No. 22, and you can almost recognize him when he walks into the gym in his street clothes. Since you're only dealing with seven people on an average, you know a bunch of players and only need to learn the new people who come in to the program. Kentucky's an exception to that rule because they use about 13 players. It's not difficult at all to get ready for a basketball game.

> *Jack Cristil loves life, loves Mississippi State, and I think he loves what he does. He's a good, fun-loving, personable guy.*
>
> ⁂ *Bob Harris, Duke University*

In basketball, I don't rely on numbers as much as I do on their physical appearance. For instance, Eric Dampier is a tall guy, while Darryl Wilson is a short guy, which immediately differentiates those two out of the five. Russell Walters has a crew cut. Whit Hughes wears a knee brace.

These things you pick up because in basketball, by the nature of the game, a lot of times you are screened from numbers. And it's so fast you don't have time to look down and figure out who No. 4 is. You learn basketball players by physical appearance more so than anything else.

With that in mind, I don't think the way I have prepared for either sport over the years has changed much. Obviously, the longer I have stayed with Mississippi State, the more they have influenced me, and it goes without saying that I want them to win. You have to try desperately to keep that prejudice, or bias, or enthusiasm out of your broadcast and try to make it as unbiased as possible. That becomes increasingly difficult because all of these things you've experienced over the years add to one another. Sort of like a big cake where you keep adding layers, and layers, and layers, and it becomes sweeter and sweeter. That's really been the thing I've had to work at most over the years and keep in mind during preparation.

That's sort of the way it is here. I've tried to be objective in what I'm reporting, but I know a lot of times you can't be. I know that 95 percent of the people who listen to my broadcasts are Mississippi State fans by the very nature of it. But by the same token, they've got their own ideas and their own opinions, and I'd like for them to be able to exercise those even though they're not seeing the game.

THE LEGEND OF JACK CRISTIL

I'm old, if that's what is meant by "legend." (I always equate legendary with ancient.) I don't ever really think about the impact I have had on people. I think possibly, if you're a stock broker or a banker you might think along those lines, but as a broadcaster, no. The only reason people turn on a radio broadcast, or a TV broadcast for that matter, is because they can't be at the game. They don't care who's doing the ballgame; they just want to know what's going on.

Now, people come up to me almost every day and tell me how they always listen to the games, or they used to listen with their dads, or whatever. You get that on almost a daily basis. You were a part of their life for a given amount of time, on a given day of the week. But I have never thought about being an impact on them, as such.

I think my responsibility is to myself. Since I elected to do this thing, I better do it the best that I possibly can. Obviously, you want to represent the university for which you work and the athletic department the best you can. After all, these are the institutions of higher learning and turning out the leaders for tomorrow. If they are to have any influence in the community, then this is the way you ought to approach it.

I don' t know that I would classify myself as a "fan" of Mississippi State, per se. Obviously, I want them to win; that goes without saying. You always have a great feeling for the individuals who are involved, whether they be coaches, or players, or faculty members, or administrators, or whatever it might be. I don't think it would be hard to be a fan for ANY college or university. I think it would be an honor to be a representative of that university, for the things that they stand for.

Currently, the university's broadcast rights are owned by a communications group, and I'm an independent contractor, so I work through them and not through the university. In the contract, and I think most schools are like this, the athletics director has the final say as to who will represent the school as their play-by-play broadcaster. I do not work for the school or state, as such, because I'm an independent contractor.

Still, when you have this opportunity to be a part of an organization that has some credibility, then you have to feel good about the organization. Unfortunately, many times we equate the quality of an institution of higher learning with its athletic program.

The accomplishment I'm most proud of is the fact that I've worked 44 years at Mississippi State, and they haven't fired me. I feel good about this organization.

I don't think I have professional accomplishments as such during this 44 years. Life has been very, very rewarding. I've had an opportunity to meet great people from all walks of life, from all parts of the country. Having associations with them and enjoying their company, whether you're with them once a year or once a week, has been rewarding. And having the chance to see so many other parts of the country and to talk to other people at other colleges and universities; people in the media, and with the support staffs with the various athletic departments ... that's been a great reward to me.

As far as personal accomplishments, I haven't set any goals, and don't feel that I've accomplished a great deal. I've just been very fortunate in my career to be able to do something I enjoy.

Now, even though it wasn't a goal, I think probably one thing that stands out in my mind for an event that I would like to have broadcast would be 1980 when the American hockey team beat the Russians in the Olympics. That would be of such magnitude that

Cristil was recognized by the Mississippi Broadcasters Association for 25 years of service with MSU, June 16, 1979.

you would want to be there, just like you would want to be there when David beat Goliath. I would like to have described that. But a game's a game, and sports are sports.

RADIO AND TELEVISION: THE CONSTANT STATIC

Television has affected the radio business; it affects everything we do in every phase of our life. It's the most influential one thing that has occurred in this country.

First and foremost, television dictates when you're going to start a game and when you're going to finish. They dictate many, many times the tempo of the game by commercial time-outs, which have been built into the broadcast. This has changed the game itself, so obviously as the game changes, our reporting changes.

Now, as a radio broadcaster, people think we're in competition with television, but we're not. If people are going to watch television, they're going to watch television no matter who's broadcasting the game. As I mentioned earlier, the only reason they're going to listen to us on the radio is because they can't be there. And if it's available, they probably feel that if they can't be there, the second best thing is watching it on television.

Television has affected the potential audience in radio, obviously, but by the same token there have been a lot of plus factors. With the cost of doing business for anyone in this day and time, you have to sell radio advertising to keep radio broadcasts alive. And it gives you the opportunity to sell more radio advertising because television demands more timeout periods which gives radio more time for commercials. It makes it easier on us to get our commercials in than it would be if those things had not transpired.

> Jack is like old man river. He said he was going to retire when I did but evidently he out-lasted me. We started in the SEC in the same year. What used to amaze me is that Jack used to go into the booth like the Lone Ranger without any type of help; he did play-by-play, color, and he was the engineer. I've heard Jack do a lot of games, and I think he's very good.
>
> ~ Cawood Ledford, University of Kentucky

I've never really given the popularity of radio much thought. You know, it's a strange thing about radio on any level, once you open the microphone, you've been taught to talk to one person. If there happen to be 5 million listening, that's a marvelous thing, and if there was only one person listening, you have to do identically the same job.

I don't think television has affected the actual way we do a broadcast, but I'm sure it has affected the number of listeners. Television measures its audience in thousands—radio measures theirs in tens. That's the very nature of the business.

When you're doing a ballgame—for example Mississippi State's playing Vanderbilt in Nashville for a midweek night game that's not on television—you'll have a better radio audience than you would if it was a Saturday afternoon game on television. I've never thought of audience size, as such, because it's of no consequence.

The Business

There's no question about it that I take the approach that this is a business. Having once been in sales I can say that this is just putting together sales presentations. You have facts and figures available to you. You try to know the philosophy of the people you're dealing with when you make this sales presentation. Nothing in this world happens until somebody sells something.

It's the same thing in that sports broadcasting is strictly a business. In business how do you present your product when you go to sell it? Are you the only guy on the block that's got this thing, or do you have heavy competition? Is it price-oriented, or service-oriented?

It's the same thing in radio broadcasts, but you determine your own style and your own philosophy. I've always had the philosophy that the broadcaster, as such, is a very poor substitute for the person being at the game. Nobody stays home to listen to a broadcaster; they stay at home because they can't get to the game, whatever the reasons. So I'm to deliver the information in regards to the game as accurately as I possibly can, as unbiased as I possibly can, and with color and emotion and enthusiasm that they would experience if they were sitting at the event themselves. That's the approach I've taken in my business.

In this business we are after-the-fact reporters. Some schools have the philosophy that they want their broadcasters to be cheerleaders, and that's fine; I have no problem with that. If that's what the school wants—"hooray for us, and the hell with the other guys"—that's fine. Mississippi State has never been that way. In fact when I got the job, in my interview the late Dudy Noble, who was the athletics director at that time, told me, "Son, I'll tell you what I want you to do when you broadcast these games. You tell that audience what the score is, how much time is left, who's got the ball, and cut out the bull." That's the greatest advice I've ever had, because that's what the radio audience wants to know: what's the score, how much time is left, and who's got the ball. That's all that's important.

Paul and The Babe

I've worked with so many coaches here, I wouldn't know where to start to think about some of the ones I've had good relationships with. I'd like to think I had pretty good relationships with all of

Jack Cristil (right) chats with MSU athletics director Larry Templeton.

them, but obviously you can enjoy some more than others.

In football, for example, I really enjoyed working with Paul Davis when he was the head coach in the early 1960s. Paul's wife and my late wife, Mavis, went to high school together and were teammates on the girl's team, and that sort of thing, so we had a good rapport with them. We had a natural camaraderie. He enjoyed a certain degree of success as a football coach at Mississippi State, and I got to know him very, very well not only as a person but also as a coach. We had an excellent relationship.

I enjoyed working with Charley Shira when he was the head coach and athletics director at Mississippi State. A lot of people don't remember this, but there was a cribbing scandal at West Point in the late 1940s (they work on the honor system, academically and so forth), and Coach Shira was caught up in that. After he left West Point, I think he always fought to overcome that image. He was just an absolute true gentleman, extremely hard worker, and he appreciated the people around him and the opportunities that he had. He didn't enjoy a lot of success as a coach at Mississippi State as far as winning and losing were concerned, but he was a great guy to work with.

As for my relationship with a couple of the basketball coaches, of course you have to go back to Babe McCarthy. I was friends with Babe before he became coach at Mississippi State. Babe was coaching junior high basketball in Tupelo, Mississippi, when I first moved there, so I knew him then. In 1955 Babe went to work with the Standard Oil Company as a salesman and was still around to see all of the high school basketball games. I'd see him at the various gyms we worked. When he became the head basketball coach at State in 1956, I was pleased he got that opportunity. Then we started doing their basketball games in 1957.

Babe was an excellent basketball coach, but he was as fine a salesman as you'll ever meet. He could sell an idea as well as anyone I have ever seen; and he sold his kids on the idea that they could play basketball, and they could win basketball games. He sold fans on the idea that this was the greatest attraction since the Barnum & Bailey Circus. Babe was a winner in all respects.

Richard Williams I think is a very, very intense individual but also a very intelligent individual. He's very well read and knows a great deal about a great deal of things including basketball. His basic background is teaching, and he's one of the best teachers I've ever been around. I love his methods of teaching.

The Opposing Coaches and Their Antics

Unfortunately, I didn't get to know a great many of the opposing coaches closely. Obviously, in football you have to look at guys like Bear Bryant at Alabama, Vince Dooley at Georgia—these types of people who have been so very, very successful in the things they did. Coach Adolph Rupp at Kentucky in basketball, Dale Brown at LSU; people that have contributed so much to the game.

Wimp Sanderson has always been one of my favorites. I thought Wimp never got the credit he deserved while he was at Alabama. He is a very intense individual, but if he likes you as a friend, he's one of those types that'll do whatever he possibly can for you to help you out. Wimp came in behind C. M. Newton at Alabama after being his assistant for many, many years. Because of that I think Wimp had to inject his own personality, which he did with the plaid coats and the ranting and raving on the sidelines, which is showmanship. Wimp is a great showman, but he's also a great basketball coach and a great friend to have; you have to admire him.

There have been a lot of coaches around the league who I have admired.

Some of these guys like Wimp had some unusual antics on the sidelines. I always liked Hugh Durham at Georgia; he was a stalker on the sidelines. He was constantly shouting out on the floor to his players or the officials. He had great knowledge of the game as a floor coach. I always liked his philosophy of changing defenses. When you played, particularly in a close ballgame, you saw every conceivable defense that basketball can offer. He'd play a man-to-man, then a 2-3 zone, then a match-up, then a triangle-and-2, then a diamond-and-1, then a box-and-1. You'd see it all. Maybe he did too much, I don't know, but I do know I always enjoyed watching him operate. I thought I would've liked to have been around him a great deal, although I never got the opportunity.

> *I worked a game with Jack one time. There was a doubleheader game with Tech playing Mississippi in the first game and Mississippi State playing Georgia in the second game. Jack asked me to work the game with him. He is a great guy. He's a legend in Mississippi.*
>
> &. *Al Ciraldo, Georgia Tech*

I've seen so many different coaches through the years that it's difficult to pick them out.

I like the "young" coaches today like Lon Kruger and Eddie Fogler. Like all aspects of this thing in college athletics, you're getting much better coaching and better facilities—everything just seems to be on the way up, and I really like it.

In football it's really hard to say who the great coach is or who the poor coach is because now they have such huge staffs, and everybody's a specialist. The coach is more of the CEO of the team. The head coach makes the ultimate decision, but you really don't know who's making the contributions and who isn't.

BASKETBALL, 1963

I think the basketball season of 1963 sticks out in my mind, not only from a athletic standpoint but a historical and philosophical one as well. And not just for the team, but for entire the state of Mississippi. Prior to that time, teams in Mississippi and Alabama, and probably elsewhere, did not play integrated sports.

Mississippi State had won the Southeastern Conference championship in 1959, 1961, and 1962. At that time the SEC champion had a bid to go to the NCAA tournament, but Mississippi State declined that invitation because they could conceivably play integrated teams. Kentucky was second in the league at that time and represented the conference. Auburn won the championship in 1960 and also declined an invitation to the NCAA tournament.

OFF THE AIR WITH SOUTHEASTERN LEGENDS

At the 1983 homecoming game, Jack Cristil was honored for his 30 years at the university. Here he is seen during the halftime ceremony with MSU President Dr. James McComas (right).

In 1963 when Mississippi State won the conference championship, every conceivable effort was made to prevent the team from participating in the NCAA tournament. There were court injunctions and a lot of legal ramifications, and it finally did come to pass for the team to go to the tournament.

In the opening round, they played at East Lansing, Michigan, against Loyola University-Chicago which had four black players and one white player. Loyola won the ballgame by six or eight and eventually went on to become the National Champions. That broke, to a degree, the color barrier. It was a great philosophical and social event not only in Mississippi but also in the South. It had tremendous ramifications. That has to stick out in my mind because of the things that transpired at that time.

1980: THE YEAR STATE BEAT 'BAMA

Alabama was rated No. 1 in the country when Mississippi State played the Tide in 1980. The fact they were rated No. 1 was not unusual because they were generally rated No. 1. They had won the national championship in 1979. We had a solid football team in 1980.

This was the only football game I saw that if you removed one play from that game, theoretically, you could have changed the outcome of the whole thing. We've seen games where you could remove a half, or a quarter, or a series, and it would not have affected the outcome of that game, but this was the only game that I have ever seen where every play was critical to the outcome.

State had kicked two field goals; Alabama kicked one. State led 6-3 when Alabama put on one of their patented late fourth-quarter drives. They drove the ball down to about the 1-yard line. It was fourth-and-one with seconds on the clock, and the Tide did not have any time-outs left. The Bulldogs held Alabama and took over possession of the ball.

MSU was trying to run out the clock, when the Alabama nose guard reached down and slapped the ball as it was being snapped. The ball was fumbled, and nothing was called on the slap of the ball, even though it should have been. Luckily it made no difference who landed on the ball, because the clock ran out on the play. So that ballgame literally went down to the very last snap of the football. Obviously it was a big win for us, since we knocked off the No. 1 team in the country.

The Bulldogs

I've seen a lot of good athletes for Mississippi State. First and foremost, when you think of basketball, the first one to come to mind is Bailey Howell. He was such an outstanding athlete, not only in the collegiate level but in the pro ranks as well. He is a member of the Hall of Fame.

Today's ballclub has a guy like Darryl Wilson who is just an outstanding basketball player. I think of Jeff Malone when he was at Mississippi State. Ray White was a great athlete. There have just been so many of them.

I like to think in football about the Billy Stacy and the Jackie Parker era and D. D. Lewis when he was the linebacker. I think of Frank Dowsing, a defensive back who was a great player, and Richard Webb, who was a defensive tackle. Arthur Davis played back in the era when guys went both ways on offense and defense, and he was a great halfback and a marvelous defensive back.

There have just been so many of them who, in their particular way at their particular position, have performed as well as you could ask an individual to perform.

The opposing players are just as difficult to pick out. Obviously, I've seen some great basketball players from Kentucky and some great football players from Alabama, Ole Miss, and LSU.

Tucker Fredrickson from Auburn was one of my earlier favorites. I thought that he was just an outstanding, superlative athlete. He was like Arthur Davis, playing halfback and defensive back. He had a shot to play with the New York Giants but hurt his knee. He would have been a great pro player.

Again, when you roll all those years together, there have been so many great athletes that it gets tough for them to stick out. Especially when you think about some of the Alabama football teams we play every year and some of the athletes they have had. You'd like to be able to watch them play 10 times a year, but you only see them once.

Mississippi State-Ole Miss

At one time the Mississippi State—Ole Miss rivalry was probably the biggest thing that happened in the state whether you played football, or baseball, or basketball. Now fans are so much more knowledgeable about what goes on in other places, I think the rivalry has diminished a great deal. People find out that things exist other than whether State or Ole Miss won the game; it doesn't have the magnitude it once did. There are still some die-hard generals who believe your season is a success if you win that particular game, though. With most of us you see so many other great games that take away from the rivalry.

The College World Series

I remember the baseball season of 1971 when we had the opportunity to go to the College World Series in Omaha, Nebraska. It was a great event then and is tremendous now. Rosenblatt Stadium was an excellent place to play, and there were excellent teams there.

The University of Southern California came in there that year having played 60 or 70 games, while State had only played about 30. Two of our pitchers were unable to compete because they were freshmen. (Our league at that time allowed freshmen to play, and these two guys had played as freshmen. But under NCAA regulations, players who had participated as freshmen could not play as seniors in the World Series because they had already used up their eligibility.) So our No. 1 and No. 2 pitchers didn't get a chance to play.

We got beat by Tulsa, 5-2, then we got beat by someone else. It was a great experience for us and sort of set the stage for Mississippi State baseball on the level that its played today. It was a great stepping stone for the university and the baseball program.

"Nothing Humorous Ever Happens at Mississippi State"

Nothing humorous ever happens at Mississippi State. Humorous things happen to those people who win with a great deal of regularity because they find a lot of levity in things that happen. We don't have that worry at State.

We've been very fortunate because we've had a minimum of problems in the press box over the years, and we have a great camaraderie with the people we work with. We kid one another a great deal, but usually when the ball's thrown up, we get down to the business of being businesslike and try to do our job in a businesslike fashion. I don't guess we've always succeeded, but we've endeavored to this.

One of the strange things—the late Joe Phillips, who ran a radio station in Starkville, Mississippi, had the broadcast rights to Mississippi State athletics for a number of years. He was also the producer of our radio network. He and Bert Banks, who owned some stations in Tuscaloosa, would always make a bet on the Alabama-Mississippi State game. Bert was a great Alabama fan. He is to this day, and is a superb gentleman, who incidentally wears the purple heart after being a survivor of Corregidor, the Death March on Bataan.

> *Jack is a fine, steady, hard workman. He became a sales manager and tied in the Mississippi State football, basketball and baseball play-by-play, and made a killing. He lived in Tupelo his whole life and is still there to this day. He's now 70 years old; he's still doing the play-by-play, and he's still in sales. Just a great man.*
>   &*Larry Munson, University of Georgia*

We generally played Alabama at Alabama for years and years because they drew the larger crowd and would pay us a nice gate. Every year we went to Alabama, and every year Bert and Joe would argue before the game. Finally, Bert would give Joe "x" number of points for an "x" dollar bet. Bert won every time because Alabama won.

One year we were over in Alabama, and we just had a very ordinary team while they were a very, very good. Bert and Joe argued and argued until just before kickoff. We were in the middle of a break, and Bert came in the booth and said, "Joe, I'll give you 40 points and Mississippi State for $100."

"By golly, you've got a bet," Joe told Bert.

Alabama won the game 41-0.

You would think over the years with as many games as I've covered that there'd be some ludicrous things and humorous things, but, really, it's never happened. That's very, very good for us.

THE CROW'S NEST

Facilities during the early stages of my career weren't designed for the media. I remember we played Delta State out of Cleveland, Mississippi, and this may have been the first radio broadcast out of their coliseum. There was a stage at one end which would have been ideal, but instead there was a huge overhang that came out over the court from the ceiling. You had to go up a ladder then across a catwalk to get to that thing, and then broadcast the game from there.

I don't know why that observation area was even there, but it was. That's where they ran the telephone line. Back then your equipment weighed tons. This particular night I drove to Cleveland and did the game by myself. When I got there, I had to shinny that equipment up the ladder and across the catwalk. There was one little guard rail around the area, so I had to loop my arm around that guard rail and was doing the game looking straight down on the court. And you talk about hot—heat rises, and it was hotter than the hinges of Hades; I was wringing wet.

Unfortunately, it was a close game, so I had to work very, very hard to get to the end of it. That may be the worst I have ever experienced, but it was no fault of theirs because no one had ever done a game from there before.

We've been at some football stadiums where the facilities weren't necessarily poor, but the weather was. We faced North Carolina State in the last Liberty Bowl game played in Philadelphia, in 1963. Mississippi State won 16-12. The temperature was about 8 degrees, and I've never been as cold in my life. There was an outdoor area that we broadcast from. The stadium held about 60,000 people, and there were probably 9,000 there at that time. Again, that was a good experience for us to be up there. So I guess 1963 was a very big year for Mississippi State athletics, even though it was the coldest in my life.

"Wrap This One in Maroon and White"

I really don't know that I've got any phrases that I use regularly; I've never tried to develop any. I'm sure I use some phrases over and over again which may be redundant. The only thing I ever consistently use and that has really become a habit, after an exciting game I'll say, "Wrap this one in maroon and white." That's really the only thing. I probably use other phrases that I'm not consciously aware of, but I don't try to establish those each season. I'll leave those to the television people, they don't have anything else to talk about anyway. And I'm not saying that demeaningly, but by the very nature of the business they have to paint a picture in addition to their picture. There are television broadcasters who have their pet phrases, and some of them are good; I've just never operated in that way.

No Regrets

I have no regrets whatsoever about getting into this business. I've made a lot of mistakes I'd like to correct, but no regrets. It has been very good for me and very good for our family. It offered us an opportunity to do some things that other families would like to have done. It exposed our children to the atmospheres of various colleges and universities prior to them having to make a decision as to where they wanted to go when they graduated from high school. I think it was very, very beneficial, and it provided an opportunity to make a living, which is important, too.

On near games the family got to travel with me, like to Ole Miss or Memphis State. When LSU would come to Jackson, they'd go to those games. We went in the car as a family and ate as a family and stayed together as a family, which was very rewarding for me.

At the same time, there's no question about whether broadcasting is tough or not on a family life. It's just like any traveling job; you are very, very fortunate to have a spouse that is understanding and children that are understanding. You're going to be gone, you're going to be away from home; you're never going to be there when the washing machine breaks down or when the plumbing goes bad, and this type of thing.

I would have to assume it would be very difficult on the spouse, but if you have an understanding spouse who knows this is a part of life as far as making a living is concerned, then it's no more difficult than a businessman who travels a few days each week. Statistics say 25 percent of this country is on the move every day, so I guess I wasn't in a great minority. When you're on the road, she or he or whoever it is can turn on the radio and say, well, he made it to the ballpark, he ain't dead yet, and turn the damn thing off because he'll be home tomorrow.

My Advice ... Don't Do It

Broadcasting today is so different than when we got started, so my advice to a young broadcaster is don't do it. When we first got into the business, it was indeed a business. It was a source of information to the people who couldn't be at the event—to the point where they got some reality into what the event was and what was transpiring.

After the advent of television (and television rules the sports world today no matter what anyone says), it became first a business, then show business. It's no longer reporting sports, as such, for the intrinsic value of the game; it's all showmanship. Radio broadcasters this day and time are, I guess, a necessary evil. If people had their druthers, they'd druther be on television. There are only a handful of people who actually appreciate what radio has to offer. It has outlived its usefulness because on a day to day basis radio doesn't do anything.

Radio stations right now will advertise the fact that they play 12 songs in a row. What the hell is that? What are you contributing to the community? When you do this type of thing, then you lose all credibility for anything else. They simply make a minor contribution. At one time they were very, very major in what they did. So I wouldn't advise a guy to go into radio broadcasting today.

> *Jack Cristil is a dear friend. He is as competitive on his broadcasts as his football or basketball teams are on the field. I see a lot of Jack in me. He will get on the officials and say how the Bulldogs were robbed. I remember when I was first with Vandy, we sat in the same little booth at Mississippi State. Vandy beat the Bulldogs on a last second shot, plus there was a wild call at the end, but Jack would not talk to me after the game. He was mad at Vanderbilt and the officials and mad at me because I was excited about it on the air. I've always laughed about that. Jack loves his Bulldogs.*
> ❧ *Paul Eells, University of Arkansas*

I really have a great deal of compassion for the guys who are coming along now in the business at this level. Rarely have any of them had a chance to emulate the people in radio broadcasting; it simply isn't there. They have to pattern themselves after these television people. And don't get me wrong, I don't have a problem

The Sportscaster's Dozen

The Mississippi State football broadcast crew, 1978.

with television people personally because they all have their niche, but they're doing an injustice to their audience. If you understand the television business, it's not the fault of the anchor guys or the play-by-play guys or the analysts; it's the directors and the producers because they're in show business. When it's show business it's all of this slam, bang, loud music, all these graphics, and all of the embellishments thereof, and the event becomes secondary.

It also doesn't help these guys that college athletics have gone from being almost 100 percent entertainment to 100 percent business. It's turned 180 degrees. Football used to be something you'd do on Saturday, and basketball was something you'd do between spring football and fall football, and baseball was something you'd do when the weather was nice and kept some boys out of the pool room.

Now everything is predicated on wins and losses and the dollar and the till. That may or may not be an unfortunate thing, I don't know. It's played on a level now that's absolutely fantastic as far as exceptional coaching, great facilities, and tremendous athletes. I guess if you were setting up an engineering department or a mathematics department, you would want those apexes to be reached at some point where you would have all of this exceptional equipment and great teachers and excellent students and an administration that was for you 100 percent. Maybe as a part of the overall university picture, it was supposed to grow in this direction.

The Future ... Knock on Wood

I'm not going to give you a short answer of how long I plan on doing this because in my stage of the game I don't make long-range plans. I don't plan to have supper tonight with any given individual at any certain time because it is strictly up to providence now as to how long I'm here. Right now I'm enjoying what I'm doing.

I watch a little television, very selectively, and I do a little reading, very selectively. I also have a neighbor down the street who is a very, very dear friend, and has always been at my side when I have needed help. But he has a lot of woodworking equipment in a shop that he has never had the opportunity to use. Now that he's retired, he has that opportunity, and he is a very good craftsman. I'm his gopher. He's taught me how to use a few pieces of machinery like a table-saw and a band-saw and a radial-arm saw, and so forth, and we build little things like kiddie rockers and kiddie high chairs, bird houses, and planter boxes, that sort of thing. We make these things more to occupy our time, and he does sell them to a wholesaler, but we don'tmake any money from it. It's not a money-making proposition.

In August of 1994, I made up my mind that I was going to retire from the television station when December 31st rolled around. So in August of 1994 I went to our athletics director, Larry Templeton. Had a nice talk with him, the gist of which was that I wanted to continue to do the ballgames if I was serving the purposes of the university and the athletic department the way they wanted it served. He assured me that I was and that I could continue to do the games. I asked him as my boss and a very, very dear friend to be the first one to tell me that I had slipped to the point where I was not doing what I was supposed to be doing the way it was supposed to be done and let me graciously get out. He assured me that he would.

Well, to this point, he hasn't come up to me yet and told me it was time to go. So I'm still here.

WOODY DURHAM
UNIVERSITY OF NORTH CAROLINA

Henry David Thoreau once said, "If one advances confidently, in the direction of his own dreams and endeavors, to lead the life which he has imagined, he will meet with a success unexpected in common hours." ¶Woody Durham, the voice of the University of North Carolina Tar Heels, had never really imagined a career in broadcasting until he reached high school. Since that time, he's been able to carve out a career of which dreams are made.

> *The toughest thing about success is that you've got to keep on being a success.*
> — Irving Berlin

Like many boys growing up, Durham enjoyed playing sports. He had his favorite teams, and had his favorite players. Also like many boys, when Durham played basketball or football in the neighborhood, he provided the play-by-play. Still, broadcasting was not a dream career.

Woody Durham spent most of his childhood and high school years in the town of Albemarle, North Carolina, a textile town of about 12,000 people 40 miles east of Charlotte. With his parents as fans already, Durham began following the University of North Carolina and one of its early football stars, Charlie Justice.

Justice was the All-American guy and All-American athlete who had the hearts of most younger Tar Heel fans. He wore Carolina blue from 1946-1949 and quickly became one of the most popular athletes in the state of North Carolina. Justice did it all for the Tar Heels, including punting, rushing, and passing duties, all of which helped him become a two-time Heisman Trophy runner-up. He helped lead Carolina teams to appearances in two Sugar Bowls and one Cotton Bowl.

Editor's Note: At the request of Woody Durham, his chapter was written in third-person by Matt Fulks.

Like a lot of Justice fans, Durham scrambled after games to try and get Justice's autograph. (Little did he realize at the time, Charlie Justice would later become one of his best friends.)

Growing Up a Tar Heel ... Becoming a Demon Deacon

The 1956-1957 basketball season proved to be an important and exciting one for Carolina fans, as the Tar Heels went 32-0 on their way to capturing the NCAA national championship. The season reached its pinnacle with back-to-back triple overtime wins against Michigan State and Kansas in the national tournament semifinals and finals.

Durham was 15 years old when the Tar Heels won the title.

"I had followed Carolina basketball," he says, "but I really didn't follow it avidly before the 1957 season. That year the entire state got caught up in what the Tar Heels were doing.

"Now I'm close friends with all five guys from that team, which is a very special and unusual part of my life and my career. Very few boys get to grow up and be friends with their boyhood heroes."

The year continued to be an exciting one for Durham as he got his first radio job a week before his 16th birthday.

The manager for one of the two Albemarle radio stations had judged an oratorical contest in which Durham had competed in the spring of that year. The manager was looking for a high school student to be on the air to work the weekend shift.

"I had a couple of friends who were working at the other radio station in town, and I would go visit them when they were doing their weekend shifts," Durham remembers. "When I went to visit them, I could tell that it was work, but it looked like they were having a good time.

"When I started doing it, I realized how much fun it was."

Within a few months of working weekends at the station, Durham added an hour-long morning shift as well as an afternoon slot to his schedule.

> *It's strange now with Woody and his son, Wes, in the ACC that I can be in the car and dial up a game not knowing if it's Woody or Wes on the air; they sound identical to me. Woody paid me a high compliment a few years ago when he was talking about me to an interviewer and said he remembered when I came into the conference that "Clemson hired a guy from the North; he won't be around long." I found that very complimentary.*
>
> — *Jim Phillips, Clemson University*

Besides working at the station and going to school, Durham played football for a very good Albemarle High School team. In fact, the Albemarle teams at that time were so good that they were the top draw during the season in the small community. Football was all that people talked about during the week and going to the game on Friday night was the thing to do.

For home games the 8,000-seat stadium was packed an hour before kickoff. For road games there were times the Albemarle crowd was as large as the home crowd.

By the end of his high school career, Durham realized playing football was not going to be an option for a career. As with many young athletes, however, he struggled with the idea of not being involved anymore in sports.

"Eventually I realized that broadcasting was the way I could stay connected with sports," Durham said. "I figured I could use my interest in broadcasting to bridge that gap with my love of sports."

Durham enrolled at the University of North Carolina where, even though he spent two summers working at the Albemarle radio station WZKY, he studied for a career in television.

"I really thought at that point that I had done my last radio," he admits.

As part of their schooling in TV and radio, UNC students took an annual trip to Charlotte where they observed at radio and TV station WBT. Durham was also fortunate during college in that he was able to do some ACC games on television. When he graduated from college in June of 1963, he had developed a good resume with plenty of practical experience.

Even though there were no full-time sports jobs available in the area, Durham had an opportunity to go to work in South Carolina.

"Bill Melson was the personnel director at what was then Jefferson Standard Broadcasting (now Jefferson-Pilot Sports)," Durham recalls. "He called me one day and told me they had a job open at their station in Florence, South Carolina. It wasn't a full-time sports job, but I would be one of the four staff announcers."

So Durham left Albemarle on Friday to meet with the program director, George Burnette, on Saturday. The meeting on that May day went so well that Burnette offered Durham the job before he left the station. Durham and his fiancée at the time, Jean, were set to be married on June 23, so he took the job.

The plan was to spend about two years at the station, get some good experience, then try to find a full-time sports job. Three months later, Durham received a call from WFMY-TV in Greensboro, North Carolina. Charlie Harville, who had been at the station since it went on the air in 1949, was leaving to go to a new station in High Point, North Carolina.

C. D. Chesley, who had originated the ACC games on television, recommended Durham to the management at WFMY. After the weekend interview, Durham felt he had done well enough to get the job, but thought the $125 weekly salary he requested was too high.

"They called me midweek and offered me the job," Durham said. "That was November, 1963. I was there for 14 years."

In the meantime, during the spring of 1964, Wake Forest University had hired a new football coach, Bill Tate. With that change the search was also on for a new radio color commentator for the football games. Durham received a call from the WFU sports information director, Marvin "Skeeter" Francis, offering him the color position. After receiving permission from WFMY's management to also work at Wake Forest, Durham accepted the position.

The quarterback on that 1964 Wake Forest team was John Mackovic, and the running back was Brian Piccolo. Brian led the nation in rushing and scoring that year, and Wake Forest improved its final season record at 5-5. (They had gone a couple seasons in the early 1960s when they didn't win a game.) Things never materialized past that point, so Bill Tate was fired at the end of the 1968 season, and the clean sweep they made included the broadcasters.

Durham was able to pick back up with the ACC basketball games on television in 1968, but he wanted to find a way to somehow keep his hand in football play-by-play. That opportunity came calling soon. The director of athletics at Guilford College, Dr. Herb Appenzeller, called and offered Durham their play-by-play job. To some it may seem like a step back to go from Wake Forest to Guilford, but it was perfect for Durham.

"My wife, Jean, and I figured it would be very convenient because the school was close to where we lived, and the team never took long trips," Durham says of the Guilford job. "It was the bridge that kept me in football."

As Durham was working football at Guilford College and ACC basketball games on television, Bill Currie was broadcasting the University of North Carolina games with Jack Callahan. Currie, who was also the sports director at WSOC-TV in Charlotte, left

Woody (right) with color analyst Mick Mixon during a Tar Heel basketball game.

Carolina in February of 1971 to go to work at KDKA in Pittsburgh. Bob Lamey, one of Currie's associates, finished out the season for the Tar Heels.

Homer Rice, who was the University of North Carolina athletics director, called Durham to meet with him about doing Carolina games on radio. Although Durham wasn't sure he wanted to do the Carolina games, he decided to meet with Rice because the television games weren't going as well as he had hoped.

When he walked in to meet with Rice, the AD caught Durham off guard as the two shook hands.

"Woody, I learned something interesting about you yesterday."

"What's that?" Durham asked.

Rice replied, "I just learned yesterday that you graduated from Carolina."

Durham says that's one of the biggest compliments anyone has ever given him, because, as he replied to Rice, "If I've been doing ACC games for four years and you didn't find out until yesterday that I went to school here, then I've done a pretty good job, haven't I?"

The two laughed about that. Ironically, about 24 years after Rice hired Woody Durham at North Carolina, as the athletics director at Georgia Tech he hired Woody's son, Wes, to do the Yellow Jacket games.

The Sportscaster's Dozen

The Football Trio: Bill, Dick, and Mack

"Bill Dooley was a very, very solid football coach," Durham says. "Whatever Carolina enjoys now in football—and Mack Brown really built an outstanding program here—can be traced back to what Bill Dooley did here back in the late 1960s."

Dooley took over the Tar Heel program before the 1967 season and immediately started recruiting the state of North Carolina, trying to get the best players from the state to become Tar Heels. One would think that would be a fairly simple thing to do, but the Tar Heels went through a period where they were not getting a lot of the better players in the state; a lot of them were either going to N.C. State or Duke.

"Bill was a very solid coach and was very loyal to the people around him," Durham remembers. "He was very conservative in his speech and also in his style of play. We used to laugh all the time that his philosophy was, "Why throw the ball down the field when you can run it?"

The 1,000-yard runners that Carolina has had so many of, started while Dooley was the coach. If the Tar Heels threw the ball 15 times in a game, that was a lot. The coach just felt that you should run right at the defense and knock them down. As a former lineman at Mississippi State, he had been the offensive coordinator with his brother, Vince, at Georgia. When he went to Carolina, he took that old style of SEC football with him.

Dooley later had a desire to be an athletics director. He thought that Carolina should consider him to be both coach and AD.

"If that philosophy held true, [basketball coach] Dean Smith would have held down both jobs years earlier," Durham says.

Dooley had a chance to go to Virginia Tech to be the athletics director, so he left Carolina after the 1977 season. During his 11 seasons, Dooley posted an overall record of 69-53-2.

Dick Crum took over for Dooley in 1978.

"Dick knew a lot of football," said Durham. "I think he could have been a very, very good coach here. He was an outstanding coach at the University of Miami-Ohio. He had a terrible first year here based on who he had coming back, and then the real turning point came the next season."

The 1979 season was one which made people think Carolina was headed to the next level. The Tar Heels opened the season with an impressive 28-0 win over rival South Carolina. Things continued to go well for Carolina that season, as the team went 8-3-1 and earned a trip to the Gator Bowl in Jacksonville to face Michigan. After trailing 9-0 in the second quarter against the Wolverines, the Tar Heels rallied for 17 straight points and won 17-15.

The Tar Heels kept heading to that next level for the next three seasons under Crum. In 1980 the team went 11-1 and beat Texas in the Bluebonnet Bowl, 16-7. In 1981 Carolina went back to the Gator Bowl and beat Lou Holtz's Arkansas team, 31-27. The bowl streak continued in 1982 with a 26-10 win over Texas in the Sun Bowl.

"Even though the Tar Heels went to the Peach Bowl in 1983, the talent started to run out; we were starting to get lean again," Durham points out.

To start off that 1983 season, Carolina won its first seven games before playing at Maryland at the end of October. The Tar Heels lost the nationally televised game, 28-26. After that, it was apparent to Carolina faithful that the team was starting to go in a slide. In fact, a lot of people still point to that Maryland game as the turning point.

People did not handle that loss very well. Crum did not handle that loss very well.

"He really went into a shell," Durham says of the football coach. "He was an introvert anyway, so he did not help himself after that Maryland loss. Dick was an old-time football coach in that all he wanted to do was coach football; he didn't want to have to deal with the media, he didn't want to have to deal with the alumni, he didn't want to have to deal with the fans, or anything like that. By being that way, it was difficult for him to communicate with anybody."

During the 1987 season, both the university and Dick Crum realized a change needed to be made. Crum, in fact, initiated the conversation with the university about getting out of his contract.

"Apparently there were some conversations that went on around mid-season, and they put a gag clause in there so nobody would talk about the situation until the season was over, and that if the story broke prematurely, the buy-out would be renegotiated," Durham recalls.

Guess what? The story broke prematurely in the *Raleigh News & Observer*. Rather than $350,000, the university ended up paying Crum $850,000. He left Carolina bitter, thinking the university had run him off. The university was bitter because of what happened in the final months of that agreement, and because they were basically left without a football team.

Durham with legendary UNC basketball coach Dean Smith.

Before the 1988 season, school officials were able to get Mack Brown as Crum's successor.

From the outset Brown was the polar opposite of Crum. Whereas Crum was an introvert almost to an extreme, Brown was an extrovert to the extreme.

"Mack's strength was communicating with people around him as well as with the media. If you work in this business, you hope that one day you're going to be able to be associated with a Mack Brown," Durham says. "He made this job enjoyable and easy for you. He was willing to do, within reason, whatever needed to be done to make his program better.

"Dick Crum and his staff had alienated the high school coaches in North Carolina by coming in and telling everyone how much better the high school football was in Ohio. It was so bad that we had recruits coming in to look at the school and current players at the time telling them they shouldn't come to Carolina because of the atmosphere of the program."

Brown went out and rebuilt those recruiting bridges very quickly, despite suffering through two 1-10 seasons (1988 and 1989). He went through the first 1-10 season because there was very little talent for him to work with. At the start of the 1989 season, it appeared things might be getting better. But before the season began, Brown suspended his top tailback, Kennard Martin, for academic reasons. Brown told Martin that he could stay on scholarship and have an opportunity to come back the following year. As it turned out, Martin left, went to the Canadian Football League and lasted less than a year.

"Even after the first 1-10 season, Carolina fans could see by the things happening off the field that Brown was turning the program around," said Durham. "I told him on the air in an emotional locker room at Duke (which was a very tough 35-29 loss to end the 1988 season) that, 'I've been around the Tar Heels a long time, but I've never felt better about Carolina football than I do right now.'

"We've had a lot of laughs about that since then, because they turned around and went 1-10 the next season."

The 1989 season was a situation whereas the Tar Heels had an offense and no defense Brown's first year. The second year they had an improved defense, but no offense to move the ball because they were missing their top quarterback.

In 1990 Brown had his first winning season at Carolina, 6-4-1, and possibly missed out on getting a bowl bid when Illinois beat Purdue with a last-second field goal.

Each season got a little better for Brown and the Tar Heels, as the coach was able to mend the recruiting fences and rebuild the University of North Carolina football name around the state.

In conjunction with spring practice, Brown started a high school coaching clinic. In his first clinic, he had 38 coaches show up. In the spring of 1996, he had 855 coaches. He has also continued to graduate players. The only year UNC wasn't recognized by the College Football Association was when the team had an unusual number of guys go to the NFL. When the players did that, some of them didn't finish their last semester. Most will probably get their degrees eventually, but they haven't as yet.

"It was a complete reversal with Mack," Durham said. "We thought at one time that it was going to be like that under Dick Crum, and maybe it could have been, but Dick's personality wouldn't let it happen. Whereas with Mack, when he decided not to go to the University of Oklahoma in 1995, that was a big difference; it made people think he was here for the long-haul.

"It's just amazing what Mack Brown has done in this state."

In December of 1997, however, three days before the Alliance Bowl announcements, Brown announced his resignation from the University of North Carolina. He had accepted the head coaching position at the University of Texas. Yet, over the past ten years he had taken the Tar Heels to the next level.

The Dean of College Basketball

Woody Durham was an undergraduate at the University of North Carolina when Dean Smith became the head basketball coach in 1961. The two had gotten to know each other a little bit while Smith was an assistant because Durham was working for Channel 4, the university's educational station, at the time. Sometimes they would set up what they called "broadvision" where the station would televise a basketball game but wouldn't do any play-by-play (they encouraged people to listen to the game on the radio). A lot of times when they would do the sports from there and couldn't get head coach Frank McGuire to go on the air, Coach Smith was available.

In the summer of 1961, when Coach McGuire went to the Philadelphia Warriors, Smith was named the head coach. When he was named head coach, Carolina was about to go on NCAA probation because of recruiting problems under McGuire. So immediately Smith inherited a program with a number of sanctions imposed like no off-campus recruiting, and the team could only play 17 games in his first year (he was 8-9 that year).

When Dean Smith was named head coach, very few people knew who he was. Back then who knew assistant coaches anyway? It's not like today with someone like a Roy Williams who had been an assistant before going to Kansas. When Smith was named head coach, people thought the administration was de-emphasizing basketball at Carolina. (Little did those people know.)

> *I think Woody is a good broadcaster. He has a good voice, and people in Chapel Hill love him.*
>
> — *Bob Fulton, University of South Carolina*

After going 8-9 in that first season, Smith had some winning teams early, going 15-6, 12-12, and 15-9 during the next three seasons. Coach Adolph Rupp at Kentucky signed a 10-year deal with Coach Smith for a Kentucky-Carolina series. Coach Smith beat Coach Rupp seven out of the 10 years. Some of those early wins the team was getting against Kentucky, as well as a couple against Indiana, were serving notice to people that this guy did know basketball. Guys like Larry Brown and Billy Cunningham were on Smith's first basketball teams. In fact, Smith gives his early players credit for helping him build a tradition.

When Smith was inducted into the Basketball Hall of Fame in 1983, he said, "Had I not gotten Rusty Clark [Rusty was the first big man under Dean Smith at Carolina] to come to school and the other guys who came with him, I probably would have lost my job."

Dean Smith took teams to three straight Final Fours (1967, 1968, 1969), and that was the thing that got him over the top—everybody knew then that this guy could coach.

Smith's priority is not necessarily winning as much as seeing that he has good players around him who want to get an education. He proved that you don't bring people in just to win games or just to use them. Even during his final seasons with so many players leaving early to go to the NBA, he still recruited guys looking for an education.

"He is the guy that set the standard for everything good in athletics that has happened at North Carolina during his time," Durham said. "He proved to people that you can be successful, and you can also graduate young people."

Things may change like they did for players like Jerry Stackhouse and Rasheed Wallace in 1995 (each of whom only stayed two years), but Smith would not recruit players who did not intend on getting their college education, regardless of how good of basketball players they were. In fact, he still gets hit with comments on Stackhouse and Wallace, but as Coach points out, who would have known that at the end of their sophomore season these two players would be two of the top five NBA lottery picks.

"The philosophy of Coach and this program is that during the season they make decisions based on what's best for the team; when the season's over they make decisions based on what's best for the individual," Durham explains. "Keeping along those lines he says, 'If you're going to be a top-five pick in the NBA draft, and you have anybody at all handling your money (even with the salary cap), not only should you be comfortable for the rest of your life, but your children should be as well.'

"The example he has always used when people ask him about turning pro early is: 'Let's say your son or your daughter is in journalism school at Chapel Hill, and the *Wall Street Journal* came to campus and offered your child (who is a junior) $5 million to go to work with them ... would you tell them to stay and get their degree knowing that they could get their degree by correspondence or by coming back in the summertime? What would you tell them?' The logical answer, and the one he points out, is to go work for the *Journal*. That's exactly what he's done with his basketball players.

"Away from the court, Dean Smith may be the most caring man about those around him that I've ever been around in my life. It's just amazing the sensitivity he has for other people."

Smith has had a hard time with changes in the game of college basketball. There was an incident a couple years ago when Jerry Stackhouse was airborne and got shoved by a Clemson player. That incident provoked some problems between Smith and Tiger coach Rick Barnes. On a play like that, Coach Smith doesn't just see one player getting pushed; but rather he sees Kenny Smith go down, he sees Steve Hale go down, he sees Derrick Phelps going down. He sees all of those injuries to players that spoil seasons and possibly ruin careers. From that aspect he had a hard time with the change of the game.

1996-1997: Passing the Baton and Hanging Up the Whistle

The 1996-1997 season was one of excitement and celebration for Carolina fans; the 1996-1997 postseason was one of shock and sorrow for Tar Heel faithful.

Toward the end of the 1996-1997 season, Coach Smith broke Adolph Rupp's record for most career wins by a college coach. In fact the entire 1996-1997 season turned out to be pretty special. For the Tar Heel faithful it would have been nice to have had a national championship at the end of it, but just getting to the Final Four was something not many people expected after the team started 0-3 in ACC play.

The Tar Heels went to Europe in December and played a terrific game against the Italian National Team but then came back to the States and were defeated badly against Wake Forest in Winston-Salem. Then the team turned around and lost a 22-point lead and the game to Maryland at home.

Very few people expected this team to go on a 16-game winning streak, and in the process of that winning streak help Coach Smith establish the all time wins record passing Rupp.

"Doing the two national championship games in 1982 and 1993 would, by far, be the highlight of my basketball career following the Tar Heels," Durham says, but adds, "Certainly doing win number 877 with Coach Smith in Winston-Salem against Colorado in the

Woody clowning around with former Tar Heel standout Michael Jordan at a fund-raiser for the Jordan Institute for Families in the UNC School of Social Work.

NCAA tournament, with the atmosphere and the people who were there and the way Coach Smith handled the entire weekend, was just terrific.

"It's been a terrific thrill for something like that to have happened and to be a part of it. I don't think we're going to see anybody do this (break Coach Smith's record) anytime soon."

On October 9, 1997, after 36 years as North Carolina's coach, Dean Smith announced his retirement. Smith had coached over 1,133 basketball games at Carolina. On the radio Durham was with the legendary coach for all but 274 of his games.

Bill Guthridge, Smith's assistant of 30 years, took over the helm of the Tar Heel basketball program.

JIMMY V.

The relationships the broadcasters have with the coaches are not limited to the ones they work with on a daily basis; there is also an opportunity to get to know some of the opposing coaches. It's generally not a close, personal relationship, but rather one in which both the sportscaster and coach feel comfortable.

There was one ACC coach, however, that Durham did have a close relationship with. He lived in Cary, North Carolina when Jim Valvano became the head basketball coach at North Carolina State. Since two of the Durham's best friends lived on either side of the Valvanos, Durham got to know Jim and his wife, Pam, in a lot of social settings before the N.C. State coach won the national championship in 1983; and, therefore, before he was diagnosed with cancer. The Durhams were very close to the Valvanos.

"Jim can say that he didn't change and that he was the same guy with the cancer as before, but he did change," Durham sadly admits. "It wasn't a change for the better. He was still funny to the public, but a lot of the things Jim had time for ... he lost that time.

"It was tough watching him go to cancer because he was so full of life. To just watch all of that leave him was tough."

One of the friends the Durhams that had lived next door to the Valvanos died of brain cancer. She died before Jim was ever diagnosed with cancer.

"It was very difficult for Jim to go see Liz when she was sick because he didn't like that side of it," said Durham. "Then for him to have to go through what he did made it more difficult."

Valvano had an uncanny way of getting everybody to like him. He and Dean Smith liked each other a lot, which was a contrast to Valvano's predecessor, Norman Sloan. Sloan and Smith had never hit it off. The State fans and the Carolina fans saw that as a little extra to add to the rivalry.

"It's interesting that Valvano and Mike Krzyzewski of Duke came in to the league at the same time, because Mike came in as a disciple of Bob Knight at Indiana, who is a very good friend of Dean's," Durham pointed out. "You would have thought coming in that Krzyzewski would have been the one voicing the respect for Coach Smith, while Valvano would come in and keep up the N.C. State thing that Sloan had. It was just the opposite; Jim came in as the one voicing the respect for Dean and Carolina basketball, while Mike came in with a chip on his shoulder."

The last time Durham saw Valvano alive was when the former coach was at UNC broadcasting a game for ESPN. Valvano was already very sick and was only exerting enough energy to do what he had to do. He was sitting behind the table when Durham went down to talk to him. They didn't have a chance to talk very much, it was basically a handshake and chance for Durham to tell Valvano he had been thinking about him.

Phil Ford

Former Tar Heel player and current assistant coach Phil Ford is amazing in the fact that he still has an incredible impact on the people around him. Durham has had an opportunity to see Ford not only on the court or with players but at various speaking engagements. At Educational Foundation meetings at the university, Mack Brown or Dean Smith were usually asked to speak. If they couldn't make it, they usually sent one of their assistant coaches. A lot of times Smith would send Phil Ford. Durham said there has never been a time when he has introduced Ford, that the former guard hasn't gotten a standing ovation.

Phil Ford (who played at UNC from 1974-1978) is still the university's leading scorer with 2,290 points. He's second in assists with 753. He wasn't a great shooter, but there seemed to be stretches where he was almost willing the ball to go in the basket. If Carolina needed a basket, he got it. That ability helped earn Ford three first-team All-America selections in 1976, 1977, and 1978.

> *Woody is a great announcer. He could probably could go to the pro sports if he wanted to, but he has found a niche at North Carolina.*
>
> ~ *Al Ciraldo, Georgia Tech*

"The team was practicing a couple years ago during exam period, and they didn't have the full team. That day when the blue team— which is the team that the starting offense works against—was out there, Coach Ford got on the floor in his coaching pants and shirt as one of the guards," tells Durham. "He deflected a pass, knocked the ball toward the scorer's table, and went diving into the table to save the ball. When he fell into the scorer's table, he split his pants.

"That day they were taping practice. After that play, Coach Smith blew the whistle and said, 'I'm going to show that to all of our prospects so they will know how Carolina basketball is supposed to be played.'

"Coach Smith told me about it later and said, 'Isn't that amazing? Even this many years after the fact, a loose ball and he'd go after it like that.'"

The general consensus is that Phil Ford is going to be an outstanding head coach. Who knows ... maybe someday he'll be the head coach at Carolina ... someday.

Perkins and Worthy

It seems natural to mention Sam Perkins and James Worthy in the same breath. In fact for Carolina faithful, it doesn't seem right to talk about one and not the other.

Perkins played for the Tar Heels from 1980-1981 and finished his collegiate career with 2,145 points, 1,167 rebounds, and 245 blocked shots. Like Phil Ford, Perkins was selected three times to the first-team All-America team.

Because of his 44-inch sleeves, Perkins did things so effortlessly that people a lot of times were under the impression that he didn't try hard. A ball would be coming off the rim or backboard after a missed shot, and Perkins would just reach out and grab it without appearing to need to fight for it. He took big shots.

"If you open up the Carolina media guide today, there is one player who is in the top five career scoring and top five career rebounding at Carolina ... he's the guy," Durham said. "He outdid Ralph Sampson about every time they played against each other.

"Sam was one of those guys that had a terrific smile and very enjoyable to be around. I think people now realize he was a much better at Carolina than he got credit for being when he was here."

Worthy is another tremendous competitor. He would do whatever had to be done in order to win.

In the 1982 national championship game against Georgetown, Dean Smith advised Worthy early in the game that Patrick Ewing was going to block some shots and goaltend some shots, but to keep taking the ball to the hole. The first 10 points in the game for the Tar Heels were off of Ewing goaltends. Worthy was doing what it took to win.

"In my office I have the scoring charts that I used from the 1982 and the 1993 national championship games. My wife had them framed with some of the credentials," Durham says. "I often notice on those scoring charts that Worthy scored 28 points against Georgetown, but he scored his last point with 12:30 left in the game. He had two free throws late in the game, both of which he missed.

"Sleepy Floyd, who grew up in the same town as James Worthy, was playing in that game for Georgetown. There was an out-of-bounds play near the Georgetown bench when Sleepy pushed Jimmy Black. Within the next 30 seconds there was a loose ball James scooped it up, was headed for the basket with Sleepy as the only Hoya back to defend it, and James dunked the ball so hard that it came out of the net and hit Floyd on the head. James never said a word or taunted Sleepy in any way immediately after the play, but you could almost sense that Worthy was sending a message to Floyd not to mess with Jimmy Black."

After a super junior season, Worthy decided to enter the NBA draft where he was the first player chosen, picked by the Los Angeles Lakers. In his three seasons as a Tar Heel, 1979-1982, Worthy finished with 1,219 points.

Sam Perkins and James Worthy will always be remembered as two of the best North Carolina Tar Heels of all-time.

"BE LIKE MIKE"

Another player who will be considered one of the best ever to wear Carolina blue, and one that Durham is proud to have followed and gotten to know, is Michael Jordan, who played from 1981-1984. Even though today Jordan is one of the most recognizable celebrities in the world, he remains one of the most humble; a trait he was reminded of as a freshman in college by his head coach.

"When Michael Jordan first came to Carolina he had this jacket from his high school days that had the name 'Magic' on the back of it," tells Durham. "He was in the basketball office one day with that jacket on. Coach Smith came out of his office, walked by Jordan, gave something to the secretary, spoke to Michael a minute, then walked back toward his office. Coach has got a way of just driving the nail right in a person.

"He turned to Michael and said, 'You know, if I were you, I think I'd get my own nickname.' Then he walked into his office. I don't believe Michael wore that jacket again."

The cover of the preseason basketball issue of *Sports Illustrated* on November 30, 1981, had Smith diagraming a play with Matt Doherty, Jimmy Black, James Worthy and Sam Perkins standing behind him. Freshmen can't be interviewed until they've played their first game, and therefore freshmen can't have their picture made for *Sports Illustrated* until they've played their first game. So Jordan wasn't on that cover. (The preview issue two seasons later had Jordan and Perkins on it.) Little did people know that at the end of that season, Jordan would make the shot to help the Tar Heels win the national title.

"Michael told me one time that he thought the best game he ever played at North Carolina was the night they played Virginia in

Durham posing for his Albemarle High School football picture in 1958.

February of 1983," Durham said. "I asked him why he thought that was the best game he ever played. He replied, 'Because I think I did everything that night.'"

He did do everything that night; he rebounded, he scored, he played defense. The Tar Heels trailed by 10 points with 4:15 to play. Late in the game Jordan stole the ball in the backcourt from Rick Carlisle of Virginia and dunked it for the go-ahead basket, 64-63. With seconds remaining Carlisle missed the possible game-winning shot. But as Ralph Sampson was going up for the rebound, two hands came up behind him and snatched the ball out of the air ... it's Michael.

In covering Jordan's collegiate career, Durham had an opportunity to see some spectacular games and even more remarkable plays from the future hall of famer. One play in particular that sticks out for the broadcaster is from an ACC game on the road against Maryland. The Tar Heels were leading late in the game when Jordan had an open court after getting the ball off a steal.

"Michael ran down the sideline, veered toward the basket at the last minute (the whole Carolina bench stands up), and did his first collegiate windmill dunk in a game," Durham explained. "I later found out that Matt Doherty, who was on the bench at the time, turned to the guy next to him and said, 'Watch this.' Michael had done this dunk before in practice but not in a game. The place went absolutely crazy!

"I got a call from the basketball office the next day before we did Coach Smith's television show and Coach said, 'Woody, have you edited the highlights for the show yet?'

"'No, Coach, we're just getting ready to do it,' I replied.

'Don't put Michael's dunk on there.'

"I asked, 'Coach, it's been on all the highlight shows, why don't you want it on here?'

"He said, 'I don't want people to see my show and get the impression that we're rubbing it in.'

"So we did Coach Smith's show on Sunday, and the dunk never appeared."

As a Tar Heel, Jordan did some things that led people to believe he was going to be pretty good and might make a decent professional player, but nobody dreamed his career would turn out as it has.

"He still does things that amaze me," Durham reveals. "It's just amazing that when games are on the line, through the years we've

The Sportscaster's Dozen

seen guys who just run because they don't want the ball Michael always wants it. The thing about it was the consistency with which he delivered. A lot of guys try to make plays but don't always make them; I'm sure Michael doesn't always make them, but his success percentage is pretty darn high."

Jordan's spectacular ability and personality have earned him (or convicted him with) worldwide popularity and fame. As the commercial slogan says, "Be like Mike." Jordan has said on numerous occasions how difficult it is for him to do the smallest things in public, including taking his children to the mall. He even has a to have a private dining room in his own restaurant in Chicago.

"I don't believe I've ever seen anybody have the kind of adulation that Michael's had, and handle it any better than he does," Durham said. "A couple of us were having dinner with Coach Smith one night in Columbus, Ohio, prior to the Carolina-Ohio State game. There were about seven times our dinner was interrupted by people wanting Coach's autograph. One of the guys asked if he minded being interrupted like that. Coach said, 'This is nothing if you've ever been out with Michael.'"

Ultimately, Michael Jordan will go down as not only one of the best ever to wear Carolina blue, but the best ever to play the game.

The 1982 Title: Michael's First Big Shot

Although Jordan may best be known by basketball fans around the world as "Air Jordan" who helped the Chicago Bulls dominate the NBA in the 1990s, No. 23 put his stamp on Carolina and college basketball with his shot with 17 seconds left in the 1982 title game against Georgetown. He would admit today that that shot at the end of his freshman season in New Orleans was the start of it all for him. That was the first title for Dean Smith as the Heels beat the Hoyas 63-62. Jordan says that shot got him some attention. Durham can still remember it like it happened last season.

> *I have enjoyed listening to and hearing him do North Carolina broadcasts. Woody's one of the extremely sincere professionals in this business. I've gotten to know Woody over the years and think he's a tremendous gentleman.*
>
> * Paul Eells,
> University of Arkansas

As Durham tells, "I was with Michael one night and he started to laugh and said, 'This all might not have happened if I didn't hit that jumpshot.' The thing about that shot was that Coach Smith knew Michael was going to take it. Some of the guys from that team have told me over the years that during the huddle, Dean said he knew that even though he wanted the ball inside, Georgetown coach John Thompson wasn't going to let James Worthy and Sam Perkins open for a shot down inside.

"In fact when Michael left the huddle, Dean slapped him on the rump and told him to make it, because he knew Jordan would have to take it."

As the play took shape, Smith knew when the ball rotated a second time toward the wing in front of the Carolina bench, that Jordan was going have to take the shot.

"We had been to Final Fours before and so many people had said how Coach Smith couldn't win the big one," Durham remembers. "The team that year had taken that theme of Dean not being able to win and talked openly about it, particularly Jimmy Black. During the midweek press conference before the Final Four, Jimmy said, 'Sure, we want to win it. We want to win it for Coach Smith so it'll get the monkey off his back.'"

Carolina started off the game very aggressively, but it was obvious Georgetown was going to come back. Ewing was terrific as well as several other players for the Hoyas. When it got down into the late stages, there was such tension. Durham has said it was even difficult for him to relax.

(Late in the game, Jordan hit an incredible shot that has been overshadowed by his game-winning basket. He went into the middle of the lane, and, as Patrick Ewing put his arms up to block it, Jordan released the ball up over the top of Ewing's hand and banked it off the top of the square. When Jordan hit that shot, Smith grabbed then-assistant coach Bill Guthridge's arm and said, "Did you see that shot?!")

When Jordan hit "the shot," some, including Durham, were surprised at the time because the Hoyas had a timeout but didn't use it. Coach Smith would do the same thing. He says you should teach the team what to do in late stages so you don't have to always worry about taking a timeout then, because your defense will react after a timeout.

"As Jordan hit the shot with 17 seconds left, the only thought in my mind is 'What am I going to say if Carolina loses?' As I'm getting all of this worked out in my mind, less than 10 feet away, Fred Brown of Georgetown threw a bad pass right to James Worthy, who was fouled with :05 remaining," said Durham. "The Tar Heels start celebrating. All of a sudden I see Coach Smith on the sidelines trying to settle the team down to make them aware that the game is not over. When I saw him, I sort of settled myself down."

Worthy missed both free throws. A Georgetown player got the rebound, and with a couple seconds left, flung the ball toward the basket.

Durham remembers, "Even at that point I'm still wondering, 'What if the darn thing goes in?' You see heroic shots like that go in sometimes. Luckily he missed it and the Tar Heels had indeed won the national championship."

That championship was more of relief for people close to the program because of all the talk around it about how Smith couldn't win the big one. Those thoughts and relief helped make the 1993 Tar Heel title one of celebration.

"I think I had thoughts in 1982 that it could be a special season," said Durham.

One of the losses that season was in Chapel Hill to Wake Forest, a game in which Sam Perkins did not play because he had a bad virus. As the season kept going, the Tar Heels lost to Virginia in Charlottesville. But there was still a thought that something a little special was happening.

The ACC tournament championship game that year was really something to see. It was a game that helped bring about the shot clock. Smith was criticized that game for holding the ball so long, but he held it because he wanted Virginia's star center Ralph Sampson to come out from under the basket and play defense on someone. One thing that gets overlooked from that game is that with 3:00 left, Virginia had to foul Carolina three times to put the Heels in the bonus. Those three fouls needed took about 1:30 to commit. As Durham points out about that ACC title game, "Dean just outcoached Terry Holland that day."

The College Rivalry: Carolina-Duke

There have been some fascinating rivalries in college athletics over the years, whether it has been Kansas-Missouri, Alabama-Auburn, or UCLA-USC. But possibly none of those compare to the rivalry between North Carolina and Duke.

The Tar Heels have had some good ACC rivals such as North Carolina State when David Thompson was there in the 1970s, Virginia with Ralph Sampson in the 1980s, or Wake Forest with Tim Duncan in the 1990s. None of those compare with the marquee match-ups between North Carolina and Duke.

Why this has been such a big rivalry through the years can be debated. It could be due to the fact that the schools are located less than 10 miles apart, or to the fact that both basketball teams have been at the top of their game for so long. Regardless of why it's such a rivalry, Durham has been through it all.

"It's been amazing the rivalries through the years that Coach Smith's teams have withstood," Durham said. "The Duke rivalry is unique because it is probably the most extended run against Carolina, with Carolina, that any team in the league has done.

"I know a lot of people around the country have difficulty appreciating it because of the locale; I'm sure a lot of people find it hard to believe that these schools are eight miles apart."

With the two schools being so geographically close, it is possible to walk down Franklin Street in Chapel Hill and see Duke basketball players or go to Duke's Cameron Indoor Stadium during the summer and see some Carolina players playing with some of the Blue Devils. Maybe a lot of that is why it is so hard to believe the intensity of the rivalry during the season, a rivalry that has produced some unforgettable games.

"It's hard to describe this basketball series because about the time you're ready to say that last game was the best in the series, the next one might top it," Durham points out. "A few of the games over the years do stand out, though."

Durham recalls the 1974 game during his third season with the Tar Heels, in Carmichael Auditorium in Chapel Hill where Duke was up by 8 points with 17 seconds left to play. Carolina managed to tie the game and send it into overtime on a dramatic 35-foot bank shot by Walter Davis. The Heels overcame a 3-point deficit in the overtime to win the game 96-92.

The game in 1979 at Cameron Indoor Stadium is one that sticks out with a lot of Carolina and Duke fans. Coach Smith decided the Tar Heels would hold the ball on offense in attempt to bring the Blue Devils out of their zone. That night, Duke chose not to come out, so it turned into a game of just holding the ball. The two teams were able to play a little in the second half, each scoring 40 points. Duke won the game, 47-40.

One week later the two teams played for the ACC Championship in Greensboro, which Carolina won 71-63.

"Coach Smith has never admitted to this being the case, but to this day I still believe that he played that game in Durham knowing that those two teams might meet again a week later, and he knew it would be difficult to beat Duke at home with a certain strategy," Durham said. "He didn't win with that strategy, so he changed it a week later and won the ACC tournament."

The 1989 ACC tournament championship game at the Omni in Atlanta sticks out for the Carolina broadcaster because it was a war. It was the J. R. Reid and Jeff Lebo team from Carolina against the Danny Ferry and Johnny Dawkins team from Duke. Those teams disliked each other about as much as two college basketball teams could dislike each other. Carolina won the game, 77-74, as Ferry missed a shot from the backcourt at the buzzer that would have tied it.

"Our broadcast position that year for the tournament put us almost in the Carolina huddle," Durham remembers. "Listening to the players during a timeout was like being in war room."

The Carolina-Duke rivalry hasn't been limited to the players and fans, however. There have been times that coaches Dean Smith and Mike Krzyzewski have gotten in a few shots at each other. Durham remembers one of the first times the coaches got involved.

"Very early on after Coach K took over at Duke, maybe his second year over there, Mike comes into the media room and says there's a definite double-standard in the ACC. 'They (the officials) call them one way for the rest of us and call them another way for Carolina,' he said. Things went downhill from there.

"Now that Mike has been successful over at Duke, I think there is that mutual respect. It's mellowed a little bit, but there are still those jabs every now and then."

And the rivalry continues.

Consorting with the Rival

Sportscasters generally get to know each other after being in the business and at the same schools for an extended period of time. They don't always get to hear each other broadcast games, but they have been known to socialize on occasions.

The relationship between Duke broadcaster Bob Harris and Woody Durham, has been a unique one. The two have been friends since childhood. Although Durham was a year ahead of Harris in school, the two grew up in Albemarle where their dads worked together in the textile mill. Both boys were involved in sports together from little league up through high school. In high school Harris was the team manager on the Albemarle High School football team when Durham was playing.

"I'm surprised that more people haven't picked up on that story through the years because it is unusual," said Durham. "It's been interesting that only a few of the media people in the Chapel Hill-Durham area have known about us, and there have only been a couple feature stories done on our relationship."

The two even went so far as to share the same car ... sort of.

"During my junior and senior years of high school I drove around in a gray 1951 Plymouth," Durham says. "When I left to go to school at Carolina, freshmen couldn't have cars, so my father sold the car to Bob's dad for Bob to drive." (Harris contends it was a 1952 Plymouth.)

> *Woody is a professional. He is always prepared. He does his homework, and he knows his subject matter. Woody has been a friend for a long, long time.*
>
> &z Bob Harris, Duke University

Harris started his radio career in 1967 doing high school football games in Albemarle. At that time Durham was working in television in Greensboro.

After Durham had been at Carolina for four years, Harris joined the Duke radio broadcasts. Part of the interest lies in the fact that Durham had known long before landing a job at Carolina that he wanted to get into broadcasting; Harris had worked for Goodyear Tires and an insurance company before getting into radio.

"It's odd that both of us came from the same small town of about 12,000 people and ended up at two of the more successful universities in the country. It's a real compliment to the community where we grew up and the people who helped raise us," Durham points out. "We have our loyalties when we go home; the Carolina people are glad to see me and the Duke people are glad to see Bob."

Fans of both schools, not only in Albemarle, are happy when Durham and Harris hit the airwaves for a broadcast.

TAR HEEL FANS

"The Carolina fans can be different sometimes, but there are times I think it's because Coach Smith has spoiled us a lot! I think that has been a big thing for us to overcome in regards to the enthusiasm of our fans," Durham said. "We sometimes have fans who take for granted that we could be awfully good."

Durham points to two instances which have affected the Carolina fans in the Smith Center.

Florida State joined the ACC and started playing the conference basketball schedule for the 1991-1992 season. On their first trip to the Smith Center, with guard Sam Cassell, the Seminoles beat the Tar Heels 86-74. With that win FSU also won its first conference basketball game. Later, Cassell referred to the Carolina crowd as a "wine and cheese crowd." That sparked the Tar Heels fans.

The other wake-up call that Durham points to came in the 1996-1997 season when the Tar Heels lost a 22-point lead against Maryland and eventually lost the game. There was a forecast that night of an ice storm. A lot of people left the game early. ESPN, who was doing the game nationally, showed people flooding the exits on their way out.

"I criticized the crowd on the air over our network for leaving early," Durham admits. "Evidently Dick Vitale really ripped them on the air about how Dean Smith alone deserved more support than that. From that game on, our crowd in the Smith Center last year was absolutely terrific."

Why are the Carolina fans like that? Are they spoiled?

"I think it all goes back to expectations. We win so often and we have found ways to win in the late stages of games, that our fans expect wins and won't settle for anything else," said Durham. "Other than that I don't know how to explain it, except to say that Carolina fans are extremely loyal."

Advantage from the Catwalk

When the Dean E. Smith Center opened for the Carolina basketball team on January 18, 1986 (fittingly against the Duke Blue Devils), it was one of the top basketball arenas in the country at any level. It still is with state-of-the-art architecture and 21,572 seats.

In each corner of the arena there are video boards which mainly provide stats and replays. There is a communications center, home of various UNC sports radio and TV shows. The radio booths are situated at the back of the first level of seats, almost at midcourt. The spacious booths feature not only a great view, but TV monitors to get a little closer to the action. (Not to mention the arena's breathtaking Carolina blue and white, which is visible right down to the rafters and air vents.)

"We're spoiled now in the Dean Smith Center," Durham admits. "We have a very spacious booth for basketball. (We have an equally spacious booth for football.) We also have a spacious area in both press boxes for some of our sponsors to come see games. Now that we've got professional teams (like Charlotte) that we're competing against for the advertising dollar, special events for the sponsors in top facilities is a little way that college athletics can compete."

Not all of the schools Durham has broadcast games from feature wonderful amenities or even good views, though.

"The broadcasting position at Duke is difficult to get to. The vantage point is good; you're suspended from the rafters on a platform," Durham said. "You have to climb up a ladder to get to it, so you don't easily get out or get to it, but your vantage point as far as the ballgame is concerned, is fine.

"Reynolds Coliseum in Raleigh where North Carolina State plays is especially tough. Again, the vantage point, once you get in position, is fine, but you have to go up to the top of the Coliseum (remember this was built in 1949), climb up a narrow walkway, go through a cubbyhole, then to a suspended platform out over the crowd. There is one bare light bulb above you. The area up there has been partitioned off for the camera crews and things like that, so you may have an area that is just a few feet wide to fit four people from the broadcast crew."

Cole Field House where the Maryland Terrapins play is another old building. There the broadcasters are far away from the floor. It's not a real high building but the seats go back at a low angle and the broadcast position is at the top of that, a long, long way from the playing floor.

Regardless of the difficult places Durham and other sportscasters have endured to broadcast a game, their job is to do just that ... broadcast the game.

"One of the things I've done all through the years is to never make a big deal about where we are working from, because the audience doesn't care. All the audience wants to know is who has the ball and what's the score," Durham points out. "I know the first time I ever went to the old Sugar Bowl (Tulane Stadium in New Orleans), I was so disappointed. Here I had gone to this place that I had heard about for years, that had been the site of these fantastic games, and we get up to the old press box where the steel is rusting.

"My engineer has reminded me that one of my lines that night to the crew before we went on the air was that these weren't the best conditions in the world, but the audience doesn't care if we're sitting on orange crates and doing the game by candlelight. All they want to know is the score and who's got the ball."

"I Left You There for a Little Bit"

A sportscaster in any sport relies on his color commentator to help provide an extra voice between plays in a baseball or football game or to provide quick snip-its during a basketball broadcast.

One year the Tar Heels were playing in the Big Four Tournament in Greensboro, North Carolina, a tournament which featured Carolina, Duke, North Carolina State, and Wake Forest. Durham's basketball color analyst that season was Bob Holliday of Chapel Hill.

Holliday worked for the network's flagship radio station in Chapel Hill, and the parent company had just gotten into the television cable business. Holliday was involved heavily in that, so he was really burning his candle at both ends. He was getting up early in the mornings to do his main job, then he would work the basketball games at night with Durham.

During the Big Four Tournament the two were doing all the games which means they would do four games in two nights.

"This particular year, the second game on Friday night was awful; it was one of those you thought would never end," Durham said. "We were talking like normal during the course of the broadcast. A lot of times I will make a comment without looking at the guy who is working with me or without calling his name, then I just stop and wait for his reply. Something happened in this game that I made a comment on and then stopped ... Bob didn't say anything. I didn't look at him to see why he didn't say anything, I just went along with the broadcast."

They got to another point shortly thereafter and Holliday still hadn't said anything.

"About that time I heard somebody behind me laugh," Durham continued. "I looked to my right, and Bob was sitting straight up in his chair fast asleep."

Holliday had gone sound asleep during the game! Evidently somebody hit him or nudged him to wake him up, because all of a sudden he started right back in like nothing had happened.

"He admitted during the broadcast that he fell asleep by saying, 'I left you there for a little bit.' I guess the people listening at home thought he had just stepped out of the booth for a minute. I have never ever had somebody go sound asleep on me like that during the course of a broadcast, but Bob Holliday did."

The Pride of the Tar Heels

As with a lot of people, what they know about a college or university is through what the athletic teams have done. Generally the only person they know or hear from the school is the radio sportscaster. The same holds true with the Tar Heels and Woody Durham.

"I'm very conscience of the fact that every time we go on the air, one to a lot of people are listening, and I'm the link for a lot of them to the University," Durham says.

Durham knows this idea to be true from his own experiences while he was growing up. He remembers listening with his dad to Carolina broadcasts on cold, wintry nights. Those thoughts often come back to him as he's doing a broadcast.

"I've always said that the ideal sports radio fan is someone driving down the road at night by themselves, because if you can make that one person understand what's going on then everybody else will follow," Durham said.

He remembers how the broadcasts of those competitive teams helped mold his perceptions of the University of North Carolina. Whatever success he enjoys now as a broadcaster, Durham says, can be attributed to the success of the teams he has covered. (Not to mention some of the national analysts who have covered those teams.)

There was an honorary society on campus that Coach Smith spoke to one night. As a surprise to Durham, that night he was inducted as a member of The Order of the Golden Fleece, and there was a dinner later that night.

"After the dinner, everyone was asked to get up and say a little something. I got up and was trying to thank them for this nice honor, and I said, 'I need to thank the coaches for the student-athletes they bring here. I need to thank the student-athletes for being so successful. I would be remiss if I didn't thank Billy Packer and Dick Vitale.' (You could see people turn to me like I was crazy.) Because if it hadn't been for Packer and Vitale, thousands of people wouldn't be turning down the sound on their televisions to listen to us.'"

The crowd loved it; Coach Smith loved it. In fact the coach asked him to tell it again two or three times that spring on the Educational

Foundation circuit. One night when Coach asked Durham to tell the story again, the sportscaster politely declined because it had been told so many times. When Smith spoke that night, he told the story.

Durham is very proud of that because it shows that Coach Smith loved that story. Durham also takes a tremendous sense of pride in being the voice of the Tar Heels.

"I take a great deal of pride as an alumnus, but I also take a great deal of pride in representing the university—a university that has done things the right way both academically and athletically with a very good mix," he explains. "It makes me feel good to be able to represent a school like Carolina, a school that does things the right way. Sometimes I wonder how the guys who work for some of those other schools that have been in trouble with the NCAA or have a reputation for not doing it the right way do those games. I don't know."

The University of North Carolina has developed a reputation for doing things the right way by running a clean program. Durham gives most of that credit to Dean Smith, who showed everyone that you can do it the right way, have a 95-plus percent graduation rate for over 35 years, and still be successful.

Only eight players to play for Coach Smith in 35 years do not have their degree, including players like Jerry Stackhouse and Rasheed Wallace who left school early for the NBA. Due to a clause which Smith helped design for their NBA contracts, which says the player will receive a monetary bonus upon graduation, the eight players could very likely graduate.

"I tell a lot of people who want to get in the broadcasting business that a degree is only important when it comes time to check that box on your job application that says you're a college graduate," Durham said. "I had a real good friend in Greensboro once that was the best newspaper writer I had ever read. He wanted to be a sports editor. He lost out on two jobs because he wasn't a college graduate. It was just one of the requirements.

"He got out of sports writing, went to the city desk area where he was an editor so he could go to school. He got his degree. The next sports editors job that he applied for, he got. Getting that degree didn't make him a better writer, but not having it was denying him something he wanted to do. I tell young people that the door will never be shut on you when you've got a degree; nothing can stop you."

My Two Sons

Durham's advice hasn't had to travel far to fall upon listening ears. Although he never pushed them or encouraged them, his two sons, Wes and Taylor, are both carving out successful sportscasting careers of their own.

His oldest son, Wes, went from Elon College, to Radford College, to Marshall, to Vanderbilt, before ending up at Georgia Tech. His younger son, Taylor, was nearing the end of his first year at Elon College when he told his dad that he'd like to do the same thing. He went to Elon as a business major, wanting to get into the golf business in some way but decided he liked radio a little bit better. He's just in at the ground floor right now, but he has potential to do well.

"It has been very special to me and has made me very proud that Wes is in broadcasting and that Taylor wants to get more involved with it," Durham says like a proud father. "The first time, however, that I worked the same game as one of them was extremely special."

> *The first time we did a game together was the hardest; it was weird, but each game since then has gotten easier. Now each time Carolina and Georgia Tech play, it's special. One of the reasons I took the job at Tech was so I could do some games with my dad.*
>
> ~ Wes Durham, current voice of Georgia Tech

The first time was when Wes and Woody were working the Carolina-Georgia Tech football game in 1995 in Atlanta. The younger Durham quickly got the upper hand in the series as the Yellow Jackets won that football game, 27-25. In fact, the eldest Durham started out 0-3 against his offspring as Tech swept the basketball series that season from the Tar Heels. Regardless, each time the two are in the same stadium or arena doing the same game, it's still unique.

"It was a matter of pride; pride not only in what he was doing, but pride in that I was the guy he came to for advice on how to position himself, and in the way he did things. To know that the way I taught him, based on the way I do it, can be that successful tells me that I'm doing it the right way," Durham says. "Even though I started out 0-3 against Wes, it's still something special to be able to work the same game as him."

Wes's story is fairly different in that he reached the Division-I level and achieved success there while he was in his 20s. By today's standards that doesn't happen very often.

"He is awfully, awfully good because he worked and works hard,"

Durham said of his son. "Just because he achieved success in his 20s, he's not resting on his laurels. You always need to work hard to be as good as you were, and you need to work hard to get better."

Even though it is the dream of most fathers to see their sons take over the family business, Woody and Jean Durham never pushed their sons to enter broadcasting. In fact if they were pushed at all, it was to make their own decisions. That may be part of the reason why Wes' decision before his junior year of high school caught his dad off-guard.

"It really kind of caught me by surprise when he first told me he was interested in broadcasting, because he never really showed that much of an interest, and I had never said anything to him about it," Woody said. "I told him how he had been around broadcasting, but he had never been involved in it. So the first thing we did was get him as much practical experience as we could."

Wes got his practical experience in most facets of radio and television sports broadcasting. It was Woody's way of making sure Wes knew the whole realm of the business and how things are tied together. For instance he worked with the Tar Heel Sports Network for a couple years as a network reporter or production assistant. One summer he worked as a sales intern at Capitol Broadcasting. The next summer he worked in the promotions department at Capitol. He also spent one college summer interning at a Greensboro television station.

The best experience, however, may have been at Elon College where the only outlet for their athletic teams is their FM station. The administration knew he was coming there, so athletics director Dr. Alan White called Wes and talked to him about it. Through working in college, Wes got an unbelievable four years of experience.

Now, Wes has more experience in the sportscasting business than most graduates, so it's time to get the first "real" job, right? Well, yes, but not that easily.

"The worst time I had during this was after he had been out of college for about three weeks, and there was an opening at Radford College in Virginia," Woody explains. "He sent a tape up there, but about a week later he got a very nice form letter back informing him that they picked three people for interviews and he was not one of them."

In the meantime, Woody had suggested that Wes send a tape to the Radford basketball coach, Oliver Purnell.

"When that rejection letter came, you couldn't have gotten Wes

Woody Durham and his son, Wes, who is the play-by-play announcer for the Georgia Tech Yellow Jackets.

off the floor with a spatula; he was really down in the dumps," Woody continues. "After it came I told my wife Jean how nervous I was about the whole situation. I thought what if Wes came in to me and said, 'OK, Dad, I've done everything you've told me to do. I did it exactly the way you told me to do it. Where are the job offers?' I didn't know what I would say. Luckily I didn't need to know."

The very next day, the telephone rang while Wes happened to be at home; it was Oliver Purnell. The basketball coach told Wes he was about to go in a meeting, and he was going to recommend Wes for the play-by-play job. Wes was assured that even though he got the form letter from the personnel office, Purnell and his staff were making the decision. As it turned out, Radford officials brought in Wes and a guy from Baltimore for an interview. Wes got the job.

After spending some time at Radford, Wes accepted a job at

Marshall, where he worked for one season. He had planned on spending three to five years at Marshall, but a different opportunity came knocking loudly.

While watching North Carolina play Ohio State in the NCAA Regionals in Lexington, Kentucky, Wes started talking to a family friend, Eddie Fogler, who had just taken the head basketball coaching position at Vanderbilt. The school's announcer, Charlie McAlexander, had just left to go to Kentucky. (Cawood Ledford had just retired from radio at Kentucky.) Fogler asked Wes if he'd be interested in Vanderbilt's radio job. One week later the ball started rolling for Wes to go to Vanderbilt.

"He felt so bad for leaving Marshall after only one year because he was afraid it would give people the impression that he didn't stay in one place very long," the elder Durham explained. "I told him not to worry about that because of where he had been and the natural progression he took to get to this level from Radford to Marshall to Vanderbilt."

Deep down Wes had wanted to get into the ACC, so when the Georgia Tech job opened, it worked out great for him. Yellow Jacket fans are happy things worked out for Wes to get to the ACC.

"I Didn't Like Him, but He Sure Did a Good Job"

All three Durhams have done whatever it takes to improve their broadcasts. Perhaps that work ethic goes back to Woody's father, who worked hard in the textile mill. Perhaps Wes and Taylor have seen their father work hard and excel at what he does. After all, it's not uncommon to see Woody on the day of a game with his "game face" on.

"Broadcasting a game is as close as people who have never played the game will come to playing it," Durham explains. "I was not very good, although I was good enough to be a part of great football program in high school, which made such an impression on me that a lot of times now when I'm getting ready to do big games, my body reacts as though I'm getting ready to play. It even includes a rush of adrenaline."

As with any player, when the game broadcast is over, Durham knows whether or not he did a good job. He doesn't need to be told if it was a good broadcast or not, or if he told the true story of the game or not.

Part of doing a good job, in Durham's eyes, includes not sounding like he only sees Carolina blue and white.

As Durham says it, "I'm never a 'we' guy. Somebody asked me one time why I'm not a 'homer.' I told him that it's against my principles. Everybody listening knows who I want to win. When we come on the air we say it's the Tar Heel Sports Network. It's the Carolina version of the game and with that we see things with a Carolina perspective. You only have to listen for a little bit to know who we want to win.

"The best way to describe what we do is with the term partial-objectivity. We're partial, you're darn right we are, but I think we're also objective about what we're doing because if the team is not playing good or is playing good, then it's our job to say so."

Through his 30-plus years of broadcasting experience, Durham has found the way to paint a picture, even if it isn't always a pretty picture, in a way that has made the game as exciting for the listener as for the fans in the stands. If all goes well, he'll continue doing it for another 10 years.

"If my health stays good, and it has been good, I could maybe see myself doing play-by-play until I'm 65 years old. That would be the cutoff point for me. You don't want to keep doing the games and have the audience tell you when it's time to quit," Durham said. "I've been fortunate that the football and basketball teams that I've broadcast for over the last 27-plus years have combined to win about 80 percent of their games. That's helped me sound awfully good."

Since he hasn't had to think about it too much, Durham doesn't know how difficult it will be when he turns off the microphone that final time, but in the meantime he says he has no regrets at all about getting into broadcasting. He feels fortunate to have made some great friends through the University and has been able to see some exciting games over the years.

When it's all said and done, though, he'll be happy if he's remembered as a good guy that did a good job. He'd like to know that people liked him as a person (keeping in mind that if a person is not a Carolina fan then they may not have liked him, but hopefully they had respect for him and the job he tried to do for UNC).

Durham adds, "I guess the nicest thing someone could say about me was that they didn't like me because I was the voice of Carolina, but add, 'Boy, he sure did a good job.' That would be the ultimate compliment."

Paul Eells
Vanderbilt University
University of Arkansas

I was at the University of Iowa on a baseball scholarship in the fall of 1954. My aspirations like all guys who loved baseball, was to be the next catcher for the Yankees and follow Yogi Berra and Elston Howard. When I first got to Iowa, freshman could not play in games, but they could practice. You had to be at least a sophomore to play on the squad, so I did that for two years. In the fall we played in the Iowa Fieldhouse because it was too cold in the fall to play many games outside.

> Who you become depends on what you do for others along the way.
> ~ Unknown

While I was at Iowa, I forgot that you had to actually be eligible to play baseball. During my junior year, I took a course called Spanish, and the second semester I failed it. I was just devastated when I found out I was going to be ineligible to play. I lost my scholarship, which was room and tuition. I went down to the local University-owned radio station to visit a friend of mine, Doug Brown, from high school days. I went in and told him I was going to have to go home because I didn't know what I was going to do. He offered to take me on a tour of the radio station with the idea that I might be interested in working there.

While we were on the tour, he introduced me to the program director. As fate would have it, the full-time play-by-play announcer, Bob Zenner, got a job as the voice of the Nebraska Cornhuskers and was leaving. Bob was a wonderful announcer. A month after he left he was diagnosed with leukemia, but he called the games for the Cornhuskers for three or four years before he died. He never complained or let anybody know about how ill he was, but he was a terrific announcer.

When Doug Brown introduced me to the program director he commented on me being a baseball player and asked if I knew anything about basketball and football. I told him that I did and thought they were terrific games. "Great, you're our new sports guy if you want to come to work at the radio station." Up to that point, I wanted to be a professional baseball player or a coach; my brother was a coach. I thought being a high school coach was good enough for me if it was good enough for him. So for the rest of my junior and senior years in college, I did all of the Iowa football and basketball play-by-play on radio for the university-owned station.

When I finally graduated, a guy in Keokuk, Iowa, said that if I couldn't get a job when I got out of the service, that I could come work for him in his radio station. When I got out of the Army, I called him and the rest is history. I've had three jobs—outside of that little radio job. I worked for a station in Cedar Rapids, Nashville, and now Little Rock.

Almost

Before I talk too much about the early part of my broadcasting career, I do want to tell you about the time I almost got into a Big 10 game. This is the most bizarre thing that's happened to me that I want to share. I was in the bullpen, as always (I was never behind the plate in a real game), and we were playing in Columbus, Ohio.

Ohio State had Frank Howard and Howard "Hop-along" Cassidy, playing on their baseball team. Howard, who was about 6 foot 7, came to the plate with Cassidy on third base, and for some reason Ohio State decided they wanted to try a suicide squeeze. Our regular catcher, Don Bock, was 5 feet 8 inches tall and weighed about 215 pounds, but he was a terrific catcher. The pitcher winds up, and Bock sees it coming as Cassidy breaks to the plate. For some reason Bock just jumps up and shoves Frank Howard out of the batter's box, catches the ball, makes the tag, and of course it's interference. Bock turns around to argue with the umpire, and Frank Howard just hits him on the top of the head. And he's laying there, the tools of ignorance, knocked out, and I'm thinking I'm going to get in the game.

Otto Vogel, an old coach at Iowa for years and years, relayed to bring in Eells. My problem was that when I threw, I had gotten in to one of those things as a catcher where I would guide the ball back to the pitcher. So Vogel didn't trust me. I could throw to the bases, but I would've been better off letting the umpire throw back to the pitcher, and Vogel knew this.

The bullpen got word that I was to come in, and here's Bock laying in the dirt. I get to the edge of the dugout, and Vogel looked at me and said, "No, go back to the bullpen." And he took the third baseman and made him catch the rest of the game.

Years later after I got out of school, I talked to Otto before he passed on and he said, "Paul, I know how bad you wanted to play, but I just couldn't do it. The reason I carried you on this ballclub is because you're just a nice guy." Then I became ineligible because of the Spanish deal. So that's the closest I got to catching in a Big 10 game.

Tricky Beginnings

The most difficult thing for me early in broadcasting was trying to fool people into thinking that I knew something about football. At my high school, we didn't have football so the only football I remembered at that particular time was watching my brother, who was five years older, play in a town where we had moved from. So I knew very little about the game of football.

I didn't have a color man when I worked for the university station, so during the broadcasts I was pretty much on my own. I had an engineer but not a color man. We would read our own public service announcements during time-outs since it was a noncommercial station.

Forest Evashevski was the Iowa head coach. I went over to introduce myself to him and he took me in his office and said, "I'm going to give you some advice. When you come over here for the pregame show, I want you to be prepared because if you ask me any stupid questions, the interview is over."

I said, "Coach, let me just ask you a question right now, and if it's stupid, I'll know I'm not meant to come over here. But I really need some help." I told him what the situation was and how I was just starting out, and he told me he would help me out a little bit and that he thought we'd get along just fine.

The first game they still say I had a guy running from the 45 to the 50, to the 55. Difficulties like that and trying to learn that you had to know the other team a little bit took awhile for me. Some of those broadcasts, though, were just awful. I mean they were really bad.

Growing Up an Iowa Hawkeye

I grew up in a little town called Mechanicsville, Iowa, a town of 600 located in the eastern part of the state near Iowa City and Cedar

Rapids. Growing up I really loved the Iowa Hawkeyes. I don't think I ever got to see a basketball or football game in person at Iowa, but I would listen to them on the radio. Also, dad would take me over to Iowa City and show me around the town.

I listened to whatever Iowa ballgames I could on the radio. Tait Cumins was the first announcer, and then there was Jim Zobel, who recently celebrated his 50th year of doing Iowa games. I never gave much thought to the people I was listening to because I never really did picture myself as being an announcer. But I loved Iowa so much that those were the two people I listened to call the games.

I just thought I wanted to be a coach of any kind. My brother, Norman, was a terrific athlete—probably a better basketball player—but I just played basketball and baseball. Norman went to school at Upper Iowa University in Fayetteville, Iowa. He was a defensive back on the football team. Not a real aggressive head hunter-type, but still a good enough athlete to play for them. He was also a terrific guard on the basketball team.

Personally, I figured on the high school level I didn't want anything to do with coaching football. I grew up five years younger than my brother, and we were living in West Branch which had football, but when we moved to Mechanicsville, they didn't. I thought since I hadn't played football, I certainly couldn't coach it, so I would stick around some town like Mechanicsville and coach high school baseball and basketball and maybe one day be a college coach. For some reason, there must have been a plan or fate that didn't make me very serious about coaching because once I got a taste of the radio thing, I knew this was it.

On the national scene, I remember listening to Herb Carneel and Halsy Hall doing some of the Minnesota Twins games. I also remember Dizzy Dean and Buddy Blattner who were doing the national telecast of the week on whatever network had it at the time. I really liked Buddy Blattner.

Looking back, when I finally got into radio as a student, I talked to Zobel an awful lot about what I should do. He told me to just be myself.

Another guy who later turned out to be a good friend in Cedar Rapids was Bob Brooks. He and Milo Hamilton went to school at Iowa together and Bob kind of took me under his wing. At the time any station in Iowa that wanted to carry the games could. So when we would travel on the road, we'd go into Ohio State or Michigan, and Iowa would have about seven or eight different stations with seven or eight different announcers. The university station sent me on the road also. So I got to know all of these guys pretty well over that two-year period. They took care of me because they looked at me as a young kid, certainly not threatening their positions at all.

Holy Smokes

I went to Nashville in 1967 as the sports director of WSM-TV and radio, as well as basketball and football voice of the Vanderbilt Commodores. I was there from 1967-1978. We didn't do TV simulcasting at all; it was strictly radio. In fact, I don't think we ever did a TV game of any sort with Vanderbilt. I remember a suggestion I made when I first came to Nashville that didn't go over very well. My first year at Vanderbilt was also football coach Bill Pace's first year. We were meeting with several other people to talk about his show, and they told us that on Saturday nights Vanderbilt's games would be on the FM station because of the Grand Ole Opry on the AM. I suggested that they delay the Opry and run it after the football game. That didn't go over too well in Music City. So before I got started I was almost gone. I found out quickly that the Opry was sacred and Vanderbilt football was not.

I think for the first five years I was at Vanderbilt, I was close to losing my job because I was always compared to [Larry] Munson, and I was no great shakes as a TV guy. Then WSM-TV hired Dan Miller and Carol Marin as the anchors, so we had really great people who interacted very well. Those people were really good, and all of a sudden the ratings went up.

We had a lot of fun in Nashville. Bob Jordan, who is now at WGN-TV in Chicago, worked at WSM-TV (now WSMV-TV) at the time and offered to do the weekend sports because our other guy had left. So Bob went back one day and just grabbed the stuff off the wire not realizing it was scores from the previous day's baseball games. He read the scores and mispronounced some of the names. And then a guy named Irving Waugh, who was a pretty good sports fan, knew the scores were from the day before, and I think he said something about it. But Bob ended up reading the same stuff for both Saturday and Sunday. Shortly after that Rudy Kalis was hired; he's still there as the sports director.

WSM had a basketball team back then called the Holy Smokers, a tag stemming from my "holy smokes" expression when calling games. I'm not sure why I started using "holy smokes;" it just appeared during the early years of doing Vandy games. I didn't do it at Iowa. I finally became aware of it because people started to say something about it during my second year of doing games there.

To define a great run or a good basket, I would say, "Holy smokes, what a play!" That became my tag.

I left Vanderbilt and Nashville in August of 1978, after accepting the job at Arkansas. I never realized the impact I had on people until I went back to Nashville. The people there were great to me and still remember me.

From Commodore to Razorback

The Arkansas job was a unique one because at that time the university hired the announcer that they wanted, and whomever the Razorbacks chose became the sports director at KATV in Little Rock. While both parties had to pretty much agree, I think at that time it was up to Frank Broyles to name who was going to do the job. So when I came down to visit, I not only talked to the station people and visited with them, but they also flew me then to Fayetteville where I talked to Broyles, then-football coach Lou Holtz, and the basketball coach at the time, Eddie Sutton. I don't know whether it was just to get their blessing. I had sent them a couple Vanderbilt basketball and football tapes already so they knew how I sounded.

I later found out that Dave Cawood, who is now with the NCAA, had recommended me for the job. I had never met Dave, but he had been a former Arkansas sports information director and had listened many nights to Vanderbilt basketball when we were on the AM.

I didn't know what I was getting into when I moved on to Arkansas, but I decided the opportunity was really good, and I was going to take it. When I went, there was a little bio in the *Arkansas Gazette* that I was coming to town along with some information. Whoever wrote that thing said, "I hope he doesn't bring that 'holy smokes' with him." It was like all of a sudden it became such an old habit, that I was intimidated a little bit. It didn't help matters that the article also talked about how I was the third guy to follow a legend in Arkansas.

What sold me on making the move, though, was that WSM had talked about the possibility of dropping the Vanderbilt play-by-play, and we were getting cut down time-wise in sports. When I went down to talk to them in Arkansas, they told me I would have five to eight minutes for sports. I would also do the basketball games which were being simulcast on TV and radio, plus the football games and coaches shows. I just thought the enormity of all of this was just wonderful. What a way to satisfy your appetite for sports!

It didn't take long for me to be accepted at Arkansas. I had always thought that whomever was the voice of the Razorbacks was accepted because the state is crazy about Arkansas football and basketball. While there are other smaller schools there like Arkansas State, it's the influence of the Hogs. And if you're the spokesperson, you're the guy that's OK because you're the intermediary between the players and the coaches. The fans just treat you great. Vandy has a close-knit following, but at Arkansas it's statewide.

> *I love Paul dearly. I first ran into him while he was at Vandy. He has always had a lot of class about him, is an intelligent guy, and I like the way he does his ballgames. Paul probably does a better job in television than radio because he looks good. He makes a really good appearance on television and obviously knows what he's doing.*
> — *Jack Cristil, Mississippi State University*

I was going into Arkansas on the heels of a basketball team that had gone to the final four and a football team that had upset Oklahoma, 30-6, in the Orange Bowl. When I got there they still had winning football, so you went into the games knowing that you had an opportunity to win, which I wasn't accustomed to doing, with all due respect to Vandy. Of course, the first game I did at Arkansas was against Vanderbilt, which is still the wildest deal because I knew more about them than I did Arkansas.

Vanderbilt: The Sportscaster's Springboard?

I always looked at Nashville as a great city and a great place to work; in fact I wanted to stay there forever when I left Iowa. In my case, I think it was the lack of emphasis put on our daily sportscasts at WSMV-TV and the lack of commitment to Vanderbilt that scared me a little bit. All of a sudden I had a chance to go to a smaller market (Little Rock is the 54th market in the country—Nashville at the time was 29th) with the opportunity to do more on the air, have a bigger sports commitment by the station, and follow a very successful Arkansas football and basketball program. I never saw Nashville as a "springboard" to bigger things.

For awhile, while I was in Iowa and working as the No. 2 guy there to Tait Cumins, I probably patterned everything after him. Tait was very easygoing; he loved to talk to people. Nothing ever excited him. I was influenced an awful lot by him. He told me one time, "It doesn't make any difference where you go or what you want to do, just remember that it's people that are going to take you there. You treat people the way you want to be treated. And don't do things that the coaches will distrust you for. Stay above board in everything you do, the best you can." I always remembered that. I asked Tait, who was a longtime sports editor with a newspaper in Cedar Rapids, if he ever wanted to be any other place as a writer. He told me that he was home.

Well, there was a time in Iowa when I thought I had to get to the network and broadcast major league baseball. The closest I ever came to that opportunity was while I was at WSM in Nashville, and Ernie Johnson gave me the courtesy of a visit. It may have been shortly after Larry Munson left the Atlanta Braves broadcasts. That would have been ironic to first follow Larry at Vanderbilt, and then follow him in Atlanta. Of course, I didn't get the job, and now I'm kind of glad I didn't because I've always loved the college game.

I've really been lucky because I haven't had to worry very much about covering professional sports or had any type of conflict with the college deal in Iowa, Tennessee, or Arkansas. At the same time, I don't think there are as many people who dislike me in Arkansas as there were in Tennessee. Since loyalties in Tennessee are split and I was the voice of the Commodores, I could get a call at the TV station because I didn't cover Tennessee enough, be criticized for being a "Vandy lover." I've been fortunate that while I've been criticized, no one has beaten me up or anything like that.

JOHNNY LARSON AND ANATOL AHEAVICH

On the field there have been a couple funny things happen that I've been able to witness. There was a high school basketball game I did one time—although I can't remember the town right now—but there was this big, heavy guy named Johnny Larson.

Johnny Larson was such a big guy that he had to wear track shorts because they didn't have basketball shorts that fit him. (Obviously he didn't match the rest of the team's uniforms, so that's one thing against him already.) He went up for a rebound one time, and he ripped those things out. There was nothing he could do! He just

Paul Eells (left) catches up with his old friend Rudy Kalis of WSMV-TV in Nashville during the 1996 SEC basketball tournament in New Orleans.

covered himself with what was left and ran right straight off the floor.

There really weren't a lot of things that were really that funny. I've heard a lot of people talk about embarrassing moments or really bizarre things, but I may have been one guy who missed out on all of that.

I have seen one backboard shattered when Oklahoma State was working out at the Final Four in 1995 in Seattle. "Big Country" [Bryant Reeves] shattered it, and coach Eddie Sutton was out picking up pieces of the backboard and putting them in his pocket, which I thought was strange. (And by this time there was security trying to keep fans from coming down.) So I asked Coach what he was going to do with it. He said, "That's a big souvenir; we'll remember this for a long time." Keeping some shattered glass? All of a sudden these fans kept saying, "Throw us some glass, we've gotta have that ... we've gotta have that." I didn't see Reeves actually make the dunk, but I heard it; it sounded like a rifle shot. There must've been 10,000-15,000 people in there at that time.

Just because I haven't seen a lot of humorous things doesn't mean I haven't been a part of any embarrassing moments. We were at an Iowa-Ohio State basketball game in Ohio. At that time the press rows were up a little bit off the floor. Ohio State had a kid by the name of Anatol Aheavich playing for them.

Iowa came down the floor and missed a shot, that puts Ohio State on a fast break. I said something like, "Johnson on the wing, feeds to Jones in the middle of the court, Jones to Aheavich, and Aheavich shits ... shoots, shoots." There were about two rows of fans between the floor and us, then all of these announcers. It seemed like everyone just stopped. It broke me up, and I couldn't stop laughing. We pitched it to a commercial, and I was scared I was going to get fired because I swore on the air. Luckily, I didn't, but that's the worst thing I have done on the air.

> Several years ago, when Lou Holtz was about to become their football coach, I had an opportunity to interview for the Arkansas play-by-play position. I chose not to go interview. Shortly thereafter, Frank Broyles hired Paul Eells. When Paul and I met a couple years after that, we had a good laugh about how everything turned out. I've gotten to know Paul through the years, and I respect him a great deal and enjoy listening to his work.
>
>   *Woody Durham, University of North Carolina*

PREPARATION:

THE IMPORTANCE OF A GOOD SID

I usually start preparing on Tuesday for a Saturday game. I will get the information, usually, through the other school's sports information director, and through our SID. With fax machines today, it's pretty easy to get what we need. I usually concentrate first on the two or three-deep lineup, so I can make my own spotting boards. When I get the spotting boards made up, I'll start writing the information on stats — leading defensive tacklers and things like that. I write all of that on the spotting board. That way it'll be in front of me. I used to try and memorize all of this stuff, and knew I couldn't do it. I finally found out that if you start getting numbers mixed up, that the easier way was to just look down and the information was right there.

About Wednesday or Thursday I'll take the wide receivers and other offensive people and start memorizing names and numbers, and making that association. I get the advantage of going to Fayetteville on Tuesdays to see them practice and talk to Coach [Danny] Ford a little bit. If I get there early enough, they let me sit in on some film on the other team. Mostly we go up to Fayetteville to do our shows and get some interviews, so you get a hands-on feel about the game through them. By Friday I've pretty much committed to memory the numbers of the running backs, quarterbacks, wide receivers. I've really been blessed working with Rick Schaeffer. He's the Arkansas SID, so he's there all the time and knows all the players and all the stats. The system we have now, I don't worry about the pregame at all or stats during the game. I concentrate on down, distance, score, time, and offensive players for both teams.

When we get in the booth Saturday, Rick and I will talk over what we're going to do—what he wants to be led into in the pregame portion that he and I do. I found that getting all of these numbers and stats out of my head has made me much more clearer to just do the play-by-play and rely on my color man.

THE WHITE HOUSE

I haven't tried to call the White House, but if I needed to I think I could. [Bill] Clinton was in the KATV station in Little Rock a lot as Governor. They'd come over and be on the news live, so I got to know him a little bit that way because he was a particularly big basketball fan.

When the Razorbacks won the national championship, we were invited along with the team to go to the White House. That's the last time I have actually seen Clinton in person. He went to two or three of the Arkansas games the year they won the title (1994). Then he was at a game over the holidays in 1995, and I got to see him briefly.

The most significant thing now is when you want to go shake his hand and say hello, how inaccessible he is as president compared to when he was governor. I was standing in the White House thinking, "Bill and Hillary ... I've seen them every day." But when you hear his introduction, hair just stood up on my neck, and I thought, "Man, this is awesome. This is the President, and I know who he is!" Even though it didn't get me anything but a handshake again.

They had the little deal where he went down the line and shook hands—they had about two or three hundred people there with Arkansas ties. When he got to us all I could remember to say was, "Mr. President, man wasn't that a great ride through the tournament?" He just said, "Yeah, and good to see you," then walked on. He had other things on his mind and was busy going through the reception line. It was brief, but it was very nice.

It was a really great experience going to the White House. The biggest experience for me was getting in and all of the security you have to go through at the gate. You have to go through all of that in advance. I remember my wife Vickie was with me, and we had to walk from the hotel to this gate, and I put her high heel shoes in my briefcase. She just had a pair of flats on. I didn't know they were going to search my bag, but when we got there, they took us into the guard gate one at a time and checked us for weapons or whatever. The guy opens my briefcase, looks down and sees her high heels, looks up at me, then back down at the briefcase, and then he just winked at me and said, "Go on through." I was so flustered that I didn't know what to say. I wanted to joke with him about it, but I just went on. When he winked at me I thought they were going to keep an eye on me all day. (An hour later, those darn heels gave me blisters ... ha, ha.)

I think the most impressive thing about the White House is the room where they have the press conferences. It is a long and very narrow room. I always thought it was a big room, but it's not. I found out that the swimming pool is underneath the floor in that room. That was the White House pool for John Kennedy, then I think Richard Nixon had it filled in. I was very impressed how all of those news people work in that little confined area. There was a reception on the White House lawn. I just thought this would be some kind of great place to live.

We got to see about two rooms. Hillary took the basketball team on a very quick tour of the White House except for the private quarters. We didn't get to see the Oval Office. We spent most of the time in the press room. That's probably the biggest personality I've met. Before Clinton became president, I used to think Lou Holtz was the most important person I had met.

The "Other" Most Important Person I Had Met

I first perceived football coach Lou Holtz very much the way that he is ... an intense perfectionist. He was coaching at Arkansas when I got there. He didn't have a lot of time to waste. In fact he wore his watch with the face on the side of his wrist. I asked him one time why he wore it that way. He told me it keeps him from having "wasted motion" because it keeps him from having to turn his hand to look to see what time it is. That, I thought, was a very good example of what he was; anything wasted was precious to him, and he didn't have time for that.

He was committed to winning ... winning was everything. He was comfortable at Arkansas, but I don't think he loved recruiting so he had his assistants handle that. But he was intense with them also; he demanded everything from them. He'd have a practice for two hours, and if he didn't like something that happened in either the first or second hour, then they would start all over again. He was a brilliant offensive mind.

There were times away from football that he could be very gracious. Yet there were times that if he started to think you were too comfortable or that you were getting too close to him, he would stop it without saying anything, you knew. An example of that is before the Arkansas-Texas game that opened the 1980 season. It was going to be the kickoff to the decade of the '80s. ABC was televising from Austin, Texas. Our station that week decided that we were going to do a 90-minute special, taped live. So I went to Fayetteville and another guy that worked with me went to Austin to cover the Texas side of it. I spent all week with Lou covering practice and such.

On Thursday before the team left for Austin, Lou had asked me what I was doing that night and invited me to his house. I was kind of shocked because we didn't socialize at all, and that was the first time he ever invited me over. So I went out to his house, and when I got there he was smoking his pipe and working on that card he carries that has all of his plays. I asked him about the plays he had written down. He said, "If it's an off-tackle play, I have a play off-tackle for every possible defense that I can think of them throwing at us." That's basically what was on that card. When we were through with that, he asked me if I wanted to listen to some motivational talks. He had been a graduate assistant with Woody Hayes and loved Woody's talks. We went back in his bedroom, and he had the old 78 records of some of their motivational talks and some of their talks that they had given in the locker room. We laid on the floor and listened to those, and I could see the admiration that he had for those coaches. Evidently he got a lot of his habits and a lot of his perception of the game from Woody Hayes. I was taken back by him, and he was very relaxed and very comfortable.

The next morning I was to do an interview with Arkansas' defensive coordinator, Don Lindsey. Lou wanted Don to get a little extra money so we did an assistant coach's show each week. I went to the office and Lou was coming down the hall and I said, "Coach, I really had a great time. It was really nice of you to invite me out last night."

He said, "What time are you going to tape Don Lindsey this morning?"

I told him about 9:00. Well, about 10 minutes before nine, Don came to the field and told me we couldn't tape at nine because Lou had called a staff meeting. Later I found out, not from Lou but Don, that Coach knew we had that interview, but it was Lou's way of saying that we'd do it when he wanted us to. I then perceived it later that I should have gone to Lou and asked him when he wanted me to interview Don.

Yet, Lou Holtz was a very generous man. He asked me one time if I had any stock in this penny stock thing. I told him I didn't, and he related a story that he had wanted some of his relatives to get in on this stock, and he was testing them. All of them turned him down even though he told them he could increase their investment within two weeks in the penny stock deal. He told me none of them had enough faith in him, so he went and invested their shares anyway and then gave the profits to the kids for school. He told me this story and then turned right around and said, "Do you have a couple hundred dollars? I want to get you in this stock."

I said, "Gosh, Coach, I sure don't."

I knew then what the deal was, but I didn't say anything about it. A week later we were coming back from a loss at Baylor and he was disappointed by the game, but he opens his briefcase and writes out a check for $200. He told me it was my share of the stock I had invested.

"Coach, I didn't either. I didn't invest anything, so I couldn't have made anything."

He said, "You take that, that's your share. I went ahead and bought the stock, and you made 200 dollars."

I argued with him about taking it until he said, "If you don't accept it, it'll really upset me because this is yours."

I took the check and a couple days later told my station manager about this bizarre thing. He said, "Lou called me and told me what had taken place." It was strange, but it was just the way he was.

He loved to play golf, but golf that was fast. He had to hit the ball, get in the cart, and immediately hit it again.

He's a marvelous and tremendously intelligent person who takes pride and ended up where he had probably always dreamed of going: Notre Dame. He told me one time he had always wanted to play at Notre Dame, but obviously he never could. He's an interesting study.

We worked together from 1978-1984. I got a call from him at home on a Sunday in December right after the football season was over in 1984 and Arkansas had gone 6-5. It was the first year that things really didn't look good. He said, "I've been fired."

I said, "Lou, what are you talking about?"

"I've been fired."

"What can I say? Because I'm going to have to break this news."

"What did I just tell you? Say anything you want. The reason I have called you is because I want to get a hold of Dale Nicholson (the station president) to see if I can keep the car for a little longer until we know what we're going to do." We had given Lou a car to drive, and his wife had been using it. I told Lou I would call Dale and have him call Coach back.

I got to the station and talked to Dale and the news director, and they told me to go on with the story. So I go on the air and say that Lou Holtz had been fired. Shortly after that the university released a statement that said Lou had gone through burnout, and he just felt it was best to get out of coaching for awhile. I called up to the school and talked with Lon Ferrell who was an associate athletics director and told him what Lou had told me.

> *I met Paul when he first came to Vanderbilt. He has always been very smooth and has always done a really good job.*
>
> ~ *Cawood Ledford, University of Kentucky*

He told me, "Your statement is not true because the university's statement which was just released says that the athletic department and Lou Holtz have come to an agreement and arrangement."

So at the station we fell right in and released the statement we received from the university. We got calls from all over the country because the wire had picked up my story about Lou being fired. The university denied it. Lou denied it. I probably looked like the biggest boob in the world at this time.

A few days later he accepted the coaching job at Minnesota. A couple of newspapers up there called and asked me why I reported that he had been fired. I told them to talk to Lou because I would rather have him explain it and tell them why.

"No, he told us to call you."

So it was another one of those deals where I just didn't know how to figure him out. For a period of about three or four weeks, radio and television stations from Minnesota would call me. I just told them, "He told me that he had been fired."

I haven't talked to him much since then. I guess a few years ago when he was in Little Rock to speak was the last time. Every time he's in Little Rock, he likes to play golf with a friend of his by the name of Pat Wilson. When I found out that Lou was going to be in town, I went out to the Country Club of Little Rock, and sure enough there he was. He was very cordial. It was like a day hadn't gone by; it was like he was still at Arkansas. He did an interview with me four years ago when he was in town, but on this particular time when he saw the camera he walked off. He is still very revered in Arkansas. I still have people come down from South Bend and tell me that Lou told them to say hi or was wondering how I was doing. In a way that surprises me and in a way, it doesn't.

The Coaches

Over the years I have dealt with some great coaches ... almost too many to name. But Bill Pace at Vanderbilt is one I liked very, very much. He was a terrific offensive coach. He was also accessible, which was very nice. I could call him and tell him I wanted to come over and do an interview, which made him different from previous coaches I'd worked with. Bill Pace was the first guy who was a coach and also a friend.

Roy Skinner was a great basketball coach at Vanderbilt. I loved Roy. He was so laid back, while inside he was churning and eaten up with nervousness. He taught me how to eat oysters one time in Baton Rouge. I never really learned to play poker, but I think Roy would've stayed up all night and played poker if he could, then go tip it up on the court. I can see why players really loved to play for him. He was just not like a lot of coaches, hollering and yelling, but the players really respected him.

There was a stretch in December of 1967, I think, where Vandy beat North Carolina, Davidson and, I think, Wake Forest. But Roy Skinner won three big ballgames against top competition, and I thought this was really a classy basketball program. Another great experience I can think of was when Perry Wallace became the first black player in the SEC. I was still at Iowa and Ralph Miller was the Iowa basketball coach recruiting Perry Wallace. (He was one of the top Iowa recruits at the time.) And I remember Perry visited Iowa, and I met him then.

Miller was telling me how he had a great guy coming out of Nashville, Tennessee, named Perry Wallace. That summer I ended up taking the job in Nashville, and Perry, being an outstanding student, opted for Vanderbilt over Iowa. Of course, I came out of Iowa and had gone to school with blacks, so I never thought anything about it.

But the experience that young man went through was unreal. We went to Ole Miss, and they just gave him the worst time. I couldn't believe some of the things that were being said. It got so bad during the warm-ups that the team started to laugh, and Roy sent Perry to the locker room. Perry didn't start that game. When he came in, he got hit above the eye and had to come out, but he got back in the game and scored 20 points and had 12 rebounds. The crowd gave him an ovation.

Every place we went that year was the first time for Perry. I couldn't believe a kid could be talked to and treated like that and respond the way he did. I have often thought of Perry because the courage he must have had during all of that was something. Roy was great with him and great for him. That's one of my most memorable things about Vanderbilt, especially to have that experience during my first year there.

Former Tennessee basketball coach Ray Mears told me he loved to come into Vanderbilt and almost incite a riot with one of his players warming up on the unicycle and his bright orange sport coat. He told me later, "Basketball is a great show, and I love to do that at Vanderbilt." Mears would go into the dressing room and tell his players about how unfairly they were being treated by "Vanderbilt officials." He told me he got the players so psyched up that he could go out with any of his teams and beat Vanderbilt at Memorial Gym. I don't know if I ever met anyone like Ray Mears.

My Favorite Coach

Overall, basketball coach Nolan Richardson is probably my favorite. I admire him so much as a man. I can only try to imagine what he went through when he lost his daughter to an illness. I just can't conceive the struggle that he and Rose [his wife] went through—to go through the move to Arkansas at the same time.

He would fly to Minneapolis where the hospital was to be with his daughter and Rose, then have to come back even though the athletic department was trying to get him to step aside and let his assistants help while he was away. Then there were people who were critical of the team losing and his style of play. These same people tried to jump on the bandwagon as success began, and Nolan made it very clear that he knew who his friends were. Still today, there are some newspaper people that he has no time for whatsoever. A couple of them who were very critical of him have never even picked up the phone and asked him about the ballclub. I think he was that hurt over some of the things that happened during that time.

One story was published in the paper that he had a cross burned in his yard. Well, at the time he lived in a condo that had no yard and backed up to a golf course. The guy that wrote it either heard it or made it up. But that was the kind of thing Nolan had to go through during his first two years at Arkansas.

I admire him as a person, but I also admire him as a coach because of the way he treats his players. These players are family to him, not only while they're playing, but he'll keep up with the kids after they leave. He would help them with whatever they needed for the rest of their lives. He's just that way.

I think our relationship has been headlined by trust more than anything else. When he first came, we did his coach's show, and he was much maligned by the media. The newspapers really hammered him for losing in his first year. They compared him to Eddie Sutton, who had won quite a bit. Through all of that, we got together every Sunday to do his weekly coach's show.

I liked him immediately because there was just something about Nolan that was very friendly; he had feelings, and he was willing to talk. In fact, he talked about some of the hurt from the papers where they would say that he wasn't doing a good job at Arkansas. They said he didn't have good players, when really it was Sutton's players that weren't very good.

His second year the papers continued to beat him to death, and he still won 19 ballgames. Nolan would always talk to me, and I think he appreciated that I never gave him a bad rap. I never did anything but be supportive of him. Although we don't socialize a lot, we've played some golf, and he's invited me over to the house to barbecue when his players were over there. He's always been very supportive and very cooperative.

The success that he's enjoyed winning the 1994 national championship makes him very proud. He's battled very hard for the black athlete and the black student. A very trying time for him was during the national championship run, when the Black Coaches Association talked about the possibility of boycotts. He made it very clear that he was committed to helping the black athlete. I was really proud of him for that. He and Georgetown coach John Thompson were steadfast about that.

THE BATTLE OF SIDNEY AND THE BIRD

At Vanderbilt, I think Jeff Fosnes was a great shooter. Tommy Hagen was a great player. Tommy won so many ballgames for them with last-second shots and great plays.

Sidney Moncrief at Arkansas, I thought, was one of the most exciting players, and basically, it was because he wasn't a great player: Sidney was a self-made player. When he came out of high school, he wasn't offered that many scholarships, but he just worked and worked and worked. He was also a great person; he had so much class about him. Even in defeat I could go up to Sidney, and he would give us an interview or talk to the media. That kind of aura affected everyone on his team. They were all class people.

The greatest game I ever did involved Sidney, when Arkansas and Indiana State played in the regional semifinals in Cincinnati. Larry Bird was on Indiana State's team that year. The game went right down to the wire. Arkansas was trying to get back to the Final Four for the second year in a row. This was the 1978-1979 season, and Rick Schaeffer was doing the games with me on radio. It was a beautiful game, going back and forth. It had a great flow to it.

Finally, as the game drew down to the wire, Eddie Sutton [the Arkansas coach] put Moncrief on Bird to try and keep him down. Bird and Moncrief had a great battle. Bird would put a head fake on to draw Moncrief in, then he would swish a jumper. At the other end of the floor, there would be two or three guys on Sidney, and he would hit a big shot. For Arkansas to lose the game, 73-71, on a last second shot in the lane by a no-name guy was incredible. I thought that was the greatest game I had ever been involved in and the most thrilling.

Another game Sidney was remarkable in was during his senior year between Arkansas and Houston. Arkansas was down by 25 points at halftime against a really good Houston basketball team with guys like Clyde Drexler. But in the second half, Sidney almost single-handedly brought the team back. Arkansas won the game, 60-57.

Scotty Thurman's shot that won the national championship—I wasn't involved in the broadcast, but that was one of the great thrills as a spectator who had to then cover it for the television station. I was so thrilled for Nolan.

The Sportscaster's Dozen

Eells prepares to tape an interview with Arkansas basketball coach Nolan Richardson at the 1996 SEC basketball tournament.

Nolan and the Razorbacks were down by 12 points late in a game with LSU in Baton Rouge during that championship season. Thurman hit a couple of threes. Alex Dillard hit a couple of threes, and all of a sudden, the game went into overtime. In overtime Thurman hit a 25-footer to win the ballgame for the Razorbacks, 108-105. Again, that was quite a season.

The Football Players

Chip Healey was a great football player for Vanderbilt and went on to play for the St. Louis Cardinals. Iowa had two linemen I thought were great. One was a friend of mine, Alex Karras, who was a fantastic football player. He and Evashevski didn't get along. The thing that sticks out all of a sudden about Alex is that during his sophomore year he was an All-American, and Coach didn't give him a letter because at that time Alex wasn't a big practice player. Years later, Jerry Burns had told me that Alex met him in Green Bay when he was playing with Detroit. Alex told Jerry that he never liked Forest Evashevski and he never would.

"Someday," Karras told Burns, "you won't like Forest Evashevski, either."

Jerry couldn't believe it.

Shortly thereafter, Evashevski had to fire Jerry. A couple years later when Jerry was a defensive backfield coach for the Packers, he went into the shower where Alex was after a game with Detroit and said, "You know, Alex, you were right, I don't like Evashevski."

Calvin Jones was another All-American at Iowa. Maybe the reason I remember these guys so well, is that I was a student and lived in the athletic dormitory with those guys. But Calvin Jones was killed the year after he graduated from Iowa. He was playing Canadian football and was killed in a plane crash.

I loved watching Burt Jones.

Archie Manning may have been one of the most exciting players I ever saw. One thing that sticks out is when he had a broken arm, and it was in a cast, and they came into Dudley Field. He did everything but whip Vandy by himself ... with one arm! I met him in Little Rock a couple years ago, and we talked about that game. He was a super guy. He was the best player that I can remember in college. Now his son, Peyton, is a carbon copy.

Texas Christian and Memorial Magic

I did a high school football game one night in Keokuk, Iowa, and I could only see about 65 yards of the field. I had a guy with a two-way radio standing at about the 30-yard line, and he would let me know where the yard markers were. That is probably the most unusual deal because they had a little, tiny pressbox at the 30-yard line of one end of the field.

The most difficult place to do a college game for me was at Fort Worth, Texas, at Texas Christian University. Their pressbox is almost 19 stories above the field, and they played night games. Their uniforms were purple with white numbers, but the pressbox was above the light towers. In the pressbox you're looking down above the lights, and I could not see the ball when it was thrown in the air. I could see when the quarterback was going to throw it, but I could not see the ball.

When that happened, if the receiver turned and started running, I would say that it was complete. If he didn't run, I knew it was incomplete. I felt like I was always about five seconds behind the play. That's the most difficult place I've had to do a game from. Tennessee, for a time because of their orange and white numbers, was the most difficult until doing the games at Fort Worth.

A lot of people talk about Memorial Gym at Vanderbilt and how difficult of a place it is to play and broadcast. The two things most unique about Memorial Gym are the coach's bench on opposite ends and broadcasting from up in the third deck. So many announcers would come in to Vanderbilt and not get used to it. Because you're so high up, everybody looked inproportionate. I loved it up there finally; I got used to it. You can really see things develop so much better. I even got to the point in Memorial Gym where on certain shots at certain angles I could almost call it good before it went in the basket. I would try and see if I could do that every once in awhile. I just saw it so well looking down on top of it. That's another one of the more unique places I've ever done a game from.

Simulcasts: Combining Radio and Television

I have to admit I enjoy the radio booth better than the television studio. Play-by-play is the thing that's kept me, I think, motivated and interested in the business. I think it's more exciting, and you get a chance to get around more coaches and players. The studio gets too routine. Even though I'm out of basketball play-by-play on radio, I really enjoy times like when we go to the SEC tournament and do our sportscasts on the road.

At first when the station decided to televise so many Arkansas games, I thought about it as just doing the radio broadcast. Everyone kept telling me not to worry about anything because people were going to know that it was simulcast and on radio. We had another guy open the telecast, host it, then throw it to Rick Schaeffer and I.

I would, at times during the broadcast, catch myself realizing that I was describing what people could see. So I might pause, or miss a pass here or there. But then I realized that I also had a radio audience out there, and they wanted every pass and every double-dribble. So it was difficult for me to handle at first, in that regard.

We started the simulcasts in 1978, my second year at Arkansas, and we did 15 games. The next year we did 20 games. We did it for three years, until the university decided we were doing so many television games that they wanted their own separate deal. Coach [Frank] Broyles asked me if I wanted to do the radio. Unfortunately the TV station said, "You don't have an option; you work for us." When I first went to Arkansas, I was paid by both the university and KATV, but that stopped in 1981. I really miss it.

I don't know if simulcasts affected my style as much as it may have affected my delivery—a little bit, because I would hesitate a little bit. For the most part, I did a straight radio broadcast. And if I slipped or let up a little bit, there were people who would remind me either listening on the radio or watching on television. I don't think there were a lot of people who realized we did the simulcasts. The guy who does the radio now is named Mike Nail, and our voices sound similar. What's so interesting is that a lot of people still think that I do the radio games. They'll come up to me and say, "We turned the TV down because we wanted to listen to you." I'll basically thank them and go on from there. When Mike took over he grabbed some old tapes of mine, and he now uses a lot of my phrases. So if people are critical of the broadcast, I say, "No, I don't do that anymore." If they like it, I just say, "Thank you very much."

I miss doing basketball on radio very much; it was my favorite. If I could grade myself on whatever I did, I would say I did a better job with basketball than football. Maybe it's because I don't know football as well; because I played some basketball but I didn't play football. It's hard for me to equate a guy going up for a pass and getting torn in two while holding onto the ball. I think it's a great play, but I never did experience that. I think that basketball is more intimate and has a flow to it, where football is snap the ball, the play is over, and you have 25 or 30 seconds to set everything up and get ready for the next play. Tommy Owen, a former high school coach in Nashville, told me one time that if you put a clock on actual football plays in a 60-minute game, they play seven minutes—there are seven minutes of action.

Basketball, to me, is intimate. I still go out and shoot hoops in the backyard. I get excited over football, but I think I trust myself more with basketball than with football.

I love the radio more because I think it gives me more room to be creative. Not that I want to create something that isn't there, but I think it's more challenging to describe something so well that the listener can understand what's going on. I've always looked at it that if I can paint a picture for someone who couldn't see it, and they feel comfortable and satisfied, then I've done a good enough job.

I look at TV as more of, "See that?" This is where we got in trouble, I think, when we did the simulcast. Because I'm telling you so many things that you're seeing, the challenge was to tell you something that maybe amplified what you were seeing. That was very difficult for me because I was so used to doing radio. Even now when I do the TV games there will maybe be a fast break, and I'll sometimes call it like bam-bam-bam-bam when I really don't need to do it, but I want to see if I still can. Plus I've never felt real comfortable on TV because I'm a little paranoid about the way I look.

The Paul Eells Style

Even though I've been in broadcasting for so many years, I still get those butterflies and nervousness before the opening game of the season ... my palms sweat. I get nervous every day before I go on in front of the camera. Believe it or not, I'm kind of introverted, even though I love people, and I'm kind of self-conscious in front of that camera. There's a different kind of deal from being on television every day than the excitement and the nervousness of doing the radio broadcasts.

Doing radio, I'm excited more about the anticipation; is our ballclub going to play well, or what could happen in this game that could be significant? Those types of things. Because I don't get to talk to the coaches on a daily basis, I'm more keyed up about it. Once we start a broadcast, though, it feels good.

To a certain degree, my style could be considered that of a "homer." I try to give credit to the opposing teams, though, whether it be a good play or a good player. I want to make sure I give them credit, but I do get more excited that the Arkansas slam dunk is a little more spectacular than the Kentucky slam dunk, for instance. People have said that I have a saying now of, "Oh, my." Dick Enberg of NBC says that, and that may be where I got it. But that may have replaced my saying, "Holy smokes." My "oh, mys" get a little more dramatic for an Arkansas play.

Thinking more about it, yeah, I'm a homer. Particularly doing games in Arkansas, where the Razorbacks are basically the team for everyone in the state, no matter what sport. I've never second-guessed a coach, and I've never criticized a player. I'm not qualified to do that. Maybe it's the era I grew up in, but back then you just didn't criticize a player or a coach; you didn't read about his personal problems. That's the biggest thing that's changed that I dislike about our profession.

Even though I don't criticize the coach, when I was at Vanderbilt I used to get on the officials a lot. I was wild, and would say things like, "Oh, man, that was no foul ... he didn't touch him." A lot of people liked that, but conversely, that was the first time I was told not to do something on the air. It wasn't Roy [Skinner], but it was a Vanderbilt fan who said he didn't want to hear about the bad officiating. But I think I had an early reputation in the SEC about criticizing officials.

I don't really do that anymore. I really don't even insinuate that there was a bad call, especially if the game is on television, because people can see for themselves. I don't try to second-guess a call.

If I Had to Work for a Living ...

I want to be able to do radio play-by-play as long as I can, whether it be until I'm 65 or 70 years old. I know I'm being ridiculous. Television will get rid of me, I think, in the next three or four years; TV is such a "young person's" media. Our television owns the rights to the Razorback radio broadcasts, so I'm hoping that I can maybe get back into it. That's how I see me being phased out.

Up until the last couple of years, I have never really given much thought of all of this coming to an end, and having to give up this great ride; it's got to be hard.

I don't consider myself a "legend." I really feel that I have been so lucky to get into this business, almost by accident. To have been in the business now for 39 years, and to have worked at three really great schools, and do what I've wanted to do; I really feel very, very lucky.

I got a call not long ago from a man who is a paraplegic and had to listen to the football games on the radio because he couldn't get to the stadium anymore. He said, "You bring me so much happiness because I can keep up with the Razorbacks. I like what you do, and I enjoy it." When somebody tells you that, it's really meaningful; then I feel even more fortunate to be doing this. I've had so many people come up to me and tell me how much they would enjoy doing what I'm doing. I think it must really be something if other people would love to do that too, and here I get to do it.

There are some great moments in this business. If I had to go to work for a living, I don't know what I'd do.

JOHN FERGUSON
LOUISIANA STATE UNIVERSITY

In the days of early radio, I was attracted to people in the sports field. I was not big enough to do what I would like to have done as a competitor, although I went out for football, played basketball, ran track, etc. But I was a good student of all the games, particularly football and basketball. And I followed all the men who described these events on radio, men such as Ted Husing, Graham McNamee, Bill Stern, and others.

> *The quality of a person's life is in direct proportion to their commitment to excellence, regardless of their chosen field of endeavor.*
> ⊱ *Vince Lombardi*

To state that I was thrilled to listen to far-away events via radio is really an understatement, since radio was our only contact with the so-called outside world. There were not many stations so listening was intense, very much as TV viewing is in these days. It was always special when "special events" were broadcast.

As the years rolled along, I had opportunities to meet several of the pioneers of sports broadcasting. I also was privileged to work games with some of them.

There was one man whom I considered to be the best football broadcaster ever, who had all the properties to be "great." His name was Kern Tips. Kern was one of those pioneers. He announced games in the old Southwest Conference. He had the extensive vocabulary, great delivery with a Texas flair, and set standards for being the best prepared broadcaster in the business.

For a long time, Kern Tips was the lead announcer in the Southwest for a network that covered all games of that storied conference. Kern hired me to be a part of that team from 1951 through 1954. I learned a lot from him, especially from the standpoint of being prepared for a broadcast.

Kern Tips and others whom I admired had the great, distinguishable voices. As I listened to them in the early days, I concluded that if I were able to perform comparable work, I would have to be my own man, set my own standards, and do my own work, not copying any other human being.

Preparing for a Career

When I was an early teenager in Claiborne Parish, Louisiana, to me radio was just about the most exciting thing in existence. Frequently, I would make up games and simulate broadcasts; practicing, as it were. It was fun to do that, and I guess that it was not surprising that I gravitated into dramatics in high school and college.

College for me was Louisiana Tech. Although I had wanted to attend Texas A&M, there just wasn't enough money to handle that, so to Tech it was. I learned to love it, because it was a fine school. Still is. My scholarship covered all fees—$10.00—and the cost of one semester's room, board, and laundry was $112.50.

Since I was so very young, my dad talked to Dean Mitchell, Dean of Men at the time, to ask that he look after me. I, therefore, was assigned to a room adjacent to the Dean's housing accommodations in the old freshman dorm. (The building still stands today.) Anyway, at Tech I concentrated on the sciences and graduated with a B.S. in Biology, a minor in Chemistry and a dozen other subjects. Really, I took almost everything at Tech except Home Economics. And, much to the distaste of some of my professors, I developed an increasing interest in dramatics. In fact, I played the lead in several plays, many plays, during my four years in college. Not only was it satisfying work, but I found that stage work was an excellent avenue to voice development. This kind of development doesn't seem to be as important to students these days, but it is a point of worthy consideration.

I guess I am saying that at Louisiana Tech I got a well-rounded education, of which I am very proud. And I have always been appreciative of the time and effort that my professors spent with me so many years ago. I am sure that my dad sighed with relief when my diploma was awarded.

During my junior year at Tech, it happened that a reasonable amount of radio equipment was made available to the Department of Speech. A whole new world was suddenly opened for me. Our class produced a great many programs; generally, we learned a lot about the radio business. My voice had developed a good bit by this time, so I was usually selected to act as the announcer for our school programs which were carried by area stations, notably KWKH in Shreveport.

We didn't cover any sports events, but I would handle public address chores for high school football games whenever possible. When I graduated the war in Europe had started, but I wanted to try the radio industry as long as possible. So, I applied.

THE RADIO BUSINESS

My application was at KELD radio, El Dorado, Arkansas. Mr. Fletcher Boles, the station manager, asked me what made me think that I should have a job at his station. I relayed that I thought I was better than anybody he had. It wasn't true, but he hired me on the spot at $17.50 a week for 70 hours of work. I was some happy. I made some fine, lifelong friends, learned a little, grew up some, and got exposed to living on my own.

While at KELD I got a chance to announce professional baseball in the old Cotton States League. My first game was El Dorado against Clarksdale. There were a number of future major leaguers on the two rosters.

In that first fall, KELD's football play-by-play announcer (a part-time employee) was going to be away, so Mr. Boles asked if anyone knew anything about broadcasting football games. I volunteered and got the assignment. With Mr. Boles looking over my shoulder at the start, I did my first football announcing job with a high school game between El Dorado and North Little. Incidentally, several players off both teams later played in the first LSU game I did in 1946.

That high school game was exciting, with many big plays, turnovers, and touchdowns. I don't recall who won the game, but I was in hog heaven. I guess I did a pretty good job, because I was asked to do more games—for which I was paid nothing extra, by the way. But, at the time, who cared?! The radio bug had bitten me.

But, there was war.

THE WAR

I grew up quite a bit during World War II.

My service was in the Army Air Corps, later the U.S. Air Force. After serving as an instructor pilot in Pine Bluff, Arkansas, I was assigned to the 5th Ferry Command at Love Field, Dallas, Texas. I

The Sportscaster's Dozen

and a bunch of talented pilots flew everything the country had at the time throughout the country. We also went through officer's training at San Antonio, before being sent overseas.

My out-of-the-country duty was served in Jorhat, India, in the Air Transport Command. We flew the "Hump" from India to China in B-24 type aircraft, carrying gasoline, bombs, and other materials to be used in B-29 raids over Japan. This experience was, of course, a once in a lifetime opportunity.

Earlier I said that I grew up in this period. It's no wonder, either. It was either grow up or not make it back. I learned that a person had to depend on himself, keep his head on straight, make cogent decisions, and be tough when the situation demanded it. I also learned that no person is ever alone, certainly not pilots in that theater of operations.

Just talk about this with any man who flew the "Hump" and you find out exactly what I mean. By the way, there is an Association of Hump Pilots that exists today. It's membership is comprised of nothing but "heroes."

> *John was a good announcer for LSU in Baton Rouge. I could hear him at night because the Tigers used to play all their games at night, and they were on a clear-channel station. I would get to hear his football sometimes at night because Vanderbilt rarely had a night game. Fergie and I did four or five bowl games together, including some Gator Bowls and Bluebonnet Bowls. He was a great guy.*
>
> — *Larry Munson, University of Georgia*

After reassignment to the Ferry Command at Dallas, I was discharged and ready to try that radio business again.

Radio After the War

There was a stint at KWKH, Shreveport, for me for about six months after World War II. It was then that I decided an extra degree would be good insurance for the work years ahead. So, after trying to attend Iowa University, I ended up at Louisiana State University. I was very happy at LSU's Department of Speech, in view of the fact that the faculty was truly outstanding. Those men—Drs. Gray, Wise, Shavers, McCleod—and Miss Borchers had a lot of influence on my thought patterns in later years. Besides, I was sort of like a mental sponge with that group. They were brilliant individually and as a group.

In the end, I earned an MA degree in Speech and wrote a thesis on imagery in sports broadcasting. It's a pretty interesting study about the principle objective people face in live radio sports.

In the summer of 1946, the announcing position for the LSU football games became open. I applied and won the audition. Radio station WJBO had the rights and offered me a $50 fee to announce the games. We compromised at $100.

Roy Dabadie was the manager and served as producer of the broadcasts. In our first game, Mr. Dabadie put so many notes on the window of the radio booth that I could hardly see the field. A postgame meeting settled that issue with the help of Vernon Anderson, a senior supervisor at the station. Things got smoother, and we made it through a season which was one of the best LSU has ever had in football. The 1946 season was not the first brush I had with the Tigers. The first was in about 1932.

I saw a game between LSU and Arkansas at the Louisiana State Fairgrounds in Shreveport, site of the series for many years. Everybody in north Louisiana went to the state fair—everybody. A lot of those people went to the football game. Shreveport was a center for college football then since Centenary had one of the nation's best teams and played a big-time schedule. Incidentally, I saw many of Centenary's games against schools like Texas, Texas A&M, SMU, TCU, Oklahoma, Rice, etc. in the 1930s.

Anyway, back to LSU and Arkansas. The tickets to the game were either 50 cents or a dollar, which was too much for me, so I waited until halftime when the ticket takers would leave the gate. That day I walked up the ramp at the half, and looked out at the field with the LSU band playing, while spelling out the word "H-E-L-L-O" from one end of the field to the other. I thought it was the biggest thing I had ever seen. I still do!

Imagine now, a small kid, alone, walking into the 12,000-seat stadium to see the magnificent LSU band in their white pants, purple jackets with the tall, parade-type hats ... I was impressed for a lifetime.

The years rolled along. My wife and I had two children, and we made Baton Rouge our home. All the while I was announcing LSU football games. There were many great seasons, more great players, and increasing experience. I did the LSU football games for 32 years. And I enjoyed every minute of every game. I don't know how many games of all types that I have announced, but it's a big number; over a big area ... the whole world, in fact. And, I don't know how many people may have heard some of my work ... that would also be a big number. What all this means is a matter for someone else to decide.

But, I tried, every time.

To fill in a few of the gaps, here is the way my play-by-play announcing has worked out through the years:

  1946-1948   LSU football
  1949 regional networks
  1950 LSU football on the Liberty Network, doing color
  1951-1954   Southwest Conference football
  1955-1957   LSU football
  1958-1960   AFL football on television
  1961-1985   LSU football, included television
  1965-1983   SEC-TV basketball on TVS and NBC.

[Also hundreds of high school football games; LSU basketball on radio; track meets; auto races; boat races; US Forces radio football; and 24 football bowl games, including the first televised Sun Bowl and the first televised Peach Bowl. Many NCAA basketball tournament games, including the Final Four. PGA golf on NBC, including the US Open and the Tournament of Champions.]

PREPARATION: RADIO VS. TELEVISION ... FOOTBALL VS. BASKETBALL

If you are a quick study in memory work and so forth, if you were good at memorizing Shakespeare, then you might be good at preparing for information for football. Ideally you have to read a lot. You need to know about all the details that you wish to cram into your mind to remember and to make notes about: of schools, of people, of coaches.

You'd like to have an explicit knowledge of the contest and the rules, speaking ideally. Today that is not necessarily followed by a lot of people, but the old-time guys, the other men in this book, you will find that they all have been, were, and are meticulous preparers. They worked at it. They thought about it. They thought about devising different means of describing different events under different conditions so they don't always repeat. That way an off-tackle play for three yards inside the 15-yard line doesn't turn out to be the same play in 1985 that it was in 1955.

So being generally prepared and generally intelligent would be keys.

For me the actual preparing was a four- or five-hour job a week, but it's not the type of thing where you just sit down and spend four or five hours at one time from 10:00 to 3:00 preparing for a game that's going to be at 7:00. You might be doing a few little things on Monday or pick up something you want to use on Wednesday or in a chance conversation.

Television is vastly different because you're not having to paint pictures, so your preparation direction is different.

And generally the approach to television sports coverage is in variance with radio as far as preparation is concerned. Radio is a tougher game for that standpoint, by far, because you have to paint a picture. I wrote my master's thesis on how you paint a picture; how I'm able to make you see what I'm trying to tell you about. These men in the Southeast, and others, are masters at that and have been for a long time.

You approach television preparation from a background standpoint, and the rest is dependent upon personality and performance. It makes a big difference if the picture's already drawn in front of you. You don't have to describe Michael Jordan over in the corner, as he prepares for a 25-foot jump shot with the score 53-to-53 toward the end of the game. You don't have to describe the flex in his knees or how the ball rotation goes in a certain way and how he follows through. So for that, football preparation was the most difficult for me.

As the years went by, I never prepared any less. In fact, I may have prepared more. A lot of people talk about broadcasting football games as fun, and we liked to enjoy what we were doing, but I wasn't really interested in fun. We were interested in broadcasting the games from a professional standpoint.

I was much the same way in the booth, I guess, as I was flying airplanes in the military—it was a serious business. We thought about it, and we planned it. We were not there to have fun and joke and play tricks on each other or that kind of stuff; we were there to broadcast a game.

The reason was we knew we were representing Louisiana State University. We knew that because almost nobody else played night football at that time and because we had two very large clear-channel stations on our network, we knew we would have a nationwide audience.

In my case, for example, when I was a kid and would hear Bill Stern or Ted Husing, you knew that they worked at their professions and tried to perfect their professions with their performances.

We would think about that fact and approach our football broadcasts in much the same way. Now I don't want to make too much of it, but that's the way we did it. When people would tune the radio dial around and would come to a place and it would be the LSU

The Sportscaster's Dozen

broadcasts, nobody would have to be saying anything and you would know that it was LSU. We worked at that. It wasn't because we hung a microphone out of the window as some people still do, because we wouldn't do that.

We worked very hard at recreating, or transmitting, the sound that you would get if you were in this place at LSU; a stadium which has a great deal of presence, a stadium which is vibrant and where people respond because they can't help themselves because the whole spirit of the event is fed back into them. We wanted you to know that when you were fiddling around with the dial in your car and you would come across the frequency that had LSU's broadcasts, that you would know what it was even if Walter Hill and I said nothing. We worked at that.

The band was an integral part of our operation because we used them, although not a great deal, to recreate this exact mood. We knew that the public relations window that was open to us was very, very important. I can tell you without any fear of contradiction, that before every game we did, particularly at night because we had the great coverage, Walter and I would say every time, "Well, there's no telling how many people we have listening to us this game, so let's make it the best one we've ever had." That's how we would start every time, and we didn't mess with it. We knew what we were about and we worked at it.

There is a lot of talk about various phrases, trademark phrases, that a broadcaster uses in the course of a game.

A lot of people would write things down, write down their ad-libs; Kern Tips was big on that. He had so many of them, he would catalog them and take a notebook to the broadcasts of a game and put a check mark or tear the sheet out, when he used one so he would never use it again. There have been a number of books written suggesting phrases to aid in the broadcast of games to describe various plays and various conditions. A lot of people use those suggestions.

Not all of the broadcasters will catalog like that, but most of them, the good guys, will write things down to remind themselves to mention something during the course of a broadcast. Most men would go with a notebook or a stack of papers a few inches high into a game, so they can remind themselves of something they want to mention. You can't remember everything, plus the fact that sometimes you run into situations where you will need to have a lot of material at your fingertips.

In Texas when I announced games in the Southwest Conference, Mr. Tips and his company, which had the rights to the SWC games for many years, required that you had a certain amount of material prepared before each broadcast.

The producer of the broadcast helped in organizing people like me so that if something happened and a game were interrupted, you would have plenty of material and would never have to sit around the booth and say, "Well, let's see what they're doing now," or "Well, there are some people down there now, I wonder what they are saying." It wasn't like that at all.

An example of how that worked ... Eddie Barker, who later turned out to be the top newsman on television in Dallas on KRLD, and I were doing a game between Rice and Florida. This was the first game at Rice Stadium when it was built in Houston. There was 1:25 left before the end of the first half in this new stadium. The lights went out on one side of the field, and they called the game.

The game was interrupted for right at an hour. They decided to play the final 1:25, take a one-minute break, which served as a halftime, then play the second half.

Well, Eddie and I never missed a step during that broadcast. We never did say, "Well, the lights are out, and we're not sure what they're going to do. I guess they're going to get an electrician. Boy, what a terrible thing this is. I'm sure they're embarrassed. I wonder what those players are doing?" You're talking about extraneous material when you do that. We never missed a beat because he and I had proper material already prepared. The bottom line is that preparation is important.

> *John is one of the few people I would cry the towel to during some of those LSU-Florida battles. The Gators would be favored, and I would go in and tell him there was no way we could win that game ... sure enough Florida would lose. John is a class person.*
>
>   ❧ *Otis Boggs,*
>   *University of Florida*

During that break, we read about everything having to do with the game, with the conference, with the school, with the experiences which we may have had, stories of the coaches like Jess Neely, who was at Rice at the time. Jess Neely was one of the storied coaches. One of the features I remember off hand was the story about his screen pass.

The screen pass to Jess Neely was not just a play; it was a "convoy" pass. It was a beautiful play which is seldom used anymore. The pass would be completed behind the line, then the receiver would be convoyed down the field by four, or sometimes five, other players.

We also talked about the Southwest Conference which, instead of breaking up as it has done, was preparing to admit Texas Tech. We talked; we didn't just grab some guy walking down the hall to come in and talk to us. The fact of the matter on the games in the SWC, we didn't have guests at halftime.

Interviewing guests during a radio broadcast at football games, while interesting, is generally a crutch. Not everybody agrees with that, but that's the position the SWC took, and I tend to agree. Even on our LSU games through the years, we seldom used guests at halftime.

The LSU Field Leaders

I have worked with so many outstanding coaches here at LSU. The ones with whom I worked include Bernie Moore, a longtime friend who later became the commissioner of the Southeastern Conference ... Gus Tinsley, with whom I'm still in contact, who is still one of the most knowledgeable football people in the world and the greatest player this place has ever produced. I thought on occasions Gus was as good a football coach as there was in America. Paul Dietzel replaced him; an organized, younger guy at the time and a fine football coach who won a national championship, the only one that's ever been won here ... Charlie McClendon for 18 years. Charlie is still around. Retired, of course, and went to be the director of the Citrus Bowl and later became the secretary of the coach's association. He and I have been friends for a long time ... Bill Arnsparger, master coach. Knows more about the game than any man I have ever known and was more in control of the game as it would be played than any man I have ever known.

I found the coaches with whom I dealt here at LSU to be extremely agreeable people, intelligent men, aggressive guys. I did not, nor do I today, think it was the province of the broadcasters to try and invade the field which the coach occupies. After all, the broadcaster is not the coach; he is not there, I think, as an editorialist. The broadcaster is the man who communicates what he sees to the people who listen. That's his job to do to the best of his ability. The rest of his opinions, and so forth, are inconsequential to the contest.

Now I understand that's in variance with what radio business is today; everybody has an opinion and wants to editorialize. Talk shows are prime examples of that. But, it's always been my opinion that people were not interested in what we thought, they were interested in what we could tell them about what was going on. Then they could make up their own minds about how they responded to what was going on. What happened on the field was the coach's business and his decision, not ours. We would tell you what it was, the conditions and consequences on either side, but for him to make up his mind was his business, and for us to comment on it was out of bounds. That's one of the basic principles on which we operated.

Even though I had a good relationship with some of the coaches, it really didn't help at all in the booth. While I have said it was not our position to editorialize on what the coach did, I felt likewise that it was not the coach's business to try and broadcast the games. We didn't have that problem with the coaches, but we did have that problem with some listeners.

One of our other basic rules to broadcast a game was that we did our level-best to be impartial. We recognized fully that 22 people were required to play the game: 11 on one side and 11 on the other. Also, we knew that while we wanted you to know what you were listening to, we also wanted you to know that we understood that 22 people were required to play the game.

We knew that among the vast audience that we had, that everybody who listened to the games was not an LSU grad. There were thousands and thousands and thousands of people who were listening to football for the sake of the game and the love of the game. Therefore, we did our best to be impartial.

One night in the 1960s Ole Miss came over here, which has been a storied series between the two schools, and was outplaying LSU the entire game. LSU ended up winning. But during the game, Walter and I commented on the fact that LSU was being outplayed by Ole Miss because Ole Miss came prepared to play, and there wasn't much LSU could do about it during the course of the game. It was a report on how the game stood. Oh, I was called into a meeting Monday morning because it was reported by one of the faculty members that we were being derogatory toward LSU. (The athletic department wanted us to be enthusiastic when LSU did something well and less than enthusiastic when the other team did something.) But once and for all, we were able to establish the fact that we were going to be impartial.

The Sportscaster's Dozen

The Opposing Coaches

Some of the top names of opposing coaches that come to mind ... Bob Neyland at Tennessee, Wally Butts at Georgia, and Johnny Vaught at Ole Miss.

Mattie Bell at SMU. I did a game between SMU and Notre Dame. Imagine this, now ... you really don't know what's going to happen, you think you know what's going to happen at the beginning of the game, but you don't. I can't remember if it was in South Bend or Dallas, but SMU received the opening kickoff and threw 16 straight passes. Sixteen passes ... that'll get your attention. That's the way Mattie Bell was.

Darrell Royal at Texas. Of course a whole line of successful coaches at Texas A&M. "Bear" Bryant at Kentucky then Alabama; a good, tough guy who was always nice to me.

Then doing pro games for a long time, I've seen and dealt with a lot of the great coaches.

Each coach at both levels had their own mannerisms, but there really aren't any that stick out as unusual. Lou Holtz constantly walks, for what reason nobody knows. Sometimes their personalities come out on the sidelines.

The King of the Hill

In my opinion the best color announcer in the game of football is Walter Hill. Walter joined me on broadcasts of LSU games in the fall of 1961 and remained in the booth until 1983. He and I shared the professional desire to perform at our peak every time we hit the air. As he proved throughout our many years together, Walter was always well-prepared and left nothing undone as he displayed his considerable talent to the very large audiences of LSU football on radio.

Our Saturday night network was big and enthusiastic, reveling in the on-the-air excitement that all started when Walter announced, "Here come the Tigers!" to the whole nation. He is well-educated via Southeastern Louisiana University and well-trained by rigorous years in an exacting profession. There won't be another like him ... or as good.

Till He Gets It Right

Eddie Einhorn hired me on a free-lance basis to be the play-by-play announcer of the SEC-TV "Basketball Game of the Week." The year was 1965. Eddie, now part-owner of the Chicago White Sox, took a big gamble in trying such an innovative project. But he made it work and soon controlled the majority of college basketball TV in the country, not to mention a lot of NCAA playoff games.

Our first game in 1965 was LSU versus Georgia. To camouflage the fact that very few people were in the stands that Saturday afternoon, Eddie directed all fans to take seats on the sideline opposite camera positions. However, through the years the fan base increased, and all schools in the Southeastern Conference built new arenas.

It is pretty universally accepted that early TV, starting in 1965, is largely responsible for the meteoric rise in popularity of this fine sport. Although I have always considered my part in this venture to be not of major proportions, I, nevertheless, did play a role, of which I'm proud. As I have indicated previously, the announcer is the messenger, not the president.

However, as Mr. Einhorn will attest, I did indeed play my role in basketball TV in the SEC while Eddie stated repeatedly, "I am going to ask John to announce the SEC basketball games until he gets it right." After 17 years at the TV mike, I guess I finally did.

1946: The Best LSU Team, or at Least the Deepest

There is not a particular team that means more to me personally, but in my opinion the 1946 team was the best team ever here at LSU. That was the team, coming out of World War II, that was about eight deep at almost every position.

One player on that team was running eighth string, and he went to coach Bernie Moore and he said, "Coach, I'm not getting to play enough." Coach said, "Well, son, I've got seven other guys who are going to play." The player said, "Coach, that's why I came to see you. I've been asked to play somewhere else." Moore told him that he might as well go ahead and take the opportunity because he wasn't good enough to play at LSU on a regular basis. The guy's name was Joe Glamp. He started Sunday, that Sunday, and did for a long time with the Pittsburgh Steelers. That shows you what kind of team LSU had.

In those days one of the big practices was punting. We had a great punter on that team named Rip Collins. It was a thrill to see Rip and the other punters on the team try to kick the ball out of the stadium. It doesn't sound like much, but to kick that ball out of the football stadium was something spectacular. They occasionally could do it.

That was a great team.

I didn't have any particular loyalties to one team over another. Again, I took the position that I was only a medium at which you followed the game. I was your connection between the team and what was happening on the field.

"Let's Go Down to the Sidelines": The Advent of the Field Reporter

> John, I thought, was extremely colorful in his presentations. He was very professional and very knowledgeable. John probably carried himself a little better than the rest of us; he was a little more suave and debonair. He was always more business-like.
>
>   ~ Jack Cristil,
> Mississippi State University

We originated the sidelines reporter here in the early 1970s. We were the first crew in the country to use a third man. The first man we used was Pat Screen, he was a former player here in the sixties and later mayor. It worked out pretty well. Later, we had Doug Moreau who is now district attorney here. In about 1980 we moved Doug up to the booth. Now they just use a two-man crew, but for us the three-man crew worked out very nicely because it was a way of providing more information.

The Chinese Bandits

The Chinese bandits were a defensive unit formed by Paul Dietzel in the 1950s. The substitution rules at that time dictated that you could send in an entire team but you could only do it once a quarter. In order to take advantage of the rules, Coach Dietzel devised a system, which was unusual, whereby he had three teams: white team, go team, Chinese bandits.

The white team was comprised of a team that could play both ways; Billy Cannon was on that team with Johnny Robinson, Warren Rabb and others. The gold team was a team that specialized in offense. So Coach Dietzel would send in the white team to start the game. The white team would play a quarter and maybe a half or so. When the other team was getting worn down a little bit, all of a sudden here comes the gold team with fresh offensive guys led by their halfback, Scooter Purvis.

Then when they would get in the situation where it really required a big defensive effort for a pickup or to turn things around, then Dietzel would put in the Chinese bandits, which was comprised of a bunch of guys who were not very good, but they would knock your block off. They were not big, 165 to 175 pounds, but they would come in and turn things around. The people just adored them and took them under their wings. And LSU won a national championship using that system.

Still today, sometimes when great defensive plays are made, you'll hear part of a Chinese song played by the LSU band.

Bert, Cannon, and the Rest of the Tigers

There have been so many great athletes at LSU and at the various schools which I've covered. Here at LSU, Bert Jones is the best quarterback I have seen in the purple and gold, ever. His individual performance in that 17-16 Ole Miss game was, in my opinion, the most outstanding single performance on this field. The big play occurred when Jones threw an incredible pass to Brad Davis in the end zone as time ran out.

A close second, or maybe tied with that, would be Billy Cannon's run. Cannon was just the perfect running back: big, powerful, fast, intelligent.

The most graceful player LSU ever had, in my opinion, was Tommy Casanova. Charlie Alexander, who works in the office here with me, is one of the great running backs in the history of the Southeastern Conference. Y.A. Tittle was a fine quarterback when he was here. The school has had hundreds of All-Americans at the different line positions, or at kicker, or wide receiver.

It was interesting that LSU through the years had a lot of outstanding linemen, but LSU's reputation was built on the lineman who was 6 feet 1 or 6 feet 2, long-waisted, barrel-chested, short legs and long arms, and weighed about 240 pounds. In my mind's eye, when I think of LSU playing exciting games in the 1960s and 1970s, I can see all of those guys rushing toward the ball carrier and all hitting him at the same time. They had such a swarming-type defense.

"Pistol" Pete

Pete Maravich was the greatest basketball player with the ball that I have ever known. He revolutionized basketball in this section of the country. I think he was directly responsible for our having a lot of great places to play in this league now.

Everywhere LSU went, the houses were full. "Pistol" Pete Maravich was really a showbiz guy in basketball. He didn't care too much about defense, but his greatness attests to the fact that he still owns the scoring record in the NCAA.

When he was a freshman, people would fill up the place to see the freshman play. Then they would leave before the varsity game was played.

All of these antics performed by guys like Michael Jordan—Pete originated all of those things. In fact, he used to play here in one of the toughest parts of town, outside, with a bunch of black kids who could do these types of things. That's how he developed a lot of those moves. He could do it all.

One day LSU was playing Kentucky. The game was on NBC nationwide, so Joe Dean and I were doing the game. Prior to the game, Joe interviewed Pete's father, Press Maravich. Press said, "Well, we're going to give the ball to the boy, and let him do his thing. If he can do it, then we can beat Kentucky."

I interviewed Coach (Adolph) Rupp and asked him what the Wildcats were going to do. He said, "Well, we came to see the show. We know this boy is the greatest player in the game, maybe in the history of the game. I'm interested in watching him perform. We really want to see what he can do. So we're going to watch him; we're all going to watch him, and we're going to try and stop the other four." That day I think Pete had 63 points, Dan Isell had 54, Mike Pratt had 35 or 39, Louie Dampier had 26, and Kentucky won the game something like 120-115. It was a great shoot-out.

But Pete was a competitive person.

Impact

Some people talk to me, occasionally, about the impact I have had on them. While I've worked hard at broadcasting professionally, I didn't take myself that seriously. It bothers me today when I see and know of people, particularly on the talk shows where opinions are spouted all the time, who think the world won't turn unless they give their opinion on things.

In a general sense, I'm pleased that I did stick to my guns and maintained my outlook on the manner in which I was to conduct myself professionally. I feel the same way about my life I had flying as a transport pilot stationed in India in the military. I'm glad that I adhered to the standards that I did. I don't know how I did all of that. Sometimes I feel that way about broadcasting. I sometimes can't believe that I did those things ... but life goes on.

It's interesting. I was invited to make a speech a couple years ago at the Lions Club. It was January 8th. They introduced me, and I got up and something had occurred to me so I said, "I know you want me to talk about football and so on, but let me tell you that it just struck me what today is. It's January the 8th."

I told them that 50 years before that I had an experience that I wanted to talk about, that I had never discussed before. So I told them about this experience that I had, a very close call. At the end of the speech for about 30 seconds (and 30 seconds is a long time when there's no sound) you could have heard a pin drop. Suddenly a man I had not seen and did not know, stood up in the back corner and said, "He's telling you the truth!"

There was another time, when some people had invited me to go to a Texas Rangers baseball game. We're sitting there in the stadium eating popcorn and drinking ice tea, having a discussion. There are people on two sides of us, and the ladies behind us recognized my voice. And what did they want to talk about? The LSU Tigers. I guess that proves you just can't get away from yourself.

Missing the Business but Catching Up with the Family

I retired from play-by-play broadcasting in 1985. After doing something for 32 years, there are times I miss it. The reason is that you're on the cutting edge of the excitement; you're there when it's happening. You can get accustomed to that and you miss that. I was never one who felt a need to get away from things after the season, because I never did get tied up in the games or emotionally involved in the games. I was not going to get a heart attack by getting excited or screaming my lungs out. Because of that, I never really felt the need to get away.

It's kind of like when I was a kid and on Sunday afternoons during the summertime when nobody was around, I felt like the whole world was on vacation and out of town, except me. At the end of every football season, it never failed, and it's true still to a certain degree, that I had to do an about face and come down to earth.

It was not an easy schedule, though. There was a time when I was doing a high school game on Thursday or Friday, LSU games on Saturday, and then some pro game on Sunday. Doing all of this I was out of town every weekend for many years on an average of 30-32 weekends a year.

It just gets tough to do that. You miss your son, who grows up a lot while you're gone. And your little daughter is growing up, and she's wearing the cute little dresses and going to parties and so forth while you're in Laramie, Wyoming; or Denver, or Detroit, or Athens, Georgia; or wherever. Then you rush back to do a TV show. Then you come home and you have to do more work. It's just not a good business for a family life. In some respects it can be worse than being a coach or a player.

That's probably the only regret I have about getting into this business, just that it took so much time away from my wife, Marion, and our two kids. If you're going to do that job in that business, then you better get ready to dedicate yourself, otherwise you're going to do a half-ass job.

I went to New York and visited with people who owned the company that was the forerunner of the ABC-TV sportscasts. I decided I was better off where I was. I enjoyed doing what I was doing, I was in a section of the country where I really wanted to be, and I could spend at least a little more time with my family.

The Tiger Athletic Foundation

Since I retired, I have worked with the Tiger Athletic Foundation. (I've actually been involved with it since 1975.) It's an independent company, a small company trying to raise additional funds for the athletic department. It's successful, not as successful as it could be, but I guess all of these types of companies feel that way.

The school didn't have a fund-raising group here so I was hired by Carl Maddux, the athletics director, to do it, even though I had never done that kind of thing before.

To start with they gave me 20 tickets to sell to see if I could get a contribution of $100 plus the price of the ticket. The next year they gave me 60 tickets, and they wanted $300 a piece on those. So, a new career was begun. And now the Tiger Athletic Foundation is a productive, contributive organization in support of LSU.

I'm happy with the way things have gone overall. We've raised more money per person for the tickets we have, than anyone in the country. But we still don't have all the tickets. There is a policy here that states if you buy season tickets then you own those season tickets as long as you pay for them. We have a lot of people in that situation.

The Future for LSU

Louisiana State University is an exciting place. We have a professor who could show you a strawberry as big as your fist. Since this is one of the top research institutions, you could see them working on a cure for the AIDS virus.

Another professor here has perfected a way to clean up hazardous waste, and so on, using microbes to go in and take care of it and then eat each other. There are just a lot of exciting things going on here. This is an exciting place to be. This place, as a special place, will continue to improve and make its mark. It's like Tennessee, or Georgia, or Alabama or Florida; all of these are good places with a lot going on.

Advice

There are three things to remember in the play-by-play business: what's the score, who's playing, how much time left. That's it. What else is there? If you can put that into the mix and come out with something, then you've got a job.

Also, remember to speak the King's English. A lot of guys today murder the King's English. It takes just as much breath to say it right as it does to say it wrong. There's no excuse for murdering the King's English. I'm not talking about accent or dialect, Ifn talking about the words you use and how you use them.

I don't really have a Southern dialect. It's not a thing that I worked at or a thing that I have learned. My father had none of that, my mother had none of that, but my wife does. She has that very ladylike Southern dialect. I guess I never did, so I never had to work at it. There's nothing wrong with a Southern dialect, or accent, as long as it's used correctly. Again, just speak the King's English.

Those Were the Days

One more story that comes to mind was a time Paul Long did the Esso Report on KWKH. All news was really rehearsed. I did the sports at 5:45, and he did the Esso Reporter at 5:55, then we alternated on another show for Falstaff Beer at 6:30.

From 6:00 to 6:30, Paul and I then would very quickly go to the Columbia Restaurant which was in the building next door on Market Street in Shreveport. We drank a couple beers. The object was, or the game was, to see which one could make the other one's tongue slur when he got on the air with that program. So more than once one of us would slur the words.

So I'm on the sports this particular day while Paul and Bob Mahoney, the news guy, came into the studio and undressed me down to my underwear. What am I going to do? No off switch, so I just went ahead and did the show. When the show was over, Jimmy Stone came over from the other station and asked me what I was going to do to them. I didn't know what, but I told him I was going to get them.

When Paul starts on the Esso Reporter, and no sooner than he gets into the newscast, which he had rehearsed, I went in with a cigarette lighter and set fire to his newscast, his copy. Guess what? The pro that he was, he went right through the whole thing and never missed a word.

Those were the days.

John Forney
University of Alabama

I was 15 years old in January of 1943 and was a senior at Tuscaloosa High School, Alabama. (I had skipped a grade). Radio station WJRD, which was the only station down there at the time, was owned by a man named Jimmy Doss. Jimmy looked kind of like Mr. Magoo, and he was a character. At the time he had one of the best announcer staffs because it was in a college town, so he got great speech students from the university. But it was January 1943, and everybody was getting drafted for World War II. Jimmy would hire a guy, and 10 days later the guy was gone.

> *Accept the challenges, so that you may feel the exhilaration of victory.*
> — General George Patton

So Mr. Doss called the high school and asked them to send him someone who wasn't going to get drafted for at least a year. I went down to the station with two other guys for a competitive audition, and I got the job.

It was a very exciting time and Lord knows it was one of those life-changing deals because I was going pre-med (my dad was a doctor). Fortunately, I joined the U.S. Navy two years later, and I changed my mind while I was overseas, because I would have been the world's worst doctor. Instead, I was one of the world's worst broadcasters. No, I was a pretty good communicator I'll say immodestly.

At any rate I have an inordinate interest in World War II because I was doing the news everyday and just followed it from then on. I went into the Navy in April of 1945. When I came back out, I got in touch with Bert Bank, who was a veteran of the Bataan Death March and lived near us growing up. He opened a new station in Tuscaloosa.

I just kept at him and finally started doing a sports show daily on WTBC in Alabama. I did sports with them and did the first play-by-play basketball games in 1947-1948, which were also carried in Birmingham.

This was a break for me because Maury Farrell, sports director for WAPI in Birmingham, was hired as a third man on the New York Giant broadcasts (with Frankie Frisch) just about the time I graduated in March, 1948. Because management had heard me on basketball, I was interviewed to replace Farrell, and I got the job.

Thad Holt, the station manager and a very intelligent gentleman (after all, he hired me!) told me I would learn a lot about radio in a short time, and proceeded to work me seven days a week. I did staff work in the mornings and afternoons, then did Birmingham Barons baseball at night and on the weekends. I opened the station on Sundays and emceed a number of religious programs on the station. To top it off, I was assigned to do a late night band pick for a half hour from 11:30 til midnight from the Tutwiler Hotel! This sometime necessitated racing from Rickwood Field or the FM studio where we did out of town games on Western Union replay.

> *John Forney and I did bowl games together every year for 10 or 12 years on the Texaco Network. He really had a passion. We had some good times at those bowl games. He and the Texaco guy could stay up all night the night before a bowl game, or at least it seemed so to me; I would leave them at 3:00 in the morning. Forney loved to have fun, I really liked him.*
>   ⍟ *Larry Munson, University of Georgia*

Back then there were no exclusive rights to Alabama games and there were basically three "feeds" that covered this. One was from WAPI, which was also contracted to do Auburn games. They did this by doing both games, alternating between AM and FM.

It worked out because Maury Farrell, for whatever reasons, decided to come back to Birmingham. Maury was and still is a very good friend of mine and was one of the best ad-libbers I have ever heard. You could drop him down in the middle of a crocheting contest, and he could describe it beautifully. With both of us on staff we alternated on Alabama and Auburn games and also on AM and FM. I did five Auburn games that year which may surprise some of my current Auburn buddies.

At any rate when Maury came back I was sort of in a second banana situation which the station did everything they could to make up to me ... there were never any hard feelings. But I decided to make a move.

I had always fancied myself as a writer, and that's what I really wanted to do. Being single, footloose and fancy-free, I went to New

York in 1949 and worked up there in the advertising agency business for almost four years. When I came back in 1952, the season had just begun, and I wasn't doing anything. In the summer of 1953, I was in Birmingham and my wife and I had one child with another one on the way, and I was wondering if I should try to sell apples or pencils on the street corner. I got a call from Lionel Baxter, who was a wheel at WAPI, along with Bert Bank and G. H. Johnston, and he said, "Bert Bank and I have the rights to Alabama football. Maury Farrell's going to do play-by-play, do you want to do color?" And so that began in 1953.

Some of my Influences

Growing up, Bill Stern was just the be-all and end-all broadcaster to me. I didn't really like Ted Husing because he had broadcast an Alabama Orange Bowl game and was so biased to Boston College that all of us native Alabamians generally hated him. My grandmother lived in Evanston, Illinois, so I would spend three or four weeks every summer there, and I really think an influence in all of this was Bob Elson of the Chicago Cubs. Down here in Alabama you couldn't get much nationally. When I was at WAPI, I did baseball for the Birmingham Barons, but they didn't have any exclusives so three of us did those games.

New York, New York

I spent almost four years working in the advertising business in New York, at BBDO and the Biow Company. It is funny that sports just sort of followed me. In the spring of 1950, I was assigned to the group that did TV production for Schaefer Beer's telecasts of the Brooklyn Dodger games. (That was the first year that Vin Scully joined the Dodger broadcast team, and happily, he is still there; a great announcer, then and now.)

It was a fascinating thing working with the Dodgers because they had built a little studio (this was in the very early days of TV) in the bowels of Ebbets Field near the Stadium Club. It was an area about 14 feet by 14 feet, and we had a little refrigerator in it. There was no air in this studio, and it was hotter than hell.

There was a bar in the commercials, and I was the bartender but you never saw our faces, it was only our hands. Red Barber or Connie Desmond would say, "Mmmm, somebody's brought up a wonderful Schaefers, make that two." And they would continue, but everything was done voiceover by whoever was in the booth, whether it was Red or Connie or Vin.

I mentioned the heat, this is a true story. Remember this was in black-and-white TV days, and in the early days they got a beautiful platter of cold cuts and cheese and stuff like that and put in the refrigerator. But we would bring that platter out and make it part of the ads ... only we never changed the platter. We bought it in April and, of course, with black-and-white you couldn't tell things were green and purple and was just horrible looking, but they looked great on TV. Well, one night one of the sponsors from Schaefer Beer came out to the stadium, but we made sure we got rid of that platter!

We worked for the Dodgers the whole summer, and it was a great experience. Red Barber was there with Connie Desmond as the number two guy. Red was a titan. He was a great announcer without question, but he was not easy to get along with, especially for a young guy in the agency business. He would come in, ostentatiously, I thought, to the stadium club and have a copy of the *Saturday Review* and the *New York Times Book Review*. He just seemed to want to be above everyone else. I think Desmond hated his guts.

As I mentioned this was Vin Scully's first year. Barber gave Scully the opportunity, but Vin was a bigger hit than Red had bargained for. We felt like Red was really starting to sock it to Vin halfway through the season, but no one could really understand it. One day Red said, "There's a grounder, Reese scoops it up, throws to first, and the ball arrived concomitant with the runner. Now Mr. Scully wouldn't know what concomitant is."

With that Vin said, "Well, it comes from con, meaning with ... " He just parsed the whole thing right down to the end. Red was infuriated!

Red did one great interview that I never will forget. He interviewed an umpire named Larry Goetz and asked him, "Larry, what's the closest call you ever had to make?" With no pause whatsoever, Larry said, "None of them are close, Red, they're either safe or out." I never will forget that.

Mel Allen was a good friend of mine from Tuscaloosa. To me, Mel had an excellent voice. He went from CBS to the Yankees. When I went to New York in 1949, I wrote him a note and told him that I really wanted to see him and sit in the booth with him one time. At that time there really wasn't much room in their booth, but he went to great lengths to get me a seat right next to him. He just went out of his way and couldn't have been nicer. He called me about a couple years ago when he was in Alabama for a function and wanted to go to dinner. He was a good friend. I'm really going to miss him.

One of the most fascinating things I ever did was while I was in New York, was when I produced the "Joe DiMaggio Show." The first year he retired, the Yankees gave Joe a 10-minute pre- and postgame show. DiMaggio was my idol; he was the best baseball player there ever was, I guess, in my mind, anyway. He was like a caged lion, having been in those pinstripe flannels ever since he was about 15 years old.

Before the show he would always say, "You're not going to show me up, are you? You're not going to show me up." So the Yankees hired this guy named Jackie Farrell, who was a cretin at best, and he would write in big letters on cue cards for Joe, who was obviously reading the cards. It was, without question, the worst show in the history of the world. You couldn't say anything about it, though, because Joe didn't want you to show him up. It was quite an experience.

Southerners and Alabama Football

I think one thing about the Southeast, as far as why it has bred so many great broadcasters, is the economy of the place. The people in the area were probably still struggling from the Civil War when us old guys were growing up. I think Southerners are good storytellers. Particularly in baseball, where you're not just an announcer but you're also a showman a little bit, and you're a narrator, which is something I just really think is ingrained in Southern people.

> *I always admired the way John covered the Tide, and I missed hearing his voice when he left.*
>
> ⁊ *Otis Boggs, University of Florida*

Football, no question, is the sport I enjoyed most. I couldn't do basketball now, and I really admire the people who do it, but I used to think I could do it. Growing up in Tuscaloosa, my uncle was the president of the university from 1935-1941, so I could always go to football practice and all the games. There was nothing other than Alabama football. In fact I kick left-footed today because Johnny Cain (1931-1932) was a left-footed kicker. I was four and five years old when I started doing that.

Preparation

I was an avid reader of sports, especially football information. I never did spend countless hours in preparing to broadcast games. I always took one night and did my own charts on corkboard. I took all the statistics and would fill in all the information on the charts. I would read all the releases and make various notes on things I wanted to talk about. Having done color I was always looking for that color-type angle on each player or something like that. I would spend about four or five hours on that.

Really, it was mainly that one night, which was usually Wednesday or Thursday night. Back in the early days, I used to try to go to bed early and behave myself on the night before a game. Later Doug Layton and I would go out on Friday night, but I did a lot of work before getting to the weekend.

In 1989 I began a pregame show on the full network with Gary Hahn and then the next year became part of the network again doing a full network call-in show. Now that I'm doing that, I'd be lying if I said I put very much preparation into it.

I am surprised and thankful that I have such a good memory which really helps. I can't remember to take this pill for my diabetes with each meal today, but I can remember a whole lot that happened in 1938. We might get a guy call in and ask about a specific play or player from 20 years ago, and I will remember it. A good memory is definitely a key to succeeding in this business.

The Bear

The main thing I really tried to be conscious of when I came back from those years in New York was trying not to bait officials and trying not to be a total homer. However, in the words of Paul "Bear" Bryant, "Hell, he better be a homer."

Coach Bryant was a big influence on my life. When I was five years old, I was a page with a cupid outfit and gave away the favors at the Cotillion Club dance at Alabama. Coach Bryant and Mary Harmon were two of the people there. He was a player then. He was such a charismatic person, even at that age; he was like a radiating magnet.

He was very popular as a player. In fact he and another guy had a dry cleaning establishment because Bryant gravitated toward rich people. They had an instinct for him, and he loved them.

As I wrote in an article for Kirk McNair's *BAMA, Inside the Crimson Tide* magazine in August of 1985, Bryant's first experience with a summer camp was as a counselor at Camp Winnipe in Eagle River, Wisconsin, while he was still a student-athlete at Alabama. Growing up in rural Arkansas provided few luxuries for Bryant other than moving picture shows at the Lyric Theater where he would one day wrestle a bear to earn his famous nickname. Camp Winnipe was the summer home for approximately 90 teen and subteen boys, many from the deep South. A number of these were from the Birmingham area, sons of the wealthy and well-to-do, even in the depths of the Depression.

Capture the flag is a staple of summer camp athletics, and Winnipe was no exception. Walter Perry, a Birmingham entrepreneur, remembers well a flag-tag game when one of the smaller campers got the flag and began to run up field toward the opposite goal. One of the opponents—a larger camper with a reputation for being a bully—headed him off and instead of tagging the smaller boy as he easily could have done, laid him low with a vicious tackle. The smaller boy writhed in pain on the ground. Bryant and some of the other staffers had to minister to him as he left the game.

A bit later the bully got hold of the flag and took off down the field. Bryant, on the sidelines, had apparently been waiting for this. At full speed he ran on the field and hit the bullying camper head on. The sound and the severity of the collision is still in Perry's mind. Bryant got up slowly, dusting himself off. The camper lay on the ground, then finally was able to sit up, moaning.

"Get up, boy," Bryant told him. "You're not hurt. You just learned a good lesson today." Bryant pulled the camper to his feet. "No matter how big you are," Bryant continued, "there's always somebody around who's a little bigger."

When he was coaching, Bryant used to have a party down at his cabin at Lake Martin every summer. It started off small, he'd cook steaks, and it was a lot of fun. Alabama was wearing white jerseys more and more because television was just coming on strong and so you had to have the white jerseys. I think they must have gotten them out of moth balls from the 1920s because they had real small numbers.

So we're at this party, and I'd had a couple pops and said, "Coach, I just wanted to see if you had any thoughts to making those red numerals a little bigger on those white jerseys, because they're really pretty small."

He paused for a second and looked at me with a hard eye. "John," he said, "you ought to know the players with no numbers at all."

I swallowed and said, "Coach, that is just what I was saying. If there is one thing I wouldn't do is touch those white jerseys!" I'm happy to say he broke into a grin.

To me, Coach Bryant was a singular, idolatrous person as far as I'm concerned; I just thought the world of him. Whenever he walked into a room, everything just quieted because they knew he was there and whether they admit it or not, everyone was looking around at him.

He taught me one thing ... if you have something to do, do it. Do it quick, don't worry about it, don't go into anxieties. If you have a decision to make or something to do, do it right now.

I never will forget an example of that. We were going to be on TV with Auburn—big game, obviously. Birmingham had just been named an All-American city. A lot of the founding fathers had a meeting on a Sunday afternoon before the game the next week. Jeff Beard was there from Auburn and Coach Bryant from Alabama, and they talked about how they wanted to get some acknowledgment on TV (and this was an Alabama home game).

So we all talked about what we could do, and at the end of it, Bryant said that he would call Tom Gallery at NBC and tell him what we had in mind to do. At my house the next morning, about 20 minutes before eight, the phone rang. It was Coach. He said, "John, I spoke with Tom Gallery, he'll be expecting your call later this morning. You tell him what you want to do, I think he'll work with you."

Of all the things he had on his mind to do with the game, that was something that Coach said he would do, and he did it. I feel like I learned something from that.

But it's really hard to say what he was like. I had a stroke in 1980 and he called my wife, he called my daughter, and he wanted to come see me but the doctors didn't want anyone to come. So he wrote me handwritten notes and sent them to me. Then my phone rang one afternoon at home.

"You want some company?"

It was Coach. I told him I did, so he and Billy Varner came out to see me. He asked me how I was feeling and told me that he wanted to hear me talk. I tried talking to him. I'm sure I wasn't talking all that well, but he said I sounded fine. I was on the air shortly after that even though I probably shouldn't have been, because he wanted me to be.

He did things for people like that, that nobody really ever knew. Consequently he could get people to do more than they ever thought they could do. I really think the thing that meant the most to him was seeing an average player reach and be better than average in a key situation. That meant more to him than anything.

John Forney signs a copy of his first book for a fan.

For example, when I did the show with him, I never knew what it was going to be like. We might have gotten beat the day before and I'm thinking how I have to face him, but he'd walk in and say, "Hey buddy, how are you doing? Tell me about so and so." Then there were other times we'd beat somebody 45-7 the previous day, and he'd come in solemn and just say hello and walk on by. I guess he was that way during a game, too; you just never knew what he was going to do.

Jerry Duncan tells a great story about, I think, the Tennessee-Alabama game which took more out of me than any other game I've been involved in, with the rain in Knoxville in 1966. Tennessee led the game 10-0 at the half, and the team went in the locker room just frightened to death and terrified. Bryant came in and said, "Well, we got ém right where we want ém." Duncan asked a teammate if Bryant was watching the same game!

There was an LSU game in Alabama when it just poured rain all morning long, and it just looked awful. I can't tell you how bad it was. The team came out onto the field, and it was still raining. Then Bryant walked out behind them and the clouds parted, and it stopped raining ... literally.

He was an incredible motivator. If he asked you to do anything, even if it was help him look at a stock in the paper, anybody would drop whatever they were doing and try to do something for him. His players did, too.

One year we were going to play Miami, and we were pretty heavy favorites. Miami had a 26-year-old Vietnam War returnee who was a real good linebacker and was getting a lot of publicity because he was a veteran and a good player.

There was a little motel outside Tuscaloosa called Moonwinks, and it's where the team spent the night on Friday night. It just so happened that Layton and I went down early to eat breakfast at Moonwinks; we had no plans to impose at all.

It was an old motel and they had those dividers on tracks in the restaurant. We were eating on one side and heard the team shuffling in on the other side. Coach Bryant got up and talked to the team. He didn't talk about the game, it was more about generalities.

He said to the team, "What you've got is class. You had it when you got here and you have it now. They (Miami) won't beat us, but if something strange happens and they do, you walk off that field with your chin high. Anybody have any questions? Then let's get ready to catch the bus."

> *I rarely got an opportunity to hear John broadcast because they were basically playing about the same time we were. Obviously, he was well-liked in the state of Alabama and did a great job for the university. I enjoyed the little association I had with John, even though it was more on a social level than a professional level.*
>
> & Jack Cristil, Mississippi State University

Nobody said anything and we could hear the chairs move around and the guys get up and start to leave. Then Bryant's voice said, "Oh, wait a minute, wait a minute. I've got one more thing to say. I don't want to read in tomorrow's newspaper how we made an All-American out of that linebacker."

We won the game 30-6.

Coach Bryant was also a man who took the blame when things went bad. I don't know where he learned that, but he really did do that. I'm not sure that he meant it, in all candor, but he certainly gave an imitation that he did.

Jerry Duncan tells another great story about one time, however, when they played Missouri and the Tigers beat the hell out of them in the Gator Bowl, 35-7. We were awful. Bryant started yelling around, "Get Ron Derby! Where the hell's Ron Derby?" (Duncan was a student coach, and Ron Derby had been an offensive tackle and had graduated about three years before.)

Duncan didn't know what to do, so he went up to Sam Bailey and told him that Coach was yelling for someone who had already graduated. Sam said, "I know that he's graduated. You know that, and I know that, but Coach doesn't know it, so don't worry about it."

The Bear Bryant Show

I did a live show with Bear Bryant for six years. It was a lot of fun, but he would say things during the show like: "That thing is sticking out there like a wagon tongue. John, you don't have any idea what a wagon tongue looks like, do you?" I'd start to tell him what I thought it was and he'd just say, "Never mind, never mind."

The man who produced the show was named Frank Taylor, and he had all sorts of secretaries who would have tall stacks of papers with various stats and play-by-plays from the games on them and that sort of thing. I don't think Coach Bryant ever looked at those papers.

As I said we were live and so the only time we had breaks were the first quarter, at the half, and at the third quarter. These breaks were only a minute or minute-and-a-half. Frank would come out at the end of the half and he might say, "We're kind of heavy on the third quarter so let's get into it quick," or something like that. I can't say how many times Frank would come out just before we started and would say, "We're a little short on film for this first quarter so I want you to kill about a minute-and-a-half or two minutes before you get into it."

So the show would start and I would say, "Hello everybody, John Forney and Coach Bryant, Golden Flake, Coca-Cola," and whatever else, then, "Coach, it was fine day in Mississippi at Memorial Stadium."

"Let's get into the film, John," Coach would reply. So what do you do? You get into the film, that's what you do.

(I tell this story at Quarterback Club speeches a lot.) We were in our halftime break one show, and Frank came out and said, "Take about a minute-and-a-half before you get into the third quarter film, we've got a little problem."

Looking at the clock, I knew we had less than a minute before we went back on the air, so I said, "Well, the defense really shut them out in the second half. Do you want to talk about that for a minute, Coach?"

"John, I don't believe so, no."

So in the meantime it's tick, tick, tick, and I said, "We're about midway in the season, and I'm sure everybody wants to know how you feel the season looks to you down the stretch. Do you want to talk about that?"

"John, I don't really think so, I don't believe so."

So I'm looking up, I've got beads of sweat coming down. Coach looked around and started to grin and said, "Well, we gotta talk about something, don't we?"

I have no idea what we talked about, but there we were and somehow we made it through.

Life After the Bear

After Coach Bryant retired, I wondered how much longer he would live, and I think he did, too. At some point he said how he wouldn't live a week without football. He actually made it five weeks.

We've got a long way to go at Alabama before another coach will survive in Coach Bryant's shadow. When Gene (Stallings) was first here, I thought that he'd be the one to take Bryant's place, and I was for him when they hired (Ray) Perkins in 1983. I was certainly still for Gene when they hired him. But I think Gene is a changed man; he's a different man. When he was down here with Bear, if there was anyone as tough as Bryant, it was Gene. Man, he was a killer.

As I mentioned earlier, I began with the Alabama Network in 1953 doing color until 1965 and then play-by-play until 1983 when coach Ray Perkins "retired" me.

I don't really know what happened with Coach Perkins. He chose to make a broadcasting change, and I don't think he had any idea of the anger and resentment and the subsequent outpouring of 'Bama fans for me. I guess the only person more surprised than Ray was me!

Lord knows it was flattering to me and, I guess, gratifying. But it was really awkward because I was primarily in the advertising agency business, so the media explosion (the stories in the sports pages and on the talk shows in Alabama) was actually pretty uncomfortable.

I wrote Ray a letter and told him there were no hard feelings on my part because he had to replace a legend and whatever he felt he ought to do, he had my respect. *Sports Illustrated* ran part of that letter later.

After Perkins left Alabama for the Tampa Bay Buccaneers in the NFL, he told some friends of mine that replacing me was the second biggest mistake he made when coming back to Alabama. (The biggest mistake was taking down Coach Bryant's tower.)

Ray was a very intense guy and he marched to his own drum beat. I believe that we are friends. He has certainly indicated thus, and I hope that's true. I have heard it said about Ray Perkins that if he heard somebody disliked him, he would take the rest of the day off to go all the way across the state to insult them! Ray fought the New York media and the Alabama media; they are both tough.

When Bill Curry came on board as head coach, there was another explosion with plenty of 'Bama fans in shock. I really felt Bill was out of place at Alabama, and Alabama was a wrong place for Bill. He was certainly always nice to me and a true gentleman.

I did a call-in show one season with Bill, and in 1988 the University of Alabama powers-that-be decided to make another change, replacing Paul Kennedy, a good announcer and a very nice person. Tommy Limbaugh was Curry's administrative guy who did a great job of recruiting for Alabama and who, I think, was the big influence in bringing me back to the Alabama microphone.

At the press conference announcing my return, I came up with, I thought, a pretty good line when I said, "As I was saying before I was so rudely interrupted." That got a big play in the press. Unfortunately, I was having some eye trouble and really did not do a very good job behind the mike.

Because of my longevity in the booth, you always accumulate some people against you, and I think a lot of younger people wanted to see somebody younger doing the games. At any rate my tenure was short-lived but for one thing this at least brought me back to the Alabama Network. In 1989 I began doing the pregame show and the next year started doing the call-in show; I've been doing that ever since.

> *I didn't get to know John as well personally as I would have liked, but in the broadcast booth, he was at Alabama during some exciting times with Bear Bryant and the national championships. He was around some incredible Crimson Tide history. John had a huge following at Alabama.*
>
>   ~ Paul Eells,
>   University of Arkansas

THE OPPOSING COACHES

I want to take this time to give coach Shug Jordan credit because he was a helluva guy, and I was very fond of him. When I went to New York, and was up there four years, Auburn was awful. The only really good player they had was Hal Herring. I came back and Coach Jordan had been there one year, and the first game I saw after 1948 was the Auburn game of 1952. Alabama won it that year, but you could just tell there was a remarkable difference when Auburn ran out on the field. They were better conditioned, and I just remember there was a big difference.

Certainly Joe Paterno would be high on the list of opposing coaches. I watched him during one of their national championship seasons. They played a game at Bryant Denny Stadium. I was in my "retirement" years and was sitting on the seventh row behind the Penn State bench. I have never seen a coach into a game as much as Paterno was then. Everything he did, it was just electric to watch him. Penn State beat us 20-3 that year.

Bob Neyland was quite a coach, too. He was absolutely as tough as Bryant was. I met a guy named Jim Honeycutt, who played center for Neyland on Tennessee's championship team. He had talked about Neyland a lot. Bryant had recruited Honeycutt and really worked like a dog trying to get him. He ended up signing with Tennessee. Honeycutt said when he went home he saw Coach Bryant's car outside of his place, and Bryant just told him he wanted to wish him the best.

Anyway, Tennessee was playing Kentucky, and Honeycutt was snapping the ball and felt the presence of someone around him during pregame practice. He looked around and there was Coach Bryant just a few feet away from him. Bryant said, "Honey, you see my All-SEC center over there, Jay Rhodemyer? If you had come with me, you would have been an All-American."

But when Neyland and Frank Thomas (when he was at Alabama) would face each other, it was just like a chess game. It was wonderful to watch them.

Vanderbilt, Tennessee, and the Wishbone

Coach Bryant really loved working with Vanderbilt, and he loved Nashville. It was a major thing for Coach Bryant in his career because when Red Sanders brought him to Nashville he was still raw-boned, country-tough, and mean as a rattle snake. Fred Russell (*Nashville Banner* sports writer) had a lot to do with his happiness because he took Bryant out and played golf and various things like that. In fact, Mary Harmon Bryant (Bear's wife) told me one time that she thought that was the happiest she had ever been in their marriage.

The loss to Vanderbilt in Nashville at Dudley Field in 1968 was tough. I remember that somebody ran the kickoff back for the touchdown, and we ended up losing 14-10. The thing I remember is Bryant leaving the stadium and all these people yelling at him, but he was reasonably serene.

I guess the toughest game on me personally was the 11-10 Alabama win in Knoxville against Tennessee. The Volunteers led 10-0 at half in a driving, driving rain.

Ken Stabler was our quarterback, and we couldn't have won it without him. We scored and then Stabler threw a two-point pass to Wayne Cook, who was a boy from Montgomery, and no one could have knocked him down. He was determined to score, which he did. That made it 10-8.

Then Steve Davis kicked a field goal to make it 11-10 with 1:04 to go in the game. The Tide kicked-off and Dewey "Swamp Rat" Warren threw a pass to Charlie Fulton, who threw a halfback pass to Austin Denny (who later went to the Chicago Bears). Suddenly Tennessee has the ball inside our 10-yard line. It was such a stunning shock that all of this is happening. We made a couple big defensive plays which forced Tennessee to kick (which is all they needed anyway). It was kicked from the hashmark, and I had a perfect line on it. There was a Tennessee trainer in orange rain gear right back of the sidelines. The ball was snapped and the kick started to veer off. Then I saw that trainer just drop his head to the ground, and I didn't even wait on the signal I just started yelling, "It's no good! It's no good! It's no good!" What a game!

Another big game was when we unveiled the wishbone and took it to the University of Southern California. Before we left Alabama, Bryant had Charlie Thornton contact us. So Doug Layton and I went down, and they gave us a little wishbone class to let us know what it was. But we had to absolutely swear that we wouldn't say anything.

Layton and I were saying later how we were afraid we'd say something in our sleep or be out eating chicken and yell out, "Wishbone!"

Anyway, I went to the Southern California Sports Luncheon while we were out there. Mike Walden, who did the play-by-play for Southern Cal, came up to me after the lunch and asked me if things were pretty much the same for us. I told him it was and just flat-out lied to him through my teeth.

We got to the contest, and Bryant had sent up word that he didn't want "wishbone" mentioned at all until it was actually run. Doug

The Sportscaster's Dozen

Forney was always comfortable behind the microphone.

and I laughed, because probably the closest station to us was New Orleans and how were they going to get word back that quickly? Well, we won the game 17-10 which was Bryant's 200th win, and the start of the wishbone era where he won 100 games in a 10-year period.

Victory #314

I called Coach Bryant's 314th victory which came at Penn State. It was a fascinating thing because they tape recorded Bryant on all of his pregame stuff. There were 85,000 people in Happy Valley Stadium, and we came out and looked like the Green Bay Packers in their heyday, leading 24-3 in no time flat. It was incredible.

What Bryant had done, and this thing was taped, is tell the guys he wanted them to play the game like they were two touchdowns behind, regardless of the score. He told his friends that he didn't want them to shoot a scared stick. He had said, "I wanted the coaches, players, everyone, to be balls out; just giving it all they had and not trying to guard anything." And they did.

There was a time-out called with just a few seconds left in the first half, and it was the quietest 85,000 people that you ever heard. It was scary. Field announcer Jerry Duncan agreed.

There are certain games like those which stick out in my mind. I never really did any of the national championship bowl games. We didn't do any major bowls because whoever had the TV got the rights to the radio.

That reminds me of the toughest loss, in my mind, we ever had which came in the 1973 Sugar Bowl against Notre Dame. It was one of the best games I've ever seen. We had a chance to win it so many different times. We had an All-American defensive end named LeRoy Cook. When Notre Dame got the ball on the one-foot line and threw the ball out to ice the game, the players on the field said that LeRoy really had a good shot, but his foot slipped in the end zone and he couldn't quite get to the quarterback. But he was really on it. Anyway, Notre Dame won, 24-23. It's tough because we had so many opportunities to win it.

Oops!

We were playing in Jackson, Mississippi, with a hellacious wind, an unbelievable wind during this particular night game. Greg Gantt was our punter, and when he got the ball up in the air, it would go. He kicked one from his own 5-yard line to their 5-yard line; it was an incredible kick! I said, "Well, Doug, there's an example of that wind we've been talking about. That wind is really something."

Doug replied, "Yeah, because you know watching Greg warm up, his balls just seem to hang right in the air."

He looked around at me, and I looked around at him, and we just busted out laughing. That's all we could do.

Layton and I used to bet pretty good on games. (He claims he hasn't lately, and I know I haven't.) Back in the old days, we'd bet a couple hundred a game, or something like that. We were playing Florida State in 1975. Florida State, out of 106 Division I teams, was 106.

Darrell Mudra was the Florida State coach, and he was trying to do something different. He was seated in the press box and directed the game from up there to the coaches on the field. Before the game there wasn't even an official line or point spread, and Doug said, "John, do you have anything on this one today?"

"No, hell, I think 34 points is a homemade line. I think that's too much and I don't want to fool with it. Do you?"

He said, "Yeah, I got 100 on it."

Right before we went on the air he said, "John, I want you to have part of this; you take $20 of my $100 bet."

"OK."

Florida State takes the opening kickoff down and scores, 7-0. It's still 7-0 at the end of the third quarter. We're thinking this is going to be the most stunning upset in the history of football. We're just playing awful. It's still 7-0 with 10-minutes left in the game when a time-out is called.

We're sitting there and I said, "Doug, don't worry, all we need is six quick ones." We didn't get those six quick ones, but in the fourth quarter we kicked a field goal, then they gave us a safety, and we kicked another field goal to win the game 8-7.

By the way, Coach Mudra was so unhappy about being beaten that he kicked a large hole in one of the walls in his particular booth. It was a real gaper. Later on I mentioned this to Coach Bryant, who replied grimly, "I know all about it. I sent him a bill for $600."

I feel like I have to tell this story about another legend, the great Larry Munson, who has broadcast for Vanderbilt, the Atlanta Falcons, and is practically enshrined by the University of Georgia fans. He and I teamed up in the early seventies on a nationwide radio network for a Bluebonnet Bowl broadcast.

Back in 1948 he was doing Class AA Nashville Vols baseball games. And on wire-recreated games, Larry had one of the most involved productions you could ever imagine—sound effects of a crowd, soft drink and peanut sellers, even a block of marble and several sticks that he would use as a bat meeting the ball. One stick for a single and different tones for extra base hits and homers.

The people I worked for in Birmingham were trying to promote our FM, which was new, and they would send me to out of town games on weekends which was the only way you could hear the Barons "live."

So I was sent to Nashville for a big series with the Nashville Vols and the Birmingham Barons. Birmingham won that series, and it was a lot of fun. Anyway, I went to WKDA and asked the receptionist if Larry was around. She told me that I needed to talk to someone else. So the sales manager came out, and I introduced myself and told him I was looking for Larry Munson.

"Oh, haven't you heard?" he asked. You know it's never good when someone says that. The story goes that Larry was doing a ballgame with Little Rock and it was 12-2, and he reached over and thought he hit his cough button and said, "What a f—n' way to make a living."

He hadn't hit his cough button, and those words went out all over Central Tennessee. We went into his office one time later, and he showed me about four telegrams. One of them said, "Dear Larry, it sure is, but dont say it."

BROADWAY JOE AND THE SNAKE

There have been so many incredible athletes at Alabama, and I could pick a couple as the "greatest," but I would have to qualify that. I would have to say Joe Namath when he had two good legs was the best. (Ken) "Snake" Stabler with all of his talent and ability and the guts of a burglar—it's really a terrible choice to have to make.

But again Joe with two legs, I think, was the best. We played Georgia in Vince Dooley's inaugural and the first game of Joe's senior year and beat the Bulldogs 31-3. It was like boy's playing with a grown man. He was back of the week that week.

Another one of the greatest athletes I ever saw was Ozzie Newsome, who started every game he was at—a total of 48. You can't beat that.

My Favorite Team

People always ask me which was my favorite Alabama team while I was broadcasting. My pick would have to be the 1961 team, the national championship team for Paul Bryant at Alabama.

The 1961 guys were an exceptional group. I felt, and I believe, they bonded closer than any other team did. Ends were Bill Battle and Tommy Brooker; tackles were Billy Neighbors and Bill Rice; guards were Jimmy Sharpe and George "Butch" Wilson (who could also play flankerback); center was Lee Roy Jordan; quarterback was Pat Trammell; halfback was Billy Richardson; fullback was Mike Fracchia (who tore up his knee between his junior and senior years, or else he would have been a cinch All-American and maybe a Heisman Trophy winner).

Substitution rules back then allowed to replace one player offensively and defensively, and Darwin Holt subbed for the late Pat Trammell at linebacker. I might add that Coach Bryant would put Pat on the field in the prevent defense. Pat would simply stand in an aloof manner about 35 yards behind the line of scrimmage. No one ever broke through the line of scrimmage or caught a pass, which was fortunate for their health. Pat would have handled it with dispatch, as they say.

Going into the ninth game of the season, the Tide were undefeated and ranked No.2 behind Texas. 'Bama was in a tough, tense game against Georgia Tech when the public address announcer reported that Texas Christian University had upset Texas, 6-0. Shortly thereafter Fracchia took a pitch from Trammell, went around right end behind a great block from Butch Wilson and scored. Alabama won 10-0 (their only halfway close game of the year) and became No.1 in the United States.

The next week they clinched the season with a big win over Auburn. Frank Taylor arranged for a celebratory cake for the last Sunday show, and Alabama won all the honors, climaxing the year with a hard 10-3 win over a tough Arkansas team.

"The" Comebacks

There have been a lot of great comebacks over the years; maybe as many great games as there have been great athletes.

I really would have to go back to 1938, though, when I was just a kid. It was a game against Vanderbilt when they had good teams and were substantially ahead of us. Alabama came back and scored three times in the fourth quarter, and back then you didn't score at will like some teams can do today. We beat the Commodores that day, 25-21.

There was one game we kind of got robbed of, up at Penn State when we had a pass go into the end zone, and one of our players caught it, but they say he was out of bounds. He was really in. Penn State beat us, 34-27. But the thing about that game was that Penn State was up 34-7 in the fourth quarter. Even though we didn't win, it was still quite a comeback.

ADVICE

So much has changed over the years that it makes it tough to give advice to aspiring broadcasters. I think you have to be pretty good at being a talk show host in sports in addition to having play-by-play talents. I think young broadcasters should read, especially sports books, and they should tape and listen to people that they like. There is a guy here in Birmingham named Lee Davis who has an incredible memory and is a super, unbelievable trivia expert in practically any sport. I don't think Lee will ever be a play-by-play man, but he can make a living in sports broadcasting.

> *John was a very good friend of mine. He was a talented gentleman. John symbolized the Alabama spirit and accurately represented the Tide.*
>
> ~ *John Ferguson, Louisiana State University*

I think sports talk shows have their place. I guess I better say that since I have one here on Saturday mornings. But at the same time I think some of them can get carried away and overdone. Some of them need to pause before putting foot in mouth in many cases.

IMPACTING A STATE

I didn't used to think about the impact I've had on people, but I do now. It means a lot more to me that I did have an effect on people, because it was a unique time in football and a unique time in Alabama, and I was a very, very integral part of it. I am truly grateful to have been, because it was something really special.

Ralph Hacker, the long time announcer for the Kentucky Wildcats, told me he would tune in to an Alabama night game and when I said, "It's football time in Dixie!" his excitement tempo reached a peak. That made me feel good hearing that from a peer.

Another pleasant thing happened at the Birmingham Quarterback

Club in 1996 when Tim Brando—one of the best of the new breed broadcasters—spoke. Tim does a marvelous job of imitating some of the better known voices, and interrupted himself to say that there was a gray haired gent in the back of the room who had some great broadcasts in the past. It was me, and the ovation from people who knew me was most gratifying.

When Alabama was on TV, it was a big, big deal. But when we weren't on, then I was it with the radio broadcast. It really makes you feel humble and grateful knowing that. I've had a lot of guys tell me about how last fall their dad died and how they used to listen to me together. That really means a lot to me.

If I'm to be remembered, I hope that people remember that for several brief shining moments, I was the voice that brought Alabama football from field to home, all over the state and all over the South.

Editor's Note: On July 31, 1997, John Forney died of cardiac arrest in Birmingham after attending the SEC Media Days. He was 70.

Bob Fulton
UNIVERSITY OF SOUTH CAROLINA

Broadcasting is something I always wanted to do—or at least from the time I was six or seven years old and would throw a tennis ball against the side of the house, and pretend I was broadcasting a ballgame. In fact, one of the prophesies in my high school annual was that I would be a major league baseball announcer, which turned out to be true.

> *Imagination is more important than knowledge.*
> ~ Albert Einstein

At the age of seven, I wanted to be a baseball broadcaster. I didn't think about football; I thought about baseball. Actually, when I was growing up, there weren't a lot of games broadcast. The Phillies, for example, didn't have any broadcasts at all because they were so bad. They played at Baker Bowl in Philadelphia that seated 15,000 people, and they never sold it out. That's how bad they were. All the attention was on Shibe Park where the Philadelphia A's had all those great teams under Connie Mack in the late 1920s and early 1930s, with guys like Jimmie Foxx, Bob Johnson, Mickey Cockrane, Mule Haas, and Lefty Grove.

So I went to as many games as I could, and I would sit in the stands and broadcast the games to myself. This is what really helped me, I think, in recreations later on, because I had done so much stuff just sitting in a room or in the yard. I practiced all the time, so it was really just a matter of being able to match what I could see and putting it with what I had learned.

I got into the business in 1942, while living in a suburb of Philadelphia, Pennsylvania. There was an ad in the *Philadelphia Enquirer* for a broadcaster in Camden, New Jersey, at WCAM. It was a station that shared time with two other stations. Never having done a bit of radio work, I answered the ad and heard from them.

I was as nervous as a cat. I went to Camden for the audition, and WCAM's studio was on the 18th floor at City Hall. The night I went there must have been 30 or 40 other guys in there, and I choked. I just knew there was no way I would be hired there, so I left.

I got back on the elevator, went downstairs and across the street to the all-night coffee shop. As I was sitting there, I realized I had nothing to lose, so I went back for the audition. I read the copy they gave me, and I was brutal; I was so bad.

The guy came in there and asked me if I could ad-lib some sports ... now, he's talking my language. I sat there and did a make-believe baseball game for about five minutes. (It just so happened that they were not only looking for a straight announcer, but they were also looking for a backup sports man to do horse racing and wrestling.) I was invited back for another audition, and I got the job ... for $25 a week.

The money wasn't a big deal, but Camden was right across from Philadelphia and it was a launching pad for announcers into WCAU, KYW, WIP, and all the big stations in Philadelphia. So some guys would have worked there for nothing just to get their foot in the door, because in those days everyone was into radio since there was no television.

That's how I got started.

Bill and Ted's Adventure

When I was growing up there were two top sports announcers in the country: Ted Husing and Bill Stern.

Ted was the top man for CBS, and was probably the most profane man I've ever been around. I didn't work with him, but I worked next to him doing horse racing in New Jersey. He had a great voice; he could even make your telephone number sound good. I heard him do tennis matches, and he was great. They used to say if you're a coach, you'll listen to Ted Husing; if you're just a sports fan, you'll listen to Bill Stern.

Bill was the first real (what I would call) "showbiz" announcer. He had a great voice with great inflection. He never let what was happening truthfully stand in his way. He would do anything with a ballgame, to the point where he was almost recreating some of the live games he was doing. That's why when television came in, those guys were in trouble ... because you could check them out.

Those two were at the top, then Graham McNamee, who did some top boxing bouts in those days. I would say they were the three top

Bob Fulton (left) was honored at Clemson University during his final broadcast there in 1994. Longtime friend and legendary Tiger announcer Jim Phillips prepares to make the presentation.

men in the business, but for a long time you thought only in terms of Ted Husing or Bill Stern.

Then Gordon McClendon came around with the Liberty Network out of Dallas with the recreated baseball games in the late 1940s and early 1950s. He did a great job at recreating, but I feel I did better. That is one thing I could do, and I added so much to what he did. I used to do games sitting in bed! Recreations were the best thing I did. I make fantasy tapes now because of it. It was just a talent I had; we all have talent, and that's one thing I could do.

I listened a lot to the "Old Scotsman," because he was good, but I thought I did just as good of a job.

Peers and Role Models

In a sense some of the pioneers were my peers. Really, though, my peers would be guys more like Vin Scully, who I knew and worked with, plus Red Barber. There are a lot more that I can't remember, but I remember Barber, and I remember Scully very well.

Vin Scully was a nice guy. But even though I remember him very well, I never really got to know him too well. I told him once that he didn't know the romance of this business. I told him I've done games sitting in trees or out in the middle of nowhere, whereas he came right out of Fordham and started doing major league baseball. I'm glad I started right at the bottom, but some of those guys didn't have to do that. Vin is one of them. Don't get me wrong, though, Vin is an excellent announcer.

The man who was my role model was Byrum Saam, who did the Philadelphia A's and then Philadelphia Phillies games. When I was trying to learn something about this business, I would go up to Philadelphia and old Shibe Park. He had one of these booths that jetted out over the field, and you could sit behind him. I would sit back there and listen to him. (I even paid my way in, believe it or not.) Years later when I was doing the "Game of the Day," I ran across him as he was about to close out his career. I said to him, "Byrum, I want to tell you something; when I was a kid and you were up doing the Philadelphia A's games, I used to sit right behind you and listen to you do the games."

He said, "Why didn't you tell me? If you were that interested in broadcasting, I would have gotten you into any game you wanted."

I said, "Well, it's a little late for that now." And we laughed about it.

He was good. Our voices were very similar, and I used a lot of his phrases (nobody's original in this business ... we're all composites of something whether it's good or bad).

I also knew Jack Brickhouse very well. He was a good announcer in the Midwest. My office was next to him at WGN in Chicago. We traveled together a lot as he was doing the television for the Cubs and the White Sox, and I was doing radio for Mutual. I like Brickhouse; I thought he was an excellent announcer.

I'll tell you something about Brickhouse that's interesting. He had done a lot of wrestling, and I asked him if it paid pretty well. He said, "Bob, I make more money doing wrestling than I do in baseball."

I got to know Curtis Gowdy. I knew Curt when he was doing Wyoming basketball, and I was doing Arkansas basketball. He had less preparation for a broadcast than anyone I have ever heard of, but he was very good.

When I was at Mutual, I got to know Mel Allen real well. I thought he was excellent with a great voice for baseball. He never really did any work. His brother would get everything together and put it in the booth, and Mel would walk in two minutes before he went on the air. I would be scrambling around going from dugout to dugout trying to get the lineup together, but Mel's brother got everything together.

Lying to Be a Razorback

Arkansas was my first college job. I lied my way into that one. In fact, I kid you not, I've lied my way into every job, because you had to get started and get that experience.

In the early 1940s I got turned down by the service because I have a bad foot, damaged after a big tube fell on it working in a shipyard one summer when college was over. The job at Arkansas came open, I told them I had some experience, and I got the job.

They weren't doing the whole season then; we just did a few games. But here's the type of schedule I had: I would do a junior college game on a Thursday night for Little Rock Junior College; a high school game on Friday night (we called it the "Pick of the Week"); a University of Arkansas game on Saturday afternoon; fly in a private plane Saturday night to wherever we were going to do an Arkansas Intercollegiate Conference game (for college teams like Monticello and Arkansas Tech); then recreate a Philadelphia Eagles football game on Sunday because the Razorbacks had a former All-American, Clyde Scott, playing for the Eagles. So I was doing five games a week! Today I could barely do one! I was busy, but I loved it. Boy, did I love it.

It was more fun then, than it became later on, because today sports is all about money. I recall when I came to Columbia back in the 1950s, Rex Enright was coaching. After a game, win or lose, we'd all go over to Rex's house and have a good time with a little party. Could you imagine something like that happening today? Of course things change, but today after a game the coach has to be with recruits, he has to do a television show, or whatever. You just don't always have the fun you used to have.

Sneaking into the Ballgame
(Not to Watch ... to Broadcast)

Let me tell you a very, very funny story about how I got into baseball broadcasting. By 1950 I had done everything from basketball and football to horse racing and wrestling, but I had not done baseball. I was living in Little Rock, Arkansas, and got a call from an agency in Denver that handled Coors beer in the Midwest. The guy told me they had just fired a guy in Pueblo, Colorado (a Dodger farm team at the time), and needed an announcer down there. He asked me if I had done baseball. (When he called that day in May, I had just come in from the pool I was burned, and had all this stuff on my face like Noxema to cut the pain down, and I looked like a mess.) I told him I had done baseball and asked him how he knew about me.

"We called Buddy Bostic [a station manager in Waco, Texas], and he said you had fed him a lot of Southwest Conference games when you were at Arkansas, and he gave you high marks," the man told me, then continued, "How about getting one of your live tapes and sending it to me? We need it in a few days because we need to get someone in Pueblo."

> Bob is a true legend. I've had the opportunity of doing the same game with him many times and being in the same booth with him, on one occasion, actually to do a professional game. Bob is one of the true legends in sports broadcasting.
> ⓚ Bob Harris, Duke University

Well, let's see, I had never done baseball in my life! But I got my sound effects together with Little Rock players in mind and ad-libbed a game against Chattanooga. I sent it out to Colorado. (This sounds awfully self-serving) ... I got the job. They were desperate, and the guy never checked my background. I had told him I worked with the Little Rock Travelers for seven years. Up to that point I had never done a live baseball game or a recreation ... never!

So my wife and I got in the car, and we drove to Pueblo. I didn't know anything about baseball's scoring rules. So all the way there when she drove, I would go over the scoring rules; then when I drove, she asked me questions about the rules. By the time we got out to Colorado, I had a fair idea of what the rules were all about (it's a long trip from Little Rock to Pueblo).

When I got there I asked the guy why they fired the announcer before me, Johnny Special. I was told it was Johnny's first year, and he didn't have enough experience. (And I'm sitting there thinking I had never done a game.) Anyway, I finally asked them again what the last straw was for Johnny to get kicked out of there. The guy told me how one night the manager, Ray Hathaway, who was also a pitcher, was getting lit up pretty good on the mound. So Ray the manager decided to take himself out of the ballgame. This is how Johnny Special described it: "Ray Hathaway has decided to relieve himself on the mound."

Johnny was gone right after that.

I got through with a lie all year. But toward the end of the season the organization wanted to get a look at one of their young outfielders, Bill Sharman (who later played basketball with the Boston Celtics), so they moved him from Pueblo to Elmira, N.Y., a Class A team. That way they didn't have to go out to Colorado to watch him, they could stay relatively close to Brooklyn.

When Bill left Pueblo, the club collapsed and lost 23 games in a row. The problem with this was, Little Rock had the record for the most losses, and I started getting calls from everyone (including the *Sporting News*) wanting to know what it was like to broadcast for the two teams with the most losses. Oh, brother! What could I say?

We went up to Denver for the game that would either set a new record or end the streak. We played a 12-inning game against the Denver Bears, and our catcher Merv Dornberg (I'll never forget his name) hit a grand slam home run in the top of the 12th inning to win it and end the streak.

After the game my wife and I went to dinner at a popular place in Denver, and for the first time this thing was finally off my back ... it was like Christmas! But if Merv hadn't hit that grand slam and Denver won the game, my lie would have come out and I would've been in trouble, because when we arrived in Pueblo the newspaper (which had partial ownership of the ballclub) had a full page ad with my picture welcoming me. It said how I was one of the most experienced announcers coming out of the Southwest. Seven years of baseball. "We welcome him to broadcast the Pueblo Dodgers. Tune in tonight on KCSJ, the station of stars."

When I got to the motel, I looked at that and was scared to death. I thought I was in over my head. Luckily the team didn't set the record and Pueblo never found out.

LIFE IN HORNELL

After leaving Pueblo in 1951 (on my own accord), I went to work for a team in Hornell, New York, it was a Class D Dodger farm club. It was another case of the guy getting fired shortly after the start of the season. Hornell was a railroad town. One of the other teams in the Pony League with Hornell was the Bradford Phillies.

Bradford had a steam train that ran right behind the ballpark. When this one fella' was working the games, on the recreation he would put the sound effects of a steam train. Well, he left and this new guy came in, but what he didn't know (everyone in Hornell knew because it was a railroad town) was that they had switched from steam trains to diesel trains. So the first game he does when they are playing at

Fulton (far right) being inducted into the University of South Carolina Hall of Fame in 1994.

Bradford, he's using a steam train sound effect. They got calls all day because of that. He was through. He had to leave because they were really trying to create an illusion then that they were doing the games live, but it exploded in this guy's face and he left.

So I got up there, and near the end of the season another team from a small town, Wellsville, and Hornell were fighting for the pennant. We went over to Wellsville—we didn't have a curfew then. Their ballpark was sort of way down in a hollow, and beyond the fence there was some type of pond or river. Anyway, we started the game in front of a packed crowd, and it was a close game. Around 10:00 a thick fog started rolling in over the field. It got so bad I could hardly see beyond the second baseman toward centerfield. The umpires should have probably called the game, but they didn't. We got to the 12th inning, and it was about 1:00 in the morning, and we got a couple runs to take the lead.

Wellsville came up in their half of the 12th, and loaded the bases with two outs and their big gun at the plate. What each of our ballplayers had done was put a baseball in their pocket. This guy teed off on one, and by the crack of the bat you could tell it was out of the ballpark. All of a sudden here comes our centerfielder, Andy Greener, out of the fog holding the (or a) ball up. Umpire signals it's an out and Hornell won the game. It was almost a riot; they had to get the police to protect the umpires. As my wife and I were leaving the ballpark, there was a long hill going out of Wellsville, and I looked down and could see all the fans out in centerfield with flashlights trying to find the ball. They weren't going to find that ball in the outfield, because it was hit so hard it was out in the swamps somewhere.

Because of that game, the next night we won the pennant. By the way, Andy later admitted that he never knew where that ball was.

Major League Baseball and the Mutual Network

In 1952 I came to Columbia, South Carolina to do the Columbia Reds games on WNOK radio and WNOK-TV. While I was doing the Reds games, the president of the league was Dick Butler who later became president of the Texas League and then became the man who was head of the umpires in the American League.

Butler liked the work I did, and he told me once that I shouldn't stay at Columbia too long; that I should move and go some other place. I don't know if he was trying to get rid of me, or what.

Paul Jonas was the sports director at the Mutual Network at the time, and Butler was a good friend of his. Mutual fired a man, and had to get somebody to replace him. Word got out that they were looking for someone, and they received a bunch of tapes. Everybody wanted to go there. Butler told Jonas that he had a guy in South Carolina that he thought could do the job. So I made a tape and sent it up there to Chicago.

It was interesting how they picked the finalist in this. They got down to seven or eight tapes, went out and got a group of people who represented various cross-sections of people, and brought them into the studio. The eight tapes were played for this group of people, and they were told to pick the man. Luckily, I got the job.

It was not an easy time, because I worked with Al Helfer who was not an easy man to work with. It was difficult because he wanted a friend of his to get the job and not me. So when I went there, it was a very cool reception. I was nervous to start off, because here I am on a network with over 450 stations in the country and on the Armed Forces Network.

Just to give you an idea of what Helfer was like, I was in the bar one night in St. Petersburg, Florida, at Treasure Island with [Harry] Caray who lived in the same hotel with us, and Helfer. Well, Helfer kept drinking these double stingers. When Al went upstairs, Harry turned to me and said he counted Helfer drinking 16 stingers. The bartender said, "A little bit too much; he had 14." I'll never forget this ... 14 stingers! But he weighed about 320 pounds. He was a huge man. He would be on a diet and be drinking doubles in the morning.

One of the funniest things about Mutual is that they wouldn't broadcast in major league cities. So my wife in Chicago couldn't listen to the games, but her sister in South America listened all the time.

Anyway, we had Al Helfer, then once a week we had Dizzy Dean and Buddy Blattner. Buddy was my favorite to work with from Mutual. He had played with the Phillies. We did a lot of games together. Buddy would work on off-days, outside of Wednesdays when Dizzy wasn't working. Buddy and Diz never got along too well.

Dizzy had an ego which was unbelievable, and you had to play to his one-way street. Blattner, on the other hand, wanted to get together for breakfast the morning of a game to go over the two teams.

I'll tell you a funny story about Blattner. We're over in Detroit, staying in a hotel there. They had a ping pong table downstairs, and Buddy wanted to play me and he offered to do so left-handed. We got down there, and he cleaned me out—beat me left-handed. I asked him how long he had been playing. He said, "I'll tell you honestly, I was the world champion in doubles one year with another guy." They were the best in the world, and I had felt sorry that he was playing left-handed with me!

He was a genuinely nice guy; I really liked Buddy. We had a very nice relationship. It was a very nice relief going from Helfer, whom I did not like, to Buddy.

With Mutual I was stationed in the West and worked out of Chicago, where I covered Chicago, Detroit, Milwaukee, Cleveland and Cincinnati. How it worked is like this: if they had a game in the East, I went on standby to Milwaukee or Cleveland, or wherever, in case the East game was rained out. When the game was in the West, then there was someone on standby in the East. Helfer was the swing man and worked both the East and West.

We had some interesting situations like once when there was a game scheduled in the East, and they had a rain situation. I was in Chicago at the time, and they called me and said you have to go find a game. So I called the Cubs—keeping in mind that the Cubs would rain out if even a cloud moved in. They wanted to play doubleheaders to draw more people and make more money.) The Cubs told me they didn't think they were going to play that day. So I hopped a plane and went to Detroit. Well, wouldn't you know it, Detroit was rained out and the Cubs played. This type of situation happened twice while I was with Mutual that year.

There was a lot of pressure with Mutual, though, because you had to find games. I had a guy at the weather bureau I worked closely with, and I had a guy at United Airlines so we could jump on a plane in a hurry. But the pressure was in making the connection, not in doing the games. I was nervous at first when I was doing the games, but after a few I got used to it. We covered all the teams and had a tremendous audience.

I enjoyed working in Chicago. While we were there I got to know Chicago Cubs announcer Harry Caray, because I worked beside their booth a number of times, especially at Wrigley Field. He was with the St. Louis Cardinals at the time.

Harry was probably the hardest worker of any broadcaster I ever knew. He kept the best set of statistics; if some guy hit a foul ball to right field, Harry knew how many he had hit in the season. On the air he really pumped it.

Away from the mike he was a nice guy. I still like him and the way he does games today. He's an anachronism to what's going on in this business, but I like him. He's from my day. What he does with television is give you a radio broadcast. He tells you a pitch was a curve ball, but you can see that. Heck, you can probably see it better than he can because he's had five Budweisers (although I understand he doesn't drink anymore because of this heart problem). I really like him.

> *Bob was a great announcer, and he is a great friend. We worked for the same guy, Dick Frick, who controlled the Texaco Gasoline account. Some of the voices in this book were so outstanding, they were what we considered a network-caliber voice. When we all started, if a guy had a network voice, we would say that guy's got an NBC voice, or a CBS voice. If a guy had one of those, he could do anything and any kind of play-by-play. Bob Fulton had one of those voices.*
>
>   ❧ Larry Munson, University of Georgia

We had "Mutual's Game of the Day" in Columbia, South Carolina, a couple of times. At Mutual they didn't feel too good about competing with the minor leagues, but they were with their games in the afternoon. To compensate for this, they would visit a minor league game during a major league off-day. Monday used to always be an off-day.

For instance, when I was at Mutual we would go to Wichita or Jacksonville or in Iowa someplace; and we would put on a "Meet the Mayor" and have parades, and all that type of stuff. Mutual was the world's largest network in those days. I was humbled by that. Ever since then if people say I'm a legend or a celebrity here, I say I'm not. But for that one year, I felt like I was at the top ... it was nice.

My Highlight: Indians/Yankees, 1954

The main highlight from my time with the Mutual Network was in 1954 when the Indians clinched the pennant in Cleveland. There were 85,000 people at the game; it was the largest crowd they had ever had at Municipal Stadium. Normally the bullpen was beyond the centerfield fence (where Larry Doby used to lean over and make those great catches). That day there wasn't any bullpen because it was all fans. Unbelievable!

Al Helfer and I worked only the first game of the doubleheader that day, then I left. When I left that day, I rode with Mel [Allen]. He had some commitment back in New York that night, so he left, also. Anyway, that's the day the Indians won the pennant.

The funny thing about all of that is what happened to me with my father-in-law at the end of the season. He was a lawyer in Little Rock, Arkansas, and I was working out of Chicago. He called me one day and after the Giants had won and said, "Bob, I'm going to put some money down on the Series. Who should I bet on?"

I said, "Floyd, the Indians have pitchers Bob Feller, Bob Lemon, Mike Garcia, Early Wynn, and Ray Narleski in the bullpen (which they never had to use, because pitchers back then pitched nine innings; it wasn't like it is today with the bullpens). There is no way anyone can beat this staff."

You know what happened, don't you? The Giants won it in four straight games.

The relationship between my father-in-law and I went downhill from there ... I can guarantee it. He called me after that last game and just gave it to me! They still might have had the best staff ever in baseball.

The Indians had a great team. The one player I remember so much is Doby. I saw him make catches that were just unbelievable. On that team Bobby Avila was the second baseman, and Al Rosen was at third base. I don't remember all the players, but those are a few that stick out.

I did a lot of games out of Cleveland. I liked to work there except in April when it was so cold they were chopping up wood in the stands and building fires. The wind coming off the lake and straight into the ballpark ... it was bad!

The Yankees

A couple of the Yankees I remember from that 1954 season include Bobby Richardson (who has since become a good friend of mine after coaching at South Carolina for several years) at second base, and Mickey Mantle in centerfield.

Speaking of the Yankees, though, I had mentioned going to Philadelphia games when I was growing up. Doing that I got to see some great teams and remarkable players.

The best Yankee team I ever saw was the one with Babe Ruth, Lou Gehrig, Bill Dickey, and that crowd. They were incredible! Dickey was the catcher on that team. I got to know him when we were both in Little Rock, Arkansas. He told me he never got an injury to his "meat" hand ... never. But then again, he had hands twice the size of my hands, and mine aren't small.

I saw Ty Cobb and Tris Speaker play when I was about 5 years old, and my father would take me up to Shibe Park to sit on that 75-cent bleacher. Philadelphia for a long time had the "Blue Law" which was no Sunday baseball, so my father and I would go up there Saturday and get in line early so we could get a good seat in the 75-cent bleachers. That's all we could afford in those days.

When the Yankees would come to town with Ruth, Gehrig and that gang, and Lefty Grove pitching for Philadelphia ... to see a Gehrig go up against Grove was worth the price of admission. It was either hit out of the ballpark or three strikes and you're back on the bench. Connie Mack was coaching the Philadelphia A's at that time and Joe McCarthy was coaching New York. That was the best Yankee team I can remember.

The Managers and Players of 1954

I got to know Eddie Stanky the St. Louis manager pretty well, but he was disliked by all of us because he would never give us the starting lineups. We'd ask Stanky for it, and he'd say he didn't have time to give it to us. So Jack Brickhouse and I decided we had enough of that so we used to make up our own lineups.

As far as other managers are concerned, I got to know Freddie Hutchinson from Detroit pretty well. I say you got to know them "well" which means you'd see them every 10 days or so, and they were always nice. They would say they remember you, but most of them didn't.

One thing that was nice about that arrangement at Mutual was that we moved from league to league, so we got to know more people. League to league is how they should play today on a regular basis ... not just a few games.

I also got to know Al Lopez at Cleveland pretty well. I can definitely remember the broadcaster in Cleveland at the time ... Jimmy Dudley. I felt for the poor guy who worked with him because Jimmy was bad; not to me but to this poor fella' he had working for him. I used to go down to his booth to get the Western Union tape, because Dizzy (Dean) bet on EVERY game. He'd bet at least $5,000 a day, which in those days was a lot of money. He'd make me go down to Dudley's booth and get the scores off the ticker. When I went down there, I would just stand in the back and listen to Jimmy give this guy with him all kinds of grief ... it was terrible.

Dizzy; I could talk about Dizzy from now until we all went to bed tonight, because he was a character.

Dizzy Dean

Dizzy was like a big kid; that's the best way to describe him. If Dizzy liked you, he would do anything in the world for you. If he disliked you, he would do anything in the world to hurt you.

The year before I was with Mutual, Dizzy and Helfer didn't get along. They were two big egos, and they got in a fight in New York in a taxi cab one day. Both of them rolled out of the cab fighting each other in the street in the middle of New York City!

I arrived next year and of course Dizzy could no longer work with Helfer, but I worked between them. So every time I was with Dizzy he told me what kind of a jerk Helfer was, and every time I was with Helfer he told me what kind of a jerk Dizzy was.

I will never forget I was going to Cleveland one night near the end of the season, and Al and I were in a cab getting ready to leave from Chicago when he started off on Dizzy again. I finally got tired of it, so I told Helfer, "Al, I'm sick and tired of all this, but I haven't said a thing about it."

That was the end of our relationship. He hardly spoke to me for the next few weeks, until we left for Milwaukee—the last time I saw Helfer—after we had done a game there and were getting ready to go back to Chicago. We stopped at a restaurant, and he looked across the table (he was a very emotional person) and said, "Bob, I want to tell you something ... I've been a real jerk to you." And he started

Fulton is greeted by fans at a banquet following his induction in the South Carolina Hall of Fame in 1990.

to cry; tears were coming down his face.

"I just want to apologize to you," he continued, "You were pretty good, you hung in there with me, and you helped me." (I used to give him notes all the time to help him; anything to build some relationship with him.)

That was the last I saw of Helfer. I left him at the airport in Chicago, and he died a few years later.

The End of My Mutual Days

The unusual thing is how things work out for you. I couldn't make up my mind at first whether or not I was going back after the first year. About a month before the crew had to leave for spring training, Paul Jonas called me and said, "Bob, Helfer is quitting because of health, and we're going to make you the number one man. We don't feel the other guy is a heavyweight, and we think you can do it. You'll be stationed in New York."

I thought that sounded great, but at the same time, when I came to Columbia I had to leave my wife the day our first child was born. Now, they're making this great offer, but she's due again and I would be leaving about the time she was to go to the hospital.

When Jonas called, I honestly didn't know what I was going to do. To add to that, he called the day I had to make a decision. I was in the apartment by myself when the phone rang at 1:00. I swear I wasn't sure when I walked across that room to answer the phone, what I was going to say. Jonas said, "Bob, we're all set. We'll be staying at Treasure Island right outside of St. Petersburg."

I said, "Paul, I'm going to stay here." I thought he was going to fall over. He asked if I was kidding. I told him I wasn't and explained how my wife at the time (she has died of cancer since then) was pregnant, and how I just didn't think it was right for me to take the job.

The travel was so bad; I figured I went 145,000 miles in six months on airplanes! Back then, the planes weren't as good as they are now, either.

I second-guessed myself at the time, but since then I haven't. There have been times I have had regrets about that decision, but not a lot. Once you make it to the major leagues, if you keep your nose clean, you're going to have a job. What really upset me was at the end of the season when I decided not to go back, Bill McKechnie was the General Manager in Cincinnati, and I had worked for the Cincinnati franchise when I was in Columbia, so I knew Bill. When I was at Mutual I also did a lot of games at Cincinnati.

Bill called me in Columbia and said, "I want to tell you something, and this may be bad news to you but yet there's some good news about it. When we needed an announcer in 1954 near the end of the season, your name was the first name that came up because we knew you from your work in Columbia and with Mutual. In fact, we were ready to hire you until a guy on our board said that we couldn't get you because we wouldn't be able to pay you what Mutual was paying you."

"Let me tell you," I said, as I was starting to laugh, "I worked for a tight-fisted sports director, and all you would have had to say to me is, 'Cincinnati's open ... come on in.' I would have been there regardless of what you were paying me, because I love the town and I love chili, and it's the chili capital of the world."

When he told me that, I was sick; I would have gone there in a heartbeat. I can understand where they were coming from, though, because people think if you're at a network you're making a lot of money, but that wasn't necessarily the case.

I don't think a "Game of the Day" format could work today,

because there is too much television in games today. In the 1950s there weren't a lot of broadcasts in major league baseball from a network basis in the afternoon or at night mainly because they didn't play a lot of night games at that time. One reason I was stationed in Chicago is because we had nothing but afternoon games at Wrigley Field. Of course, with the White Sox it was different.

I don't think that format would work today because the rights would be too high and so many of these ballclubs have contracts that wouldn't allow for it.

Moving Up to Columbia

Going back to 1952, the year after I worked in Hornell, New York, I decided I didn't want to go back there or back to Pueblo, Colorado. There was an ad in *Broadcasting Magazine*, which back in those days was the magazine you got jobs through. I saw the ad, sent in a tape to South Carolina and also one to Columbus, Georgia.

There were three finalists for the job at Columbus, and I actually thought I had it. The father of the guy they gave the job to was on the board of directors for the ballclub. That knocked me and the other guy out of the running. So I called USC, and they told me they had three finalists for the job and wanted to meet with me. I got the job.

That's how I got into Columbia, South Carolina, ostensibly only to do baseball, and then I was going to return to Arkansas for football and basketball. After the baseball season was over, they came to me and asked if I would consider working at the university doing football and basketball. My wife loved Columbia, I liked it, and I was tired of bouncing around. So we decided to stay.

Not only did I do baseball, basketball, and football at the university; I also did boxing, some soccer, and a lot of other things.

When 1965 came up, I was having problems keeping the television show. The problem at the university for me, during my 43 year tenure there, is the fact that I worked for nine football coaches, 10 basketball coaches, 13 athletic directors, and eight university presidents. So I would have to redefine myself every time a new guy came in there.

For instance, when Jim Carlen came in there to coach football, he wanted to use his own man for television; so that knocks me out of that box. Believe it or not, I lost the show nine different times. It's not right, but I just hung in there.

In 1965 I lost the television show. Marvin Bass was the football coach at the time. At the same time, I had an opportunity to go to work at Georgia Tech. I called Marvin and told him that I wanted to stay at South Carolina, but I wasn't going to if they were going to take the television show away. He told me he would work on it, but he had no clout with the board, so I lost the show. I decided I would still do basketball at USC (which I did) and football at Tech. Had they let me keep the television at South Carolina I would have stayed. But they didn't, and so I didn't.

I worked with a guy for a few years named Johnny Evans. Johnny was at a station in Charlotte, North Carolina, and he's the one who got me the job at Georgia Tech in 1965. Georgia Tech was looking for a man, they called Johnny, and he recommended me. I sent a tape in and got the job.

I liked Georgia Tech because it was a very professional-type operation. They had a large network around the country, they paid me well, we traveled first class, and we stayed at the best places. Football coach Bobby Dodd was one of the most unusual people I had ever been around. Because of the size of the network, that was one place you had to broadcast straight down the line without any type of bias. I worked at Tech in 1965 and 1966 with Al Ciraldo. The two years I was there, we went to bowl games which was great because they took me and my family ... it was nice.

Dodd wrote me a great letter when I left, one of the nicest I've ever received. He used to tape every game and listen to them. I've been to his practices, and he'd be sitting at one end of the field talking to someone from a national magazine while the team was down at the other end practicing. I know some of his former players who say they never worked hard during the week, but when the bell rang on Saturday afternoon, Bobby Dodd took over, ran the ballclub and they'd beat you. But he never sat with anyone on the plane or the bus, and once you got to the hotel, he would disappear and you wouldn't see him the whole time we were there.

Before I came back to USC, I was offered the job at the University of Georgia. Texaco handled the network at Georgia, and the announcer had left. So the people at Texaco (who had also handled the network for a time at South Carolina) told me they were going to give me the job if I wanted it. I decided if I was going to make a move, it was going to be back to Carolina full time because I missed it. So I turned down Georgia.

Tech was alright but when you do the games then jump on a plane and go back to the other place, you don't feel like you're a part of everything. They made it tough, though, when they offered me a 10-year contract. In this business that is unheard of.

Paul Dietzel was the coach at South Carolina at the time, and I told him I would come back if they would make me a part of the athletic department, with all of the benefits that go with it. That was a smart move on my part, because it has really paid off for me. I got the television show back (but then lost it again in about three years).

The problem I had at Carolina was the constant turnover, and I think it hurt the school. Look at the University of Nebraska, for instance ... who do you think of when you think of football coaches? Bob Devaney and Tom Osborne. I can't even think of any other coaches at Nebraska. Georgia Tech was the same way up through Bobby Dodd, but after him it was a revolving door. But Dodd was only the fourth coach there, dating back to the days of [John] Heisman. Where you don't find a lot of turnover, you find pretty good athletic departments and pretty good teams.

I think now at South Carolina they have the right people in the right place. I think Brad Scott is excellent for the football program, and I think Eddie Fogler is probably one of the best basketball coaches in the country. Mike McGee is a real pro as an athletics director.

I'm not saying it means a whole lot to me, even though I miss some of it. This is true of a guy who's gone through it so many years as I did ... you miss some of the things that used to be. You used to be able to take your girl and carry a blanket to the ballgame. If you do it now, you're almost arrested because they think you're messing around—I'll say tongue-in-cheek.

When I stopped, I was burned out. I told basketball coach Eddie Fogler, "Eddie, in the basketball games I started looking at the clock in the last 15 minutes or so, not to see if we had time to get back into the ballgame but rather to see how much longer I had to work." When it gets to that point, it's time you leave; that's one of the reasons I left. It wasn't the same anymore.

Frank McGuire: The Fiery Gamecock

I spent 16 years with Frank McGuire. He is one of the most interesting people I have ever met. He was an Irishman, and he marched to a different drummer's beat, I'll tell you. I could talk all night on Frank. I don't really know where to start with him.

Frank and I were very close friends. We traveled together for 16 years. We always got a suite of rooms together, and he taught me a lot.

He taught me a lot about how to handle defeat. He was one of the best. Although at times I had seen him falter after a loss, but usually after a win or a loss we would get on the plane and it was party time. Once we got on the plane we wouldn't talk about the game at all. He demanded that on the plane I sit across the aisle from him.

I only saw Frank pick up a piece of chalk once in our 16 years. We were in the studios at Channel 10 here in Columbia, and were going to do a deal where he would diagram some things on a chalkboard. Frank got a little chalk dust on his hands, and it looked like he thought he was never going to be able to get it off. It was obvious he hadn't had it on there very much. That's the only time in my life I saw Frank pick up any chalk.

> *I didn't know Bob personally, but I know of his work from baseball's "Mutual Game of the Day." He also did a wonderful job with South Carolina. He gave the Gamecocks a touch of class that they might not otherwise have had.*
>
> *&. Otis Boggs, University of Florida*

There is another absolutely true story about Frank McGuire that I love to tell at various talks. There was a guy named Bob Zawoluk who lived in New York City and later turned out to be an All-American. He was a great high school ballplayer. McGuire wanted him, but the boy's mother wanted him to get out of town. This is when McGuire was coaching at St. John's University. Coach felt he had to get this guy.

Frank called the boy's mom and said, "I want to come over and talk to you about your son." She agreed, so he went over there, and they talked for about an hour about how she wanted her son to leave town and that type of thing. When they finished she asked him, "Coach, do you dance?" He told her he did, and she asked him to dance.

This lady had one of those old RCAs with the horn-looking speaker coming out of the top of it. She cranked that old 78 up and they danced for about half an hour. And Frank was a good ballroom dancer. They finished dancing, and as he was getting ready to leave, she asked if he wanted to come back the next day.

He went there three days in a row, and all they did was dance for those three days. Around Thursday of that week he went back down to St. John's, and when he walked in, the athletics director asked how things were going with Zawoluk.

Frank said, "Can you dance?"

By the way, to finish the story, Frank got Zawoluk, and he was a great strong player and became an All-American.

During the 1976-1977 season at South Carolina, we were supposed to play St. Bonaventure (I still don't think the Bonnies know how I got him to cancel this game). We were playing a game in Philadelphia against Temple and won the game by one point, 49-48. That gave Frank 499 wins.

We were scheduled to go to New York and play St. Bonaventure the next day, which could be a tough place to play. We had played at St. Bonaventure a couple years before and were lucky to win. They had some good teams, and we figured he probably wouldn't win his 500th up there. Plus I really didn't want to go there to play.

Another friend of mine and I worked on Frank and said, "Frank, you don't want to get your 500th win in the Pit, you want to get it at home. There's a lot of snow around here, so just tell them we can't get up there."

Well, St. Bonaventure is a Catholic school, and Frank is Catholic. And he knew all the priests up there. He didn't call them; he had Tom Price our sports information director call them. They were upset because they had the game sold out. They even offered for the state police to go to Buffalo with a bus to escort the team. They wanted to speak to Coach McGuire, but he wouldn't talk to them.

As a result the game was cancelled. We went home, and he got his 500th win in Columbia against The Citadel, 85-66.

I would say McGuire was a street fighter. He had grown up in a family of 13, and he had to learn early in life to take care of himself. His father was a cop, so Frank knew all the police in New York. He knew the rough element in New York, and he knew the mafia in New York. Some of his friends were mafia people.

When he was with his ballclub, he was in charge. During a game nobody called a time-out except McGuire, nobody did anything except for Frank.

There really wasn't anything for sports people in this state to cheer for until Frank got here. University of South Carolina basketball became a religion in this state. The following he had here was just fantastic.

He was one of the strongest individuals I think I've ever met, and a very interesting one. It's a funny thing when I talk about his profanity; if you and some ladies were sitting at a table with him and somebody at the next table had been drinking too much and started swearing, Frank would get up and tell those people, "Either clean up your language or get out of here." That's the way he was.

Frank never answered the phone, he always got someone else to

The Sportscaster's Dozen

Fulton broadcasting a game at USC's Williams Brice Stadium.

do it. He never even signed a check until his first wife, Pat, passed away. Speaking of which, she was great and very direct. For instance, there were times we would be sitting in a room with Pat and Frank when somebody would knock on the door and start to come in. Pat would say, "Has anyone invited you in here?"

She was direct. The first night I was out with them we had a banquet at Forest Lake Club in Columbia. She was at the bar with some woman, who was one of these name droppers, behind her. Pat turned around and said to the woman, "Hey, you're a name dropper." I thought that woman was going to faint.

But Frank was good to me. You always knew where you stood with Frank. I consider him a very close friend. I miss him, I really do miss him.

Officials

I remember we were up in North Carolina one night, and Coach McGuire was sitting on one of the trainer's tables in the dressing room and he said, "You know, those people back home think I'm putting a lot of X's and O's on the board." The funny thing about that was that Frank was not an X and O coach; he was a motivator. He got a lot of great players through friends of his, and he was the best manipulator of officials I've ever seen in my life, and this is often where you win.

[University of North Carolina coach] Dean Smith is one of best, by the way, but he operated differently than Frank. One of our biggest wins at Carolina was in 1968. They were heavily favored and had us down by 19 points. We came back in the second half for the win. Where we won that game was on our way up to the floor. I was with Frank, and one of the officials came out of a dressing room and said, "Hey, Coach, it's good to see you." Frank never offered the official his hand and basically told the official that if he blew the game, Frank was coming after him. That official turned as white as a sheet of paper!

In the second half when we were down by 13 points at Chapel Hill, where fouls normally aren't called against the Tar Heels, this official was pumping out fouls. We had little Bobby Cremins now a college coach going to the line to make eight-out-of-nine down the stretch (and he was normally one of our worst foul shooters), and we won the game. It was mainly this one official from the hallway calling the fouls against North Carolina.

He was just one of the best in the business I've seen at working officials. I've seen him do it so many times. For example there would be two officials during a time-out standing about three or four feet apart. He'd go up to one official and say, "Hey, you're a good official, and I know that. But that guy you're with—I think he's incompetent and a thief. Now if you don't take charge of this game, somebody's going to get hurt because it's getting too rough."

What he has done, he's already got this official in his pocket, and the other official is thinking to himself that here's this nationally known coach talking to the other guy, maybe I'm not doing what I should do. So before he's finished, he has both officials.

He was unbelievable.

Coach McGuire would start working the officials early in a game. We put a microphone on him one year during the games, and at the end of the year literally about 95 percent of it had to be cut out because of the language.

We were playing up in the Milwaukee Classic one year in Wisconsin, and Al McGuire, who had played for Frank, was coaching at Marquette. They were the host team in this tournament and were supposed to go to the finals. South Carolina played them the first night.

That afternoon Frank told me he was going to get about three technical fouls. In those days you could get three or four without getting tossed out of the game. Frank told me how these were Big 10 officials and how Al uses Big 10 officials all the time, so he figured he had to do something.

Sure enough he got three technicals. Al McGuire came down to the scorer's table where Frank was and said to the official, "Can't you see what he's doing? Don't you know what he's doing to you? I know this guy, I played for him."

You know what happened at the end of the game? A Marquette player hit a basket to put them up by one point in the last second, and the official called offensive goaltending. We won the game, and they were the host team.

We were doing a game down in Florida one night against a small school, Florida Southern. We had a much better team than they had, but we were getting screwed by the local officials they were using. Frank came by the table before halftime and told me he wasn't going down to the locker room with the team. Instead he was going to go down to the officials' dressing room to get this straightened out.

He told me later he went in there and said he told the officials, "I'm going to report you two to the NCAA, and if that doesn't work I know some of the mafia."

Guess what? The first 12 fouls in the second half were called on the home team. It was remarkable what he could do with officials. Not every coach can do that, but Frank had such a good reputation as one of the top coaches in the country.

Football Was My Sport

I enjoyed doing football. I was fast I covered things well, but I could tell the slippage near the end when my mind wasn't as quick. You're as good as you prepare, but a lot of guys don't prepare, and I can tell. A lot of listeners can tell five or 10 minutes into a game if a guy prepared or not. If the guy does good preparation and gets a good night's sleep and gets out there early and really gets with it with a good crew, then it should be a good broadcast.

I had a brother-in-law who was a psychologist tell me, "Everybody when they get up in the morning should look in the mirror at themselves and laugh, because they're not nearly as smart or nearly as important as they think they are." There is a lot of sense in that. That's why I would try to keep my crew loose and tell them before the broadcast to just have fun and make it interesting. The game is not a war; the game is a game. We tried to keep it that way. When you had a real close ballgame and the ball is down in the 5-yard line, you've got the listeners where you want them.

There was a football game we played in 1969 against Virginia Tech at Blacksburg, Virginia, that we had to win to go to the Peach Bowl. Tommy Suggs was on that team as the quarterback. The Gamecocks are down two points with about seven seconds to go. Virginia Tech was on the verge of breaking a long losing streak they had.

We had the ball and were going to attempt a 48-yard field goal by Billy DuPre, who was about 5-foot-6. You think about all these guys with clipboards, but you can throw all these away because the game is on this kid's shoulders—whether Tommy can handle the snap, get it down and Billy kick it through the uprights.

When you've got something good like that as a broadcaster you don't give it away. You've gotta pause and let the audience jerk around a little bit. Plus on this play, for instance, somebody could jump offsides, so don't give it away too soon.

I had it like this: "The ball's down. The kick is up, and it is ... (I drew that word out; by the time I say it the listener is probably going nuts trying to figure out what happened. Just don't give it away because you have worked your tail off all day for a moment like this.) ... good!"

When we got back to Columbia all the coaches' wives were there at the airport and asked me why I waited so long to say it was good. That was fun.

My Idea of a Good Coach's Relationship

I think it helps to have a good relationship with the coaches, but I don't think you should have a close association with the players because you can lose your objectivity. Obviously, this can happen with the coaches also, although I would rather see it in the coaching profession than around ballplayers. I've been close to some coaches, but not close to the point where I smother them or feel that I'm obligated to say something good or whatever.

One thing I don't do, however, is bother coaches. In other words, I don't call them a lot, even if we're good friends. I just believe they are bothered enough. If they want to see me, they'll call me and offer to get together. I do not hang around coaches, and I never have.

I have coached high school football and basketball, and I know a coach has enough problems and things to worry about. I don't know how coaches at this level do it; I don't know how they survive.

Bobby Richardson: From Yankee to Gamecock

I had mentioned Bobby Richardson earlier from his days with the Yankees. I can't say enough good things about Bobby Richardson. He's one of these guys who is involved with the Fellowship of Christian Athletes and doesn't talk out of both sides of his mouth. He's a straight arrow. He's just a great person. He's convicted in his religious beliefs, but he doesn't use it in a bad way.

I remember when he was coaching the Gamecocks, and I was doing some baseball announcing. After a game on the road, some of the players would follow me when I went to get a beer, and they had to get away from Bobby. If he'd walk into the room, they would push their beer over. Sometimes I would have four beers in front of me. I'm sure there were times Bobby thought he had a drunk working for him. He also didn't allow any bad language.

South Carolina was playing at Clemson one day and Jeff Grantz, who was a great quarterback here and a very good shortstop, was at the plate and the umpire was very inconsistent. Finally Bobby walked out of the dugout and went to the plate.

He went to the plate and told the umpire, "These guys are all confused and don't know what to swing at; you're taking the game away from them." With that the umpire pretty much let Bobby have it, and told him to get out or he was going to get tossed out.

Bobby took about four steps away from home plate, then turned around and said, "And phooey on you too." Grantz said he about lost it when he heard Bobby say that.

Opening Day

Opening day was special to me, particularly so in football. In that situation you're learning two teams, the one that you're following and the one that's coming in. Normally I would memorize before the first game, around 100 numbers. I could do that because I had done it all my life. It's really not that difficult because there's nothing else up there cluttering my mind. I can remember numbers back to the Baylor team in the old Southwest Conference when they went to the AAU in 1948. Everything is in the mind, it's just a matter of learning how to trigger it and get it out. I could memorize numbers so fast, although not the last few years. The last few years it became a chore for me, and I could tell I was slipping.

I figure you have to know the numbers of the linebackers, the skill people, etcetera. I used my spotters as an addendum to what I was doing. The forgotten people in football are your offensive linemen, so we would mention them when they made a big block or some other type of big play. Every time your eyes leave the field you're missing something, so you better know the numbers. I used my spotters as something extra, not to give me the meat of it. Because if, for instance, they had been out at a bar or out late the night before, I'm just as good as they are, and they're in bad shape.

Getting ready for the first football game was a lot of work. Once you got through the first game, you learned your own ballclub. Then it was just a case of learning the opposition.

I would pick up a lot of things about the opposition, generally it would be something on their background. I figure you don't use more than 5 or 10 percent of all the material that you get ready for, but that 5 or 10 percent could make the difference between a fair broadcast and a damn good broadcast. You'll have some lemons for ballgames sometimes, and you better have something else to talk about.

Lindsey Nelson was great at this. I really liked Lindsey personally and as a broadcaster; he was a real pro. I heard him do a Brooklyn Dodger game one day, and he had a lemon. It was a 12-2 ballgame, but the pitcher had walked so many that he was about to set a record. Lindsay did it in such a way that he kept you in there. That is the mark of a good broadcaster — if you can possibly keep people interested.

Game Day Butterflies

If you're not a little bit nervous I don't think you're going to do a good game. What I liked was the countdown to when you went on, especially at a football game where you had a big name and you knew you had a big audience. When the countdown starts, 10-9- ... I like that.

I was a little nervous, but I got to a point where I never thought of an audience. After awhile you don't even think of who's listening. One thing — I learned this from Marvin Bass's wife Audrey. She told me when Marvin was coaching Carolina and they were playing out of town, she literally got down on her hands and knees in their kitchen and prayed because this was her husband's career.

That got me to thinking that if I presented a game where I didn't offend the coach's wife, then I've done a pretty good job. So I used that as sort of a beacon. And it worked pretty well because then you don't second guess. If I acted like I was talking to one person, I acted like I was talking to the coach's wife.

That was hard in some of these games where you're losing 52-0, but it worked.

Bud Wilkinson and the Other Opposing Coaches

One of the greatest coaches with whom I was ever associated was Bud Wilkinson when he coached at the University of Oklahoma. He was one of the nicest guys I have ever been around. Little Rock High School went to Norman, Oklahoma, to play a game one time. Earlier in the day of the game a sportswriter took me to OU's practice and introduced me to Coach Wilkinson. They were getting ready to play a big game against Missouri, and I asked Bud in passing if he would come up to the booth at halftime of the high school game to be with us.

I never thought he would come up, but sure enough he came up there. He gave the best dissertation on the kicking game of football that I've ever heard. You talk about a class individual; he was a class guy. I have never met a finer man in the coaching business than Bud Wilkinson. When I got back to Little Rock after that game, people came up to me and told me how great the halftime show was with Bud Wilkinson.

One night I was flying to New York when I first took the job with Mutual, and Bud was on the same plane. I went up and introduced myself (of course he didn't remember me) and thanked him for doing that interview. If I had to pick what a coach should be, it would be Bud Wilkinson.

Eddie Fogler: Turning Around a Program

I can say nothing but good things about basketball coach Eddie Fogler. One of the amazing things about him is that for 25 years he was never associated with a losing team. All of his years in high school, all his years as a player at North Carolina, all his years as an assistant to Dean Smith at Carolina, and his years at Wichita State and Vanderbilt, he was never associated with a losing team.

I really thought he was going to stay at Vanderbilt and that we were going to hire Bobby Cremins. I was up at Lexington, Kentucky, for the SEC tournament, and I met Eddie for the first time. I congratulated him on the fantastic job he had done at Vanderbilt. He asked me who was going to get the job at South Carolina, and I told him I thought it was going to be Cremins.

Then it turned out that Cremins stayed at Georgia Tech and Eddie came to South Carolina. I told Eddie when he first came to Columbia that he might have a tough time keeping that 25 season non-losing streak alive. The team had a rough first couple of seasons with him, but they're doing alright now.

Eddie is a very intelligent guy. I sit right behind the bench during the games, about two rows back, and I watch time-outs. I judge coaches a lot by what they do on the sidelines or what they do on the bench. If you watch the players and they're looking up in the stands to see where their girlfriends are, then you don't have a good coach. Eddie has the complete attention of his ballplayers. I've been to a few of his practices, and he's tough, but he's not unfair. He has a quick mind and a good way with officials.

> *Bob Fulton is one of the best. He was a good baseball announcer. You meet very few great people in this business, but Bob is a great one. He did a very good job.*
> — *Al Ciraldo, Georgia Tech*

When he first came to South Carolina, I didn't think that he would be here long. In fact, I, like a lot of people, thought he would come here and then try to go to North Carolina when Dean Smith retires. Before I left the program, Eddie told me he plans on staying at South Carolina as long as they'll have him. I think he would like to build stability here with his family and the program and then maybe retire when he's 55 or 60.

Former Athletes Are Good ... as Analysts

I think it's good to have former athletes in the broadcasting booth, but only to an extent. When I left Mutual, they brought in Mel Ott to replace me. Instead of making former athletes analysts, Paul Jonas made them play-by-play men, which I think is ridiculous.

So I'm in Columbia that year and Mel comes to town on his way north from spring training wanting to have lunch with me. I had never met Mel Ott before. When we met for lunch, I could tell he's a very nice guy; a class act.

He said, "I want to tell you something. They [the people at Mutual] think I should get excited when there's a home run, or even a grand slam home run. When I was with the Giants in New York, I saw so many go out of that ballpark, that I didn't get excited even when I hit one." I told him that he should be an analyst and not doing play-by-play, but that's the way Mutual wanted to do it.

In fact, Mutual brought former Cleveland pitcher Bob Feller on the next season to do play-by-play. He told me that he should have been an analyst and not a play-by-play announcer. Paul Jonas insisted that Bob be a play-by-play man, but he wasn't good at it.

I think it's good to have former athletes come in, if they come in as analysts. If they don't talk too much (even though there's too much talking in the booth today, anyway), then it's OK. You just don't want to analyze it too much; when you do it too much you take something away from the fans. Fans can see a lot, and they aren't dumb anymore. They are pretty knowledgeable because they read a lot of books, they listen to a lot of television, they go to a lot of clinics, they know what's going on.

For instance, former major league pitcher Steve Stone who is with the Chicago Cubs as an analyst, does a super job. He fits in with Harry Caray. You have to fit in with the guy in the booth with you.

In football John Madden is great. He might have a bad ballgame, but he is so good that he'll find something to keep you in there and make it interesting. I know Pat Summerall very well from when he was playing basketball and football at Arkansas, and I asked him at a banquet one time how he stands Madden jumping in all the time. He said, "If it weren't for Madden, I might not be there anymore." But Madden is funny without trying to be funny. He gets the game reduced to a face in the dirt and dirt all over you, instead of all these X's and O's. He talks the way a guy at a bar talks about a ballgame.

Tommy Suggs: A Top Former Athlete in a Busy Environment

I worked with Tommy Suggs at South Carolina for 22 years. He was a former Gamecock quarterback, so he was very knowledgeable and good to work with. He also had a good sense of humor. When you work with the same man for that long, you can have a lot of fun.

Tommy and I had what I call a loose broadcast. We weren't structured, which went along with my idea of a good broadcast which is to keep it loose. The problem you can run into with young guys who don't have a background in announcing, is if they're following a team closely that gets behind, then the young announcer can get discour-

Bob Fulton publicity photo.

aged and get out of it. This (when you get behind) is one time you need to dig down and find something that the fans can hang their hats on to keep them in there. Working with people who don't have much of a background, then that is hard to come by.

I used to tell Tommy before we had a potentially one-sided game that anybody can work a close game because that carries itself. "You're going to have a helluva job keeping an audience today," I'd say to him. "If we get behind and some team is clobbering us, then don't give the score very often."

Tommy was good, and he's the college color man I remember most.

Some broadcasters—especially young ones—think that people stay on one station regardless of the score of the game. The fact of the matter is they don't. They're going down the radio dial, or they're going to watch television. So I would say give the score a lot if you're winning, but don't mention it as much if you're losing a one-sided game.

> Even though South Carolina wasn't in the SEC for awhile, Bob and I touched base on occasion while he was at South Carolina for 199 years. I probably got to know him best over the last three or four years, when we would sit down and chat like old-timers do. Bob was greatly admired by everyone who knew him and worked with him.
>
> — Jack Cristil, Mississippi State University

Along those lines I think the best broadcaster, if you maybe give it four or five more years, is Bob Costas. When you talk about a guy that can do it all, it's him. He is the best interviewer, he can do play-by-play in baseball, and he can do play-by-play in football and basketball. Costas gets right to the meat of things, but he's not vindictive and he pours it right in.

If there is one fault today, I think it's that there is too much going on in the booth for the most part. Like our college games here at South Carolina: We have two former quarterbacks, Tommy Suggs and Todd Ellis, and now they're both analysts (one in the booth and one on the field), and they dissect every play. As a listener, you get tired of that after awhile: You need a little time to think for yourself what is going on in the game.

As a play finishes in football here, they go down to the field to Ellis who talks about something, then up to Tommy and he talks about something, then over to the play-by-play man, but, hell, he hasn't had time to give you the wideouts. There's just too much talking at times.

We can't all do a game the same way. For instance one announcer who is the exact opposite of me—and he's a good friend of mine—is Larry Munson at the University of Georgia. I have told him that if I took his place they would fire me in a week because I see two teams, whereas he only sees the Bulldogs. There's nothing wrong with it, only I can't do it. I like Larry; he marches to a different drummer's beat.

For me, though, my idea of a good broadcast is a fair broadcast. If you're not honest, who in the hell is going to believe what you say?

Have a Coke and a Smile

I didn't use many phrases because I don't believe in getting caught using cliches. It's OK for some people to use them, but I tried to stay away from it. I don't think I had any identifying phrase. What I had that people could identify with is my voice; I was able to use pretty good voice inflection. I would say a lot of the announcers today sound generic when you go down the dial. They all sound alike. Today there just isn't a lot of inflection or excitement in these voices. I was different. I thought I did a pretty good job. I was my toughest critic, which is why I left. I started making mistakes.

Jim Phillips and I worked the College World Series together one year. I'll never forget it, not because of what happened on the field, but rather what happened in the booth. Bob Bradley is a former sports information director at Clemson, and he was with us in the booth. Well, Bob is a tobacco chewer. When it came time for me not to have the mike, I had a Coke beside me, and Bob had his spit cup next to it ... you can guess what happened. That made me sick; I threw up in the booth.

For the Love of the Business

I was never in this business for money because I never made that much; I was in it because I loved it. If you don't love it, you're not going to do that good of a job, regardless of what your job is. When I was going to retire, I talked to a man who was the head of a men's department at a store here in Columbia, and I asked him when he was going to retire. He said he could tell me exactly how many minutes, how many hours and how many days until he retired. I thought to myself that he was doing something he didn't like to do.

When I did that last basketball game against Auburn and we got down to about five minutes left, I knew we were going to lose it. At that time I started having these flashbacks, and thought how I wasn't going to do another basketball game and that was my favorite sport. I could remember the first basketball game I did; Arkansas played Phillips 66 in Little Rock in 1943. I kept thinking that I was never going to do another game. That's a helluva feeling; it was tough.

Pilot Life had a camera in front of me, and they were going to use it at halftime of the SEC Championship game. These guys are shooting me, and I'm sitting there with tears; I choked up. I was having all kinds of trouble because I didn't want to cry in front of the camera. Later I saw Pete Carill from Princeton, who I always thought was one of the best coaches in the business, walk out on the court after his last game. He had coached Princeton for 25 years, and tears were streaming down his cheeks. I figured maybe it's not so bad to have tears like that.

All the other announcers were coming up to me and patting me on the back. What really set me off though, was when the commissioner of the SEC, Roy Kramer, came over, grabbed my arm and said, "Bob, we just want to thank you for all that you've done for your school but the conference as well." Plus a few other things. I was doing pretty well up to that point, but that got me. I cried like a baby. I thought how I had done this for 53 years, and I wasn't going to do it anymore. That's a helluva feeling because while I was at South Carolina I did over 1,000 basketball games.

My last year was 1994, and I'll never do another basketball game. That's tough because it was something I loved all those years. Even with all its problems and traveling and losses and snow and waiting in airports for planes ... it still was great. It was tough; I could cry now thinking about it. But it doesn't bother me nearly as much as I thought it would, because I'm doing other things like making fantasy tapes for people (which is still broadcasting) and making reverse fantasy tapes.

I did one recently for a guy who was giving it to a friend of his who was the head of some club. The guy had the head of the club looking like a fool, throwing an interception, and the guy I did the tape for is the one who runs the interception back for a touchdown against Clemson.

I learned reverse when I was doing high school football. At that time my first wife (she passed away in 1976) had gone to SMU, and one of her boyfriends was a football player and so I wanted to kid her about it. Well, Little Rock had a tremendous high school team that travelled all over the Southeast, but no one could ever keep up with who was on the opposing teams. So I had my wife's old boyfriend as the guy who was flagged for offsides, or fumbled the football, but nobody knew it because they didn't have any way to check it. My wife knew it; she said she used to slam the iron down and think she wanted to kill me when I got home. That was fun though.

The Clemson Tigers ... Our Big Rivalry

Clemson isn't all bad. In fact, the people there were very good to me when I left broadcasting. In my last year, the University of South Carolina put my picture on the cover of the program before the Tennessee game at home, and got the band to spell F-U (I'm glad they didn't misspell the rest of it) -L-T-O-N; and they did some other nice things.

My last game (or at least my last regular season game ... we did the CarQuest Bowl) we did at Clemson, they called me and asked if I would help them honor Coach [Frank] Howard. I told them sure. I got to Clemson, and the night before the game I went out with Jim Phillips (a very good friend of mine) to a party, and I asked him if they were lying to me about honoring Coach Howard. He told me they were just going to have a short thing for him on the field during halftime.

Honestly, at the end of the first half I was working on some statistics and forgot about the ceremony. Luckily a guy came in and got me, so I grabbed my coat and tie, and we went downstairs to the field. When we got to the north end of the field, I looked down the sideline and saw my wife there. I'm thinking it's not what Jim told me. I walked out there, and they gave me a Clemson jersey, a plaque, and drove my wife and me around the stadium in a golf cart. We got a standing ovation from that crowd of 85,000 people; I got choked up. Think about it ... this is our biggest rival, and this is the biggest compliment I could get.

After the game for at least an hour and a half, we were over by our car signing autographs. And Clemson lost the game. I'll never forget it, because I was fooled until I got down to the field and saw my wife there.

I told a good friend of mine, Larry Conley, who does a lot of basketball, about it and he said something about it on ESPN. (I knew Larry's dad, George, very well. He used to be a good official in the Midwest.) Some other guys did things like that, and I wish I could pay them back for it because it was very nice. I'll never forget it.

I'll tell you what happens to you when you stay 43 years in a place. People used to tell me this, and I can now understand it. People say, "You're not only our broadcaster, you're a part of our family ... our kids grew up with you."

It's really nice when a guy who looks like he's 40 years old comes up to you and says, "I remember listening to you when I was a kid." It's nice to hear, but I guess it also shows how old I am. The people here at South Carolina have been just great to me.

But I didn't think about the impact I had on people until I made a tour around the state with the coaching staff after I retired. I didn't realize until then. I don't think anyone in this business really realizes that until they've left. But you do have a tremendous impact in this business. I don't think the guys who work really realize it; I didn't.

It's very humbling. I spoke to a group of blind people. Boy, you talk about an experience; I was one of only two sighted people in the room. When you speak to a blind group they focus on your voice. You talk about attention. They told me they would go out to the ballpark, but even though they couldn't see, they took their radios to listen, and they could hear the crowd around them, and they felt like they were right in it. When I finished they all stood up and gave me a big ovation, and it was great.

After that thing was over, I went around that room and hugged every one of those people. Then I walked outside, and I broke down. I thought why should I ever complain about anything in my life.

The Task Ahead

Sports, in general, is becoming such a big business that radio broadcasts are mainly filling up cars now, because when someone is at home they can watch it on television. Because of that more young broadcasters want to look into television before radio.

One fault I can find with most young broadcasters is that they don't get a background; they don't go to clinics; they don't arm themselves with information that they should have. They think all they should do is sit down with what the SID gives them and do a ballgame; you can't do it that way. You've got to work, but most guys don't want to work anymore. And always be sure you get good help. I was fortunate because I had very good help; I picked guys I knew would stay with me.

It's hard to say what's ahead though; I really don't know. So many things are going to change in this business over the next 10 years, that I feel I may have gotten out at the right time. America's romance with radio is over. It's not the same anymore. In radio you used to be the only communication connection people had with the ballclub. Now it's not. Shoot, television is eating up newspapers today; newspapers are going to be non-descriptive and almost obsolete over the next few years.

It's going to be tough for some of these schools to sell anything anymore as far as radio advertising is concerned. There's just so much advertising money to go around. It's going to be difficult. The small colleges—their day is over. They don't have really any coverage anymore to speak of, and they don't draw the crowds. It's tough.

What's happening in television, the Internet, and all these other things is mind boggling. I don't know enough about it, but I do know one thing, radio will always have a place.

Bob Harris
DUKE UNIVERSITY

My first "live" baseball broadcast was in Asheboro, North Carolina, in 1967. Beforehand, I called the high school to get their permission to broadcast the game and to make sure they had a phone line and electricity in the press box. "Yes, no problem," was the answer I received to all three questions. We arrived about an hour before the game, set up the card table, set up the equipment, plugged the equipment in, lights came on—it's working fine.

> *The art of getting rich is found not in saving, but in being at the right spot at the right time.*
> ~ Ralph Waldo Emerson

I plugged the telephone line into the phone jack on the little panel box, sat down and had my first high school baseball broadcast. When we got back to Albemarle, North Carolina, I called the radio station to see how everything went. In those days we had no two-way communication and I couldn't talk to the station. There were no telephones there at the park.

They wanted to know where I'd been because they didn't get a broadcast. Oops! That wonderful broadcast was going as far as my feet. Evidently I was supposed to call the telephone company to turn on the switch. I thought the line was live because the panel box was there. Inexperience showed up there.

There was another embarrassing moment doing high school baseball in Albemarle. Unfortunately we were on the air for this one. We were at one of our county schools, and the field didn't have an outfield fence so if the ball was in the gap, it was all the batter could get. One of the local kids smacked one in the outfield between left and center at a crucial time in the game, and I knew when I saw it hit the ground that it was pretty much a home run. So I took a deep breath to just bring him around in grandiose style. As I did, I swallowed a gnat or another bug of some sort—worst tasting thing I've ever had in my mouth—and I couldn't get my breath. I was coughing and sputtering so bad I couldn't say anything. By the time I said my first word, the kid had rounded the bases and was sitting in the dugout.

When you're doing the game yourself you have nobody to rely on. I just sat there and just coughed, sputtered and gagged. The perils of high school baseball in the springtime.

Growing up on "Mill Hill"

I was born and raised in Albemarle, North Carolina, a town about 40 miles east of Charlotte. We lived on "mill hill" as they called it, and I think that really set a lot of things in motion for me. Number one, it gave me a good work ethic because I saw how my dad went about his job every day. He worked 55 years in an Albemarle textile mill. I saw the loyalty that my dad had toward the company and toward his job. Regardless of the situation, Dad worked. That work ethic was ingrained in me when I was growing up.

Secondly, Dad had a great love for sports which he passed to me. One of my fondest pictures is from when I was about 4 years old and I have a baseball bat in my hands—a bat that was handmade for me by one of Dad's coworkers. I still have that bat.

Growing up I was always on the smallish side. As a sophomore in high school I was 5'9" and 119 pounds. It was obvious I didn't have a lot of athletic ability. My high school baseball coach finally told me after I graduated that a scout was watching one of our games, and on my card beside "speed" he had written, "deceptive—slower than he looks." I was too small and too slow to play football and too short to play basketball. I had always wanted to play major league baseball, but I couldn't hit the curve ball so that halted those dreams.

Since I couldn't play football, I did the next best thing and became a team manager and trainer. Watching how one of the more successful high school coaches in North Carolina, Toby Webb, handled players was an invaluable learning experience for me. We came along at an era when Albemarle was very, very good. The team was 12-0 my sophomore year and won the North Carolina championship. My junior year we were 8-3, and my senior year we were 8-2-2; so we had a lot of success. I also worked with the basketball teams in the same capacity for a couple of years. My sports background came more from observing than it did from playing.

At one time growing up, I had a little ambition to be a sportscaster, but it just didn't work into my schedule at the time. It was virtually impossible to find a job at a radio station in Albemarle during high school, because my involvement with sports took too much time.

I went to North Carolina State on an academic scholarship given by the company where Dad worked. The company offered several scholarships every year to children of employees who could qualify through academics, so it was off to NC State to major in textiles. I gave up on the idea of going back to Albemarle after college to try and cure all the ills of the textile business, so I dropped out of NC State after two years. My plan was to work for a year, then transfer to Pfeiffer and change my major to English to be a teacher; that was the plan.

In the meantime I managed to land a job with Goodyear Tires and advanced from commission salesman to credit manager, and eventually to store manager in Dillon, South Carolina, in 1966. During that four and a half years, I worked in five stores and could see another move coming soon. At that time my wife, Phyllis, and I had two young children, both under three years old. Because I was gone so much I didn't know who they were, so I left Goodyear and we moved back to Albemarle.

Hey, Was That My Dad?!

Going back to my days growing up, my earliest radio memories are from the time right at the advent of television. Not a lot of people in Albemarle had televisions when I was younger. In fact, the first 10 years of my life were spent with radio.

Mom worked at home as a seamstress, so she listened to soap operas, "Our Gal Sunday" and "Art Linkletter's House Party." At night we would listen to Jack Benny, Dr. Christian and Sam Spade, "Gang Busters," all those. On Saturday night we listened to the Grand Ole Opry from WSM in Nashville, Tennessee.

My first sporting remembrance was listening to the Shrine Bowl in 1949 when I was 7 years old. My dad got a ticket to the game in Charlotte with my uncle, and he kept telling me to listen to the game, because he was going to yell to me. I listened to that entire broadcast, and I didn't hear him yell once. (I thought I did one time, but I wasn't real sure.) That was the first game I actually remember listening to on the radio.

I also listened to the Brooklyn Dodger games at night—I grew up a Brooklyn fan. A station in Salisbury carried games in our area, and if I turned that radio just right, I could pick it up most of the time, not realizing that a lot of those games were being recreated by a guy sitting in an office in New Jersey. Before I realized they were recreated, I wondered why people were yelling "Atta boy Duke," when Snider wasn't even at the plate. Several years ago I interviewed Duke Snider, and I told him about that. He said, "You know you would be surprised how many people had told me they listened to that same thing."

As far as the individual sportscasters I listened to growing up, Add Penfield, who did Duke a couple of different times is one of the main ones I remember. (As a matter of fact, I succeeded him at Duke. I worked with Add a part of a year and then succeeded him.) He was a Duke graduate in the late 1930s and had been associated with them on a couple of occasions. He was one of the truly great voices. I have said many times and told him, I wish I had the command of the English language that he has; he is a very, very eloquent speaker.

Ray Reeve was another one of the broadcasting pioneers in North Carolina. Charlie Harville is the third. They were probably the three more influential broadcasters of the people that I listened to growing up. The network guys like Bill Stern, Graham McNamee and Red Barber, and other guys like that were the pros, but I liked the local ones.

A lot of my TV and radio memories were of sports programs simply because I loved game broadcasts, plus the old "Home Run Derby Show."

Harry Wismer, who later owned the New York Titans (which later became the New York Jets) did a prediction show on TV of the games for that Saturday. They had a unique way of getting the transition from one game to the other. They used a mock card section, which was something used a lot in the 1950s where the student sections had colored cards and at a certain signal they would hold up a certain color card and it would make into a pattern in the stands—it was beautiful. That's how Harry would transition. For instance there would be Texas A&M versus Texas in the card section, and he would go into it with the card section then show some footage. That was a lot of fun.

D-Day

With the styles of those broadcasters in the back of my mind, I still had thoughts of going into broadcasting. Unfortunately, when Phyllis and I packed up everything and moved back to Albemarle, the timing still wasn't right. On April 1st, 1967, I took a job at an insurance company with a friend of mine.

Shortly after starting with the insurance company, another friend of mine who was the manager of one of the two stations in Albemarle, was talking to me about the broadcast business. I asked him if they were going to carry high school football in the fall. He said they were, but the guy who had done the play-by-play for the previous couple of years had gotten a promotion with the company and was not going to be able to do the high school games. Kind of offhanded I said, "I'll do it for you," and that's how it all got started. I was 25 years old.

It was a daytime radio station so we taped the games on Friday night and then broadcast them on Saturday morning at 11:00. When I listened to the tape delay broadcast Saturday morning of that first football game in the fall of 1967, it was agonizing! As soon as that game ended on the air, the station manager Ralph Gardner called me. The first words out of his mouth were, "I hate a liar."

"What are you talking about?"

He said, "You convinced me you were in South Carolina working for Goodyear when in all actuality you were working for a radio station doing sports, weren't you?"

That really made me feel good.

I was packing up the equipment after the last high school broadcast, and I had a lump in my throat because I knew that this was something I really wanted to do. So I talked with the manager of WZKY and told him what my feelings were. He said, "I think you can make a good radio man, if you can wait until April or May. After we get over the first-of-the-year lulls, I can probably afford to hire you." So I went ahead and got my radio operator's license, which everybody had to have back then, and I waited.

After a staff meeting at the insurance company in the first of February, 1968, my manager and district manager wanted me to take a car ride with them for a meeting. As I look back, that became my D-Day. I was sitting in the back seat, my staff manager was driving, and the district manager was sitting in the passenger seat when he gave me the old "get in the business or get out" speech.

He said, "I want you to take some time and make up your mind and decide what you are going to do, insurance or radio."

I thought for a second and said, "Okay, I've made up my mind."

"I'm glad it didn't take you long. I'm glad you're going to get in the harness."

"No," I said, "I'm getting out," and proceeded to tell him I was going into radio full time. He almost had a wreck.

"You don't want to go to work for a radio station, working with all those dope heads and people like that." (I didn't know what kind of station he had been listening to.)

We went back to the office and I went to the radio station to tell the manager what had happened, and that I had given my 30-day notice. He said, "Well, I wish you could have waited until later, but actually it has worked out well." He had just been elected the president of the Chamber of Commerce in Albemarle and wasn't going to have as much time for all of his radio work.

He gave me an air shift from 10 to 12:30 in the mornings, a couple of sales accounts, and we started doing high school baseball—we started doing those live because they were in the afternoon—and then we did little league baseball that summer. I did two games a night at the park, three nights a week, and then we got back into the high school football and basketball the next year. In the eight years that I was there, we probably originated more sports than any other station in the state of North Carolina.

I had been in Albemarle in radio about 8 years and had looked at other jobs. Every now and then I would hear about a TV job that was open in a larger market where they would be looking for a second man, but I was always a day late and a dollar short. I did have one shot at a TV job in Charlotte. I went through the whole hiring process and was offered the job, however, our 250-watt daytime radio station was paying me more than WBTV in Charlotte was offering me to go on television.

There goes my shot at TV stardom. Everything happens for a purpose and that happened for a reason. I told them I'd let them know, but I knew when I drove out of the parking lot that I wasn't coming back. There was just no way.

Becoming a Blue Devil

In July of 1975 I was very involved in our state's sportscasters association, and we were having a board meeting in Raleigh. Howard Wilcox, who had just come to Durham in June of that year to take over as station manager, was sitting in our board meeting. At lunch we were talking about his new situation in Durham, and he told

Bob Harris with his wife, Phyllis, enjoying a Durham Bulls baseball game, July 5, 1997.

me things were so bad at the station that it would probably be a year before he could think about hiring anybody to do sports. He told me to send him a resume and some tapes and when they were ready, we would talk about it.

A month later I finally got around to sending Howard a tape on a Friday afternoon. On the following Monday morning he called me. He had not gotten the tape yet, but called me because they needed a salesman and wanted to talk to me about the job. It was a really good situation. He offered me a whole lot more money than I was making in Albemarle. So Phyllis and I thought about it, talked it over for a good while, and decided to take the offer. I came to Durham on Labor Day, 1975, to work for WDNC radio.

The following Sunday night he put me on the air doing a call-in talk show as well. I didn't know a whole lot about the Durham sports market, only what I had observed from afar about Duke, State, and Carolina, but I knew enough to muddle through. Before Sunday came I read everything I could get my hands on trying to learn as much as possible before going on the air. The show went fairly well, and it developed into a regular situation.

In the 1975 football season, Duke was using a guest color

commentator for their broadcasts. I talked with the people at Duke to see if I could maybe keep stats or spot—anything to keep my hand in play-by-play. They told me they would give me a shot at the guest commentator for a game later in the season. I got more than that—I ended up working four games. They found out very quickly they couldn't have a different commentator in the booth with a regular play-by-play man every game. It just doesn't work because there's no cohesion and no familiarity.

After doing color on those four football games, I started the basketball season doing color. The third week in January, Add Penfield had some health problems, and I finished out the season doing play-by-play. As a matter of fact I did the whole thing—they didn't hire anybody else to do color until the ACC Tournament when they got former Blue Devil, Glenn Smiley, to help out. The rest, as they say, is history. It was a matter of being in the right place at the right time and having a little bit of luck on my side.

I've been very, very lucky to be in this business for 30 years.

Falling from the Catwalk

The first few years of doing play-by-play at Duke were relatively painless ... almost. During my second year, we had a home basketball game in Cameron Indoor Stadium where we broadcast from a catwalk at the top of arena. In order to get there, you have to go up the steps to the back of the seating, up a ladder, and up into the booth.

The ladder up to the booth was not a very long ladder, but if it was blocked against the concrete wall, everything was fine. Before doing a halftime interview, I was on my way to the rest room. The ladder looked in place, but I didn't check it. I assumed that since it was in the upright position that it was blocked. Unfortunately, it wasn't.

When I put my foot down on the top step, the ladder shot out from under me. My right leg went out onto a four-foot screen wire, my right arm caught a piece of angle iron which was sticking up. I grabbed around a post with my left arm and my left leg was dangling straight down toward the steps with the concrete about 10 feet below. There I was suspended in midair. Finally somebody grabbed my leg and pushed me back up so I could get back in the booth until they got the steps back up there.

When the ladder fell, it hit a girl who was sitting in the aisle seat. Thank goodness it was a glancing blow, across her ear and onto her shoulder. If that thing had hit her directly in the top of the head, it could have been very serious. Needless to say, the next week that ladder had two metal hooks that hooked over the top of the rail on the press box.

We're still at the top of Cameron, and it's the best seat in the house.

THE NOT-SO-BEST SEATS IN THE HOUSE

Vanderbilt's Memorial Gymnasium in Nashville is the toughest place to broadcast from because they have no elevator and you have to climb "73" flights of stairs to get there. Another difficult place is the arena at Purdue where the broadcast position is with eyes almost at court level. Press row is recessed beside the court so everything is above you. That was back in the late 1970s and early 1980s.

We went to Boston to play Northeastern two years ago, and played in the arena where the Boston Celtics originally played in before the Boston Garden. When we went up into the booth three hours before game time to set up the equipment, it was 106 degrees (this was in the winter). Evidently there had been a hockey tournament in there, and they were doing the inversion to keep the ice from melting. Somehow that made it so hot! They kept telling us it would cool down. My engineer had stripped to his waist while setting up the equipment. I went out and bought a souvenir T-shirt in the lobby and wore that during the game. It was extremely difficult, because not only was it very hot in the press box, but the quarters were very cramped.

For football the most difficult place by far is West Point because you have to walk and carry the equipment up a ramp, out into the stands, all the way to the top row, through the press box, out the back door, and up another set of steps to the broadcasting level. There are no elevators, and when you have nine cases of equipment you can't let the engineer do it all himself, so you have to help out a little bit. On top of that, Army's megaphone man (the cheerleader has a microphone with speakers) is focused directly at us, and we can hear him almost as loud as ourselves through our headphones. When Army scores there are several howitzers across the lake on the far side of the stadium aimed in the direction of the press box, and they fire those. You can feel the concussion, and it is extremely unnerving.

The University of Tennessee's Neyland Stadium is difficult just from the sheer height of the press box, because you're on the ninth floor looking down. You have to have good eye sight or a good set

The Sportscaster's Dozen

of binoculars to see what's going on. The first Duke football game I ever announced was in Knoxville in 1976, but my problem that night was not due to sight. Tennessee was moving the ball in the last 1:14, and I made the statement on the air, "run, clock, run." Everybody thought I wanted the clock to run out so Tennessee wouldn't score, but being my first college football broadcast and being so excited, I had forgotten to go to the bathroom at halftime. So, there was an ulterior motive. By the way, UT missed three extra point attempts and Duke won, 21-18.

The Orange Bowl in Miami was a fairly difficult place to broadcast from. We played there in 1976 against the Hurricanes. There were three swivel seats across the front row of the press box that were bolted down. Since the two spotters were on each side of me, our color announcer had to sit up on the second row. When he wanted to say something, he had to throw a little wad of paper over my shoulder or hit me in the back so we wouldn't have cross talk.

> *I remember the first time we met; it was at the Kemper Open golf tournament in Charlotte, North Carolina, in the 1970s. He was broadcasting high school games and wanted some advice, so we talked for awhile. In fact a highlight for me was when I was inducted into the Clemson Hall of Fame, and Bob thanked me for encouraging him to seek a college broadcasting job. We go way back. I'm envious of him with all the national championships Duke has won. Bob is a very good broadcaster.*
>
>   ɞ *Jim Phillips, Clemson University*

My Right-Hand Men

Wes Chesson is, in my opinion, the best color analyst that I've ever listened to in the college game. I always had a lot of respect for Hank Stram doing the Monday night games with Jack Buck, but that's a little different situation. Wes is a student of the game. He's also had enough broadcast experience that he knows what his restrictions are, what his parameters are, and he knows who he's talking to.

So many analysts get into broadcasting trying to be so technical in their explanation of what's happened that they lose part of their audience. Wes has the ability to look at a play, analyze it very quickly, and then tell the average football fan what happened and why. He can talk on that average fan's level while not talking down to the real knowledgeable football fan.

We've been working together for 18 years, and it's almost like we have an inside communication system. There are times when it gets rather scary because we think the same way about the same things at the same time; it is almost like being married. He's so good at what he does and he knows that it's not a full time profession for him (he has a very successful insurance business in Raleigh), but he does it because he loves it.

Wes was a great player for Duke in the late 1960s, then he went on to a solid four-year professional career with Atlanta and Philadelphia. Even though he wasn't the fastest receiver in the world, he was outstanding and could get to the ball to make the catch.

Jay Bilas was a very brilliant person who has seen the basketball game from a player's standpoint and from the coaching aspect. He also could take a game apart and explain it to just about anybody. I knew the third year he was with us that we were not going to keep him very long. He had done a couple of movies. He had the California showmanship that would carry him to another level.

In 1996 Jay got a full contract with ESPN to be an analyst. He has also done some things for Jefferson Pilot for the ACC Network. Jay's doing extremely well. Away from the broadcasting booth, he is a very successful lawyer in Charlotte.

Tony Haynes is now kind of my right-hand man. He's a guy that can do almost anything. He has been doing the engineering in basketball and helping with the engineering in football. He does sideline reporting in football. He does the pregame, halftime, and postgame in basketball. He can also do play-by-play. The two years that Duke football has gone to a bowl, 1989 and 1994, the basketball team has gone to Hawaii to play in a Christmas tournament. In those instances, I've gone to the bowls and sent Tony to Hawaii. He can do pretty much anything. He's a good all-around guy, and I'm glad we could elevate him to the full-time analyst spot in the 1997 season.

Float Like a Butterfly, Sting Like a Bee

While we were down in Miami for the 1976 football game, Muhammad Ali was in town making the movie, "I Am the Greatest." On the way from the airport to the hotel, we were talking about how it would be great to have Ali as a halftime guest at the game the next night.

Phyllis, my color man Tom Mickle, and I, rented a car and went down to the Fifth Street Gym where Ali had been filming. They had finished shooting the day before and were out at the Miami Beach Auditorium. When we arrived at the auditorium, there were film trucks and equipment all over.

Harris (right) with color commentator Wes Chesson before a Duke football game.

We started in and this huge guy stepped in front of us and said in a deep voice, "Could I help you with something?"

"We'd like to see Muhammad Ali."

"What for?"

We told him we were with the Duke Radio Network, and we'd like for Ali to be our guest at halftime during the game. I also told him that I had written a little poem in the Ali-style, and if Muhammad couldn't make it to the game, we still wanted an interview with him.

"Stay right here."

He walked away while we stood there talking. We stood and stood. Fifteen minutes went by. Phyllis said, "He's not coming back, he's just put you off. We'll go." Sure enough, the man came back and told us to follow him. He took us back to this area where they were shooting a locker room scene. In the scene were Ali's manager, Angelo Dundee, and actor Ernest Borgnine.

The bodyguard led us through to a little cubicle which had a bench in the middle. Ali was sitting on the bench with a white long sleeve shirt, sleeves rolled up, open at the neck. My tape recorder was running when we went in. We introduced ourselves and invited Ali to come to the game. I told him about the poem I had written for the opening and asked if he would record it.

He looked at it, read it, and said, "Who wrote this?"

"I did," I told him.

"You're good; this sounds like me."

He yelled for people to be quiet outside as he reads through it a couple times. It was too noisy in there, so we went outside. As he's leading us outside I thought about how he didn't know us from Adam, but he trusted us. When we got outside, Ali did 13 more takes. It wasn't all that complicated, but he'd get part of the way through it, mess up, and then start over. (The poem said, "From the Orange Bowl in Miami, down by the sea, it's Duke versus Miami, this is Muhammad Ali.") We ended up using the second cut that he did on the air that night.

When we finished he asked, "How many tickets do I get for the game?" I looked at Tom, who was the assistant sports information director at the time, for the answer.

Tom said, "How many do you want?" Ali said he needed six. On Saturday morning we carried six tickets to the Fontainbleu Hotel. The tickets were used, but Ali didn't come.

That experience changed my opinion of Ali, totally, because I had not been an Ali fan prior to that. Just to get a chance to meet him was an experience. He was extremely nice, as nice as some of the coaches I've been able to work with.

The Teacher Mike McGee

Mike McGee was coaching football at Duke before I came here. But I remember when he was a player at Duke and with the St. Louis Cardinals, then when he went to East Carolina as coach. I had interviewed him prior to coming to Duke when he was in Albemarle for a speaking engagement.

During his years at Duke, Mike didn't take any of his teams to bowl games, in fact his best record from 1971-1978 was 6-5. Even though the 1975 team had an overall record of 4-5-2, the team did finish 3-0-2 in the ACC, which was good enough for a second-place finish.

Regardless of the mediocre records Mike's teams had, the 1977 team is one that will stick out in my mind. The team finished 5-6 that year, but had two great comeback victories during the season. The first one came against Georgia Tech in Atlanta. Duke was down 24-9 and won it 25-24. Earlier that season the team came back against South Carolina and won 25-21.

Overall Mike McGee was a very strict person, a disciplinarian. He was rather private as well. He was a hands-on type coach and didn't care that much for the supervisory aspect of the position. He liked to get down in the trenches and teach. Mike was a very good teacher, a very good tactician, a very smart man.

Shortly after I came here, he was embattled with the media. Several writers were calling for his hide because Duke was not going to a bowl every year.

One Sunday night the show got rather hot and heavy with callers, several of them just screaming for his tail. Then Monday at the press conference he started his opening remarks and all of a sudden stopped, looked directly at me and said, "I want to see you after the conference is over." That scared the liver out of me! I don't know what was said during the rest of the press conference because I replayed that entire Sunday night show and Saturday's game broadcast back in my mind to try to think if I had said anything that would have given him reason to be upset.

When the press conference was over, we normally went down to his office and did the radio interview, three or four of us. On that

Bob Harris publicity photo.

day he told me, "You go on down. I'll take care of the interviews here and then you and I will talk."

So we went down into his office, and he shut the door. I sat down on the couch and he sat down beside of me instead of sitting behind his desk.

He said, "I listened to your show last night." Oh, what did I say? Mike was a very imposing, physical person, being the ex-offensive lineman that he was and still a very robust individual. He continued, "After listening to the show, I get the impression that you're on my side with this battle."

"Yes."

"Good," he said, "if you're going to fight for me, you need some ammunition."

We sat there for an hour and a half, and he just poured out everything—all the problems he was having—in some cases with admissions, getting the kids in and the type of players to compete, etc. This was my second year doing the play-by-play and I got more of an insight as to what Duke was all about and some of the inherent problems that were there at that time, and I got very much closer to Mike as a person. I could see where if someone really didn't know him, they could be intimidated.

To this day we're great friends. The basketball team went to Los Angeles to play in a tournament several years after Mike left here, and I was out at the side of the court watching the team practice. All of a sudden I feel two huge arms grab me from behind in a bear hug, and when I could finally turn around it was Mike. He was AD at Southern Cal at that time. We kept in touch through the years, and I see him from time to time as he comes through Durham.

THE OFFENSIVE MASTER-MIND

Steve Spurrier has the best offensive mind I've ever seen in my life; brilliant! He is just an unbelievably self-confident person and does not believe that there a defense that's been invented, or yet to be invented, that he can't beat. It was so much fun watching him and watching him react to the players and what he did for them—the confidence he gave those guys as Duke head football coach from 1987 to 1989. They knew if they came to Duke and played for Steve Spurrier, they were going to throw the football, they were going to be successful and probably have a good shot at the NFL. Lindy Infante said one time that Anthony Dilweg knew more about offensive football than any other rookie he had ever seen come out of college because he had played for Spurrier. I'd go into the football offices on Wednesday mornings to tape the Thursday and Friday daily shows and Steve would be sitting there drawing plays. He'd say, "Bobby, come here and look at this. Do you think this will score?"

"Steve, did you draw it? Then it'll score." Standard ... it didn't take a mental giant to figure that out. Spurrier was a competitor;

he'd fight you. His philosophy has always been, and always will be, that it's his job to score, and it is your job to stop him. If you can't, it ain't his fault for running up the score. I know there are things he has done (a lot of other coaches probably feel this same way) that he would probably like to take back, but in the heat of the moment or excitement of the moment, he'll hurt you.

We went down to Whispering Pines in Pinehurst for a convention where he was the keynote speaker. Steve and I, along with the president and vice-president of the company, played golf together in a tournament for this company's employees. Spurrier left his last putt a foot short that would have given him a 65. He had never seen the course before. He didn't just swing the golf club, he attacked the ball. He doesn't just coach offensive football, he attacks defenses.

I learned so much football from Steve. When he was offensive coordinator with Red Wilson, I'd get with him on Wednesday, Thursday or maybe Friday on the plane going out of town just to find out what gadget plays he had come up with. I'd always get with him to find out what was new, and he'd always tell me. We went to Maryland one year when Ben Bennett was quarterback. I didn't have a chance to see Steve on the plane, so when I saw him about 20 minutes before the kickoff I asked him what new plays he had for the game.

"Nothing. We're just going to go with the same old stuff that you've seen. We didn't feel like there was anything that we needed to do new."

Maryland kicked off to Duke. The Blue Devils came straight from the bench to the line of scrimmage. On the first play, Ben threw a pass for about 25 yards ... ran to the ball, snapped it, threw it for about 30 yards ... ran to the ball, snapped it, threw it into the end zone for a touchdown. I couldn't even catch my breath before Duke scored. No huddle, just straight play.

I threw it to the commercial break after the extra point. The Duke coaches were in the booth next to us with glass between, and I could see Spurrier. He was standing there just dying of laughter—he had pulled one on me big time.

When I finally got a chance to talk to him at half time, I let him have it, that sorry rascal. He really got a lot of enjoyment watching me scramble. During that possession my color commentator Wes (Chesson) couldn't say a word, and I could barely tell the ball situation when they were ready to snap it again.

Away from the field Steve is still very gregarious and loves to have a good time. Yes, Steve Spurrier was a lot of fun to work with.

The Right Man for Duke Football

Fred Goldsmith is a good, genuine person to be with. Fred cut his teeth on defense. As much as Spurrier likes to score, Fred wants to see offenses stopped; he wants to play good defense. He took over the Duke program before the 1994 season and has been very easy to work with.

Fred was very surprised by Duke's first two seasons under him. In 1994 the Blue Devils got out of the blocks quickly against Maryland. We didn't have to play Florida State the first game of the season like we normally do, which gave the kids some confidence. Then the team won a couple of games that maybe they shouldn't have won. All of a sudden the Blue Devils were 7-0 and ranked in the top 25. The team ended the regular season with a record of 8-3 and played Wisconsin in the Hall of Fame Bowl. The Badgers won 34-20.

After my first meeting with Fred, I knew we were two birds of a feather. Our conversation ended up on baseball, and come to find out, he also grew up a Brooklyn Dodger fan. His grandmother and grandfather lived right near Ebbets Field in Brooklyn. His dad had played ball at Southern Cal and played against Jackie Robinson, who played at UCLA.

Fred had polio when he was small and was in the hospital in Miami, and as a favor to Fred's father, Jackie went to the hospital to visit the younger Goldsmith. Unfortunately, Jackie wasn't allowed in the all-white hospital because he was black. Robinson said, "That's OK, I'll wait until he goes home." Fred went home, Robinson visited him and brought him a couple of autographed pictures.

Coach has been a Brooklyn fan for many, many years and we've had some fun with that. Topps came out with a set of trading cards a couple of years ago where they reproduced all the Brooklyn Dodger cards from 1952 to 1955; beautiful cards. I bought two sets and gave one to Fred. He acted like a kid with a new toy at Christmas. Whenever I see or read something that's got a little Brooklyn flavor to it, we'll discuss it.

I think if anybody can take Duke football to the next level, he can. Private schools just have a tougher time than the state schools do. A school like Northwestern or Stanford will have great seasons every now and then and will then fall back. Don't get me wrong, Duke has had a couple of bright moments with the 1989 and 1994 bowl years, but I don't know whether they can compete like that every season. If they could stay in the upper division of the conference every year and go to a bowl every few years, people would be happy. The average Duke fan is not expecting a national championship from the football program.

Fred Goldsmith can take this program to that level.

THE BLUE DEVIL SIGNAL-CALLERS AND RECEIVERS

There have been several very good quarterbacks come through Duke. One that comes to mind is Ben Bennett. "The California Kid" played football for Duke from 1980 to 1983. He had more self-confidence than any football player I have ever been around. He'd tell you he could make it happen, and he could back it up. He could make it happen. He was a good college quarterback with a great arm and a good understanding for the game.

Most good quarterbacks have the ability to go to the secondary receiver if the primary is covered. Bennett was the best at going to the third receiver as any quarterback I've ever seen. He wasn't quite that quick when he had to run with the ball. As I said on the air one day, he was timed in the forty with a calendar. Bennett has more career passing yards at Duke, 9,614 yards, than any other quarterback and also holds the Blue Devil record for completions in a game with 38 against Wake Forest in 1980.

Six seasons after Bennett led the Blue Devil offense, Dave Brown (1989-1991) took over the quarterbacking duties. Brown is another player with a lot of confidence, but his was a quiet confidence. He was not the gregarious Bennett type, but he had confidence in his abilities. He has proven that in the NFL with the New York Giants.

I remember his first start as a college quarterback. The starting quarterback that season, Billy Ray, was injured before we went to Winston-Salem to play Wake Forest. Brown was set to start. Since he had not taken very many snaps and had never started a college game, the biggest question was, will he be nervous? Spurrier had an answer ready when he said, "We'll probably have Brown hand off a couple of times until he gets the feel of the game."

Brown dropped back and threw an 88-yard touchdown pass on the first play of the game. What nervousness? He was just a quarterback with a great arm, a good ability to read defenses, and he was a good kid to be around.

Brown's biggest target in that Wake Forest game was wide receiver Clarkston Hines, who had 251 receiving yards. Clarkston could get open in a phone booth. He knew where the football was going to be, and I think he knew how many steps it was going to take him to get there. Because of that, he was going to be there when the ball got there. I can't remember very many quarterbacks overthrowing him. He had speed, and he had great hands. He didn't drop balls. A lot of receivers are big play receivers, but they will drop some passes; not Clarkston. If he got his hands on it, it was going to be caught. He was a quiet, unassuming, genuine kid.

There are dozens and dozens of other football players who stick out, although maybe not for their ability or the recognition they got, but rather because of who they were. Mike Atkinson, for instance, who came to Duke from a very small 1-A high school in North Carolina, played single wing tail back, and set the state record for touchdowns and rushing yardage for a career. He never really found himself on the football field here, though. He played a good bit but was not the super star everybody thought he was going to be. He has made quite a name for himself since graduation and has done extremely well for himself.

There are a lot of those cases, even kids who were walk-ons who didn't get to play a lot, but they managed to take advantage of a few moments that they did get on the field and took extreme advantage of the classroom. Now those guys are really successful.

Included in this group is also Justin Beckett, a player recruited out of Massachusetts, and now he is one of the more successful business men in the Durham community. Along with a few other business men, he put together a venture capital to work with a lot of third world countries in Africa in development. He's brilliant when it comes to things like that.

In 1997 I saw a kid I had not seen since he graduated, although I had seen a lot of his brother on television. Jay Foxworthy played linebacker at Duke in 1982 and 1984. When I was introduced to his brother Jeff, the comedian and actor, for the first time, he said, "I know Bob, well he may not know me, but I've listened to him since Jay was playing. We used to listen to him while we were watching the games." How about that?!

THE BUILDER AND RECRUITER

Bill Foster was a builder as a basketball coach; he loved to take a program that was in disarray and build it into something. People say it is harder to stay at the top than it is to get there. I don't know which side of that line Foster fell on, but I know he was at his happiest when he was building something. Bill could work 22 hours a day, sleep a couple of hours, and get right back at it. That may have eventually brought on his heart attack when he was at South Carolina. Foster guided the Blue Devil basketball program to a record of 113-64 from 1975-1980.

Bill was, again, very easy to get along with, and we still have a very good relationship. He was a good recruiter, a very good recruiter. He brought in Jimmy Spanarkel and the class that were freshmen when I was a "freshman" (in the broadcast business) at Duke in 1975. Spanarkel was a solid Duke basketball player and a special guy. He still gets the biggest cheers when he is introduced at the alumni games. He was one of the few people to be elected Blue Devil captain as a junior and a senior. He left Duke after scoring 2012 career points. We've remained good friends through the years. Jimmy's got a special place not only with me, but with all Duke people.

> *The first time I ever met Bob was when we were playing little league baseball together in Albemarle, North Carolina. I never really knew he wanted to get involved in radio. Once he got his break at Duke, he's done it very well. The fact that he's been at Duke for as long as he has indicates that Blue Devil officials think he's doing a very fine job.*
>
> Woody Durham, University of North Carolina

The next year Foster added Mike Gminski, and the following year he brought in Gene Banks and Kenny Dennard. Those were three pretty good classes with the people that he had around him. Gminski came to Duke when he was 16 years old, after he graduated from high school a year early. That was one reason that Duke got him, because the other coaches that were recruiting him thought he was going to stay for a senior year. He came to Duke and caught a lot of people by surprise. Mike is a very brilliant man, which is apparent from academic All-American awards for three years. He realizes there are a lot more things going on in the world than just the game of basketball. He's involved in so many other things.

As a player at Duke, he was always quiet. In some cases almost introverted until his late junior and into his senior year. As a freshman and sophomore he was very quiet until he got on the court, and then he made his presence known there. Gminski is currently third on Duke's all-time scoring list with 2323 points and first all-time in rebounds with 1242.

Because of a couple things, Bill Foster got itchy feet to build another program, and he left after the 1980 season. He wanted to change some things that he perceived as improvements in the program and facilities. At the time it was just not in the cards to happen at Duke, and I think he may have gotten a little perturbed at that.

Coach "K"

We could write a book on basketball coach Mike Krzyzewski. Everybody talks about Mike's ability to coach, but I think there are other things that make him successful that are more important than his basketball knowledge. Number one is time management; he is a master at managing time. I think sometimes he has a day clock that has 28 hours in it instead of 24 like everybody else works off. He can get more things done in a short period of time and get them done extremely well because he is such a disciplined person. That goes back to a number of things like his family background, his ethnic background, and his days at West Point where everything was so entrenched. It became a way of life.

The second thing that helps make Mike successful is his ability to get maximum effort out of everybody around him, whether it be his players, his assistant coaches, the office people, me, or whoever. He just always believes that if everybody works together, you automatically get more out of it because you do work as a team and as a family. He knows something that a lot of coaches never find out; some coaches try to deal with everybody the same way, and you can't do that. Coach knows what buttons to push to get people to do things they need to do that make them special.

He will not bring in a youngster simply because he's a good basketball player, he has to fit in with the current players, coaching staff, and everything around Duke. The recruit has to feel comfortable in that fit because, for the most part, the kid's going to be there for four years. Mike's been lucky so far that none of his players have gone pro early. He's had a few transfer and a couple that have dropped out, but I think of only one person right now that has played for Mike for four years that hasn't graduated. That speaks volumes.

Coach makes all players empty their pockets when they get to Duke. They don't bring any baggage with them. It is what they do from the time they step on the court at Duke that matters to him, and he gives them all the same opportunity. He has never, ever promised a recruit any playing time. All he has ever told them, including stars like Grant Hill, Johnny Dawkins, Mark Alarie, Christian Laettner, and Bobby Hurley, is that they will have the opportu-

Bob Harris: A man for all seasons.

nity to play if they bust their tails. That's all they are guaranteed.

When Coach K goes into a recruit's house, he will talk to the family, but he may not talk about basketball for the first hour. He talks about family, the kid's family and his family, about Duke University and about what being a part of Duke University signifies and what it can mean down the road. He is one of the more brilliant coaches in the history of the game.

I would probably put him in the top five coaches of all time. There's a guy eight miles away from Durham in Chapel Hill that's pretty good [Dean Smith], a guy out in California that still rolls up the program and sits on the end of the bleachers down there [John Wooden], and several others in that category. Certainly Krzyzewski deserves to be in that category.

Coach has been perceived different ways by different people. It has even been suggested that he is not personable and only cares about winning. These views go back to the idea of some people not wanting to find out what Mike Krzyzewski is all about. He doesn't give you a lot of coach speak. There are some coaches that you can ask a question, and they will answer what they want you to know, whether it is about that question or not.

Mike's not like that. Mike will answer your question. You might not like it, but he will answer your question. The one thing not to do is to ask him a question to get him to confirm something that you have asked him in the question. In other words he will not affirm your story if you have a hidden agenda. He hates that. He loves the challenge of an interview, a good interview.

There are times I shudder at the thought of the number of questions that I've asked Mike Krzyzewski in 17 years, doing a pregame show with him for every game, a five-minute daily show Monday through Friday every day for 20 weeks for 17 years (that's 340 of those shows), his TV show now for 15 years, various post game shows, and various other interview shows. So, I've asked him a few questions. About once a year, I do take time to thank him for overlooking some of my stupid questions and going ahead and giving a good answer.

Speaking of handling reporters, a lot of people want to refer to Krzyzewski as a "Knight protégé." That's not right. Yes, he played for Bobby Knight and he coached with him for a period of time, but his tactics are totally different. They do have some philosophies that are the same, but Mike has taken the best things that Knight does and thrown out all the garbage. Maybe I'm a little more prejudiced after working with him almost every day during the season and knowing him as I do for 17 years, but with Mike, what you see is what you get. He won't BS you, he'll tell you what's on his mind, good or bad. He won't embarrass a reporter like Knight will.

Mike has an appreciation of my job and of every reporter's job who interviews him or who's in a post game press conference. He knows what that person has to do, and he respects that person for doing it. I ask dumb questions and I think every reporter who has ever interviewed anyone has asked dumb questions, but Mike will give you a good answer.

As a matter of fact, I've never had a problem with any of the coaches, nor the players for that matter, in any interview. In 22 years I have never had to trash an interview. I've never felt bad after a live interview feeling a player may have embarrassed himself. Sometimes you hear athletes on the radio or television and it is obvious they are in college for one reason and one reason only—they could either run the football or shoot a basketball. Maybe I'm a throwback, but that's not right. Sports, supposedly, are an extracurricular activity—one that you do after you complete class work. Those priorities have been reversed in many places. I've never had that problem with a Duke athlete, which points to the way they've been raised and to the coaching staffs we have had here, like we have now with Fred Goldsmith and Mike Krzyzewski.

Mike is also very family-oriented. He was very close to his mom who passed away in 1996. As a matter of fact, she became a part of the Duke basketball family even though she was living in Chicago. She was a very beautiful lady to get to know. Mike would call her after every game and let her know how they did. He's very close to his brother (they are the only two children). Their dad died when Mike was at the Academy. He values family relationships very highly.

He loves his three daughters. I was really proud of him when he walked one of them, Debbie, down the aisle at Duke Chapel when she got married. I didn't even see his lip quiver—he did a good job. (More than I can say for me when I did the same thing about eight years ago.)

Mike has been very successful and he's been rewarded for being successful, to the point where some people have taken him to task for being so rewarded. Why shouldn't he be? Nobody says anything about a great author getting a nice book contract for writing a very good book. Nobody says anything about an actor who gets a nice contract because he has proved that he is a very good actor. That's what America is all about, getting rewarded for your efforts and the good job that you do. If we didn't do that in industry, we never would have anything accomplished. I don't begrudge Mike any nickel that he has made in his life because he has earned every cent of it and will continue to.

All in the Genes

The Duke athletic programs have had some celebrity sons here like Paul Heinsohn and Larry Doby, Jr. Roger Staubach's son just graduated. Staubach and I actually go "way" back.

We made a trip with the basketball team in December, 1977, stopping in Dallas to play SMU and then to California to play Southern Cal. The trip took about five days. While we were in Dallas, we went out to the training camp for the Dallas Cowboys. They were getting ready for the playoffs. I got a chance to interview Tony Dorsett and a couple of others. I waited for a while to interview Staubach, but he was in a quarterbacks meeting when we had to leave.

We were almost ready to get in the car when Staubach came out of the clubhouse and yelled down for us to wait so I could interview him. That's the kind of guy he is. Usually we don't think of NFL quarterbacks running a reporter down to do an interview. It's been enjoyable getting to know him since his son started playing at Duke.

There are tons of great athletes whose sons have gone through the Duke programs. Getting to know some of them, like Roger, has been kind of neat. A lot of times sons have not turned out to be near the athlete their fathers were, but nevertheless, good people.

One of the sons who did live up to his dad's athletic abilities is Grant Hill. Grant is the kind of kid that if you're a man with daughters, you'd like to have him for a son-in-law, or if you had an opportunity to adopt a youngster, he's the kind of kid you'd want. He is one of the more humble super stars I've ever seen.

Hill came into the Duke program when other guys were "the man." He knew that and was totally content to be the role player. Even late in his junior year, Coach had to sit him down and say, "Grant, be you—be aggressive—be the man." Grant usually wanted to make the pass to set up Christian [Laettner] or Brian [Davis] for a shot; he didn't want to hog the limelight.

Overall, Grant was just an outstanding person. All you have to say when trying to explain him, are his parents, Janet and Calvin. They are two of the finest people that I've ever been around, and they have passed along some tremendous values to Grant. In the discipline department they were tough on him, but that paid off handsome dividends. Grant is just a super guy, not to mention his athletic ability which I don't need to comment on.

The Confident Blue Devils

Christian Laettner is a piece of work in a lot of ways. He is a bit arrogant and a bit brash, but a good basketball player with a lot of good basketball sense. The one thing you could say about Christian Laettner, he was a competitor. He and Bobby Hurley were the two most competitive people I have ever been around. They would not lose — they would do everything they could to find some way to beat you — all the way until the final buzzer went off. They wouldn't quit. They had their differences of opinion at times, but it was for that very reason — they were both so confounded competitive. Largely due to competitiveness and talent, Laettner is second in Duke history in scoring with 2460 points, while Hurley is the career leader in assists with 1076.

Laettner could be seen as obnoxious at times to some people. He loved to play games with you, and he got on one of these jags during his senior year. We name an Exxon Supreme Performer of the Game, and one game we did the interview with Laettner as the player of the game. When we got through with the interview he made a little sarcastic remark, "I'm sure glad I won this award." Then he kind of grinned at me.

I said, "Hey don't give me that attitude. I remember when you were a snot-nosed freshman, so don't give me that." He just laughed.

Christian would push you as far as you'd let him. He had that much kid in him and still wanted to feel his oats a little bit. He just needed to be taken down a little bit and respected you for that. Laettner was the same with the younger players in that if they backed off from him, he had no respect for them, but if they got back in his face, he loved it. It has always been so interesting to watch how these kids work together and how they develop relationships and their reaction to coaching.

Laettner had that ability to make something happen when it needed to happen. There were very few times that he didn't. One time he didn't was during a nationally televised game with Arizona at the Meadowlands in New Jersey when he was a freshman. He went to the free-throw line for two shots with 14-seconds left and didn't make them.

After the game I was standing in the hallway outside of the locker room with Wilt Browning, a writer from Greensboro. We were waiting on them to open the locker room so I could do the post game show. We heard footsteps coming around one of these long, round hallways down in the basement at the Meadowlands, and I turned to see who it was.

I turned to Wilt and asked, "Is that who I think it is?"

He said, "It sure as heck looks like him." It was Richard Nixon.

We knew that he was at the game because we had seen him across the arena. He came walking over to us by himself, without any type of security. As he got close to us, I turned and introduced myself to him. He said, "You've got the best job in America, haven't you?"

I said, "You're right about that."

President Nixon loved sports. I asked him if we could interview him on the post game. He said, "Sure." Our engineer at that time was a staunch democrat; believe me, we did not talk politics because he would get mad in a heartbeat. I got on the two-way radio and said, "Send it to me when this commercial is over."

He said, "Is the locker room open?"

"No, but I've got Richard Nixon with me."

"So?"

I said, "We're going to interview him for post game because he's a former president of the United States and a Duke Law school graduate. Do you need anything else? Also, send Phyllis down here (my wife was keeping stats for us at that time)." She came flying down there and we got President Nixon to autograph both of our press passes. We later had them framed and mounted. That was a neat experience.

Anyway, after we had chatted and did a post game interview, he asked permission to go into the Duke locker room. He went straight to Christian Laettner and talked to him about the missed free throws. Nixon recognized the competitiveness, I think, at that point in Laettner.

The one thing everybody remembers him telling Christian is, "I've missed a few, too. Things will work out. There will be day that you'll make a shot like that that'll win a big game for Duke." (Was this a foreshadowing to the 1992 NCAA tournament?)

Hurley was self-confident, maybe not to the cocky point that Laettner was, but still very confident. When he came into the league, however, he was perceived as a whiner and a cry baby because he had a demeanor about him. He'd put his hands on his hips and frown if a call went the wrong way, and everybody said he was a whiner. Coach put a series of highlight tapes together, not of Bobby's shots or his passes, but of his whining. He showed that tape to

Hurley. It embarrassed Bobby, because he didn't realize how that looked. That was the beginning of his sophomore year, and he turned it around unbelievably. Right before we played UNLV in 1991 in Indianapolis, Mike showed him the tape again. Bobby had a pretty good game that night.

Being a coach's kid, Hurley came in with a lot more savvy, a lot more insight into the game than a lot of players. Mike really gave the team to Bobby to run. I think he saw a lot of himself in Bobby. Being a former point guard, Mike respects those kids so much that he will put a lot of confidence in a point guard earlier than he will other players.

Hurley constantly worked to improve. In fact in his last collegiate game, a second-round game in the 1993 NCAA tournament against California, he had a career-high 32 points. He tried everything he could do that night to win that ball game because Cherokee Parks had gotten hurt earlier in the game. Unfortunately, the Blue Devils lost 82-77.

1992: An Incredible Season

The 1991-1992 national championship season was an incredible season which featured a heart-stopping game in the regional finals against Kentucky. A lot of people, myself included, think that was the greatest NCAA game of all time for what was accomplished and what was on the line. Regulation was enough, but to go into overtime and see what happened there, it was phenomenal.

The basketball fan, no matter who he pulled for, had to be impressed with that ball game. I can still close my eyes and go back there. To see the ebb and flow of the game, the momentum switching back and forth, each team looked like they were going to seize it and win it when the other team would make a run and come back. Howard Wood for Kentucky hit a soft shot over Laettner's head to put the Wildcats ahead. That shot forced Duke to call a time out with 1.8 seconds left, trailing 103-102.

The Kentucky fans knew they were going to the Final Four. I will always remember, we threw it to the break, I leaned back in my chair, put my hands behind my head, looked up at the score board, and tried to get all the scenarios down that might happen and who might take the shot for Duke. Basically I figured either Kentucky would win 103-102, or either Laettner, Hurley or Hill would hit a shot and Duke would win 104-103. 104-103. I said it over and over in my mind to make sure I had it right. (The year before in the UNLV game, I got so excited that I stumbled on the score a little bit which kept that call from being really, really good.) For some reason I never once thought about a three-pointer after that time out.

We came back from the break, I reset the scenario, and out of the corner of my eye I saw Laettner coming to the top of the key. He caught the pass, turned, and hit an incredible shot. I will always remember that Laettner did so much in that 1.8 seconds, because I described it on the air as, "Laettner catches, comes down, dribbles (and there was a question mark in my voice like why is he doing this), turns, shoots, scores!"

But then to describe all that was going on, to see all the euphoria of the Duke players—Laettner running, Grant having to chase him down to hug him—was chaotic. Then for some reason or other, I looked down in front of me and saw Kentucky's Howard Woods lying prone on the floor, beating his head into the court. He could not believe the game was lost; two minutes earlier he was the hero.

That's one of the few times that I've ever gone into an opponent's locker room after the game, not for an interview, but just to talk to the players. I especially wanted to talk to the seniors, who had stuck it out through all the probation mess and then to play a game like that. It was just unbelievable.

That was the last Wildcat game that legendary broadcaster Cawood Ledford called. After the game Mike Krzyzewski went straight over to Cawood and asked to go on with him on the Kentucky network to talk to Kentucky fans. That was something.

The 1991-1992 team sticks out in my mind more than any other because of what they did and how they did it. For a team in this day and age in college basketball to be ranked preseason No. 1, go through the season every week at No. 1, and finish No. 1 with a national championship, is truly amazing.

After the game with Kentucky, the Blue Devils went on to defeat Indiana and Michigan for their second straight title. That was a special team.

Is the Sky Duke Blue or Carolina Blue?

The relationship between Duke and the University of North Carolina is so unusual. It has a fierce, fierce rivalry, especially in basketball. The real fierceness, though, is between the fans. The players know each other, they've played against each other in some instances since junior high school and in AAU ball. They've been recruited by the same coaches, they've made recruiting trips together, they've played summer pickup games together, they go to the same restaurants on the weekends, and in some instances dated back and forth on the campuses. It is not the all-out "I hate you" type thing that people want to make it out to be, although we all get caught up in the moment quite a bit.

On the court it had developed into an interesting rivalry between the two coaches. Over the years it developed into more of a professional respect. Mike Krzyzewski was quoted early in his professional career about the relationship between he and Dean Smith, saying, "Well, we're friends, but not to the point of going out and smoking a pack of cigarettes together." (Dean was smoking very heavily at the time, and that comment kind of put things out there.) They respect each other but they don't run in the same circles, so to speak.

There have been so many fantastic basketball games between the two schools, especially between teams coached by Mike and Dean.

One great game that was a loss came in 1984 when Mark Alarie, David Henderson, Jay Bilas, and Johnny Dawkins were sophomores. The Blue Devils were leading Carolina with a few seconds left in regulation, and a Duke player was at the line for a one-and-one. All he had to do was make one and we win. He missed both of them. The Tar Heels came down the floor, and on Matt Doherty's senior day, he threw one up from left field and swished it! The game eventually went into double-overtime and the Tar Heels came out on top, 96-83. Michael Jordan was on that team. That was a great game.

The one basketball game that sticks out in my mind the most was the 1979 game at Cameron. Carolina came in and chose to freeze the ball, to hold the ball. The Tar Heels took only two shots in the first half, both of those were taken from the corner by Rich Yonakor and both were air balls. (That's the first time I ever heard the chant, "air ball.") Duke played Carolina's game for a while, got seven points, and led 7-0 at halftime. Toward the end of the half it was so bad, I started reading out of the press guide just to kill time. How much is there to say when a player is just standing there, holding the ball?

As we went to the halftime break I said, "If they hold the ball the second half, I'm going to have to sing." Evidently somebody got that word to the coaches. In the second half, Dean decided to let Carolina play. The Blue Devils went on to win, 47-40.

The Sportscaster's Dozen

The football teams have had some good battles over the years as well. One of my first football games as the Duke announcer in 1976 was a great game. Carolina won 39-38 in what became the Mike and Mike show with Mike Dunn for Duke and Mike Voight for Carolina. Both players scored four touchdowns. Voight ran in for a two-point conversion that enabled the Tar Heels to win. Some people say it was probably the greatest football game in the Duke/Carolina series. It was a fantastic football game.

> *Bob does a very good job for Duke. He has a great personality which comes through on his broadcasts. I did a professional football game with him one time in Raleigh, North Carolina, and really enjoyed working with him. In basketball he is fast and knowledgeable, which are two keys to doing basketball. He is very good.*
>
> ⋈ *Bob Fulton, University of South Carolina*

One of the more bizarre football games in the series was in 1985 when Steve Slayden helped guide Duke to a late comeback. The Blue Devils were dead in the water that game, trailing with less than 2 minutes to go in the game and Carolina had the football. Basically all they had to do was take the knee for four plays, and we couldn't stop the clock because we had no time outs. The Tar Heels ran two running plays. On the second one, the player got hit, lost the ball, a Duke player recovered it. Duke went on to score for the 23-21 Duke victory. Carolina fans wanted to fire their coach, Dick Crum. Of course, Duke fans wanted to knight him. That was a great comeback.

If it were not for the fans, I could pull for Carolina extremely easily. Some of the fans make it very difficult to do that. Some Carolina people, however, aren't too bad. A couple of years ago, Duke had an off-day after playing Army on the Thursday night ESPN game. On Tuesday I was at the press conference at Chapel Hill, and I was talking to John Swofford, then-athletics director. I asked, "Where would a play-by-play guy who was going to be out of work this Saturday go to find some good football?"

He said, "I think you can find some over here."

"Can I get a couple of tickets?"

"Better yet, how about if you and your wife just come be my guest in my box Saturday?"

I said, "Great, I need to get her out of the house. It was her 50th birthday, and if I just take her to a restaurant for dinner, she won't go. If I tell her we're going to a ball game, then I can sneak her back." (Twenty people were going to be waiting at the restaurant at a certain time.)

When I told Phyllis about it, she was fired up. John gave me a special parking pass, and we parked in his lot. It didn't take long for the people in the press box to realize the Blue Devil play-by-play announcer is in the Carolina athletic director's box. When we got in there, there was a huge sheet cake, white with Duke blue icing around it and it says, "Happy Birthday Phyllis."

That tells me that all Carolina people aren't bad. John Swofford is one-in-a-million. That's the reason he will do such a great job as commissioner of the ACC because of his demeanor, personality, his recognition of other people and attention to detail in making people feel good.

There's at least one other Carolina person who isn't so bad ... Woody Durham. My path crossed that of the North Carolina broadcaster when I was 10 years old and he was 11. Their family moved to Albemarle in 1952. Woody's dad was personnel director for the plant where my dad worked, and he later was my dad's boss for a number of years. Woody's and my path crossed quite a bit growing up through little league baseball, a couple of classes we had together in high school, mixed chorus, and through my work with the football team.

When Woody went to school at Chapel Hill, he had to sell his car because freshmen couldn't have them on campus. My family didn't have a car, so I got my drivers license almost a year late and we bought the "gray ghost," Woody's 1952 Plymouth. He says it was a 1951, and I say it was a 1952. Anyway, it was an early-1950s vintage gray Plymouth. Our family drove it for a couple of years.

Woody knew all along he wanted to be a broadcaster, and I think he wanted to be the broadcaster for his favorite school, the University of North Carolina. For me growing up, I was never really a big Duke fan. It's natural for kids to pull for the team that wins. In 1957, when Carolina won the national championship, I pulled for Carolina. Then I found out I was going to be going to NC State, so I became a State fan, and was until 1975 when we moved to Durham. It's ironic that Woody went on to Chapel Hill and majored in radio/television, and I went another direction, then several years later we came back together. I think it is one of the really ironic stories of broadcasting.

Cameron Crazies

Duke fans are the most creative fans in the country. The student fans, the "Cameron Crazies" have been maligned, sometimes justly, and a lot of times unjustly, because of their creativity. They can be funny, especially after they have been chastised. After Terry Sanford, who was university president at the time, wrote an open letter to them and tried to get them to quit using the BS chant, they started using, "We beg to differ, we beg to differ" when they disagreed with the officials' calls. A couple others include, "Thanks, Uncle Terry" and "Go to heck, Carolina."

When they were allowed to have signs, those were very creative. They used to get on Mike O'Koren unmercifully. Mike had an acne problem, and he was on the "all-ugly team" five years running (all four years in school and then the year after he graduated he was still on the "all-ugly team"). NC State had a penchant for getting players in trouble for stealing or changing price tags on underwear at K-Mart. When those players came over to Cameron the next year, all of the students came in with underwear on their head. Then when the player was introduced, the underwear came out on the floor.

One opposing player was arrested for stealing a bottle of aspirin from a drug store and when he was introduced the next year, you would have thought it was snowing with all of the aspirin flying from everywhere. Chris Washburn of NC State stole a teammate's stereo. The next time Chris came to Cameron, album covers came flying out of the stands.

Clyde Austin was involved in a story about his girlfriend having two cars. When he was introduced the next time, keys were jingled at him and some were thrown on the floor. Lorenzo Charles attacked a pizza guy and robbed him on campus. He was introduced to flying pizza boxes. Unfortunately, he turned around and scored 35 points that night against us. Mike Krzyzewski went to the Crazies before the next game and said, "I don't ever want to see anybody challenge an individual player, ever." They haven't since then.

However, the Cameron Crazies are still alive and well in Krzyzewski-ville.

The Nick of Time

For me, about 12-16 hours a week from Monday through Friday is spent getting ready for a football broadcast. Unfortunately, I will only use about 30 percent of what I prepare. But I don't know which 30 percent I'm going to need, so there no way of cutting anything out. Sometimes it can be kind of aggravating after a game to look at all the notes that weren't used. Learning how to prepare was difficult for me, but I feel I have a pretty good system now.

When we're playing a home game, I generally get to the stadium by 9:00 a.m. just in case the people I work with need something or there's a problem that I can help get solved. As soon as the engineer is finished setting up all the electronic equipment, I get the rest of my things done. Once everything is done, if I don't have any special functions to be a part of before the game, I can sit and relax and catch my breath. There nothing worse than rushing.

There have been several occasions in the past that have really been trying, shall we say, which made me glad all the preparation was out of the way.

The Blue Devils were playing down at Clemson several years back, and our radio crew was staying in Greenville. I decided because of possible traffic I was not going down Interstate 85 to get to Clemson, I was going the back way. Unfortunately, I didn't give us enough time, and we were caught in traffic. We got into the press box 30 minutes before air time. I asked the engineer what we needed to do. He said, "Set the equipment down, and get the hell out of here. Everybody!" Cables started flying everywhere as he frantically set everything up, but he had us on the air at the proper time. He was very good.

We had a similar situation in basketball during the 1984-1985 season before a game in New Jersey at the Meadowlands against Notre Dame. On Saturday morning our engineer, television show producer and myself went into the city to shoot some stand-ups for the TV show. The only problem was that we didn't realize that all but one of the tunnels out of the city had been closed. We finally got to the Meadowlands, and because we were cutting the time close, we had to run to the nearest entrance with all of our equipment on the dolly.

When we got to the door, there was a big police lady, she said, "You'll have to go around to the front."

We said, "Ma'am, we've got to get in there; we go on the air in less than 5 minutes."

"You go to the other entrance."

The engineer said, "We've got to go in here."

She said, "You're going to the front.

"I'm going in here," he insisted.

She reached for her hip (for her gun) and said, "You're going to the front."

We went to the front. When we got into the broadcasting area, the first thing out of the bag was the telephone. The engineer slammed it in and dialed up the network, handed it to me, and said, "Wait for the cue then start talking." We were that close; we were 30 seconds from air time. "Talk for at least two minutes or so, until I give you the signal."

I heard the cue and started talking. I did the opening while he was setting up cart machines and the mixing board, and then he gave me the cue to throw it to the commercial. He started the commercial, I gave him the tape recorder with the coach's show tape in it. He plugged it in, we came back from the commercial, and went straight to the coach's show. By that time he had almost everything set up.

Those are two of the more harrowing experiences we've had. I've always required the engineer to be there three hours ahead of air time in case anything goes wrong. You never know what can happen. I don't like surprises; I want things to be nice and set.

Rushing like that can throw everything off in the first part of a broadcast. I've been fortunate to work with great engineers and technical people. We've always had very good ones, and I never really had that much to worry about.

Pride and Perks

Broadcasting for an institution like Duke is the ultimate experience. First of all outsiders know the institution—the program, the people, the tradition and all the things that go into what is Duke University; those things are known from the outset. You know what's gone on before, the manner in which they did things, and the high level that they set. As a broadcaster you're always striving to keep it at a very high level.

I have to work awfully hard to maintain everything on a high plane, because I know that there are a thousand play-by-play men who would give their eye teeth to have my job. You can't live off your reputation; you can't live off what you did last year, five years ago, or 10 years ago. Broadcasters generally don't become rich financially. Broadcasting is just not that kind of business. That's good because those things keep me on my toes and constantly trying to improve myself.

The thing I'm most proud of career-wise is the fact that I have been able to work for a university like Duke—one that has so much tradition and so much prestige. Hopefully, I've been able to add to that. To have the opportunity to work with, and develop relationships with, so many great coaches and so many student athletes is really an honor.

That Duke pride, however, has turned me into a "homer" to a certain degree. I like to say that I look at the world through Duke blue eyes or that maybe I'm unbiased in favor of Duke. When you travel with these kids all the time, I don't think there are very many play-by-play guys who work with one school who can honestly say that he's not biased to a certain degree. As a broadcaster you are on the plane with the teams, in the team hotels, eating meals together; you just get to know them so well that you know how much they put into it. You know the energy they spend to mix the academics and the athletics at the high level that they have to mix them. And you're so appreciative of what they do, that you want to see them succeed. Then when things go against them, you feel bad for them.

Phyllis and I have had an opportunity to travel quite a bit with the Duke football and basketball teams. We've been to the West Coast several times, and we've been to Alaska for the Great Alaska Shootout with the basketball team. The team has been to Hawaii five times since I've been here, three trips of which I've been able to go on. The football team played in the Coca-Cola Bowl in Japan, where we spent a week. Those trips were fun from the standpoint of getting to travel and see a lot of the world that we had never seen.

There have also been some trips that haven't been quite as much fun, and it's safe to say that we've seen things we didn't need to see. In December of 1990, we flew into Boston to play Harvard in basketball. Due to snow at Logan Airport, our plane was put in a holding pattern for an hour. The runway was opened briefly, but as we were in the glide path it closed again. We were diverted to Worcester, Massachusetts, where it was snowing. Ice was everywhere, and it was extremely windy. We hit the runway, which was a solid sheet of ice. We went all the way to the end of the runway, and how the pilot got that plane stopped, I'll never know. But as soon as he turned the light off, he got a standing ovation. As soon as we got into the terminal, they closed that airport. They had to send a school bus for us, because the bus that we had to pick us up at Logan couldn't get to Worcester. We finally got to the hotel that night about six hours late. At least we made it.

In 1979 the basketball team played Marquette on a Sunday afternoon. When we arrived in Madison, Wisconsin, on Saturday night, the wind chill was 40 degrees below zero! We were told that once we got into the hotel not to leave for any reason at all because we could die—our lungs could freeze. There have been a lot of trips like that.

An Involved Family

There have been times broadcasting as a career has been difficult on our family life, mainly because of the travel and time away from home. I was fortunate when we were in Albemarle; all the high schools were in close proximity so Phyllis and the kids could go to a lot of the games. Even though they were in the stands while I was in the radio booth, we were going to the games together and coming home together.

When we came to Duke, going to the games together became more difficult because of the travel. With two small kids who had to be in school, mom stayed home with them and did a lot of the raising. When the team had a game at home or close by, North Carolina or North Carolina State, the kids usually got to go. Our family was, and still is, involved in the games.

During Mike McGee's later days of coaching football at Duke, our youngest daughter was about eight years old and was sitting in the stands for a game. When a fan started criticizing Mike, our daughter turned around with tears streaming down her face, and screamed to the man, "If you can do any better, go out there and do it yourself." Our family is involved in the games.

In our house life revolves around ball games. When one of our daughters was engaged to be married, she chose her wedding day one year in advance when there was an open football date.

While there have been some hardships and difficult times, the rewards have been unbelievable in regards to the things Phyllis and the kids have been exposed to. I think it made us all grow as individuals and as a family.

Life's Too Short ... Have Fun

The most important thing for aspiring broadcasters is to learn everything you can about the broadcasting profession, including what everybody does and what their responsibilities are. Be loyal to the people you work for, the people who work for you, and the other people who surround you.

The whole purpose for a radio play-by-play person is to put the listener in the seats, and paint a word picture that is so vivid, the listener believes he or she is actually watching the game. The highest compliment that any listener can give me is not, "You did a great job with that broadcast," but rather, "I felt like I was there." That's it; as a broadcaster you can't get any better than that. You have to develop your own style for doing that.

For my style I hope I have taken some good things from the good people that I have listened to and worked with—not only the predecessors, but contemporaries as well. A lot of the guys included in this book I listened to and still do, because you should never stop improving your style or building it. If you feel like you have it built then all that can happen is that it gets torn down. You've got to keep building all the time.

Above all else though, have fun and enjoy it. If it is not fun, then get the heck away from it. Life's too short to have to do something that you don't like or that you don't have fun doing. I made myself a promise 30 years ago that if I ever got up in the morning, looked in the mirror, and hated to go to work that day—not because of something that might be going on, but because of the job itself—then I would go in, resign and find something enjoyable. Luckily, I haven't had to do that.

As I tell people when I speak to groups, to borrow a line from New York Yankee great Lou Gehrig, "Today, I consider myself the luckiest man on the face of the earth." I have the opportunity to travel all over the world, stay in some of the nicest hotels, eat good food, work with some of the most brilliant coaching minds in history, work with great student-athletes, and usually get the best seat in the house for great games; and to top it off, they pay me to do it! What more can you ask for?

Cawood Ledford

UNIVERSITY OF KENTUCKY

I was very young when we got our first family radio, but I do remember it. We had it in our family room, which now serves as my office. I grew up in a very average home in the sense that we used to sit and listen to the radio at night, listening to whatever mother and dad liked (which meant we mainly listened to entertainment programs).

CBS used to carry a lot of baseball broadcasts which I enjoyed as well as football games on Saturday afternoons. Guys like Red Barber and Ted Husing were the two that I liked.

> *The secret of success is to do the common duty uncommonly well.*
> — John David Rockefeller

I had always liked participating in sports and listening to broadcasts on the radio but never gave broadcasting as a profession a thought.

I Can't Be Rupp So I'll Be Red

In the early 1950s, I was an assistant basketball coach at a Kentucky school which has since been consolidated, Hall High School. At the end of the 1951 season the radio station in Harlan, Kentucky, hired the head basketball coach to sell advertising and do some sports on-air. About three months later in June he called me to meet for coffee, at which time he said how he enjoyed selling and doing sports on WHLN, but he really missed coaching. He told me how he wanted to recommend me for his position at the station when he resigned.

I had never been in a radio station before in my life, but he set up an appointment for me with the station management. After I met with them, I went back and made an audition tape which was horrible. It was the first time I had ever heard myself.

Somehow after that terrible audition tape, I got the job. I was at WHLN for two years selling advertising during the day, doing a sports show, and Class D minor league baseball (which is no longer in existence). The baseball team was pretty good. It was a farm team for the Boston Braves, so some nice players came through here.

Broadcasting had never entered my mind as a career. Before working at WHLN I kind of wanted to be a coach, but I think I realized by 1951 that I wasn't going to be the next Adolph Rupp. I was just really searching for what I wanted to do when the opportunity came along.

In 1953 I left for Lexington and the University of Kentucky.

> Cawood Ledford is a brilliant broadcaster and probably has the best voice out of all of us. Of all the old-timers, nobody had a voice like Cawood. He was impeccable.
> ₨ Larry Munson, University of Georgia

There used to be a chain of theaters called Schine. The man who was in charge of those theaters for the eastern part of Kentucky (from Lexington to the east) was a fellow by the name of Bob Cox. There was a Schine Theater in Harlan and Bob was in town visiting it. When I got back to the station late one night after a game there was a message for me to call him. When I called Bob, he said he wanted to meet for breakfast the next morning.

When we met he told me he had liked the work that I had done and that if I wanted to go to Lexington and the University of Kentucky, he wanted to help me. He knew a lot of people at the stations in and around Lexington. A few months went by without hearing anything else, until one day Bob called me and said that he had an appointment for me on the following Monday at WLEX.

I went down, did the interview, and was hired about a week later. WLEX had just lost its sports guy, Jim Thacker, who eventually ended up in Charlotte. I was at WLEX for three years.

In 1956 I got two calls within two days for other jobs. One was from WAPI in Birmingham, which covered Auburn, and the other call was from WHAS in Louisville. I visited both stations before I elected to go with WHAS where I stayed until 1979. Even though I was working for a Louisville station, I was still doing UK games. In 1979 I moved back to Lexington where I stayed until after my last season in 1992.

The Movers Behind the Football Program

Even though the football teams at Kentucky have usually been less than spectacular, there have been four coaches who have made an impact on either the program or the fans; Bear Bryant, Fran Curci, Jerry Claiborne, and Bill Curry.

The University of Kentucky broadcast crew before the start of a football game.

I was only with Bear Bryant for one year, but when I first met him I was petrified because he was already a great coach. Actually, I got to know him better when he was at Alabama and found he was also a great person.

Bert Banks owned the station in Tuscaloosa, Alabama. During the basketball season when the Wildcats were down there, he would have Coach Bryant and Coach Adolph Rupp at his home. I got to know Coach Bryant very well then as I sat and listened to their stories. I'm not sure Bryant and Rupp were on the best of terms when Bear first went to Alabama, but they became close after he left.

Fran Curci had two great teams while he was here. In fact he had the best two teams here in my 39 years of calling Kentucky football. Those two teams were the 1976 and 1977 teams which both split the Southeastern Conference title. (Georgia in 1976 and Alabama in 1977 were the other co-champions.)

The 1976 team defeated North Carolina 21-0 in the Peach Bowl. Unfortunately, the team went on probation in 1977 after going 10-1. The Peach Bowl team had a 10-year reunion in 1996 and invited me. It was nice seeing some of the players and Fran, who now lives in the Tampa Bay area. Fran was an outstanding coach at Kentucky and is a good friend.

Fran had kind of let the program get a little slipshod off the field after the 1977 season before Jerry Claiborne came in and really got things straightened out. The team was off probation when Jerry came in, but they were still not winning.

Jerry took two teams to bowl games and had some other competitive, but not great, teams. There haven't been a lot of great football teams at Kentucky.

He was really strong on academics. In fact, the first and only time Kentucky led the nation in graduating players was when Claiborne was here. He was the right man at the right time.

On and off the field Jerry Claiborne is a great guy.

Speaking of great human beings, Bill Curry is a great one. Unfortunately, he could never get the program going through the 1990s.

As a person Bill is the salt of the earth. We think the world of Bill and his wife, Carolyn, and are very close to them.

The Top Cats

Surprisingly, even though the Kentucky football teams haven't been great, there have been some top athletes. Players such as Lou Michaels and Steve Meilinger come to my mind almost immediately as top Wildcats. Michaels was just awesome and Meilinger could play anywhere, in fact he played three positions in three years and kept making All-American at end even though he hardly played there during one particular season.

Lou Michaels played in the late 1950s and finished fourth in the voting for the Heisman Trophy in 1957. Art Still, who played pro ball for years, was on a couple of the better Kentucky teams in 1976 and 1977. Derrick Ramsey played quarterback on those teams but had a long professional career as a tight end.

Some of the other players who stick out from my days at Kentucky include Howard Schnellenberger who coached at Louisville until recently Ray Correll, Sonny Collins, Roger Bird, Warren Bryant, Jeff VanNote, Mark Higgs, and Rick Norton, just to name a few. Kentucky has had good players, just not enough at the same time to make many good teams.

The Baron of the Bluegrass State

Adolph Rupp was already at Kentucky when I arrived. I think without a question he and Hank Iba from Oklahoma A&M (now Oklahoma State) were the two premier coaches in the game of college basketball from the 1930s through the 1960s. When I got to Kentucky, Rupp had already won three national championships, which at that time was more than any other college basketball coach had won. He was at the top of his game when I met him.

The Wildcats were suspended from playing a schedule in the 1952-1953 season, but they continued to practice that year and came out in my first year, 1953-1954, and went undefeated.

Rupp was a great person to work with because he was very colorful. He was a tough guy to play for, though. He demanded perfection which nobody could deliver, but I think he got everything he could out of each player.

There are so few characters anymore that it made him even more enjoyable to be around. I was there for Rupp's last 19 years, so I got to know him very well and thought a lot of him.

Off the floor he was one of the most entertaining people to be around at dinner. He was a very private man, but if you could get him to go to dinner with a few friends, he was a charmer. He was very well-read and could speak on about any subject. While the rest of us were reading sports pages on the plane, he was generally reading *The Wall Street Journal, Barrons,* or the *Hereford Digest.* (He raised cattle and was president of the National Hereford Association at one time.) He was a very entertaining fellow.

I think Coach Rupp was also the most superstitious man who ever lived. He carried a buckeye and a four-leaf clover, and he always wore a brown suit on the day of a game. If he was in a tournament where they played everyday, and they won, he would go home and wash out his socks because he didn't want to take any chances. He parked in the same parking space on game day and walked the same journey from his car to the Coliseum, which included stepping on the same manhole cover every time.

He was extremely superstitious. He didn't leave anything to chance, but he would have won without those superstitions. He was a winner, there's no doubt about it.

> Cawood is the consulate; he is the sportscaster's sportscaster. Above all, Mr. Kentucky brought a level of professionalism to the microphone that you just do not find in a lot of people.
>
> — Bob Harris,
> Duke University

Without question Rupp brought basketball to the South. He beat people so badly that they got tired of it and started to go out to find good coaches and build better places to play. I know when Coach Rupp died, longtime Georgia Tech coach Whack Hyder said that without question, "He (Rupp) was the man who made basketball in the South."

Cawood (right) with the legendary Adolph Rupp.

Following the Leader

I knew Joe B. Hall really well when he got the head coaching job at Kentucky because he had been an assistant for about seven years under Coach Rupp. Rupp pretty much kept to himself a lot on the road, but we would go out to dinner with the assistant coaches, which is how I knew Joe B. so well.

Following the legend of Coach Rupp, Joe B. Hall came into the head coaching job under great pressure. It was very tough for him, but he did a great job.

I thought when Joe B. was promoted to the head coaching job that he deserved it, and I think that he proved that. In his 13 years as head coach, Hall won eight Southeastern Conference titles, won the NCAA championship one time and was runner-up another time, and he won the NIT (which was still a good tournament), in the 1970s.

I don't think Joe B. was ever appreciated for the good coach he was, but I think as time has gone by that people realize what a heck of a job he did.

Kentucky's Darkest Days

Eddie Sutton is a great guy. We always got along great, and I think the world of him and his wife, Patsy. He was a superb coach for Kentucky who just let the program get a little out of control, and, in turn, resigned under pressure. I still think he is an outstanding coach.

The Wildcat program's going on probation was very tough. The investigation for it came during Eddie's last year which was the 1988-1989 season. During that time the players didn't want to play, the fans were embarrassed, and the coaches didn't put their hearts into coaching. It was the only losing basketball team I ever followed (the team finished with a record of 13-19). In fact, it was the first losing season at Kentucky in 62 years. It was a dismal year. Sutton left at the end of that year.

He had done a great job up until then, but he was only here for four years which is a short stay. I think the magnitude of the program almost overwhelmed Eddie. He built a great program at Arkansas out of nothing, and I think he thought this would be the same, but it wasn't. It's a big program and a tough animal to fight.

Rick Pitino, who replaced Sutton, came to Kentucky in its darkest days and rebuilt it quickly. He had built programs everywhere he had been. He had the reputation of being a builder. Before Rick came here, he was unhappy with his position with the New York Knicks. Up until the time I met Rick at his first press conference, I was only familiar with the job he had done in various places.

I had seen his Providence team in the 1987 Final Four while I was there. When I saw their players I couldn't help but wonder how they had gotten there, because they didn't look like they would be that good. He had beaten a great Alabama team which was one of Wimp Sanderson's best teams. Then they came back and beat Georgetown which was a highly ranked team. Providence lost to Syracuse in the Final Four.

At that first press conference at Kentucky he was pretty noncommittal. I walked out with athletics director C. M. Newton, whom I had known forever. I told him I didn't think Rick was going to come to Kentucky. C. M. said, "We've got him." He was right. It was a great day and a super marriage for Kentucky.

The Wildcats couldn't play in a postseason tournament for the first two years Rick was here, but it was mind-boggling how quickly he built the program back up.

In the third year, when they were eligible for postseason play, and he was turned loose, Rick won the Southeastern Conference tournament. The Wildcats went to the NCAA Elite Eight before they lost to a great Duke team in overtime. That 1991-1992 game is one that many still consider one of the best in the history of the NCAA tournament.

The team came back in 1995-1996 and won the national championship by defeating Syracuse, 76-67.

Rick Pitino came to Kentucky at the perfect time for the program and we developed a good relationship. The close relationship I had with all the coaches helped. In fact about three weeks before his first game with Kentucky, Pitino called me and asked if I had any objection to moving our postgame interview to courtside and also broadcasting it over the public address system. I told him I didn't have any objections, and I didn't think anybody was going to care.

> *I didn't get to hear Cawood call too many football games, but I loved to hear him do basketball. Whenever Cawood stepped into Rupp Arena, Kentucky basketball came alive. I have a greater appreciation for the game of basketball because of him. I also loved to hear Cawood call the Kentucky Derby because that is a very challenging job, and he mastered it.*
>
>   *Otis Boggs,*
>   *University of Florida*

Rick is a great entertainer and a great showman, as Coach Rupp was. The two of them were the true entertainers of the four coaches I worked with in basketball. The crowds were tremendous for our postgame interviews from courtside. Chris Cameron, who was the SID at Kentucky at that time, had figured that the crowds were so large for Coach's postgame that it was the 16th largest crowd in college basketball.

The 1996-1997 season marked the last for Coach Pitino as he accepted the head coaching job with the Boston Celtics of the NBA. I think his replacement, Tubby Smith, will do a great job here, but Rick Pitino will be missed. Rick is a close friend, and, in my opinion, the best coach in the sport.

If Rick had left three years earlier, he would still have done such a remarkable job.

The Fiddlin' Five

The Fiddlin' Five team was a big surprise when it won it all in 1958, even though it was a senior team who had been together for a long time. At that time the conference champions were the only ones eligible for the NCAA tournament, and Kentucky had to win at Tennessee on the last game of the year to go. Then it had the great good fortune of playing the entire NCAA tournament in the state of Kentucky.

I was lucky to be at Kentucky for two basketball national championships, 1958 and 1978. Even though they were 20 years apart, they stick out very vividly. (The Wildcats won three championships before I got there and one after I left.) The championships are really special. It's always been tough to win the tournament, and if anything, it keeps getting tougher.

When tournament time came around in the 1957-1958 season, the "Fiddlin' Five" team was peaking. It defeated Miami of Ohio in the first round, 94-70, then beat a really, really good Notre Dame team in Lexington, 89-56.

The semifinals and finals were played in Louisville. In the semifinals the Wildcats beat Temple by one point, 61-60. Those same two teams had played a triple-overtime game during the regular season in Lexington with Kentucky winning, 85-83. Temple only lost three games that season, including the two to Kentucky.

The Wildcats met Seattle in the finals and were given no chance against the team which featured one of the best opposing players I saw during my career, Elgin Baylor. Kentucky worked its gameplan perfectly and got Baylor in foul trouble early. The Wildcats, which were led by Vernon Hatton with 30 points and Johnny Cox with 24, came back twice after trailing by 11 points and won, 84-72, to capture the NCAA Championship.

That 1957-1958 team was a surprise. It had six losses that season, which to that point was the most losses any team had who still went on to win the national championship.

Coach Rupp kept talking about how that team was just "fiddlin' around and fiddlin' around." He said that he was playing a Carnegie Hall schedule with a bunch of fiddlers instead of violinists.

The guards on that team were Hatton and Adrian Smith. Ed Beck was the center. One of the forwards on that team was John Crigler who had 14 points and 14 rebounds against Seattle in the finals. Cox, a great outside shooter, was the other forward.

Rupp's Runts

The "Rupp's Runts" team of 1965-1966 was another surprise team, although it fell a game short of winning the NCAA title. It lost to

Texas Western (now UTEP) in the finals of the NCAA tournament, 72-65. The team finished the previous season with a 15-10 record.

Joe B. Hall had just joined Coach Rupp's staff as an assistant coach after the 1964-1965 season. After a big-time sales job on Coach Rupp, Joe B. helped install a running and weightlifting program for the team. Coach Rupp had previously objected to weightlifting because he felt that it would make the players musclebound, which is something a lot of people thought then.

At the start of the season, this team was ranked nowhere in the world. Then the "Runts" won 23 straight games and were ranked No. 1 in the country. They lost the next-to-the-last game of the season to Tennessee in Knoxville, 69-62.

Throughout the NCAA tournament the team played well, defeating Dayton, Michigan and Duke, but then losing to Texas Western in the finals.

Larry Conley, I thought, was the heart of that team; he was a great shooter but an even better passer. Conley and Tommy Kron were the two seniors on that team, and I thought they really sacrificed themselves for the good of the team. Louie Dampier and Pat Riley were the two juniors from that team who went on to make All-American. Thad Jaracz was the sophomore who played in the middle.

They earned the name "Rupp's Runts" because their tallest players were Kron and Jaracz at 6-foot-5.

The 1965-1966 team was the best passing team at Kentucky since 1953 and mostly because of Conley. He was a tremendous basketball player who never got the honors he deserved, but he was the heart and soul. Ask any player today from that team, and they'll say that Conley was the player who really made things go.

Riley was probably the best athlete on that team. Pat was recruited more for football. He was a great quarterback in high school in the Syracuse, New York, area. He was determined, though, to play basketball, and when he came to Kentucky, at 6-foot-3, he jumped center. He could really jump and rarely ever lost a tip-off to start a game. Riley played forward as a strong player who could shoot the ball and was a great competitor.

I never did think of Riley as the coaching type. Actually in that group I saw Conley as more of a coach, even though he never became one. (I think he has found his calling in broadcasting.) I had lost track of Pat until Kentucky went to the NCAA tournament in 1975, when the Wildcats lost to UCLA in legendary coach John

Ledford and former Kentucky basketball coach Rick Pitino during a postgame interview.

Wooden's last game. Pat walked up to me at that tournament, and I didn't even recognize him because he had a huge beard. Come to find out he was doing color for the Los Angeles Lakers, where he later became an assistant coach, then head coach. He's been fantastic ever since. Riley was always a laid-back, happy-go-lucky kind of student and is the last person I would have pictured as a head coach.

THE FUTURE NUGGET

Dan Issel was a great player and a person who took great pride in being a good player. Former Vanderbilt coach Roy Skinner told me one time that he saw Issel more than any other player as one who made tremendous improvement every single year for four years.

Issel was the type of player who, whenever he got into a shooting slump, would go into the gym and put in a lot of shooting on his own. He would deny it if you accused him of working to get out of a slump or saw him in there. He was a great competitor.

In men's basketball at Kentucky, Issel is still the all-time leading scorer with 2,138 points. He did that in three years since freshmen weren't eligible to play when he was in school. Coach Rupp adored Issel and maybe let him shoot more than he would a lot of people, but Dan knew what to do with it.

The Sportscaster's Dozen

In a game at Mississippi in 1970 when Issel was about to break the SEC scoring record for a game, Coach Rupp took him out. A manager went over and told Coach Rupp that Issel only needed a few more points to break the record, so Coach put him back in. As soon as Issel got his 53rd point and broke the record, Rupp took him back out. There's no telling how many Issel may have had that night because that wasn't a very good season for Ole Miss.

Dan Issel was also very bright; in fact, he was an academic All-American for the Wildcats. After he left the University of Kentucky in 1970, Issel had a great professional career with the Kentucky Colonels of the old ABA and then with the Denver Nuggets in the NBA.

Since his playing career he has also been a coach for Denver and now works in their front office. He's also doing some part-time broadcasting. I did a few games with Issel after he got out of school, and he did a tremendous job. I think he could be a great broadcaster if he ever decides to go full-time into it. Dan Issel was inducted into the Basketball Hall of Fame in Springfield, Massachusetts in 1993.

"Goose" and Macy

In the mid- to late-1970s, Kentucky was fortunate to have some of the top players in the country. In turn the Wildcats won the NCAA title in 1978. Two of the players who helped lead that 1977-1978 team were Jack "Goose" Givens and Kyle Macy.

Jack Givens was just a really smooth basketball player. In fact one of his nicknames was "Silk" even though most people knew him by "Goose." He came out of Lexington, so he was not a secret to Kentucky fans. The Wildcat staff started going after him when he was a sophomore in high school.

"Goose" had a fantastic game when Kentucky won the national title in 1978. He had 41 points in the win over Duke and was at that time three points shy of the scoring record for a title game. He just shot the lights out.

Givens was almost a middle-range shooter on that team, playing with guys like Truman Claytor and Macy who could shoot from the outside, and the twin towers inside with Rick Robey and Mike Phillips. Jack fit in perfectly between those two groups. He could shoot from the outside and could drive to the basket, but if he was anywhere around the circle or the lane, he was a deadly shooter. He could also play defense. Givens was just a good athlete.

I was really surprised that he didn't play longer than three seasons in the NBA. He is in broadcasting now, doing color for the Orlando Magic.

Macy is a player who also went into broadcasting, although he has since left the microphone and gone into coaching. He was the missing part of the puzzle in 1978.

Kentucky had recruited him as hard as they recruited anybody out of high school, but he started out at Purdue. For some reason he wasn't happy there, so he transferred to Kentucky. The 1977-1978 season was his first year of eligibility after having to sit out one year. The year he sat out, the Wildcats lost in the NCAA regionals to North Carolina.

He started the first game he was eligible to play and was a great, great player. Macy was an All-American. He was a great floor shooter and a great free throw shooter. In fact, he still holds the record for the highest free throw percentage for a career at 89 percent. One thing a lot of Kentucky fans remember about Macy is how he always wiped his hands on his socks before he shot a free throw.

"Goose" and Macy were two great players and really nice guys to be around.

The Best Hopping to the NBA

The last three best players that Kentucky has had in the 1990s have all left school early for the NBA, which is a shame, but I think that's the trend in college basketball. At any rate Jamal Mashburn was an outstanding basketball player. He was the one player who, I think, really elevated Kentucky when it was making its comeback after probation.

Antoine Walker only played two years in college before being drafted in the first round by the Boston Celtics in 1996. Now Ron Mercer, after becoming an All-American as a sophomore, was drafted by the Celtics in the first round of the 1997 NBA draft.

> *I've always thought Cawood was an exceptionally fine broadcaster. Even though he was representing the University of Kentucky and they won the basketball game 99 out of 100 times we played them, Cawood tried to deliver the broadcast very professionally and unbiased. He had every opportunity to be nonprofessional because of what he represented, but he wasn't. He did an excellent, excellent job. He was also a prince of a guy, just a genuinely good person. I was always a great admirer of his. He and his wife, Frances, were always one of my favorite couples around the league.*
> ~ Jack Cristil, Mississippi State University

Cawood with the great Jackie Robinson.

There have been a lot of great players here, but those are the three who come to mind as possibly the best in the 1990s.

Even though I'm a college fan myself, players can't be blamed for leaving early to go to the NBA. I hate to see it, but I think it's going to keep everybody humble because teams aren't as likely to keep great players for four years.

Again, the players can't be blamed because they never know if they're going to get hurt or have a bad year in college. Most of them have also tested the waters, or at least their coaches have, and know they'll be drafted fairly high. A high draft pick means instant riches. I don't know how you can blame them. I would do the same thing.

The Games That Made the Players

Any last-second shot or play is one that you remember. There is one play from a game that comes to my mind immediately. After I had finished broadcasting, we went to Maui with the team early in the 1993-1994 season and played three games, the third of which was against Arizona.

Arizona was ahead with just a few ticks left on the clock. Kentucky came down the floor. Rodrick Rhodes fired up a long three-point attempt that missed, but Jeff Brassow was there to tip the ball in for the 93-92 win.

The biggest basketball comeback which had some memorable plays came in the 1993-1994 season during a game in Baton Rouge against Louisiana State University. Kentucky was down by 31 points with 15 minutes to go but came back in the second half to win 99-95. That was incredible!

I remember the game with Indiana in 1975 which earned the right for Kentucky to go to the Final Four. Indiana had beaten the Wildcats 98-74 earlier in the season and could have won bigger but Bobby Knight called off the dogs. It was embarrassing enough, but it could have been really bad. The Hoosiers hadn't lost all year until Kentucky won in Dayton in the Mideast Regional finals, 92-90. That same Indiana team came back the next year and did go undefeated to win it all.

The most unusual football play I remember was several years back when Kentucky was playing Ole Miss at Stoll Field. During one possession Kentucky had lost a lot of yardage on every play. They were back in their own territory on 4th down and 41 yards to go. Kentucky had a punter by the name of Larry Seiple, who went on to play for the Miami Dolphins, back to punt. For some reason Ole Miss didn't rush a single player for the block, and Larry, who was a good athlete, noticed this and just took off with the ball. Forty-one yards is no prayer, and he not only got those 41 yards, he scored a touchdown to help upset a good Mississippi team. That's probably the most unusual play I saw.

The Wildcats played at Vanderbilt one year in a stinking game; the score was 7-7 late in the game. Vandy had the ball late, and they tried a running play up the middle. The fans booed. I guess the coach felt it a little bit so on the next play, the last play of the game, they threw a pass, but it was picked off by Kentucky's Darrell Bishop who ran 60 yards for the touchdown.

There have been a lot of great games over the years, but those are a few that stick out in my mind.

The Rivals: Louisville and Indiana

The Kentucky and University of Louisville rivalry is a big rivalry even though the two teams didn't play each other for about 25 years. Coach Rupp was dead-set against playing any instate school. Then Joe B. Hall felt the same way when he became head coach. Finally word came down to Joe B. that the Wildcats would play Louisville. By the time Pitino came around, he was ready to play all of the instate schools. Strangely, even though Coach Rupp didn't want to play Louisville, Kentucky has done well and leads the series.

Coach Rupp and Joe B. didn't want to play instate schools because they felt that Kentucky was the established program and they knew that if they played these other schools some, then they'd lose some. I don't think it was right, but they thought if they lost those games then it would diminish their recruiting power around the state. I don't think that's happened, but that was their thinking.

The funny thing about that is that Louisville's program was already established when we played them. In fact they beat Kentucky the first time the two teams met after the drought. Louisville beat Kentucky in the Mideast Region finals in Knoxville in 1983 in overtime, 80-68.

Out of the conference, Indiana has been another good rival. Whenever Kentucky and Indiana play they play at a neutral site, either Indianapolis or Louisville. They started that several years ago. In fact it started out as a Big Four tournament in Indianapolis with Kentucky, Indiana, Louisville and Notre Dame. CBS decided they only wanted to televise the game between Kentucky and Indiana, which left Louisville and Notre Dame not interested in going up there without getting any television money. So it was set up where Kentucky and Indiana would play in Indianapolis one year and Louisville the next year, and they split the tickets right down the middle. It's been a great series.

In the Southeastern Conference the rivals change. Tennessee has been a rival; LSU has been a rival. Arkansas was probably the last big rivalry that Kentucky has had in the conference. The biggest Kentucky rival in the SEC is the team who can beat them every once in a while.

Year in and year out I would say that Louisville and Indiana are the two big rivals for Kentucky.

The Opposition: The Characters of the Game

I got to know a lot of the opposing coaches like Roy Skinner at Vanderbilt, Ray Mears at Tennessee, and Dale Brown from LSU. In fact, I love characters, and Dale Brown is who I consider a character. He was a delightful fellow that I loved to interview. In one of Dale's early trips to Lexington, after getting mad he took off his coat and threw it to the middle of the floor. When Brown came to Kentucky for his last time, Coach Joe B. Hall took off his coat and threw it to the middle of the floor. That was a lot of fun.

Wimp Sanderson at Alabama always looked like he was about to die on the sidelines, but his trademark was that plaid sports coat. The Tide came in to play Kentucky one time, and Pitino, who is always dressed in Armani suits, went out and found the ugliest plaid coat he could to wear to that game. I don't think Wimp appreciated that too much. The Wildcats won that night. Wimp's a great person. I hated to see him leave Alabama.

Speaking of characters, Bob Knight at Indiana is a great person to interview. Away from the court he is one of the most delightful people you would ever want to spend an evening with. Granted, during the season Bobby Knight can be his own worst enemy because he's just what he is, and he isn't going to change for anybody. I think sometimes it comes off worse than it is. He does some things that I'm sure he wishes he hadn't done when he gets up the next morning.

If you're friends with him, he'll go to the end of the world for you. Bob is a very special man.

Coach Knight was my color analyst for a final four one year. An active coach can't be an analyst anymore. Knight came to the booth well prepared and did an incredible job. He was a fine analyst and didn't try to do the play-by-play.

There were so many coaches over 39 years, most of whom I got to know — at least the ones who were in it for any length of time. Working with a program like Kentucky I've been able to see a lot of great coaches and characters who have gone against the Wildcats.

Do You Have a Telescope?

There haven't been a lot of bad places to broadcast games from, but there is one particularly difficult place: Vanderbilt's Memorial Gymnasium. It has what ought to be a football press box. It's the worst place I've ever worked. You're so far removed from the court, and you're almost looking down on the tops of the players' heads. I joked with Joe B. Hall one time before we went to Nashville, asking him if he would consider painting numbers on the top of the players' heads. The only thing you can see really well is if an official blows an out-of-bounds play because you can sure see the stripes on the floor. Vanderbilt is the hardest place to broadcast from, I think.

There aren't many bad places left, but there used to be some. Madison Square Garden in New York was really tough, but they've improved it to where it isn't bad anymore. At the University of Tennessee they put you up, but you're not far, only about halfway up. Most arenas nowadays have nice places to work. In fact, with most of them you're at courtside. That's not a bad seat.

The Blue Mist

Kentucky fans are super-duper fans. They live and die Kentucky sports. The basketball fans follow the team everywhere. I was a Kentucky fan, especially basketball, even before I started doing the games. I can be a fan more now that I'm not doing the games.

It's virtually impossible to get a ticket to a Kentucky home basketball game, selling over 24,000 tickets each game. Because of the home sellouts, when the team goes out of town, to Knoxville, for instance, to play Tennessee, it'll be at least a 50-50 crowd.

The UT administration got smart, and it packaged the Vanderbilt and Kentucky games with a game on either side, so you have to buy tickets to three or four games. Kentucky fans still buy the package and throw away the other tickets. They don't go, but Tennessee still gets that money. That was a pretty smart move for UT, I thought.

Ole Miss also had to come up with a plan to go against UK fans. It's easier for Kentucky fans in the western part of the state to go to Oxford, Mississippi than it is to go to Lexington. Fans in Paducah and places over there would buy all the tickets they could to the UK-Mississippi game in Oxford and charter 30 or more buses to go to the game. One of the Ole Miss coaches thought that wasn't a good deal, so they would not sell a ticket by mail if it had a Kentucky return address.

I guess you don't like to be outnumbered in your own arena.

Plagiarism or Research?

As a longtime broadcaster you hear certain styles that sound similar to yours, and I've heard some that sound similar to my style.

That's especially been true driving around Kentucky during the state tournament. It's flattering, though, if you can hear some of your phrases. In fact, I've heard current Kentucky broadcaster, Ralph Hacker, use some of my phrases. But how can he not when he sat next to me for 20 years as my color analyst?

When you start out in broadcasting I think you listen to games a lot. I know I did. I listened to everybody I thought was decent and stole a little bit from all of them. There's the saying that if you steal from one person, it's plagiarism, but if you steal from a lot, it's research. I think that's kind of true because it takes time to develop your own style. Developing a style, though, is something that has to be done; you can't be somebody else.

For so long people said of former Bear Bryant players that they weren't very good coaches because they all tried to be like him when there was only one Bear.

In regards to developing a style, during the course of a broadcast I think it's important to know the dimensions of the field or the court, where the action is on the field or court, down and distance, and time and score. Don't be telling stories while baskets are being made and the crowd is yelling. The most important of these things to me is the score. The most maddening thing for me as a listener is not knowing the score.

Legendary broadcaster Red Barber had an hourglass in the booth with him and would give the score every time it was time to flip the hourglass. After reading that Red did that, I did it for the first three or four years of broadcasting games. Believe it or not, that helped.

Experience is the Best Master

When I started in the business, I was rare because I had a college degree. Now it's extremely important to get a degree. A lot of times I recommend staying out of the broadcasting classes and instead get into English or journalism (preferably English because that's where you make your living on radio or TV). Then when it's time to get that first job, go work in a small market.

In the first few years of a broadcasting career, I think you're searching for the right style, some comfort and confidence. You don't get that the first day. I was very fortunate to work for a small station because it enabled me to do a little bit of everything. That served me in good stead, because it helped me better understand later the problems that other people had that I worked with through the years.

The Sportscaster's Dozen

In fact, I've talked to a lot of college broadcasting groups over the years, and I tell them that maybe instead of going for a masters degree, to look for a job in a small market station. Let that serve as their masters degree. Don't expect to start at NBC.

Get out in the small markets where you can learn a ton even though you won't earn much money. Be your own best critic. That's the only way to get better. I did critiques on myself on every game. Then when the smaller markets are mastered, try to get into bigger markets.

Where the business has changed from where I started until now is in TV studio work. It's not uncommon today for even the middle-sized TV markets to have three full-time sports guys. That's a lot of jobs. Radio play-by-play jobs, conversely, have shrunk because so many stations have gone to strictly daytime formats to get more power. This means there aren't as many jobs doing high school games and then colleges have exclusive rights with various stations. The play-by-play jobs are in short supply while studio jobs are mushrooming. Personally, I would not want a studio job because to me sports announcing means play-by-play, which is tougher.

> *Cawood's an excellent broadcaster. He has such a following that he is part of the Kentucky family.*
>
>   — Bob Fulton, University of South Carolina

In fact, in my opinion, television didn't change radio at all. One of the greatest things that happened to me is that I had been at Kentucky for so long that people would turn the sound down on the TV and listen to us do the radio broadcast.

Because of that, subconsciously, I maybe wasn't painting as good of a word picture as I had done in the past. When the games weren't on television I was painting a better picture. When I realized the difference, I vowed that I was doing radio, and I wasn't going to worry about whether the game was on TV or not.

Nowadays almost every Kentucky basketball game is televised in the area, which may have diminished the radio audience somewhat.

Regardless of whether a person chooses radio or TV, he's just got to keep at it. You can get anything you want if you try hard enough, I think. Always try to improve.

For me, obviously, I'm glad I chose radio because I've had a great time. And even though we had an idea of the kind of radio audience we had, I never really thought about the impact we had on people. I just hope we gave them some enjoyment and a good product to listen to. A lot of people grew up listening to me do the games, and I think they felt comfortable, but it's not rocket science. I just hope they enjoyed it.

I've had people tell me how their granddaddy would sit them down at the kitchen table, and they'd listen to the games. That's humbling.

Preparation: The Key to Success

To me preparation is the whole key to a good broadcast. Maybe there are people who can do a broadcast without it, but I'm not one of them. In fact, I prepared just as hard for the last game as I did for the first. I pretty much had the same routine for preparation during my 39 years at U.K., but I got a little smarter with it. Time preparing has to be smart preparation instead of spending time on things that aren't going to get you there.

I never thought about how big our audience was during any particular game. In fact, I used to imagine that there was just one person listening who was friendly and interested, and I tried to talk to just that one person instead of a big audience.

This is how my preparation generally went:

During football season on Monday night I'd listen to the tape of the previous Saturday's game. With a pen and legal pad, I would make notes as to what I thought I could have done better. Usually I would end up with four or five pages of notes.

On Tuesday I would put together my spotting boards and tried to memorize the specialty people like the backs and the ends. On Wednesday I read everything in the media guide that came out. I would highlight things I needed to know and things I thought would be of interest to Kentucky's listeners.

Generally once the football season got under way, I would go to practice on Thursday. That gave me a chance to see the game plan that was put into place and try to see what they're going to do in Saturday's game. That night I would go back and do a little more memory work. Thursday night was also a time for me to go back through my critiques and boil those four or five pages down to the 10 points I really wanted to stress and work on this week.

On Friday I usually didn't do anything unless the game was on the road. If it was on the road I did my memory work again. If we were at home, I usually took Friday night off.

On Saturday as soon as I got to the game, I opened the program and studied all the signals the officials gave. Some of the signals you see all the time while some you see only once a season. I didn't want the ref to give a signal and me not have any earthly idea what he was doing. Then I always went to the other team's sports information director to go over pronunciations of names. It's very offensive to a person to have his name mispronounced.

When the teams came out onto the field for the first time, I liked to look at the actual jerseys and see if I could call the name by the number regardless of where they were. Then I would go over the notes in the legal pad that I wanted to remember as well as the 10 areas I wanted to improve. That's pretty much the way I spent a week during the football season.

In basketball it's sort of the same way, but it doesn't take nearly the same amount of time to prepare for since there aren't as many players and you can see their faces. It's really pretty easy to prepare for basketball when you're in a league because you're going to remember a lot of the players from the previous year, or if you play them more than once in a season, you'll remember them from the previous game.

I prepared just as hard for the last game I did as I prepared for the first. I would be so nervous if I went out there not having done everything I knew I needed to do, that I wouldn't have been able to do the game.

As I mentioned to me preparation is the whole key to successful play-by-play. I can usually listen and tell when someone hasn't prepared, at least I think I can. If someone is poorly prepared, that's the same to me as not being prepared at all. I don't believe in beating people to death with statistics. That probably bothers me as much as anything when I'm listening to other announcers and they just kill the listener with stats.

Just because I was prepared though, it doesn't mean I didn't have butterflies. I had butterflies every game I ever did. If I didn't have those, especially in a basketball game where Kentucky was a 40-point favorite, it may have been tougher. Those blowouts are the worst games to do. Before a game like that I used to try to get off by myself and crank myself up. Because if the listeners are going to have the courtesy to tune you in, you owe it to them to give it your best shot and be just as enthusiastic.

During a blowout like that you try to think of some reason of why the teams are still playing. A lot of the players in games like those are players who aren't going to play very much throughout the season, so you talk about those young players who are coming up or the older players who don't get to play much. I think that's a good angle to take.

It was always important to remember that sometimes those 40-point spreads didn't always turn into 40-point games.

1992: A Heartbreaking Loss

The 1992 NCAA East Regional final game against Duke was a great, great basketball game, but of course it hurt to see it end the way it did. What made the game so remarkable to me, and I've watched the game since then, was that both teams played very well. Duke coach Mike Krzyzewski still says today that it's one of the greatest games he's ever seen.

The Wildcats and Blue Devils played to a 93-93 tie in regulation to force an overtime period. During that period Kentucky's best player, Jamal Mashburn, fouled out. (I don't know that it would've made any difference because everyone else really stepped up.) With :02 left to play, the Wildcats hit a shot that looked like it won the game for them. After a time-out Duke's Christian Laettner hit a 17-footer to win the game. He didn't miss a shot the whole game. Duke won the game 104-103 in overtime.

The thing I'll never forget is how after the game Coach Krzyzewski, whom I had never met, came over and motioned that he wanted to get on the radio with us. He talked to the Kentucky fans and told them it was a game he wished would've lasted forever because it was so great, and how fans should take great pride in their team and not be too disappointed. I thought that was a classy thing to do.

I've gotten to know Coach Krzyzewski since then and think he's a great person and a great coach.

That year I did the regionals for our Kentucky network and then the Final Four for CBS. On the years Kentucky wasn't in the Final Four, I still worked the games on radio. First for NBC, then when they lost the games, I worked them for CBS. I did network games for 18 years. Then I also did some others when I was at WHAS in Louisville and the networks weren't doing the games. In fact, one of the games for WHAS was in 1964 in Kansas City when UCLA coach John Wooden won his first of 10 NCAA titles.

I would've done the regionals for CBS in 1992, but the NCAA has a rule that if an announcer has a team in the tournament, he cannot broadcast for the network. There was a standby ready for CBS in case Kentucky would've won that game and gone to the semifinals. I think that's a great rule because if it came down to a close game, no matter how hard you tried to be neutral, it would be tough.

The years I did the games with CBS, either way you go in there and just hope that every game is close regardless of who wins because you hate to do a blowout. I just think it's a great rule for the school's broadcaster not to be involved. The NCAA doesn't have to worry about that now because the main two people doing the games are really baseball announcers—John Rooney of the Chicago White Sox and Marty Brennaman of the Cincinnati Reds. But they're both very, very good.

I went on to do the 1992 Final Four for CBS which Duke won. The hardest game the Blue Devils had in that run was Kentucky. That championship game was the last basketball game I broadcast.

CBS was great to work with, but it was strictly a business deal. The last several years I did basketball games for them, a small crew came in for radio while the big crew was with television. It was a nice relationship.

Besides broadcasting basketball for CBS, I also did the Kentucky Derby on radio for them for about 20 years as well as the Preakness four or five times and the Travers seven times.

Over the years I also used to do quite a bit of work for the NCAA. I used to record their PSAs and put a voice behind some pieces of video they had, but all of that was a long time ago.

"And They're Off ... "

When I went to Lexington to work, the station had wanted to do horse racing. A deal was worked that we would call the feature race live, but we would tape the others and play them back in the evening. Having never done horse racing, I went out and called eight races in a day. They had a 10-day meet, with eight races each day for 10 days. So I ended up doing 80 races in 10 racing days (there weren't races for 10 straight days). That put me way ahead of the game of calling races.

I love calling them. Even though I don't call them anymore, I still love the races.

Calling a race is completely different from doing basketball, football, or baseball. It's quick; the average race is over in a minute-plus. The Derby itself is about two minutes. It's different, but it's a lot of fun.

At first it was difficult calling races. You can do so little preparation for a race, unlike football, baseball, or basketball. In racing you know about the horses, but you have no idea how they're going to run. The better race you run, the more likely they are to run to form. If you call the day-to-day races, they can run every way in the world. So trying to read their form doesn't help a whole lot. You try to pick who is going to be out of the gates early and who is going to be running late.

Preparation consists of looking at, and going by, the color of the jockey's silks. They come on the track about 10 minutes before they race, so you've got to be able to memorize them and quickly wipe them out because you're going to end up having 12 or 14 different colors the next race.

Secretariat is the horse that immediately comes to mind for me as one of the top horses I saw through the years. In fact, I have a lock of his mane on my desk and two of his shoes in our living room. Secretariat won the Triple Crown [the term for winning the Kentucky Derby, Preakness Stakes, and Belmont Stakes in the same year] in 1973.

I was a big Secretariat fan, but I saw a lot of great horses. Seattle Slew was great horse who won the Triple Crown in 1977. Affirmed, with a young Steve Cauthen as the jockey, won the Triple Crown in 1978. Steve was the jockey for all three of Affirmed's Triple Crown races.

In my mind, though, Secretariat is the greatest horse I ever saw. Even when he was in the stud I used to go over to Claiborne Farm in Paris, Kentucky, and just take a look at him.

To go along with the love of horse racing for me, in the past I owned a few race horses. I really enjoyed that. They weren't Derby-type horses. They were bottom of the barrel, but I enjoyed those. I still like to go to the track in the mornings and just look around.

I'm pretty much out of horse racing now. I really enjoyed working for WHAS TV and Radio during Derby week up until 1995. But when they called in 1996, I declined because I had gone through 39

> *Cawood Ledford was a legend not only in Kentucky but all over the country. I may have been influenced by him to some point, because I could pick up Kentucky basketball when I was in Iowa, and I thought, "Man, this guy is great!" He had excitement in his voice, just like Jack Buck; it was so distinctive. Away from the mike, Cawood was laid back and very nice to me. He would call me when I went to Lexington with Vandy or when they would come to Nashville. I feel lucky that I've been able to rub elbows with him. Cawood's one of the really great announcers.*
>
> ❧ *Paul Eells, University of Arkansas*

years of that and decided that was enough. Ten days away from home is a long time. I taped some vignettes for them last year [1997], but we did those in one day for the station to use during race day.

The work that I did over the years was for both radio and TV. For television I taped a world of stuff. I taped an hour special, taped different features to be used on Derby day, and even though I wasn't calling the Derby, I did live setups of all the races. Then they used me as a race "expert" on radio. I worked in the radio booth on the roof. I had an assistant with me who would check off where I needed to be next. It was hectic, but it was a lot of fun. I enjoyed it.

WHAS starts its Derby day coverage around eight in the morning, and it ends around six or seven in the evening. That's their biggest day, ratings-wise and financially, so they carry all the races and several features throughout the day. They do a great job.

Going Coast-to-Coast Wasn't for Me

Working nationally on television is something that never really appealed to me on a full-time basis. I've done a world of television (about 150 TV basketball games), but I love radio. To me on television you're like a public address announcer because you're basically just giving names. You're not supposed to talk as much on TV, because people can see things. The main person on the TV sportscast is the analyst, the guys like Dick Vitale, Billy Packer and Al Maguire. That's not enough for me.

I like painting the word pictures and everything involved in radio. For that reason I much prefer radio play-by-play. The only sport I see where the radio and TV announcer do the same thing is horse racing because both mediums call the race.

At the University of Kentucky I had as good of a radio job as there was in America. Where would I go?

The NBA? I had a chance to go to the NBA to work with the Chicago Bulls, but that just wasn't for me. Before that time I had already been exposed to professional basketball. In Louisville WHAS radio had the rights to the games for the Kentucky Colonels of the old ABA. The Colonels wanted to bring in someone from out of town to do their games. The management at WHAS said absolutely not because we had enough good announcers at the station who were qualified to do the games.

The general manager of the Colonels Mike Storen asked me to do as many as I could and then another sportscaster, Van Vance, would do the rest. Most of the games I did were on the road, and Van did the rest. By the end of the year they liked Van as the announcer, so I didn't do any more after that. I got in enough traveling in the 40 percent of the schedule I did that I knew professional basketball was not something I wanted to do.

If the direction had gone a different way, I would like to have done major league baseball because I enjoyed the two seasons I did in the minor leagues. Obviously, the direction didn't go that way, it went more toward colleges, and I was glad to get there when I did, being in my 20s and doing UK. That was a heck of a break.

RAISING MINIATURES: STAYING INVOLVED WITH HORSES

I bought our house in Cawood, Kentucky, from my mother and dad while they were still living. This is the house where I grew up and my wife, Frances, and I had always kind of planned to come back here when I stopped doing the games. We moved back here in 1993.

Before we moved back here, I was on the team plane flying back from a game, and I saw an ad in *Town & Country* for miniature horses. I had never heard of them, but we had been looking for some type of livestock for our land. Frances and I visited some farms and went to some shows that had the miniature horses, and we ended up buying four of them.

We were on a trip to the University of Florida in Gainesville, and one of the top miniature horse farms in the country is in Newberry, Florida, which is just 10 miles from Gainesville. I made an appointment to go to the farm, thinking I'd like to possibly buy two horses. A good friend of mine named Jim Payne, who lives in Owenton, Kentucky, is a big UK basketball fan, and he asked if he could ride with me to see these horses.

When we got to the farm we were taken all around and shown the various horses, and I took some notes as to what I thought was good and not so good about some of them. By the end of the day, Jim and I were partners and had bought 33 horses.

I keep anywhere from six to 13 horses at our property in Cawood, and Jim has the rest. Out of the 44 horses that Jim and I owned in 1997, five of those were used as show horses. We show the horses in Tennessee, Kentucky, Indiana and Ohio, a total of about seven shows. Four of our five show horses qualified for the national show.

We've never had a horse win the nationals, but we've only gone two years. Regardless, we still enjoy it.

The Sportscaster's Dozen

Ledford with a few of his miniature horses at his home in Kentucky.

The Pride of the Mist

It's been great fun broadcasting for a school with as much basketball tradition as Kentucky. It's especially rewarding with some of the football teams we've had, where you labor through those three months in the fall. I think you're very lucky when you can follow a basketball program with the stature of Kentucky. It's been a great run.

In my opinion anybody who follows and broadcasts for just one team, and he's not for that team—he's in the wrong line of work. I tried to never get into the "we" or "they" or call players by their first names. It's a personal thing with me, but I think that calling players by their first names is unprofessional unless there are two players with the same last name and there isn't time to call them by first and last names every time they touch the ball.

I'm very proud to have represented UK, but as a broadcaster I think you would have pride whether you're broadcasting for a national champion or the worst team in the league. It's a lot harder when you're following the last-place team in the league, but regardless, you want to feel like you've done a good job when you walk out of that booth after a game. In that regard I don't think pride has anything to do with tradition; I think you would follow the team the same no matter how good or horrible it is.

I was lucky because I really enjoyed all the sports I covered. I think each of the sports offered a different challenge. Horse racing is quick, football is a lot of preparation, while basketball and baseball are probably the easiest.

The pride for me comes from the fact that I lasted 39 years and got to decide when I wasn't going to do it anymore. When I got out I was at an age that I felt it was time. I had actually thought about leaving after the horrible 1988-1989 season, but I thought that would've been kind of cowardly. I'm glad I stayed because it was a really fun three years with Pitino. During the last few years of working, I had become super-critical of myself and decided that 39 years was long enough, and it was time to do something else.

Going into a career you know that one day you're going to have to step away and turn the mike over to someone else. Generally, it's not a situation where you wake up one day and say, "I don't think I'm going to do this anymore." I know that my decision was something I thought about for years as far as when I would do it and how I would do it. If you have any type of a career, you know that final day is going to come.

It was a very tough decision. Frances and I agonized over it a lot. I think it was the right decision, and I'm not sorry I did it.

Fortunately for me, I had the chance to say when I wanted to leave and where I wanted to be. I feel I could have broadcast for several more years, but I just felt it was the right time to stop and do something else.

Now I have the horses, do some speaking, have five clients to do commercials for on a yearly basis, and I write, so there's enough for me to do to stay busy.

I think a sportscaster is tired when the season is over, and you feel that need to get away from things. It used to work out where the last football game would be against Tennessee on a Saturday. Then the basketball season would start the following Saturday, so Frances and I would get about five days in Florida which was really nice. Then it got to where we would play two basketball games before the last football game, so there was no break. That shot down the midterm travel. Then generally I didn't have too long after basketball before we got into horse racing, which meant there were years I didn't get to put my feet up until summer. Now, even though I'm still fairly busy, I don't feel that need to get away from things.

Sure, I miss broadcasting, but that didn't come as a surprise to me. You can't do something that long and not miss it. Even after being out of it for more than five years, I still miss it (even though it's a little less every year). Before retiring I talked to some people who had been in similar situations to see what it was like. For instance, I talked to Joe B. Hall a lot. When he got out of coaching, it was his call. His advice was to find something to do instead of just sitting around at home. He said it gets easier every year. He's been right.

There are no regrets for me about getting into sportscasting. It's the greatest thing to happen to me professionally. I was awfully lucky. I loved it from day one and enjoyed every minute of my 41 years in the business.

LARRY MUNSON
VANDERBILT UNIVERSITY/UNIVERSITY OF GEORGIA

Before getting into broadcasting, I had been interested in the music business. In fact, during World War II I had a band at General McClusky Hospital in Temple, Texas, where I was working in the recovery room. My mother was a talented musician, and my sister was a super-talented classical pianist. She could read any type of music, even though I couldn't read anything at all.

> *One person has enthusiasm for 30 minutes, another for 30 days, but it is the person who has it for 30 years who makes a success of his or her life.*
>
> ☙ Edward B. Butler

During high school I played in a five-piece band with a famous black bass player, Oscar Pettiford, in Minneapolis. He was older than I was, so he was able to take me into a club called the Rum Boogie Club up in the wrong section of town. I was 17 years old, and the only white guy in the place, including all the waiters, waitresses, owners, and all the patrons. Everybody thought I was so brave for working there, yet I didn't really think about it; it was just exciting.

Oscar Pettiford went on to Duke Ellington's band. He wrote a lot of songs and arrangements. I never forgot Oscar.

Even though I was really big into music for awhile, I actually wanted to be a high school football coach. That's really what I thought I would do. I had gone to a state teacher's college in Minnesota (Moorehead State Teachers College) but the draft for World War II came along and blew out that idea.

Nobody realizes what a war does to a guy or a girl, friends and family. When a war hits you and your generation, it just scatters everybody like a covey of quail. Hundreds of kids you've gone all the way through school with go into the service. They meet somebody, get married and don't come home to your state. Everyone

The Sportscaster's Dozen

gets scattered around the country and the world. That's just about what happened to me, too.

Tickle the Ivory ... for "Real" Money?

As I mentioned, during WW II I was stationed in Texas at General McClusky Hospital. One day a bunch of names were called over the PA system, and mine was one of them. They were discharging me. Germany had surrendered in May, but Japan didn't surrender until August. When I got home to Minnesota, guys were just starting to trickle home. Shortly after I got home, there was a radio commercial begging for announcers. During the war there were pops and moms, old timers, running radio stations all over America, but since most of the men were in the service, high school kids provided most of the help.

I took my discharge pay of 200 bucks and headed for this radio school that had been advertised. They claimed a person would have a job within 13 weeks. It was sooner than that for me. They gave me a job in eight weeks, because they were desperate for voices and for help in the radio business. My first radio job came in 1946 at KFBC in Cheyenne, Wyoming, following the legendary Curt Gowdy who was leaving.

Gowdy was a great person to know. He introduced me to Cheyenne, its bars and night life. We fished quite a bit, and he taught me how to use a fly rod. He's the one who taught me how to broadcast baseball games, a year or so later. At KFBC I was doing university of Wyoming football and basketball, as well as high school sports.

One day a piano guy, a jazz piano player, was passing through town on his way to Miami and stopped in the old hotel in Cheyenne. I was a real young kid then. He had found out that I fiddled around with the piano a lot. We started talking, and he told me that something new had just started in America; cocktail pianists. Today we call them piano bars, but they weren't called that 50 years ago. This guy had just signed a contract for $175 a week, plus all of his meals and a free room in a motel in Miami. He was going into this "glamorous" lifestyle in Miami and he said, "That's what you ought to do. This is something new. There are going to be piano guys living for free all over America."

For a few hours that night and even the next morning, I seriously thought about what he had said since I was only making $65 bucks a week. He's going to make $175, free room and board, plus the

Off the Air with Southeastern Legends

Larry Munson speaking to a group of Bulldog fans in a small town, May 1981.

night life and cocktail glasses. It was a lot more than what I was making. I came very, very close to getting on a train to find a cocktail piano job, whatever that was. Thinking about it, though, I knew I was going to have to study more before I could do it.

So I stayed true to my faith and decided I was pretty excited in Wyoming, even though the football team was losing (we didn't win a game). The basketball team was big time. We went to the NCAA tournament that first year. That was when hardly anybody made it to the tournament and when the NIT was just as big or bigger than the NCAA.

Gowdy came back that second season and said to me, "You'll never make any money in broadcasting unless you get into baseball." By that time Mel Allen had hired Gowdy to work with him on the New York Yankee broadcasts. Gowdy helped me get the AA job in Nashville, Tennessee. Since I was a hunter and fisherman and Nashville had great hunting and fishing, I settled in there with Vanderbilt. I spent a long time killing ducks and geese, and I caught a lot of fish.

Even though I don't play the piano as much today, I still enjoy jazz and collecting tapes and things like that, from musicians such as Art Tatum and Oscar Peterson.

Building Excitement

Working in Wyoming with Curt Gowdy was a blessing in regard to my baseball broadcasting career. Wyoming helped me with baseball in one main respect; we recreated a major league game of the week every Saturday afternoon with full sound effects. There was a man standing up behind a huge console that had three turntables moving at all times with various sound effects. He stood there watching you at all times. The announcer sat behind a table and read, or at least tried to recreate, from this script of a game as it came across the wire.

> *I think Larry really found his niche when he started broadcasting for Georgia; you don't get much more red and black than Larry Munson. I really love to hear him do a game. He's also a pretty good fisherman.*
>
>   ~ Otis Boggs,
>   University of Florida

For our station the idea of recreating games came out of Salt Lake City which had some big station that was doing all sports in all games with full sound effects. During the War Western Union taught Curt Gowdy and the station guys in Cheyenne how to recreate games. The station figured they would save money because they wouldn't have to send Gowdy and the engineer to various games around the country, so they did it. They were still doing it when I joined them.

They had to teach me how to read the script, even though they didn't give us much to work with. For instance, if the script had "FLGS" then you knew it was a foul over the grandstands. If it had "S1C" then it was strike one, called. "B1W" meant ball one, wide. We had to learn those types of things.

Recreating games was quite an experience, I'll tell you that.

Things were a little different with the job in Nashville. Gowdy helped me land a job calling baseball games for the Nashville Vols, a Double-A minor league team on WKDA radio in 1947. I also did games for Vanderbilt University. Since I had never done live baseball before, I had no idea it was going to be as addicting as it was; I went literally ape.

It was quite an experience with some great players. I went to the minor league spring training camp in Melbourne, Florida. In one of the games, Jackie Robinson was playing at the time with the Montreal Royals. On another team I watched Larry Doby, who broke the color barrier in the American League shortly after Robinson did so in the National League, playing with Newark. Man, he wore us out during one weekend. The Vols played against Newark two or three games that weekend, and they killed us. Doby was really something, and actually hit the ball much harder than Robinson did when we saw him.

At the end of the second summer, despite just a $225 weekly salary, I tried to buy into the ball club. As young as I was and excited about baseball, I couldn't see anything on the horizon that was going to wipe out the minor leagues. An insurance executive friend of mine, Mr. Harrison, went down to talk to the two owners of the Vols to see if I could start out and buy 10 percent. The owners couldn't believe that I was serious. I was the only real play-by-play guy in Nashville at the time, and here I was trying to buy into a ball club. The owners were professional guys, both around 60 years old and were hard drinkers and cigar smokers. They were faced with a kid wanting to buy 10 percent of the ball club. Needless to say, they didn't go for the idea, and I never bought into the team.

Working in Wyoming I had learned how to also recreate football games, so when I got to Nashville, I talked them into doing pro football. At that time there were two teams in Chicago, the Bears and the Cardinals. We got full football sound effects and did games "out of Chicago" every Sunday. Since there were two teams in Chicago, one was at home every week. So there was a permanent Western Union line up there that enabled us to do games every single Sunday. That worked for two years.

I suppose we dressed it up a little. We had good sound effects, and it was easy enough to time plays. The Western Union coding for football was a little better than it was for baseball. It would have something clearly typed, like "Johnson, right tackle, G6, T by Smith and Roberts." That meant Johnson ran by the right tackle for six yards and was tackled by Smith and Roberts. Or it might have, "Trippy pass, long, incomplete, third down." Western Union gave us that much for each play. The typewriter was giving us enough to work with because of that little 20-25 second gap between plays.

It was fun because I could get on a jammed elevator leading up to WKDA on Monday, not saying a word to anybody, and the people would be talking about hearing that announcer talking about how hard it was snowing in Chicago the day before with the guys sliding on the ice when they went out of bounds. It was difficult keeping a straight face knowing they didn't realize that it was me with sound effects sitting upstairs of that building. I really did enjoy it.

Down at the Ole' Fishing Hole

While I was in Nashville, I also spent some time on television. I had a fishing show on TV, 22 years before fishing guys like Roland Martin or Bill Vance had theirs. When I went on the air with ours, there were a couple others shows in the country, like a man in East Lansing, Michigan, and a man in Kansas City. Those guys were doing studio shows where they had two or three guys sitting around the table talking about how to tie a rod or how to cook a venison stew, stuff like that.

We didn't do ours that way. I had my own camera (no camera man), would get a fisherman, and we would go try to catch fish every Saturday and Sunday of every weekend. Before we went out, I would teach the other person how to pick up the camera and how to work it. Then early in the morning, I would get them used to working the camera by shooting me while I was driving the boat up the lake. I would then set the camera between us while we were fishing, with the F-stops set.

Whenever one of us hung a fish, the other would just throw the rod down and dive for the camera. The name of the game was get the video and go home. The guys that I took didn't always see it that way; they didn't understand why we wanted to get the film so fast. They thought just sitting and watching the other catch one was the greatest thing in the world.

The reason we did it so fast actually came by accident. We found out that when we hung a bass after casting out, within seven seconds the bass was in sight of the boat. That isn't much film. Because of that we went to lighter and lighter tackle. This started before ultra light tackle. When we got as light as we could, we timed those bass at 22 seconds ... now that's what we wanted. We wanted to see that rod bent on the film. Sometimes we put a big lens on the camera and showed the fish as it was rolling on the water. We wanted to get four boxes of film, 400 feet of film, every week. Man, when a storm hit, we were panicky.

The show started on WSM-TV then moved to WSIX. Later, they swapped channels with WSM. Then it went to the Public Education Channel, which is now Channel 8. We filmed the show on various lakes, private ponds, and reservoirs around middle Tennessee, like Old Hickory Lake, Kentucky Lake, Center Hill, and Dale Hollow. Since we had to go out every week, we used about every different place we could find.

Larry with one of his sons, showing off the younger Munson's bass.

The Sportscaster's Dozen

When Vanderbilt's football and basketball seasons kicked in gear, I still had to carry the cameras, fishing gear, and heavy clothing with me when we went on the road. There were private lakes at the schools where we traveled, so we would tape the show there. Some of the schools that had places are the Florida campus, the Auburn campus, and the Alabama campus. They would all have a guy waiting for me. Sometimes there would be muddy waters, and we would have to fight like the devil to catch fish. But I had to have fish on film every Thursday night. It was a live show and we ran that piece of film every week.

There were times when we saw bad storms coming, and we didn't have any film. But we still had to catch fish, and get the job done. Unfortunately, a lot of times we may have done a Vanderbilt game the night before and had only been in bed a couple of hours before we had our weekly Sunday morning meeting at 3:30 at the Waffle House. Man, I just staggered.

When those storm warnings were out, we'd go to the rivers down below the dam to stay away from the bad wind. We didn't want to be out on the reservoir if the storm was coming. It took us a few years to catch on to doing it that way. We met an old-timer one day who showed us that down under the dams was where there were all certain species of fish plus a lot of bass. We never knew there were bass under those dams. We used that trick quite a bit. We only had two days to make that film. It got to be kind of a load.

It wore me out for $25 a week, but it was worth it. In those days a car note was only $97.50. So I was making $100 a month off the fishing show, which also included free food and iced Coca-Cola and a free station wagon to use with a free boat, trailer and gas. I did that show for 20 years, and for a long, long time got the $25 a week. We caught so many fish, cleaned so many, gave so many away, and ate so many. I had to rent a locker in downtown Nashville where I had geese and ducks kept illegally because I had too many. Some of the people we did the show with didn't want to eat wild duck or goose, and so I would take them. For a long time I had a locker just full of stuff.

The Atlanta Braves stopped the show, technically, for a year and a half because I joined them in the spring of 1966. I took the show off the air, of course, and went to Atlanta. When the Braves put Bob Uecker in my chair after the 1967 season, I went back up to Nashville in December and put the show back on the air. That's when it was moved to Channel 8. Overall the show ran for about 20 years.

I really did love it ... I really did.

The Art of Vanderbilt

Art Guepe was my introduction to coaches at Vanderbilt. He was a tough, tough guy. He had a good build on him as an athlete and had been an All-American in the 1930s at Marquette. He went to Vanderbilt as the football coach in 1953, where he stayed until 1962. He was a little bit hard to work with on television because he would give "yep" and "nope" type answers, and he never wanted to admit that he was wrong on anything. He was not easy to work with, but we got close over time.

From my weekly fishing shows, I started bringing him a lot of fish. He would make his wife clean them, because he wouldn't. He was the head football coach and the director of athletics and at the time was making only $25,000 a year; he was desperately underpaid. At that time the Vanderbilt program was sinking. We had three or four pretty good years, and all of a sudden it started going down. In 1960 it started down hard, and at one stretch we lost 16 games in a row. It was really hard there for a while, and Guepe was caught in that thing.

Jess Neely came in later after Guepe, and tried to resurrect the program. By this time we were taping for TV all of the Vanderbilt home games and televising them later on WSIX. The station was also doing some University of Tennessee games the same way. We put the outdoor show back on the air and then whoever was home—Tennessee or Vanderbilt—we would televise their games and play it back on tape at 10:30. It was a reasonably heavy schedule.

The Golden Arm

Bill Wade was a great passer with a great arm for Vanderbilt from 1949-1951. He was also a strong Christian guy. He never quite recovered, though, from the night his brother was killed in a car wreck out in front of a theater in Nashville. His brother, Don, was a Vanderbilt center from 1950-1952.

When he was in high school and I was doing their games on radio, he would throw the ball 60 yards! When he went to Vanderbilt, their coach Bill Edwards put in a pro offense. Edwards had been an offensive coordinator for the Cleveland Browns. He put in the

Browns' offense to allow Wade to throw the ball. There were times, however, Wade wanted to force the ball and throw it 60 yards.

Edwards took black chalk, and on Wade's gold pants, wrote the sequence of plays they wanted him to call. He could go just so long, and he wanted to let that arm go. He wanted to let it fly, but unfortunately most of his receivers were not fast enough to get down there. But when he followed orders and stayed with the short game, he was far and away one of the greatest passers that the SEC has ever seen.

He won an NFL-NFC championship for the Chicago Bears in 1963 and hardly got any credit for it. What really hurt him from that game, I think, was that someone else was named the MVP. Wade had a great game and completed a ton of passes.

Polk Salad Annie

On the other side of things, basketball wasn't very big when I got to Vanderbilt in 1947. Bob Polk was the first decent basketball coach that Vanderbilt ever had. He taught me the things that Everett Shelton in Wyoming had tried to teach me. Shelton, when I was a young kid, took me into a room with a blackboard and diagrammed his offense. I was too impatient and not quite knowledgeable enough to accept what he was trying to do. He was just trying to help me. But now Polk really would work with you.

Polk had paranoia about being spied on by other teams. When we were on road trips, he would take the traveling writers, myself, the trainer, and a couple of chairs and put us out on the floor with no one around. In those days a team would play on the road Saturday and Monday one week, then at home on Saturday and Monday the next week. On the weeks we were out of town, we left Nashville on Friday and wouldn't come home until Tuesday. The team played two games every weekend in the SEC. Sunday was a big practice day, in whatever city you were in.

Since Polk didn't want any students spying on him, he would use us guys as the enemy. Sometimes we'd have a chair with us, and he'd have us in a zone defense while the Commodores ran plays around us. At times he wanted us to shuffle our feet and get over there to bother the player while he was shooting. Polk was almost an inspiration.

He ran a good offense—called it a shuffle offense. With Polk and his offense, Vanderbilt basketball got on the map. At that time they didn't even have a home gym in which to play their games. We played in two high schools the first two years I did the games. Man, Vanderbilt basketball caught on like you can't believe. It was great for me because nobody had ever broadcast Vanderbilt games.

The team started winning the moment Polk got there. He brought in five scholarship kids, four of them out of Indiana. They could all shoot. Man, he tore Nashville up even though his team had no place to play their home games. They were in a high school gym which seated about 800, and fans were tearing the doors down to get tickets. Right away Polk beefed up the schedule. He was in the SEC where they had never won a game, and all of a sudden they were winning. It was really something to see and was really a lot of fun. It was like we were building something; they had never broadcast the games on radio, and they had never had a scholarship athlete in basketball.

It took the press awhile in Nashville to wake up to basketball and to the fact that the town was going crazy. It was only on radio. There I was traveling with the team, but there was no other media. Newspaper writers wrote their stories from listening to the radio broadcast. It took them a while to start to cover the games. That's how new it was up in Nashville.

Vanderbilt was nothing in basketball, and here comes this guy who knew what he was doing. He only got $25 for his television show, and his salary was only $10,000 a year. We put a radio show on and only paid him $10. He lobbied

> Larry is a super, super guy. I've known him since the late 1940s when I was doing Memphis baseball and he was doing Nashville baseball. Larry, and I don't mean this demeaning at all, is a homer. It's "us" and "they". There's nothing wrong with that because that is Larry's method of operation. He lets you know quickly that he is a Georgia Bulldog, and you only have to listen to about 15 or 20 seconds to pick up on that; he's a cheerleader. Larry does a very, very good job. He has always had a tremendous following.
>
> ~ Jack Cristil, Mississippi State University

hard enough until he got that show on five nights a week. My boss at KDA didn't see how in the world he could pay somebody $50 bucks a week for a show, especially a Vanderbilt basketball coach. My boss was a Vanderbilt alumni, and the moment basketball caught on fire, he was glad he had Polk signed up. Those were pretty good years. We went a long way.

One of the players responsible for Polk's early success was Billy Joe Adcock, the first scholarship basketball player in the history of Vanderbilt University. He came out of West High School in Nashville.

Munson and his sons take a break during a trip to Arizona in 1990.

He was a fine shooter but not a great ball handler. There are a million point guards today who would have stripped him clean and taken his shorts off, but he could shoot. Adcock was 6'2", and because there was nobody else on the Vanderbilt team worthy of a scholarship, he stood out like a sore thumb.

In Adcock's senior year, Polk had recruited the first five scholarship kids that came as a group; he meshed in with those guys. The Commodores had some pure shooters on those five, and Adcock got to play with that bunch. That's when basketball took off in Nashville. Adcock was at Vanderbilt (1946-1950) right before the game started to change and speed up.

We used to have a wild duck dinner at the end of every basketball season for the coaching staff. My wife would cook wild duck, and Polk would come over with the trainer, the two traveling beat writers that traveled with the basketball team, and the sports information director. We would kind of have a drunken-type party, eat wild duck and wild rice. It was an event every year.

In fact, the moment Guepe heard that we were doing this, he wanted me to do it for the football team. Since he had more coaches, we had a party of ten during football season. Usually at the end of the season, we had just lost to Tennessee (we always lost to Tennessee) the day before. We would do the final TV show that afternoon at the supper hour on a Sunday and everyone would come to my house. They'd all loosen their ties, roll up their sleeves and complain about the game and the officiating or something that happened in the game that was illegal. They'd get into that liquor and out would come those ten ducks. That also became quite an event.

Being in the Right Place at the Right Time

Roy Skinner, who was an assistant under Polk, was more loosey-goosey than the head coach. Polk was more serious. We didn't think he belonged as a coach. For the most part, the town didn't think so either, and I know the ex-players didn't think so. Skinner was very friendly, but not a very impressive looking assistant coach; he was young.

Polk had a heart attack which forced Skinner to take over as acting head coach for the 1958-1959 season. Skinner immediately started playing part of the second five players who rarely saw action with Polk as head coach. Skinner made everybody happy. He'd run the second five in there that didn't have any talent, and he'd let them play a minute or two. You talk about morale ... it went up on that team. He became the full-time head coach when Polk left before the 1961 season.

We didn't think Skinner would ever recruit, but he did. In fact, he recruited some real race horses, and the Commodores really got good. We almost won a national championship with him in 1965.

Skinner loved to play cards and have a good time. We played a lot of poker. When we were on the road and the plane landed, if the trainer came up and said, "You've got to have dinner with the coach tonight," we all knew what it meant; he wanted to play cards after dinner. He would take the newspaper and radio guys out to dinner to some nice meal, and by 9:00 we were in his room playing cards and smoking. We'd be playing poker because Skinner wanted to play poker. Remember, he was not an older guy. He was younger than we were. We had great times.

There was this one newspaper guy in particular, when it was his turn to deal would say, "All red cards are wild, plus all deuces." That meant almost every card in the deck was wild! When you looked in your hand, holy smokes, you've got four kings. You knew you were going to win, so you'd bet the house on it. Well, somebody else would have five aces, because all red cards were wild. It was tough getting used to playing games like that, especially with a little firewater in you. We really did play a lot of cards and have a lot of laughter when Skinner was the coach.

With Skinner, by the way, we served quail dinners at our house. That was by accident. Skinner knew Polk and Guepe always had wild duck dinners at the end of the season. We accidentally got into quail with Skinner and his group. We were a more select group at that time, only about five or six people.

Bob Polk's name will be in history for being the first real coach Vanderbilt ever had who went out and recruited and ran that shuffle offense so well. Roy Skinner's name will always be in Vanderbilt basketball history because he had to take Polk's place on an emergency basis, then succeeded when nobody thought he could.

> *What a unique style! Larry Munson could probably run for governor of Georgia and be elected. His style's not for everyone, but it's worked for him. A Georgia game without the phrase, 'Dogs hunkering down,' just wouldn't be a game.*
>
>   ₪ *Eli Gold, University of Alabama*

Clyde Lee

Clyde Lee, a great individual, is a player who will go down in Vanderbilt basketball history. He came out of a highly religious high school in Nashville, David Lipscomb High School (which is also a part of a college, Lipscomb University, where one of my sons recently graduated from). Lee was kind of a stoop shouldered, skinny 6-foot-9 kid. He could have had more meat on his body, but he was a good shooter. He jumped well and could tip a ball back up in there.

Lee was blessed that he had a country kid from Hopkinsville, Kentucky, playing next to him at forward named Bob "Snake" Grace. He was almost 6'8" and could jump through the ceiling. It helped Lee to have Grace under there. That was the club that went to the NCAA final eight and was knocked out by Michigan in 1965. Michigan had a great bunch that season.

Lee was a great individual. He went into the NBA and played quite a few years in San Francisco. He told me of his desperate attempts to keep his weight up. Even though he hated the taste of it, when a game would end he took about six raw eggs, broke them into a milk shake, and then drank it trying to get the calories and the protein into his body. It was difficult because he was built like a race horse. He was tall and skinny without a lot of muscles on his body.

1965: The Season That Almost Was

The 1965 basketball season, Lee's junior year, is one that Vanderbilt fans still haven't forgotten. The Commodores were two points from going to the NCAA Final Four. The final eight tournament game that year between Vanderbilt and Michigan was a great game. The winner was headed to Portland, Oregon, to play in the Final Four. One thing that stands out about that night was how the coaches of the teams Vanderbilt had fought so hard to beat to become SEC champions, Adolph Rupp of Kentucky and Ray Mears of Tennessee, were in that crowd. Skinner was the coach of that Vanderbilt team. We were broadcasting the game doing a simulcast. We got permission from the network, it was either ABC or CBS, to put my play-by-play on the telecast in Tennessee only.

Most people thought Michigan would kill us with their five great athletes led by the great Cazzie Russell. The Wolverines were an 11-point favorite. Lee got four fouls in the first half. We're down eight points. Rupp, who was impossible to approach, came over to us and volunteered to do a halftime show. He had never done a halftime show with me in my life. He came over, sat down and did the halftime show with us. It was funny because he was suggesting things out loud on the air that he hoped Skinner would do to save Vanderbilt. He was pulling for the SEC team. Rupp was convinced that Lee was going to foul out, so he wanted Roy to pull him out and play him off the high post.

During the last three or four minutes of the game, the two teams were tied 80-80. The Commodores were playing man-to-man defense, and Michigan started to run a play around Russell where he was posting on the low baseline. When he did that, he would draw a foul against Vanderbilt. Mears saw immediately what Michigan was going to do. With his orange coat on, he came running down those bleacher steps to the Vanderbilt bench screaming to Skinner what Michigan was doing. Mears was going nuts, shaking his finger at Skinner and the floor. He wasn't mad at anything, he just wanted Vanderbilt to win. I saw him coming down the bleachers since it was across from our broadcast position.

The irony of that was Vanderbilt fans hated Ray Mears because Tennessee would hold the ball for a low-scoring game when you wanted to run and play a high-scoring game. He could get Vandy fans fired up as he wore his bright orange coat at Vanderbilt.

I scared the death out of my engineer that night—a big, lovable guy called Big John. He weighed 350 pounds, and he loved to fish. He was our engineer for baseball, football, and basketball. He and I were working that simulcast together. There was a timeout called late in the game with the score 85-85, and I said out loud on the air, "John, if we win this game, I'm going right over the top of this table, and you're going to finish this broadcast. Don't forget to read all these sponsors." He almost turned sheet white. It scared him to death, because I was dead serious. If the team was going to win and celebrate on the floor, I was going to go out there and get in the middle of that thing. It scared Big John to death.

As it turned out, the Commodores lost that 1965 Michigan game, 87-85. Traveling was called on John Ed Miller in the lane as he hit what would have been a game-tying shot. It was a great game.

Later that night around midnight, we get back to the motel, and Big John broke the lock on the kitchen door. He took all these Vanderbilt alumni and ex-players in there, turned on the lights, found the whiskey supply, and tried to find the food. Everybody's drinking, sitting back, with one light on in the restaurant and the kitchen all lit up. We had a party just as if we had won.

Taking on the Athens of the South
(At Least a Couple of Them)

WSM, a clear-channel 50,000-watt station in Nashville, took the baseball rights away from WKDA in the late 1950s. They bought the baseball rights mainly so they could have it for television. In order to stay with baseball, I had to go with WSM. That put me on the 50,000-watter.

Executives from the advertising agency that handled both Brave and Cardinal sales were sitting in St. Louis listening to me do Nashville baseball games. WSM's big signal just boomed out at night. Within a few days of hearing me do games for the Nashville Vols, the advertising agency called me to offer me a job with the Braves. It was an opportunity I had to hop on. After the offer I went back up to Nashville and told the family to start packing, and we put the house up for sale. The team, which had been in Milwaukee, and I moved to Atlanta in 1966.

My first assignment for the Braves was spring training in Florida. It's funny how it all worked out in Georgia. The Braves told me to get a ride to Atlanta, not to bring my car down, to let my family bring my car down, and they would have a car waiting for me at a certain dealership in downtown Atlanta. Since they told me I was going to be in the same motel room for 31 days, I packed everything, including my golf clubs and fishing tackle. My father-in-law drove me down to Atlanta from Nashville, and let me out on Spring Street in front of the car dealership. There was a newspaper box outside, so I bought a paper and carried it into the dealership with me without looking at it.

I saw this car had my name painted on the door. It read, "Voice of the Braves." Actually there were two "voices." I was No. 2 and not No.1. I loaded all my gear in the car, threw that paper in the back seat (still without looking at it) and drove 10 ½ hours to Palm Beach, Florida. I had never driven to Palm Beach in my life.

When I got down there to the motel, it was 10:30 at night. I put all my gear away, threw the paper on the bed and went in to take a shower. I had to be at my first spring training camp the next morning at 10:00. By the time I got out of the shower and put my pajamas on, it's after midnight. I lie down on the bed and picked up that Atlanta paper. On the front page was a story of how the University of Georgia announcer had quit to take the job with the Falcons, and he didn't want to do two teams. He didn't want that kind of cross country travel. The Georgia job was automatically open and the last line in the story said they were taking applications from all over because they were "desperate." The Bulldogs were replacing a guy that was really good, Ed Stalinius.

I knew that was open before I ever turned out the lamp of the bed. I called the director of athletics Joel Eaves the next morning before I ever went to camp. Ironically, he coached at Auburn for a long time, and I had interviewed him many times on the half time of Vanderbilt games since he had a good view of the game from up there. Needless to say, we knew each other well. When we talked about the Georgia job, he gave it to me over the phone. Before I ever went to that first spring training camp for the Atlanta Braves, I had the Georgia job in my pocket. The trouble was, though, technically I still had the Vanderbilt job, too. I had promised them I would free-lance football and basketball for them even though I was living in Atlanta. That's what WSM expected me to do. It took me awhile to tell WSM and Vanderbilt that I had taken the Georgia job. I didn't have the nerve to tell them that I was walking away from them.

The Sportscaster's Dozen

Hugh Durham

Hugh Durham was an outstanding basketball coach at Georgia. He diagrammed his offense for me once. He stopped in the middle of it and said, "Do you know what you're looking at?"

I said, "Well, a little bit; it's got something of the old weave that I had seen out in Wyoming years and years ago."

He told me to look at it again. I said, "Well, you've got a post up high and a post low."

"That's right; this is a John Wooden, UCLA high/low post offense. It's the same thing that Denny Crum was using in Louisville."

> *Larry is an extremely knowledgeable sportscaster. He gives you the complete picture, although he takes a different approach by being the hometown broadcaster. Because of his talent, Larry became popular and very long-lasting. He should be commended for being in the business as long as he has been.*
>
> *& John Ferguson, Louisiana State University*

I never forgot the day we got into that discussion. Durham was a heck of a coach. Since he hadn't been in the Southeastern Conference as long as I had, he would ask me stuff about Adolph Rupp, Ray Mears and all his success at Tennessee, and about Bob Polk. We would go for walks on the day of the game after the morning shoot-around, and he would ask me stuff about the league. Even though the newspaper men may have been older than I was, they had not covered basketball as much as I did. We had good times.

Durham had a volatile temper. I've seen him blow at his players, but I have also seen him have guys get hurt, and he had compassion for them. One year because of injuries, he got down to six scholarships and two walk-ons with a total squad of eight. The two walk-ons couldn't have carried your shoes, and they went all the way to the NCAA tournament with those eight men. He just simply stopped everything dead that season. He threw out his offense, held the ball, and played zone defense desperately. He didn't want any of his players to foul out or get hurt. It reminds me a lot of what Temple is still doing up East.

Durham was a very, very good coach.

Vince Dooley: Building Georgia's Football Tradition

Vince Dooley was an outstanding football coach for the Bulldogs. He coached from 1964 to 1988. When he became head coach the big wave of commercialism, endorsements, raising money, and being on

Munson (left) is presented with a plaque from Georgia Governor Zell Miller on Larry Munson Day, 1996. (Photo by Laura Heath.)

billboards, was just starting. I saw him going through all of that just as I got to Georgia. He started making more and more speeches. Not to imply that I was old and he was young, because we were both almost the same age. But he came just as the whole industry changed.

Even now, head coaches do very little coaching. The staff does almost all of it. And most coaches use the guys up in the booth during the game or on headsets who call in all the plays and do everything. The head coach doesn't even make substitutions on the sideline. All of that was starting when Dooley took over as head coach.

He was a self-disciplined man; he could control his temper and not blow at anybody. He had everybody's respect. That's true even to this day. He's athletics director now, and the people around act like he's going to crack a whip, but he's not going to do that.

He was really a football man; he really wanted to run the ball. I've looked back at that first book he ever wrote and am just amazed at the diagrams of those running plays that he had in there. It's what he believed in. He took Georgia right out of the bottom of the tub. In 1965 he took the Bulldogs to Ann Arbor, Michigan, and Georgia beat the Wolverines, 15-7. It was the first and only time Georgia has won up there. Nobody ever thought they'd win that game. That win helped people believe that Dooley was going to be a great coach.

Since I've never lived in Athens, I've never had a real close relationship with these coaches, but Dooley and I were pretty close. For about seven years, I had a roundtable talk show in Athens on Tuesday nights. When I went to town for that on Tuesday afternoon, I would get to see practice which was a first for me. When he saw me coming to the practice field and the assistants were running everything, he would start walking away and wait for me to come join him. We would then walk by ourselves around those practice fields. If somebody had just gotten hurt or if there was going to be some big change that week, he would tell me what was going on. If he had some worry about a player who had just flunked a test, and that was occupying his mind, he'd tell me about it. I never used it on the air, but we were close enough that he could tell me about it. At night we would eat dinner at Dooley's house.

The thing that got difficult for Dooley was the various things he had to do away from coaching. There were demands on his time from Quarterback Clubs and Booster Clubs, which started in the 1960s. At first it wasn't bad because there weren't a lot of those clubs. All of a sudden, they ran wild as one was put in almost every town around the state. Some members of Dooley's staff like Loran Smith and Dan McGill got some of the Bulldog Clubs started. Once these clubs were established, they wanted Dooley to come and speak. He did, but it was very demanding on him.

Dooley did a great job for the program over the years as he finished his coaching career with a 201-77-10 record. With Dooley the Bulldogs also won one national championship and six SEC titles.

Succeeding a Legend

Ray Goff came in after Dooley and was very, very suspicious of the media during his first year. He thought people were out to nail him. Goff was hired for one main reason ... his recruiting ability. He had been head of recruiting for Dooley. He was hired as a recruiter, and he let his assistants do virtually all the work, while he did, maybe, more public appearances than Dooley did.

There were some wild rumors, scandal and scuttlebutt that started almost immediately when Goff started. Nobody knew if it was true or not true. Unfortunately, that's about the time talk radio was also really taking off in the 1980s. Talk radio was repeating stuff without checking on it, but nobody knew. I was listening one day to a talk station in this city, and I heard the guys that morning say that Ray's wife was going to file for divorce that very morning at 8:30 in the courthouse in Athens, Georgia. The station had sent a reporting team to the courthouse in Athens. They had talked themselves into believing what they were hearing. Of course, she didn't file for divorce. There wasn't any reason for anybody to be at the courthouse, but by gosh, they were and they spread that story. Goff had to fight that off.

Immediately, under Goff the team was struggling. We had to screen calls during his Sunday night call-in show. When some guy would call really angry because Georgia had just lost, let's say, we tried to protect Goff. If a guy tipped his hand to you that he was going really go after Ray, the producers would screen him off, put him on hold, and take another call. To some fans Goff couldn't replace Dooley, and they weren't going to give him a chance to keep the team at the same level where Dooley had it.

Keep in mind, now, they changed all the academic rules at the school just as Dooley went out and Goff came in. He was hurt by a real change in the academic structure at the university. There was another change three years later that hit him right after he had beaten Ohio State in the 1993 Citrus Bowl. Goff was a victim of the drastic changes and the academic rules. It took him about two years to realize that all of us at WSB were his friends. We weren't out to get him. Some of us were doing talk radio, but we weren't the Atlanta station that was after him.

Goff had a good staff that recruited and coached well. He recruited two great classes when he was the head coach. One of those classes included players like Eric Zeier, Garrison Hearst, Andre Hastings,

Brice Hunter, and Randall Godfrey. He also had a great bunch of players left here when he was fired in 1995, with Mike Bobo, Hines Ward, and Robert Edwards. That group finished out their careers in 1997. In his seven seasons as head coach, the Bulldogs went 46-34-1, with four bowl appearances.

In came Jim Donnan as a replacement in 1996.

Donnan is a little bit more like a throwback. He calls his own plays for one thing, which very few coaches do. During his second season he cut back down on speeches, fund raising and things like that. He really wanted to get out of that. He had done whatever they asked him to do during his first year, but after that he turned it around and walked away from a lot of it. Coaches nowadays really have to do a lot of that stuff. They don't turn down any TV interviews, because they really try and cooperate with the press. That's great for us in the media, but it takes a toll on the coach.

The Georgia Bulldog

Herschel Walker, who came in under Dooley, was a great running back. There had been a violent recruiting war over Walker with everybody accusing everybody. Clemson stayed right in to the end with us. There were all sorts of stories about money attempting to change hands.

I was doing a live television talk show on Atlanta's channel 36 at 6:30 at night, before Herschel had signed. The recruiting's over for everybody except Herschel Walker. The decision was between Georgia and Clemson. We had a caller who was extremely excited; it was a desk clerk from a hotel in Macon, Georgia. He said that John Robinson, head coach of Southern Cal, had just checked into this hotel and was in town to sign Herschel Walker. Naturally, I believed this phone call. There was a John Robinson who had checked in, but this desk clerk just added the Southern Cal part. He had seen the John Robinson name with "paint salesman" written under his name. Southern Cal had been in the picture about a month earlier, but had dropped out. Of course it wasn't John Robinson the coach, and the Bulldogs got Walker.

Walker helped lead the University of Georgia to a remarkable 1981 season and a national championship. There'll probably never be another year like that one. We'll never know how good that team would have been, because we had a couple of very good receivers on the team, but with Walker, the other guys didn't touch

Off the Air with Southeastern Legends

Publicity flier for "Munson's Sports Editorials."

the ball a lot. We had a good tight end and a quarterback, Buck Belue, who could throw the ball.

The exciting thing about Herschel was the fact that as the team came out of the huddle, especially in his freshman year, you figured he might go 75 yards. He was always breaking a long run during his freshman year; every week he broke at least one and sometimes two. By the time they got to the end of the season in 1980, other teams realized we weren't going to throw the ball at all and hardly anybody else was even going to touch the ball other than Walker. The defenses started crowding up in the middle and bringing the linebackers up in the line, which meant we were looking at eight-man fronts.

During his freshman year, Herschel had 1,616 yards with 15 touchdowns. After that season he rarely had another really long run in the rest of his college career, yet he gained more yardage and scored more touchdowns in his second and third year than he had in that freshman year with all the long runs. Defenses were stacked in there and pounding him to death.

One day after a Florida game in Jacksonville, his body was covered with bruises that you could easily see. The coaches counted 24 bruises on his body, and when they looked back at the film, there were almost 24 late hits where people were sticking their head gear into him even though the whistle had blown. He had a specially designed set of pads that went all the way down to his waist to cover all of his ribs, because people were really sticking him and trying to hurt him.

Bulldog Tradition

There have been so many great football players at Georgia, but the guys that stick out in my mind are players who people have probably forgotten about. Glynn Harrison, for instance, was a brilliant running back from 1973-1975. He had a different style; he was so smooth and had deceptive moves. Jimmy Poulos, the "Golden Greek," was kind of a small running back before Harrison, but he had moves, too. Quarterback Matt Robinson, who saved us a couple of times in the mid-1970s. There have just been so many great players over the years.

All of Dooley's fullbacks used to be great blockers. We used to run sweeps with the fullback leading the way. We also used to have outstanding linebackers, a lot of whom came from north Florida. We used to raid Jacksonville heavily for players. Strangely, even though these were really tough kids who could play hurt and who made a lot of tackles, the Bulldogs never had a linebacker that made it in the NFL. Once Clemson moved into Jacksonville and shut that recruiting down, we weren't getting any more linebackers out of north Florida.

Dooley's defensive coordinator, Erk Russell, was great to watch. Players just worshipped him. He used to tell me that real quietly at the beginning of every spring practice, Dooley took the biggest kids and put them in the offensive line, regardless of where they played in high school. Dooley knew that's where everything was going to be won or lost with his running attack. He wanted to have the biggest offensive line that was possible to build. Doing that left Erk with what he called "the runts." He used to be really upset about it. He wasn't cursing about it, but he said all the size is on that offensive line. "Muns," he'd say, "all I got are these little guys." He did all right with those "little guys."

The "Victory" Cigar

For a long time, the "victory cigar" was a superstitious thing with our football broadcasts. Years ago the engineer of the broadcast and I would light a cigar up if the Bulldogs had a lead in the fourth quarter and were managing to keep that lead. In the beginning it wasn't necessarily a "victory cigar." We never lit one up, though, unless we were actually ahead.

We forgot about it for awhile, because a lot of places killed smoking in the press box. We did break it out one time during the 1997 season. It was against the Florida Gators in Jacksonville. The Bulldogs led most of the game. With about 2:30 left in the game, our current producer, Larry England, who can't stand smoking, told me to light one up. Even though he wasn't with us originally, he knew we used to smoke one when we were leading toward the end of a game. That was the first time in a long time that we lit up in the press box.

> *Larry is a great guy and a wonderful announcer. He may be the best football announcer in America.*
> ~ *Cawood Ledford, University of Kentucky*

It was great for me when we could light up in the press box, because I love a good cigar. I don't really have a favorite brand; I smoke anything and everything. There are so many good ones out there, and people just send me boxes. I've always got some around.

Down at the Ole' Fishing Hole ... Part 2

Doing the fishing show was a natural for me; it wasn't really even work. I've enjoyed fishing and hunting almost all of my life. In fact, I fished in some bass tournaments when they were first invented, back in the early 1950s. The first tournament I had ever heard of was at Center Hill Reservoir in Tennessee. It was a winter tournament at Sligo Boat Dock.

That year the winners were caught cheating; I'll never forget that. Come to find out, these guys had fished in the middle of the week, caught a bunch of bass, put them in a live basket, and sunk the basket in one of the creeks near Sligo. That was the first tournament I had ever been around and the winners were caught cheating. What an introduction to bass tournaments.

For all the great places I've been able to fish, including Wyoming and Tennessee, I'm hoping my best trip is the one right around the corner. As a going-away present from WSB radio in Atlanta, they gave my two sons, Michael and Jonathan, and I, a week's trip to the Kenai River at Mount Kenai in Alaska. They are sending us to Alaska to fish for giant salmon with a guide. I am hoping that's going to be the best trip of my life. We've been told that sometimes it snows a lot out there, and we need to bring a lot of clothes, but man, am I looking forward to that!

That jolted me as a gift; I had no idea that was coming.

Larry Munson Day

In 1997 the state had "Larry Munson Day" at the Georgia capitol. It was neat to go up there and to speak in front of all those guys. I looked up in the balcony and a lot of the Georgia fans were up there, and the guy that I was working with in the afternoon, Jeff Van Note, was sitting up there. I was allowed to take seven people up on stage with me. I tricked my spotter, Dick Payne, who's been with me over 30 years, that he had to talk 60 seconds. That's all he had to do, one minute. He said, "No."

I said, "Only one minute. You can say something for one minute."

He walked up to that microphone, put his hands on each side of the podium, like somebody who's made a lot of speeches (which he hadn't done), and the first words out of his mouth were, "Well, geez." Then he talked for one minute and pulled out of there.

I will always remember that distinctly.

Not everyone was happy about it, though. A non-fan in the *Atlanta Journal-Constitution* newspaper's "Vent" column, took a crack at me by saying that having me honored by the Georgia Legislature, was like having [former Atlanta Falcons' quarterback] Jeff George honored. (George is not a fan-favorite in Atlanta.) They really took a nasty crack at it.

Things like that can bother me when its unjust or untrue. If I know it's unjust or untrue, if I hear somebody lying, like a talk show guy, it really gets under my skin if it's totally unfair. I've never been able to stand anything like that. That bothers me.

Another big day for Munson on a lake in Tennessee.

Somebody saying that I should be compared with that particular quarterback, who at that time had a lot of enemies among the fans and the writers, didn't bother me, but the guy was obviously taking a lick at me.

It's really nice to be honored like that by the state of Georgia, and it's certainly something to be proud of from my career. But there aren't really a lot of career achievements that stick out to me. I'm more proud of the fact that over the years I've been able to do a lot for children. I've adopted children and have helped raise some nieces and nephews.

I was married 46 years to two different women—24 with one and 22 with the other—so there had to be something right in those marriages to go that long. Now that I'm older, I can contribute small amounts of money to various causes. I have two wolves in Yellowstone Park, two buffalo in Oklahoma and am contributing to the "Tall Grass Prairie" in Oklahoma. All of a sudden I don't want to kill geese anymore or anything like that. I've killed geese and ducks by the thousands during my life because I used to love to do it, but now it's not as important to me.

I don't know that I've really accomplished much at all in my career. The Georgia fans are very excitable, but the whole business of radio and college athletics have changed. Cable television has changed everything. When we were all real young, to be one of the network television announcers and do a football game on a Saturday afternoon would have been a big thing. Now it doesn't mean as much. There must be 200 guys doing football play-by-play on television. If you count all the games every Saturday on all the stations, there are 14 games, and they start at 11:30 in the morning and they don't quit until 2:00 on Sunday morning. Cable has changed everything, and it's eventually going to eat everything up.

The Future of Radio

There's no telling what's ahead for the young guys in the radio business. I don't know if they can last as long as us old guys did without television to help them. I don't believe these young guys can make it in this business unless they get a certain amount of television. Sooner or later they're going to have to have a piece of TV, somehow, some way, even if it's just weekends.

Radio play-by-play is a shaky thing. University of Tennessee announcer John Ward and I have talked about the future of radio. I thought at one time, radio staffs were going to be cut way down to two or three people. With cable television there might be six great games on, going against you while you're working radio. A Georgia fan, for instance, might have the Bulldog game in his ears, but he's looking at Florida State, Michigan, or Ohio State. So I figured that everything's going to be cut down.

Ward thinks it's going the other way. He thinks that in order to make it, radio is going to have to expand the crew and make the whole thing like a day-long talk show, using a lot of people, with the game part of a whole eight or 12 hour-long thing. Ward thinks that maybe that will be the way to try and fight all that cable television. I had never thought of that and it remains to be seen, but it makes sense.

We're already seeing things toward that trend. Our tailgate show is three hours long, and it can be a pain in the butt. It's hard, because you're tied up from the moment you walk in the press box. For a 1:00 kickoff, for example, we have to be in the press box no later than 9:30 in the morning. It isn't like it used to be. We always used to get to eat lunch with the press guys—guys that smoked cigars—and it was kind of fun to sit with newspaper people and talk. We can't do that anymore; all that's gone.

Some of the young guys coming up are really talented, and I hope they can stay in radio. Wes Durham at Georgia Tech, for example, is tremendously talented, quick, and what a voice. I don't know if there is enough time for a guy to make a living in radio. Keep in mind there's not much money in college sports. There might be on the television side, but there isn't on radio. A lot of guys who are making a good living on play-by-play are working more than one job. That's a tough thing to do. I did the Atlanta Falcons from 1988-1991 while I was doing Georgia games; that was hard. That's really the only way to make the radio part of the football scene pay money without getting into sales or other aspects of the business.

I turned down a lot of major league baseball jobs, primarily in the 1950s, and I turned down two more jobs when the Braves put Bob Uecker in my chair in 1967. Perhaps if I hadn't turned

> Larry is the consummate professional and a very colorful announcer. He makes you feel sorry for the Bulldogs before the game. Then they turn around and kick the daylights out of you. I followed Larry at Vanderbilt and spent a lot of time trying to overcome his popularity and image in Nashville. Larry is a super announcer.
> ~ Paul Eells, University of Arkansas

any of those down, I would have made a lot more money. There's no doubt about it. I probably would've doubled my take-home income for the rest of my life.

When I started doing the Falcon football games in 1988, CBS and ESPN picked up my touchdown calls and played them throughout the weekend and rest of the week. I was constantly getting checks from the two networks for four years. It seemed they were always playing cuts and always sending money. There were even a couple times when a cut got played during a Super Bowl.

When you start calling games in the National Football League, you sign a piece of paper that gives them the rights to do anything they want to with your call of the game. In turn, you get paid for that, and you don't really realize it until the checks start coming in. Even during the summer months, those checks were coming in because your call of a play was being used.

However, the television fishing show that I started in Nashville probably changed my life more than anything else ever has because it made me stay in Nashville for what amounted to 25 years just because I fished and hunted so much. Even back in its early days when it was worth $25 a week to me, that show influenced many decisions for me because all I wanted to do was kill ducks and geese and catch fish. It really changed my thinking; I can't name all the jobs I turned down because of that fishing show. It changed my life; there isn't any doubt about that.

JIM PHILLIPS
CLEMSON UNIVERSITY

I had never thought about getting into radio until the day I walked through that first door and was introduced to the general manager of a local station in Ohio. Radio was the thing when I was a kid, though. I was born in 1934 so I didn't see a TV until I was 14 or 15 years old. I listened to radio a lot.

> *The difference between the impossible and the possible lies in a man's determination.*
> ~ Tommy Lasorda

Like all kids I listened to the series that were on in the afternoons like Dick Tracy and Tom Armstrong. As I grew a little older and became more sports-oriented, my heroes were guys like Bill Stern and local Youngstown, Ohio, broadcaster Don Gardner. Don used to do a little bit of everything like minor league baseball, Youngstown College, the games from a team in the original NBA, assorted high school games ... he did it all. In that market he was really the only sports voice.

I grew up in a town where all of the fathers worked in steel mills. My dad was a steel worker for 46 years, so I had figured when I got out of high school, I'd just go work in the mill, which I did. After about six months of that, I decided that was enough. While I worked there, however, it happened to be the same time as the Korean War, so we were making a lot of parts which in turn helped me make more money that I stashed away.

In January of 1953, I decided to enroll in college. In 1954 I was out of school and working in radio. It's funny how things work out sometimes.

I went to a small school in Ohio called Ashland College. I was a real goof-off in school. In fact, the only class I attended on a regular basis was speech class.

When I dropped out in 1954, I didn't have anything to do, so I started working at a gas station, afraid to go home because of the wrath my parents would throw at me.

I ran into my speech professor Dr. Miley one day, and he asked me what I was doing. When I told him I hadn't been doing anything, he suggested that he introduce me to the general manager of the commercial radio station in town.

After meeting with the general manager, he gave me a part-time job on weekends. Before that I had never even envisioned myself in the radio business at all.

My radio career grew from there as I eventually went full-time there. I bounced around a few stations in Ohio until I ended up in a town called Alliance, Ohio, where I did color on high school games.

Then I moved on to Lima, Ohio, where I was again a disk jockey. In 1961 Ed Krahling called me up to tell me he was taking a job in Dayton, which would open his job up; he thought I'd be a good replacement. Ed put in a good word to management, and I got his old job. So in 1961 I started doing play-by-play for high school and a Division III college, Mount Union College. We then started adding games to where during football season we would do games about four times a week (three high school and one college). I made that magnanimous $10 a game, $40 a week, and thought I was rich!

One of my early career thrills came in the mid-1960s when I met Don Gardner for the first time. One year I happened to go to a sportswriter/sportscaster convention in Columbus, Ohio, and ran into him. We became fast friends. I told him how I had grown up listening to him. I don't know what satisfaction I gained from it, but I guess when you meet someone you've admired for a long time there is some satisfaction. It was nice. He was a great guy, and I'm glad I had the opportunity to grow up listening to him and then meet him later on.

In 1966 Kent State asked me to come do their basketball games, which I did for two seasons. In 1968 I answered a blind ad in *Broadcast Magazine* and ended up in Greenville, South Carolina, as a sports director for Channel 4 television, sports director for WFBC radio, and the voice of the Clemson Tigers.

I really thought I was satisfied where I was, and I wasn't really looking for anything, but I saw this ad one day and thought I'd take a chance with it. That was 30 years ago.

Settling into My First Job

Broadcasting wasn't that difficult for me early on, but it was really a different animal then compared to today. I was in small markets to begin with, but even in the larger markets you didn't

Jim Phillips (center, with headset) working a football game in Clemson's "Death Valley."

have to worry about ratings, so you weren't out to beat the other stations in town. As a result of being in small markets, it didn't matter if I was good, bad, or indifferent on the air, they just wanted someone to fill the slots at 75 cents an hour. If they had gone out and hired someone with experience, they may have had to cough up $1.50 or $2.00 an hour.

Once I got over the initial fright of facing a microphone and realizing that there were people listening out there, and once I began to grasp what ad-lib was all about, it kind of came natural to me.

As a player the only sport I ever excelled in was baseball. The high school I went to dropped football during World War II due to a lack of boys to play, and as a result I never got to play football. In basketball I was an average player, but baseball I was pretty good at. I knew about the other sports, though, and I followed them. Growing up I was a big Cleveland Browns fan. My playing experience and following those sports have helped in my broadcasting career.

I'll never forget the first football game I did. It was a high school game. The station I worked for carried the Cleveland Indian games, so early in the football season we were committed to carrying baseball and taping football to be played back on Saturday morning.

We drove up to Elyria, Ohio, for my first game. My partner was Jim Forest, who is now working in Columbia, South Carolina. We walked into this press box, and all it was was this big glassed-in booth with everyone in one common area. There we sat with our tape recorder doing our first-ever football game, scared to death and listening to the giggles from the other members of the press whenever we screwed up.

I remember a long touchdown run that covered 75 yards. It was a decent call except I called the wrong player carrying the football. We really heard the giggles then. At that point Jim pointed out to me that I miscalled the player. I was so concerned about that, that when we got back to the station that Friday night with the tape, I actually went into the studio and recreated that play and inserted it into the tape.

You can imagine what that sounded like because we were on a small, ancient tape recorder, then I go into studio conditions and try to put some crowd noise behind it. It was so obvious, but I would rather have done that than have put the wrong thing on the air.

I listened to the replay of the game Saturday, and I knew when that play was coming. So I was sitting there just rolling my eyes because it was so obvious. The funny thing about it was that it may not have been that obvious because there was never a lot of flack made about it. Maybe no one was listening ... I don't know.

We eventually got comfortable doing games, and people started to enjoy listening to us. From that point it got easier.

> *Jim's a great guy and dependable. Everything I know about him is good; plus he's out of Ohio, just like I am. He obviously does a very good job, or he wouldn't have been at Clemson this long.*
> — Al Ciraldo, Georgia Tech

Frank Howard: Clemson Football

Two years is all I had for the opportunity to broadcast football games coached by Frank Howard. I knew him, however, a lot of years following those first two. Since he was at the end of the line when I first met him, he didn't have as good of teams as he had earlier in his career.

I must admit when I answered the blind ad in the magazine, I knew nothing about Clemson. I did have one memory of Clemson from the service in 1959 when they played LSU in the Sugar Bowl and lost 7-0. That was the only thing I knew about Clemson; I didn't know about Frank Howard.

I remember the first time I met him, I couldn't help but be captivated because he was just Frank Howard. He was unique, he had his own language. He stepped on people when he talked about them; that was just his way. Fortunately, we had a good relationship, and he liked me.

He could tell stories, too. The thing about that was that he would tell the same stories over and over for years but no one would ever tire of hearing them because they were told in Frank Howard's unique way. The stories were always about friends of his in the coaching fraternity.

He was so much a part of the coaching fraternity nationally, that I was almost embarrassed that I did not know who he was when I first moved to South Carolina.

In the fall of 1968, I attended my first Frank Howard-coached practice. There he was, this heavy-set man out there in shorts, a T-shirt, screaming and yelling at players telling them how much the press thought they were going to be inferior to everyone in the conference.

Coach Howard was really something special for Clemson.

Welcome to "The Rock"

"Howard's Rock" was something that a fan brought back from Death Valley, California, to give to Coach Frank Howard to be symbolic for our Death Valley Stadium. From what I've been told, Coach Howard just threw it on a shelf. Then somebody was in Coach's office one day, spotted the rock, and asked him what it was. The person, director Gene Willimon, thought it should be displayed somewhere. It was decided that they should put it on a pedestal at the top of the hill. Actually, the players had been running down the hill into the stadium since 1942, although the rock was not placed there until 1966. It became tradition for Clemson players to rub the rock before they take the field.

They call it the most exciting 25 seconds in football, and I think it is very exciting. The crowd is in the stadium when this occurs. The team leaves the locker room to ride a bus up to the top of the hill. They get off the fans begin to applaud and scream because they see the team getting off the bus. Then when the band is in position at the bottom of the hill, the team rubs the rock and runs down the hill. It is very difficult to put into words, but it's really a fascinating thing.

It's interesting the way opposing coaches treat it. Some coaches want their teams out there to see that, while others don't want their teams to see it so they stay in their locker room until the Tigers make their entrance.

In 1988 Florida State came to Clemson for a great football game. Florida State won the game 24-21 with the help of the fumble-rooskie. Deion Sanders was playing for Florida State at the time, and he taunted the Clemson players as they came to the bottom of the hill. Deion was Deion, even in college. During the game Deion was able to backup his taunting with a big punt return which helped the Seminoles.

Hootie and the Tigers

Hootie Ingram came on in 1970 and had some tough shoes to fill because he was succeeding Frank Howard. He had been an assistant at Arkansas, and I don't think he knew what he was getting himself into when he became a head coach.

Hootie left his mark, though, and I'll tell you what his mark was. Hootie was the man who said let's get going and change the image around here. He knew that he couldn't recreate Coach Howard's image, which was the good ole' country boy. So he was the image behind getting the Clemson paw print created.

A local ad agency in Greenville created the design of the paw. That's credited to Hootie because he was smart enough to realize that there was no way he could step in with Howard being the coach prior to him and create something which was going to excite people.

The paw print didn't excite people to begin with because people thought it was kind of hokey. The idea really caught on in the mid- to late-1970s when the team started winning again and the paw print was painted on the highway leading to Clemson.

Hootie won the last game he coached for Clemson in 1972, beating South Carolina 7-6 to finish the season with a record of 4-7. After we finished taping his television show the next morning on Sunday, we were sitting in the hallway and he told that he had resigned. He told me that he recognized he wasn't cut out to be a college head coach. He went on from here to work in the SEC commissioner's office.

Hootie was a good guy. I give him credit, too, because he was smart enough to know when it was time to walk away. He gave things three years to materialize, they didn't, so he walked away instead of waiting around to be fired. I really have a deep appreciation for people like that, because in the case of Hootie, he was still able to remain in athletics in any capacity that he chose.

The Clemson Magician

I think Charley Pell is personally responsible for the turnaround in Clemson football. Charley coached in 1977 and 1978 and got the program back to where it was when Coach Howard was here.

Charley has a lot of people who don't like him because he walked after stirring up the fans for two years. He started at Clemson as an assistant coach under Red Parker, who later accused Charley of stabbing him in the back to get the job. Whether that's true or not, I don't know ... all I know is that Charley turned things around.

Red Parker and his staff had recruited a lot of outstanding football players like Steve Fuller, Dwight Clark, and Jerry Butler, but Charley turned them into a football team.

There are exceptions to that like Bennie Cunningham who came here and played for Red from 1973 to 1975. One of the funnier stories about Bennie here in recent times is when he was invited to play in a celebrity golf tournament that I was also playing in. Bennie's not a golfer. He arrived on the scene without any golf clubs or golf balls, or anything. He just showed up because they asked him to be there. One of the local golf pros, Tommy Mullinax, who was also playing in the tournament, went to his car and pulled out an extra set of clubs for Bennie to use that day. That's how Bennie got to play golf in this tournament.

We haven't had many tight ends since him that have been able to catch a football like Bennie could. He had a tremendous big play up at Tennessee in 1974 where he caught a 75-yard pass play in a great, close game. In that game Bennie showed what type of speed he had. Tennessee won it 29-28.

After Clemson Bennie went on to play professionally for the Pittsburgh Steelers, where he won two Super Bowl rings. Now he works in a school system in South Carolina. He is an all-around good person.

Jim Stuckey, who was also recruited by the Red Parker group, is a good ole' country boy from South Carolina. He came in to play football under Red in 1976 and played until 1979, which actually put him through Charley Pell and to Danny Ford. Stuckey was a heck of a defensive tackle. He played his heart out and Clemson fans loved him.

We went down to play South Carolina one year in late November, but it was a beautiful day. The team had arrived for the game a little early. Jim was sitting out by the pool with many of his admirers

The Sportscaster's Dozen

Jim at age 12.

standing around talking to him. As I said, he is just good people, and Clemson fans loved him.

Jim Stuckey took advantage of his opportunity to play in the NFL and got a World Championship ring in San Francisco. Now he sells real estate around Hilton Head, South Carolina, and is doing very well. Jim was inducted into the Clemson Hall of Fame in 1995.

Getting back to Charley, the first interview I did with him was the morning after he had been announced as head coach. Speaking of which, it was strange the night he had been announced. On a Monday night, Clemson played Furman in basketball. At halftime someone from sports information came down to the press room and circulated a release saying there was going to be a press conference immediately following the basketball game. Nobody really knew what it was about. Red Parker had ironically just beaten South Carolina in his final game despite not having a good season overall.

At the press conference they announced Red was out and Charley was in as the next football coach. I wasn't even prepared; I was there doing play-by-play for the basketball game, but I didn't have any type of television photographer there for the press conference. Therefore, I didn't do my first interview with Charley until the next morning.

The first thing I said to him in the interview was, "You realize you are probably one of the most hated men on Clemson fans' lists right now because of some newspaper articles where Red said you stabbed him in the back."

He paused, then looked at me and answered the question. Then we went on with the interview and became fast friends. During that first season under Charley Pell, the Tigers went down and beat Georgia in Athens. Clemson hadn't beaten Georgia in eons, but Charley took a team in and beat them. The team went on to win eight games that first season under Charley and got a bid to the Gator Bowl where they were soundly whipped by Pittsburgh 34-3.

The next season (1978) the team went 10-1 with their only loss to Georgia. The Tigers went to the Gator Bowl again, this time to play Ohio State. Charley, in the meantime, had decided he was going to go to Florida. Because of that the administration wouldn't let him coach the Gator Bowl, so they moved Danny Ford into the position.

I was in Charley's house the night of the Furman basketball game that season in December. I had taken a TV photographer with me, and we sat in front of the fireplace in his den. Charley said, "For all of you out there listening to me, Charley Pell is staying at Clemson. Don't you believe that other stuff." That was a Saturday night.

The next day a friend of mine who worked at Eastern Airlines called me and told me the University of Florida plane was out at the Stevens Aviation hangar, and he thought he saw Charley Pell.

On that Monday Charley was named the head coach at Florida. I just laugh about that now.

But Charley had set the tone for football at Clemson; he got things back on track. That 1978 conference title-clinching game against Maryland, which was a real donnybrook, is one I don't think I'll ever forget. Fuller would throw a touchdown pass to Butler, then Maryland would come right back and score. Fuller would throw a touchdown pass to Clark, then Maryland would come right back down and score. It was a great football game.

> I've known Jim for a long time. In fact, he's the oldest rat in the ACC barn. He's been doing Clemson games about two years longer than I've been doing the Carolina games on radio. I call him Onie,' but I don't tell anyone why I do that; you'd have to ask him about it. That goes back to a joke he told me years ago. 'Onie' has stuck with him ever since.
>
> ಒ Woody Durham, University of North

I will never forget that because after the game we flew into Greenville-Spartanburg Airport to a crowd of over 20,000 fans. Ever since then the airport officials have not liked it very much when we have announced what time the team would be landing. In fact, they have gone to great efforts to keep fans from getting in. Fans were everywhere! Cars were parked up and down Interstate 85, miles from the airport to greet that team when they got back from Maryland after having won the ACC championship.

Coming out through that crowd, the fans just mobbed those players. I had called back to the TV studio to the girl reporter I had working for me, Carol Sadler, and said, "Carol, you call Sheriff Johnny Mack Brown and ask him if he'll get you a sheriff's escort into the airport and out to the apron, so I can do a quick interview with Charley when they get back."

It worked. She was waiting at the apron when we got there, and we got an interview with Charley. Then the deputy took Carol back, so she could get back to the studio and get the piece on that night. That was a mob crowd. It was absolutely tremendous!

Charley Pell turned things around at Clemson; there's no doubt in my mind. He brought back the glory years that they had experienced when Coach Howard was on top of his game. Charley did it in two short years. Then he left and probably to this day still regrets it. When he left in 1978, he said he was leaving because he didn't think he could ever win a national championship here ... three years later they were national champs.

Dwight Clark

Dwight Clark may be best known for a catch he had for the San Francisco 49ers in the 1980s in a playoff game against the Dallas Cowboys. The funny thing is that Dwight Clark wasn't highly recruited out of high school. In fact, he almost went to Appalachian. He came down here to visit, and after he did he turned around and went home. He thought he had made a mistake by coming to Clemson to visit. Red Parker and his coaches wanted Dwight, so they went after him and got him to visit again.

Dwight didn't have a spectacular career at Clemson. A lot of people think that because he went on to great things with the San Francisco 49ers that he had a great career at Clemson; he didn't. You won't find him in any of the overall statistics career-wise because they didn't throw to him that much. He was always a solid football player, but he wasn't of star caliber.

The San Francisco 49ers were looking at Steve Fuller and came to campus for him to have a workout. Steve called Dwight Clark, who I think was his roommate at the time, to catch some of his passes for this workout. Dwight did and the Niners ended up being more impressed with him than they were with Fuller. That's how Dwight ended up at San Francisco with great fame out there.

In fact, Dwight Clark is one of only two Clemson football players (the other is Perry Tuttle) ever to be on the cover of *Sports Illustrated*. Tuttle was on for a catch in the 1981 Orange Bowl; then a couple weeks later Clark was on it for his famous catch in the NFL playoffs against the Dallas Cowboys. Dwight's catch, by the way, is the one that to this day 49er quarterback Joe Montana says was a ball he was throwing away. I feel very fortunate that I have both of those covers autographed (and framed) by those two players.

I still, on occasion, see Dwight when he comes back to Greenville to visit friends. He's currently working in the front office for the 49ers.

Inheriting a Winner

Danny Ford inherited all of Charley Pell's success and was immediately faced with the task to coach the Tigers against Ohio State in the 1978 Gator Bowl. Danny beat legendary Ohio State coach Woody Hayes in what would be Woody's last game, as the Tigers beat the Buckeyes 17-15.

I think a highlight from all of that would be how some people bought a Jaguar car for Charley to present to him after the Gator Bowl. When Charley said he was leaving, whoever bought the car said forget about Charley; we'll give the car to Danny. They were so upset with Charley that they were willing to give this brand new Jaguar to Danny Ford who, at that time, had never coached a game at Clemson.

At a pep rally before a game, the car was presented to Danny. I was not at the pep rally, but I have often heard that Danny said he would have rather had a pickup truck. Lo and behold, he didn't keep the Jaguar for long; he got rid of it and bought a pickup truck.

In 1979 the team had a decent year and played Baylor in the Peach Bowl to finish 8-4 that year. Then in 1980 he could have just as easily been out of a job as not. Fans were totally upset with him, since the team went into the South Carolina game with a 5-5 record ... they beat South Carolina. The track record showed that Danny, even though he beat South Carolina, could still be history. He wasn't.

It turned out the very next year that the team went undefeated (12-0) and won the national championship. Once that happened, there was no way that Danny Ford was ever going to leave Clemson as far as the fans were concerned.

The team went on probation after that season. In 1985 they came off probation to go to the Independence Bowl in Shreveport and lost to Minnesota in a bitter cold night in Louisiana. It wasn't a very exciting bowl game.

Then they bounced back and had that great string of bowl victories beating Penn State and Oklahoma in back-to-back years (1987 and 1988) down in Orlando in the Citrus Bowl. The next year they beat West Virginia in the Gator Bowl a year after West Virginia challenged for the national championship. That West Virginia game in 1989 turned out to be Danny's last game, as a matter of fact. He had a great string of wins in there.

He also had a temper. One year during a nationally televised game, Danny was out on the field because the play clock had expired several seconds before the opposing team got the play off, and he was irate. As it turned out, he did some strong cussing of that referee on national television. It just happened to be one of those games where they had everyone wired with a microphone.

The day that Danny Ford was fired was the day that this state erupted, in so far as Clemson fans go. That was, without a doubt, the biggest story ever in sports in this state. The protests against Clemson University were just gigantic! The fans rallied; as far as they were concerned, Danny Ford was going to stay. The fans wanted to fire everybody in Clemson's administration.

The university turned around and hired Ken Hatfield, who was the total opposite of Danny. Ken was hated the day he got here. He was announced on Sunday at the stadium in the president's box. There were about 200 protesters outside when he arrived, waving signs, screaming insults at Ken and various other things.

Ken later told me that when the Clemson University plane picked them up that morning in Arkansas to fly them over here, the pilot said, "I don't know what kind of reception you're going to get when we get to South Carolina." Then he started to relay all of these stories.

Keep in mind that when Danny was put out, there were demonstrations on campus. The players split into two groups: those who supported Danny and those who felt it was time for a change. It was a rough time.

Most of us in the press arrived early enough on that Sunday morning that we didn't even know the protesters were outside until we heard some shouting out there. When we looked outside, there was Hatfield and his wife coming in. Ken Hatfield is a very strong man. He is very religious and very deep in his convictions. He came in and did his press conference like nothing had occurred outside.

He went out his first season and won 10 games, including a 30-0 wipeout of Illinois down in Tampa in the Hall of Fame Bowl. With that bowl win, Ken was the first coach to win 10 games in his first season at Clemson.

The team was 9-2-1 in his second year (1991) and lost to California in the Citrus Bowl. His third year was a bad year as they won only five games. They came back in 1993, his fourth year, and had another winning team at 9-3.

That was it. He was gone after that. The administration turned him loose and brought in Tommy West.

Coaching changes like these remind me of how the field of college sportscasting has changed quite a bit over the years, and some of it I don't like. For instance, I think there's too much pressure in college

Phillips (far right) doing a Clemson basketball game at Littlejohn Coliseum with analyst Tim Bourrett (center) while Jim's son, Jeff, looks on.

athletics nowadays which can, and has, put us sportscasters at an awkward position. Coaches almost need to wear a life preserver around their neck because if they don't win enough to satisfy the alumni, then they're gone. In many instances they aren't given enough time to build a program, and in turn fired within the first five years. We've seen that at Clemson. Sportscasters can get stuck in the middle by knowing the coaches, the administration, and the fans.

I did Ken Hatfield's call-in show while he was there, and it was awful. We had a seven-second delay, but what we had to bleep out was obviously heard by Ken and myself. There were some of the worst insults hurled at that man that you could ever imagine. We had to let a lot of that stuff go on when it wasn't profane or defaming in any great degree.

It was so bad that even women would call in and cuss him out. People would call in with accusations that Ken's wife had left him. She hadn't left him. She was a barrel rider in the rodeo and would be out of town for six weeks at a time. It was terrible the way this man was treated because all he did was accept an opportunity to coach. I will always defend him for that.

He still managed to win 32 games in four years. When he was shown the back door, the fans couldn't have been happier. But then the fans weren't happy when Clemson hired Tommy, because they still wanted Danny. The only answer was Danny.

When Tommy came on board, he had to struggle his first year, but then had decent teams in this second, third and fourth years. The problem for Tommy was that recruiting had gone down under Hatfield. I'm not blaming Ken or his staff, but there was so much negative being said about the program. There were even groups who would find out who Clemson was recruiting and send letters to these kids telling them not to choose Clemson University.

I've seen copies of these letters. Some of them went so far as to say they would rather see Clemson go 0-11 every year that Hatfield was there; therefore, don't come to our school because we don't want you. It was an absolutely terrible situation. I've never seen vendettas like that in my life. That was a rough four years. I really don't know how Ken withstood everything that happened to him.

It finally started to get to him that last year when a couple of the sportswriters started to smell the possibility that there was such an uproar that Ken may not last after that year. They began to question him almost weekly about that in his press conference.

For awhile he was able to toss those questions aside, but there was one day that he lost his cool after the press conference was over and verbally confronted one of the two writers outside. Just that one day he cracked. It was in view of a lot of us who were on our way out the door.

When it was announced Hatfield was out, he and his wife were still just as cordial as could be. He even thanked Clemson for the opportunity they had given him. I don't know if I could have done that under similar circumstances.

1981: The Year of the Tiger

The 1981 football team was supposed to open the season by playing Temple. Temple made the decision in the summer leading up to that season that they were going to drop football. That meant Clemson had to schedule someone else for the opener, which turned out to be Wofford College. That was the only school with an opening for that September 5 game.

The first half with Wofford was reasonably close; it was kind of scary. In fact, Clemson only had a single digit lead at the half. Luckily, the Tigers wore down Wofford in the second half and won the game 45-10.

The next week Clemson went down to New Orleans to play Tulane. The Tigers won that one 13-5, but for the second straight week they weren't impressive at all. So the team is sitting with a record of 2-0, but no one is really giving them much consideration.

In week three the Tigers beat the Bulldogs of Georgia at home, 13-3. All of a sudden everybody started to get a little excited. The Bulldogs were the defending national champions and ranked fourth in the country before the Clemson game. By the way, that was Herschel Walker's only regular season loss as a Bulldog.

The Tigers continued to roll for the next few weeks, winning games they were supposed to win over teams like Kentucky, Virginia, Duke, and North Carolina State.

On October 31 Clemson hosted Wake Forest. The Tigers won that one 82-24 without trying to run up the score. Coach Danny Ford played everybody he had. He even made an announcement on the public address system at halftime for all of the members of the scout team who were in the stands to go down to the locker room. So those guys got suited up and played in the second half.

I'm up in the booth trying to call this game, and I don't have a clue who some of these guys are! What made it even more difficult was the fact that there were duplicate numbers on the field. For instance, there were multiple number 35's playing on the field. I didn't know who any of them were.

Back then, USA used to pick our particular game every week. They would hire a local television company to shoot the game and then the network would use the local play-by-play. So they told us before the game they were going to be doing that, and we did a stand-up for them to use before the game, then later did a closing for them. The game ran on the network by tape delay, so it ran a couple days later.

I was sitting at home a couple nights later, and a guy called my house and said, "Jim, are you watching USA?" I wasn't, but when he told me the game was on from Saturday, I decided to turn it on. It was embarrassing because we were totally confused in the second half. Anyhow that was a big scoring win for the Tigers.

The big game of the year was the following week at North Carolina. The Tigers won that one 10-8 against a really solid North Carolina team. The thing that helped make that game so exciting was that the Tigers and Tar Heels were battling for the ACC championship, and it came down to that game.

I ran into a guy in the winter of 1997 at a car dealership in town who played on that North Carolina team. He was talking about how disgusted he was when that game ended because he thought they should have won. Maybe they should have after the way they moved the ball all over the place. Late in the game Carolina threw an intended swing pass, but it turned out to be thrown behind the quarterback and dropped by the receiver which made it a lateral and a free ball. Clemson recovered it and stopped the drive that would have won the game for North Carolina.

Over the next two weeks, the Tigers beat Maryland and South Carolina and earned a trip to the Orange Bowl in Miami to play Nebraska. Clemson was No. 2 in the country after the Tigers beat South Carolina. Pitt and Penn State played the week after Clemson's regular season ended. Penn State was ranked No. 1 until Pitt beat them that game. With the Penn State loss, the Clemson Tigers became the top team in the country without having to play a game that week.

Clemson played No. 5 Nebraska in the Orange Bowl on New Year's Day, 1982 and won 22-15. That kept Clemson as the only undefeated team in the country, and they were selected as the national champions for the 1981 season.

Unfortunately, that was at a time when the NCAA did not allow school networks to do bowl games. NBC had exclusive radio rights to the Orange Bowl. So there I am, sitting in a press box, biting my nails to the quick. I was so nervous I didn't know what to do. There is a certain comfort when you're doing your job. I can't really go and just sit to watch a game and enjoy it now that I have broadcasted games for so long. I have to be doing something. I love baseball, but when I go to a baseball game, I score the game because if I don't score the game then I don't enjoy the game.

I was totally out of my element in that press box with nothing to do. The sportswriters always pack up a little early in a game like that so they can be sure to get down to the field or locker rooms for interviews. When they did that, I was left in the press box with a girl from Clemson who was there for the school paper. Nebraska had the ball for the final drive when a Clemson player knocked down the ball on a deep pass as time expired. We looked at each other and just embraced out of excitement. We did it! It was so anticlimactic, though, because I couldn't tell anybody about it except that girl, and she had seen it all.

We did go down to the locker room after the game where Danny Ford and I taped portions of his TV show from there. Then I went back to the hotel for the big party; it was fun. It was a great night and a great atmosphere. It was a position I never thought I would see the football team in.

That was an exciting year, but nobody realized how exciting it was until the Tigers started to pick up some momentum after the Wake Forest game. Then with the win over North Carolina and a few weeks later to see the polls come out with the team ranked No. 1. It was everything you could dream about, I guess.

The Perrys

Michael Dean Perry was at Clemson in the shadow of his older brother, William "The Refrigerator" Perry, all through his career. William in his freshman year may have been as good of a defensive lineman as you would ever see in a college game. He went downhill after his freshman year.

Michael Dean then came along and played alongside his older brother for a year (1984) and wasn't impressive until he got out of the shadow of "The Fridge." Then he came on, and people began to understand just how good he really was. He worked at it, which I think he may have had to do more than his brother because the game didn't come as naturally to him. Michael managed his weight and stayed in shape and went on to have a pretty good professional career at Cleveland before he went to the Denver Broncos.

He was a quiet person; I didn't get to know him too well. Fridge ... well everyone knew The Fridge. Michael Dean was more laid back. Who knows, maybe his proper role was to be in his brother's shadow while he was in school and just never really become an extrovert in any way, shape, or form.

William was just a big, happy-go-lucky guy. I remember being down in Miami leading up to the 1981 Orange Bowl game. There he was—a 300-pound freshman, a little over 6 feet tall. He was standing around joking with some of the media people. He walked over to the goal post (which is 10-feet high). From a standing position, he jumped up and dunked a football over the crossbar. His athletic ability was amazing!

William was so happy I don't think he took everything seriously. Then when he was with the Chicago Bears, head coach Mike Ditka made a legend out of him by letting him run for a touchdown in the Super Bowl. He's done everything.

It was an interesting contrast between the two Perry boys because William was so outgoing, and Michael Dean was more laid back.

Clemson-South Carolina: The Rivalry

The rivalry between Clemson and South Carolina can get a little hairy sometimes, but it's a lot of bravado and all that kind of thing. But after the game, it's the biggest tailgate party you could ever imagine. There are a lot of mixed families in the state where one spouse went to one school and the other went to the other school.

There are cars around the state that have huge Gamecock decals and stickers on one side and Tigers on the other side. Then on game day there are those magnetic signs that people put on their cars whether they be Tiger paws or South Carolina chickens.

It all builds up, and both sides talk a lot of trash before the game, but it really goes down without a lot of people who get ugly about it. For the most part, it really is an awfully good situation. The fans attend the games together, they rag each other, and the winner has a full year to keep bragging. I will say this ... I think the rapport between the fans for the two schools is pretty good for the most part. What is bad, however, is that so many times the losing school either got screwed over by the referees, or the other team got lucky, or the losing coach is so bad that it's time to get rid of him. Very seldom does the loser admit that the other team was just better.

Luckily, the game that sticks out in my mind from the rivalry is one where the Tigers didn't have to admit the Gamecocks were better. The 1977 football game where Fuller threw to Butler is the first Clemson-South Carolina game that sticks out in my mind. The first Tiger win over South Carolina that I broadcast was in 1971; that one certainly sticks out. The final was 17-7 in that game. It sticks out because Clemson had lost the first four meetings to South Carolina after my arrival.

The 1977 game really is the one that stands out without question, though, because it was 27-24 in favor of South Carolina when Clemson started its winning drive.

Steve Fuller to Jerry Butler was a great combination in the 1970s.

The 1977 game against South Carolina played out to where Clemson could do nothing wrong in the first half and led 24-0 at the half. In the second half, the Gamecocks could do no wrong, and they went up 28-24 with less than 2 minutes to go. We figured it was over. The Tigers were going to have to go down to the locker room where the Gator Bowl people were ready to extend a bowl invitation to them, coming off a loss to their greatest rival. I was going crazy because I had to go down and go live from the locker room. I was dreading it!

The Tigers received the kickoff. Fuller proceeded to lead the team downfield. He threw a pass to Rick Weddington in that series and then he threw one to Clark. At this point the clock is really running down.

On the next play, Fuller rolled out. As he was looking downfield being pursued, he threw a bullet pass to Butler who was right at the goal line facing the play. Butler reached up and caught the pass with his back arched and fell back into the end zone for a 20-yard touchdown play and the winning score.

Like I said, I was frightened to death that I was going to have to go to the locker room and do interviews with the losing team and a losing coach. When I had finished doing everything after the game in the locker room, Weddington yelled at me, "Hey voice, come over here a minute. I want to talk to you."

He said, "I bet you thought we were going to lose out there, didn't you?" I told him I did. "I'll tell you something," he continued. "We have a man at quarterback; that's why we won. We got in that huddle, and he cussed us up one side and down the other basically saying that if there was anyone in his huddle who didn't think we were going to win, to go back to the sidelines and send in someone who thought we would win, because we are going to win this game and do it one play at a time."

They did just that to win the game 31-27.

In 1977 I was still working in television. A lady from Spartanburg, South Carolina, called me at the TV station on the Monday after that game. She and her husband were in their den listening to the game that week, and when Butler made the catch, her husband jumped off the sofa and straight up in the air where there was a chandelier. He crashed into that chandelier, breaking it and splitting open his head. He was all right, but he needed somewhere between 85 and 100 stitches in his head because he got so excited about "the catch!"

Back in those days the press facilities at Columbia, where the radio booth was, had University of South Carolina fans right in front of you in the open booth. When those fans stood up, they could look right across the table where you were working and right in your face.

By the time this game had rolled down to 28-24 South Carolina, this one particular guy was in my face good. You know what's ironic is when Fuller led them down and hit Butler with the winning pass catch, that guy who had been taunting me all game shook his head, turned around, stuck out his hand and said, "Congratulations, you guys have a helluva' quarterback." It's ironic to me because this is such a heated rivalry.

Rick Weddington was less of a star and more of a blue-collar player, but he was instrumental in a lot of good things that happened for Clemson from 1976 to 1977. He was just one of those guys.

The Tigers also have a pretty good rivalry with the Georgia Bulldogs. Through South Carolina and Georgia, the Tigers have faced two of the best running backs ever in college football. The Tigers not only faced them, but fared very well against them. In fact, Clemson held George Rogers of South Carolina and Herschel Walker of Georgia so well that neither one of them ever scored against the Tigers. Both of those players were Heisman Trophy winners.

There's a story around that says whenever George or Herschel came back to Clemson after their playing days were over, a couple Tiger fans would meet them to go to lunch. They'd go to a fast food place, get a picnic lunch to go, and start driving. Herschel asked, "Where are we going?"

"Someplace you've never been before," one of the fans would say.

"Really?"

They'd go over to Death Valley and sit down in the end zone with their picnic lunch, and a fan would say, "Well, Herschel, you haven't ever been here."

They did the same thing with George Rogers. I've had people tell me it's a true story. I have no way of verifying it, but it's a great story regardless.

The Modern Day Crew Cut

Bobby Roberts is the only guy in South Carolina I know of who still has a crew cut. He was a great guy and a fun guy. I always felt he was a very good coach. Clemson at that time (1963-1970) put very little emphasis on basketball; football was the sport with Frank Howard as the coach. Bobby was just happy-go-lucky and worked very hard.

He had a couple of good seasons before I came to Clemson. I was only with him for the 1968-1969 and 1969-1970 seasons. To show you how much Bobby was thought of, Frank McGuire took Roberts on as a volunteer coach at the University of South Carolina after he was let go at Clemson because he said Bobby was as good of an X and O coach as he had ever been around.

Most of my relationship would have been through the fact that he was coach for two years. The rest of it would have been friendship, which we were and still are to this day.

One game that sticks out that Bobby Roberts was coaching would be his last game. We met South Carolina in the first round of the ACC tournament. McGuire had a powerhouse team with the Gamecocks. Bobby put the game in a slow-down, and the game ended up going South Carolina's way, 34-33. That was back in the days when only one team per conference went to the NCAA tournament.

Bobby and I still keep in touch. After Clemson he went into business with Converse shoes conducting clinics and went into sporting goods stores, that type of thing. Again, though, the thing I remember most about Bobby Roberts is his crew cut.

Building a Program

Bill Foster came to Clemson in 1975 after Tates Locke and during probation. He inherited one of Clemson's greatest players in Tree Rollins and won a lot of games during his first few years.

He really had a great team in the 1980-1981 season. That team featured players such as Bobby Conrad, Billy Williams, and Larry Nance. It was a good, solid bunch. That team lost to UCLA in the Elite Eight of the NCAA tournament in Tucson, Arizona.

Bill was, and still is, a very solid person. He was impeccably neat all the time. It didn't matter what he was doing; it looked like he never broke a sweat. He did very well at Clemson.

He may have lost an interest during the last few years he was there going into the 1980s. He just all of a sudden one day decided he would go to the University of Miami and try to revive that program. Again, with Clemson being a football-oriented school, it didn't

Off the Air with Southeastern Legends

Jim at a cow milking contest. As he says, "I think I managed to get 10 drops."

matter how good of a job you did in basketball because there was only a certain small number of people who appreciated it. Bill had successful teams and brought in successful players; the gym was still only full when teams like Duke or North Carolina came to town.

I think Bill got tired of all that and left. He retired after he finished at Miami, and then got back into it at Virginia Tech.

He has a great family and is a great guy.

Cliff Ellis came to Clemson after Bill in 1984. When Cliff came in, he inherited future NBA player Horace Grant. There were some great Clemson teams during those years. Cliff was able to go out and get players like Elden Campbell and Dale Davis to play the post.

All of a sudden he fell into a mode where he had to recruit junior college point guards for about three consecutive sessions, covering about five or six years. That is a problem because in the ACC, if you go out and recruit a point guard who is a junior college kid, it's going to take him one year to get used to the league. Then he's really only going to possibly have one really good or great year. Then he's gone, and you have to bring in another one. So in the long run, Cliff wasn't really building the point guard position. Why? I don't know. He was reasonably successful with that system, especially in 1990 when the team lost on a last-second shot to Connecticut in the Sweet 16.

In the early 1990s, Cliff was in trouble with the university. Cliff is a tremendous family man and a tremendous person. He didn't mix well with the Clemson community because he was such a good family man that he didn't want to go out and socialize a lot. He wanted to be home with his family. That didn't go over well with some Clemson fans because they wanted him out and about. He did do that sometimes, but not on a regular enough basis to satisfy them.

In the next to the last year of his final contract, he surprised some people when he went in to renegotiate his contract. He told university officials that if they would let him stay one final season, and he didn't succeed, then he would just walk away. So they agreed.

Then Cliff did a strange thing. In the preseason of 1993 (preseason in the sense that it was before their ACC schedule), he called a press conference and announced his resignation effective at the end of the season. I could never figure that one out. In fact, I think it may have hurt that team a little bit. Instead of being an NCAA team, they went to the NIT's postseason tournament. While we were in Nashville, Tennessee, playing Vanderbilt in the NIT, it was announced that Rick Barnes would be the next Clemson basketball coach.

A Tree and His Tigers

Head coach Tates Locke was trying to bring back Clemson basketball in the 1970s, and he recruited Tree Rollins out of Georgia. Tree is one of the nicest guys you would ever want to meet. He was tall and skinny when he came here in 1973, but he could block shots — which is what he did in college and the pros.

To the best of my knowledge, Tree still comes back every year to help out another former player, Chubby Wells, put on a basketball camp for underprivileged kids.

Here I am, a little 5-foot-8 guy, and here is this first legitimate 7-footer in Clemson history in Tree Rollins. He could really excite people with the way he played basketball.

Rollins, Horace Grant, and Dale Davis are the three Clemson basketball players with good NBA credentials that immediately come to the top of my head as being Clemson's big men.

Away from post players, one of my favorites would have to be Bobby Conrad who was a point guard from 1976 to 1980. He was on that Bill Foster team that went to the Elite Eight in 1980. Bobby Conrad was a hard working, stick-his-nose-in-your-face-and-play defense playmaker, and an all-around great guy. He's now an attorney in Charlotte and is still a big Clemson supporter. You couldn't ask for a better person than Bobby Conrad.

Larry Nance comes to mind as a player out of McDuffie High School in Anderson, South Carolina. Nobody knew Larry Nance existed before Bill Foster recruited him. Nance had a tremendous NBA career. He is now a scout for the Cleveland Cavs.

Stan Rome, who played both football and basketball for one year, was a tremendous athlete. Even though he only played football for one year at Clemson (basketball for all four years, 1974-1978), he went on to play football professionally for the Kansas City Chiefs. He didn't play long for the Chiefs, but he played defensive back for a couple seasons.

Those are all players that are exceptional to me as both players and individuals. I think about them a lot because they were such good people.

Basketball players are a lot easier to get to know than football players because there are fewer numbers, and when you travel, they're not under the same rigid schedule as the football team. When you travel with the football team, they are herded off to their rooms when we get to the hotel, they are herded off to eat, they are herded off to a movie, then they come back for a meeting, go to bed, get up, have another team meeting, are herded off to the game, then get on the plane and go home when the game's over. You don't have a chance as a sportscaster to be one-on-one with them. When you travel with the basketball team, it's more like a family since there's only 13 of them.

Clemson a Basketball School? Ask Rick Barnes

Rick Barnes is amazing. He has come in to Clemson and captivated this area as far as basketball goes. Normally this time of year (February), with football signing day coming up, people would be talking about who was going to be playing football for Clemson next season. There still is a little bit of that, but the enthusiasm for basketball now is tremendous.

First thing Rick did when he got here in 1994 was join the football radio broadcasts (he was asked to) on the "Tailgate Show," which comes on two hours prior to us coming on. He drives around in a golf cart with a remote microphone and a young lady, and they talk to fans in the parking lot who are tailgating. He introduced himself to the fans that way.

He has also reached out to the other Clemson coaches. To my knowledge, and this is not to knock any of the basketball coaches or any of the football coaches, basketball coaches and football coaches didn't really associate much with each other at Clemson. Now they do. During the football season I can guarantee that Rick Barnes will be one of the first people in the football office on Monday morning. If the volleyball team wins, he'll be over the next day talking to that coach. He has ingrained himself in the entire Clemson family. Everybody in the athletic department speaks highly of Rick Barnes.

During his first season, there wasn't a lot of talent left at Clemson. One of the main players, Sharone Wright, skipped his senior year. But Barnes ended up with what he called his "slab five," which consisted of a few leftovers and a couple that he brought in with him. That team went out and won some basketball games and really surprised people. The Tigers went to the NIT and were defeated in the first round at Virginia Tech. Nonetheless, he had done something nobody thought he could do ... win some games.

In the 1995-1996 season, the team had 17 wins going into the ACC tournament. They beat North Carolina in the first round, which helped get them to the NCAA tournament. And the fans really loved him. That helped the 1996-1997 season when there was a record number of season ticket sales (7,300), plus 3,000 student tickets, which means they have a sellout every game. That's how much Rick Barnes has attracted attention to the basketball program.

I think the stance he took against Dean Smith really got the Clemson fans in his corner. No one had ever stood up to Dean Smith—at Clemson, anyhow. Then here he was taking up for Clemson, Clemson fans, Clemson students, and Clemson players; they all loved him for it.

Rick is so enchanting. They can talk about how Will Rogers never met a man he didn't like ... I don't think Barnes ever met anyone who didn't like him. He just walks into a room and the room lights up. I've seen him on the road during tournaments at 3:00 in the morning in the lobby talking to people. He's wide awake chatting with people, and he's got 'em. They're sitting there googey-eyed because here's this ACC coach sitting there talking to them.

We do a weekly show called "Tiger Talk," which is an hour-long program that we do with all the coaches during their season. Barnes takes his on the road every week. There is a chain of restaurants in South Carolina called Fatz, which are owned by a big Clemson fan. So every Monday night during the season we go to different Fatz locations. When Rick gets there, the people are lined up, and they start clapping and cheering. It's tremendous the way he has gotten the people behind basketball at Clemson. I really love it, but I never really thought I would see the day when the fans would be this convinced that basketball is something less than an alternative to football during the winter months.

I think Clemson is destined to have great success in basketball with him at the head of the program. I hope he stays around.

The Tiger Faithful (And Overly Faithful)

Clemson Tiger fans are great when you're winning, but don't ever lose. Ever since the championship season of 1981, they expect football never to lose. They can really make it hard on coaches when the team does lose.

We mentioned earlier how basketball coach Rick Barnes helps us with the "Tailgate Show" during the football season. He stood up for football coach Tommy West when the Tigers got off to a slow 2-3 start in the 1996 season. Rick went on the "Tailgate Show" one day and kind of chastised the fans by saying, "You people don't really know what's going on here. You don't have a clue. You're out here talking about needing a new football coach. Let me tell you something ... I came here two years ago, and I got lucky. I had a surprise year the first year and a bigger surprise year the second year, and you all were in my corner. What if this year, when we're expected to do something good, we fail? Are you going to be after me, too?"

Irony of all ironies, after starting the 1996-1997 basketball season so well, they went through a stretch where they lost three-of-four. One of those losses came at North Carolina in a season fans thought the Tigers would win in Chapel Hill. When Clemson lost, some fans got a little rough and were vocal about that loss. Then they really couldn't believe it when the team lost to North Carolina State.

The group that makes all of the fuss is probably like the one with all professional teams, all college teams, and all high school teams; it's probably about a 20 percent group, but they are awfully vocal. They sometimes make themselves sound like they're 80 to 90 percent strong because they're always talking. They're always calling in to the talk shows, they're always writing letters to the editor.

> *I've known Jim second longest of anyone in the Southeast, because I met him before I came to Duke. Jim is the kind of guy who goes about doing his job, not for the fanfare or the recognition, but because he loves his work and he loves Clemson. He's a good friend.*
>
>   *~ Bob Harris, Duke University*

I think most fans are the type of people who get excited, and they might close their eyes during a heart-stopping play, but they're not against the coaches. The good fans say, "If it happens, it happens."

As close as I can be to a fan, I am one. I'm different from a fan, though, in the sense that I can walk away when the game is over, and I'm not affected by the outcome. I might hurt immediately following the game, but that's it. The NCAA Eastern Regional game at the end of the 1989-1990 season when Clemson played UConn in the New Jersey Meadowlands and led 70-69 with one second left before the Huskies went 94 feet on one pass and scored — I was devastated until I got off the air.

I don't even recall what I said, but I know I dwelled for some time on what type of horrible feeling it was. It was a horrible, gut-wrenching feeling because you just knew that UConn wasn't going to be able to score in one second. You just knew Clemson was going to go to the Final Eight. They didn't, and it happened just like that. Once I had wrapped up the broadcast, packed up my stuff, and walked out, I was OK.

At the same time, I don't think I'm a homer although I do get very excited when the team does something particularly well. I like to think, though, that I give credit where credit is due. In other words, if Clemson gets whipped, they get whipped. I will point out, however, if I think there is a bad call by an official. I try not to point that out until I can see a television replay.

When one defines "homer," I think that means you're not subjective at all. You're just totally engrossed with your team and to hell with the other guys. I'm not that kind of guy. I'm not a we, us, or they type of sportscaster. I do get excited when they do well. I don't think you can be a good broadcaster if you don't get excited about these games.

I love all the sports that I broadcast. Besides doing football and men's basketball, I do about a dozen regular season plus postseason women's basketball games, plus baseball. I'm at it nine and a half months out of the year. I used to be employed full-time in radio and television, but as of January, 1995, I've done nothing but Clemson.

Spending Time in Double-A

I did Greenville Braves minor league baseball games here for seven years in the 1980s. Greenville is the Class AA team for the Atlanta Braves.

We had a game in Knoxville one night when it was starting to storm something fierce. I was on the roof of a rickety, old press box with lightning all around, and I announced to the radio audience that the umpires had suspended play (which they hadn't). But the wind was blowing what felt like 80 miles an hour, the press box was shaking, and the lighting kept going off all around, so I packed up the radio equipment and ran down to the clubhouse. About 15 minutes later the team came in there. Play had been suspended and nothing exciting had happened since I signed off. The fans never knew what they missed. I was scared, and I wasn't going to sit up there in that situation!

I really couldn't have picked a better seven years because I covered current major leaguers like Tom Glavine, Pete Smith, Mark Lemke, Jeff Blauser, David Justice, and several other kids like those who came through here when I was doing the games. I had, and still have, great, great friendships with some of those people. It's nice to go to an Atlanta game with a press pass and be able to talk to friends like that on the field before the game.

I think to myself how I never dreamed I would be on a major league baseball field talking to friends of mine. Lemke, who in my opinion is just one of the most solid human beings you would ever want to be around, is missing a tooth in front and has a bridge. We were at a restaurant on the road during his last season in AA, and one of the guys thought it would be funny for Mark to play a trick on the waitress.

So Mark took his bridge out and plopped it in his glass of water. The waitress came by and Lemke said, "Miss, there is something in this water; what is this?" She was shocked and kind of screamed a little bit.

Later on I got to talking to Mark about that. He said, "You don't know how many times I almost lost that thing when I was playing. There would be a play coming in from the outfield when it was my responsibility to tell the relay man to cut or throw the ball. About a half a dozen times I turned and said 'cut,' and my bridge popped out of my mouth. Luckily, I caught it with my glove and snuck the bridge back in my mouth."

I often wonder when I watch Mark Lemke play, if that has ever happened to him since he's been in the big leagues.

In 1991 David Justice was having all sorts of problems with the press and the fans in Atlanta. He decided he wouldn't talk to any members of the press on the field. I went down to Atlanta that summer for the Cincinnati series and was down on the field talking to all my buddies. I saw Justice over by the batting cage, so I went up to see how he was doing. He just gave that big Dave Justice smile, and put his arm around me. I told him I was doing some interviews to take back to Greenville to use on the air and wanted to know if he'd do one. He said sure.

So Justice and I stood at the batting cage and talked for a few minutes. We finished; I thanked him and went on my way. Willie T. Smith, who is a writer for the *Greenville News*, told me I had every writer in Atlanta absolutely boggled because Justice wouldn't talk to anyone, yet he talked to me. They couldn't believe it.

Friendship is such a positive thing in the minor leagues because it's a terrible life. You ride that bus all the time, you stay in cheap hotels, and you eat fast food. You need friends. As a result everyone gets friendly with each other, and there are very few incidents between players because of jealousy. These guys really become close. I was fortunate enough to get close to a lot of those guys and become friends with them.

College Athletics Versus Professional Sports ... One and the Same?

I used to think that I could do major league baseball or something like that, but I'm glad I didn't. Professional sports have really disappointed me in recent times. I'm extremely upset with major league baseball because it's a sport I love so dearly, and the owners are making a farce out of it. All of this talk of realignment and so forth is crazy to me.

Baseball is America's only pure game. Relatively speaking, so very few countries play baseball. There are very few other places in the world where you can find good baseball. I get very upset with fans who say they're fed up with the players because I feel this is a free market. And if the owners are willing to pay millions of dollars, then, by golly, you take it and run with it. The owners have dug a hole for themselves. That's why I like the collegiate game.

The collegiate baseball game (and collegiate athletics in general) has a lot of flaws, the NCAA is responsible for making a lot of mistakes that I think are very costly—for example, this idea of allowing players to hold part-time jobs during the school year to earn extra money. Even though I think there should be some means for these kids to have some money, I don't think working during the school year is going to do it.

Football players report in July to start getting ready for the season which ends in December and sometimes in January. After the season they have to keep up their physical training leading up to spring practice which leads up to the end of the school year. They're busy going to class and doing all of these other things for football. When are they going to have time to work?

Basketball players come to school in August, and they have to continue conditioning until practice begins in October for a season which could go as late as the end of March or into April. Then school's out again.

Baseball players have a fall practice schedule. Then they play a 55-game regular season schedule which is all encompassed within the school year. Teams generally start their regular season games in February. The ACC tournament is in May. Then, if the team is good enough, they'll play in the playoffs to the end of May and possibly into June.

I just don't see how players can possibly work. I think the NCAA really messed up. Most of the coaches I've heard from are against it because they know that if a kid feels he needs to work for money, the coach can't stop him because it's an NCAA rule. I still feel the NCAA should come up with a stipend.

Hopefully, something will happen soon.

"Oh, Yes, They Called Him the Streak"

The old football press box at Clemson was wooden and completely glassed in. You couldn't open the windows in the radio booth, plus there was no heat and no cooling system. So when the weather was hot outside, it was terrible in the press box, and when it was cold outside, it was even more terrible inside. Our saving grace was the fact that we could take a heater in there when it was cold out to generate some heat.

We hosted the Citadel on opening day back in the early 1970s. The temperature outside this particular year was in the high 80s to low 90s. I would guess it was about 120 degrees in the press box. The press box sat on top of the stadium, which made it impossible for fans to see in there. I was so hot that I stripped down to my boxer shorts! I literally took every bit of clothing off that I had on except for my boxers.

I was still sweating profusely. Someone had told a photographer what was going on in there, so he sneaked in and took a picture of me. That picture ran in the state newspaper. That's one thing that people seem to talk about regarding me, as to improvising to try and cool off on a hot, hot day. At the time I was just doing it because I was so hot, and my clothes were soaking wet. I figured enough was enough.

> Jim is perfect for Clemson. When you're a broadcaster, a lot of your success depends on where your team is and if you can fit that team. Jim has been able to do that with the Tigers. He's not a second-guesser. He's an easy guy to work with. Jim is a good friend.
>
> ~ Bob Fulton, University of South Carolina

Former basketball coach Tates Locke had a temper. He had a temper which I believe was unparalleled with all the coaches I've been around. We used to broadcast basketball on the same side as the team benches. Now we work opposite of the benches. Tates was highly energetic and highly volatile. There were times he would almost get into fisticuffs with officials.

At that time our games were broadcast back through the telephone lines as opposed to the satellites that most programs use today. The way we did it, we had a telephone sitting there with a coupler on it. Then we would dial up our telephone line to the studio that was going to originate the broadcast and send it out to other stations.

There was a switch on the phone that you would toggle over so you could hang the receiver up, but keep the phone line up. That's how you would broadcast.

We were doing a game and Tates became irate. At some course he stomped by in front of us, picked up the telephone we were using to broadcast, and smashed it to pieces on the floor! Of course, we were off the air.

Another time when we were in Charlotte for the North-South doubleheader, we were playing North Carolina. Tates didn't like the officiating in that game, so with a couple minutes left when the Tigers were getting killed Locke got his second technical foul and was kicked out of the game. Tates was so fed up that with 2 minutes left he took the whole team with him. He got kicked out, and the whole team went off the floor and never came back.

We just simply wrapped up the broadcast shortly after that. There was an effort to get them back out, but he refused to bring them back out.

The Excitement of Opening Day

I don't get those butterflies in my stomach anymore, but I do get excited before a season starts. I have a policy, though, whereas when the baseball season ends (that's the last sport I do each year), Clemson is totally out of my mind. I block it out until about the middle of August. Then I start mentally gearing up again to get ready for the upcoming football season.

In August I go over to the university and start hanging out a little bit at their practices and talk to the coaches. Then when it comes time for that first game to be played, all of a sudden, BINGO, I get excited again.

Butterflies, though, I don't get anymore. The first game I ever did at Clemson was a football game at Wake Forest in 1968. I had some butterflies then. The game ended up in a 20-20 tie. I had no clue as to whether anyone thought I had done a good job or not. The 1997-1998 season marked my 30th, so I guess I passed the test.

My longevity at Clemson, by the way, is something I am very proud of from my career. I do enjoy a great relationship with Clemson and Clemson fans. It's nice because people are very respectful of me.

The interesting point is that through the years, since my first season in 1968, the majority of the people who listen today have never heard anyone except me do a Clemson game. The people who were, say, my age 30 years ago are in all likelihood dead by now, and so we're going back to their children and grandchildren.

I believe I do a professional job, but at the same time I do believe you can be grandfathered into a job. I'm not the greatest thing to come down the pike, but I've done it the right way, I think. But you can get grandfathered in because people don't have anyone else to compare you to.

Chances are if someone is a Clemson fan and listens to the games on radio, they have no one to compare me to. I'm it, and I've always been it. Hopefully the fans have enjoyed what they have heard and have felt that I have done a professional job.

Watching a Game ... Just Watching a Game

Ideally, I want to continue broadcasting either until I'm incapable of doing it professionally or Clemson University no longer wants me to do it. If health should force me out or if they come to me and say, "Jim, sorry but you're just not cutting the mustard anymore," then I'd walk away and feel no regrets.

The way I look at it, I would love to work until I'm at least 70 years old then not worry about it. At that point I'll just take my retirement and social security and decide if I like watching games. If I can do it eight more years, then I'd be happy, because I have no regrets about getting into the radio sportscasting business.

The only regret I have is this: I'm over 60 years old, and I know sooner or later I'm going to have to quit doing it. I wonder how it's going to be. As I mentioned earlier, it's difficult for me to just go to a game and watch it. I wonder how I'm going to be able to handle that. Based on my continuing relationship with Clemson, I'm sure that anytime I want to go watch a game, they're going to invite me and have a good seat for me. I wonder if I'll be able to go over there and enjoy it. I don't know, but I guess I'm going to have to find that out one day.

I feel like I have been extremely fortunate in that I thought I had everything I ever wanted when I was in Ohio, but then, just by coincidence, I saw that blind ad in *Broadcasting* magazine and ended up here at Clemson. I now look back and realize that I wouldn't have known the disappointment of not doing Clemson games had I not seen that ad because I never would have experienced all of this. I'm here to tell you that outside of the birth of my children and stuff like that, this job is the best thing to ever happen to me in my life.